ANALYZING INTERNATIONAL RELATIONS

Analyzing
International Relations

A Multimethod Introduction

edited by
WILLIAM D. COPLIN
and
CHARLES W. KEGLEY, JR.

PRAEGER PUBLISHERS
New York

Analyzing International Relations is based on the editors' earlier publication *A Multi-method Introduction to International Politics* (Chicago: Markham Publishing Company, 1971).

Published in the United States of America in 1975
by Praeger Publishers, Inc.
111 Fourth Avenue, New York, N.Y. 10003

Library of Congress Cataloging in Publication Data
Main entry under title:

Analyzing international relations.

Bibliography: p.
Contents: Descriptive, explanatory, and prescriptive analysis in international relations research: an overview. (etc.)
1. International relations—Addresses, essays, lectures. I. Coplin, William D. II. Kegley, Charles W.

JX1395.A54   327.1   74-20602
ISBN 0-275-33580-1
ISBN 0-275-89130-5 pbk.

Printed in the United States of America

For Debbie, Laura, and Suzanne

Contents

Preface

The theme of this book corresponds to that of its predecessor, *A Multi-method Introduction to International Politics: Observation, Explanation, and Prescription*: "The rationale for this book stems from the conviction that most introductory readers in the field of international relations have been designed merely to fit a number of well-known authors into some *a priori* substantive framework. More could and should be accomplished. Thus, our purpose in designing this book was to provide a set of materials through which the student in an introductory course could acquire *both* a substantive and a methodological overview of the field. The book aims not only to expose the student to scholarly literature about international behavior, but also to introduce him to various methods employed by scholars to study and build knowledge about that behavior. Therefore, this book seeks both to offer answers and to show how these answers are found."

While the goal of the present volume remains consistent with the basic objective of our previous reader, a number of structural and substantive changes have been made in order to accomplish that goal more adequately. Organizationally, the format has been refocused by collapsing component parts of international relations into three substantive chapters dealing with foreign policy, international interactions, and the international system, respectively. This structure is designed to accentuate and further differentiate the distinctions inherent in those three levels of analysis, while at the same time enabling the reader to appreciate further the methodological problems peculiar to the analysis of international relations at each level. This organizational structure was selected also because it enabled us to expand the scope of the book from a narrow treatment of international politics to a broader introduction to the relations of nations, both political and transactional; the consequent shift in focus thereby enabled us to incorporate reading selections from authors representing a wider disciplinary background, under the conviction that international relations is a field requiring interdisciplinary treatment. Thus, the present volume seeks to introduce the student to the problems associated with analyzing international relations but not exclusively international *political* relations and in a manner that allows him to appreciate the contributions that disciplines other than political science can make toward our understanding of those relations.

In addition to providing a substantive overview of international relations through this framework, the book seeks to provide the student with a basis for examining the similarities and differences among scholars in approaching the analysis of international relations. It would have been impossible to discuss all the methodological and epistemological issues intrinsic to the analysis of international relations. Therefore, we were forced to sacrifice comprehensiveness of treatment for a concentrated focus on what we consider to be three of the most important analytic tasks of investigation in the study of international relations: description, explanation, and prescription. These methodologically interrelated but logically distinct tasks of inquiry are not presented through long-winded methodological arguments or, as in most readers, through methodological essays from the literature. Rather, we have provided in the first chapter a brief introduction to the nature of these three analytic tasks and some problems scholars face in performing them. The subsequent three chapters illustrate the distinctions between these three analytic modes of inquiry by applying the distinction to classify the methodological posture of selected studies dealing with foreign policy, international interactions, and the international system. That is, these readings are introduced and discussed in each chapter in terms of the authors' approaches to description, explanation, and prescription. A final chapter summarizes methodological points made throughout the book by a comparison of all the readings; the problems of making descriptions, devising explanations, and providing prescriptions are again discussed here, using examples from the readings to underscore key methodological points. Its focus enables the text to acquaint the student with some of the basic methodological problems confronting the analysis of international relations, to sensitize him to differences among studies in analytic modes of inquiry, to help him to appreciate the methodological underpinnings of our knowledge claims about international relations, and to induce awareness of the existence of contending approaches to the study of international relations. It is hoped that the accomplishment of these goals will facilitate the reader's ability to evaluate critically the contribution and recognize the limitations of scholarly studies of international relations extant in the literature.

WILLIAM D. COPLIN
CHARLES W. KEGLEY, JR.

Chicago, Illinois
October 1974

Acknowledgments

The present volume is an outgrowth of the contributions of many people to whom we owe a large debt of gratitude. To the numerous instructors and nearly ten thousand students who employed this book's predecessor, *A Multi-method Introduction to International Politics: Observation, Explanation, and Prescription* (Chicago: Markham, 1971), we are grateful for the many constructive suggestions they provided for the text's improvement; where possible, we have sought to incorporate changes in this volume to reflect those recommendations. To Denise Rathbun and Praeger Publishers we express our appreciation for the opportunity to create a book in this crucial area of human affairs. To our many college students, whose questioning and interest continue to challenge our thinking and serve to stimulate our desire to provide them with this material, we owe immeasurable thanks. We must acknowledge as well the administrative and typing assistance rendered by Amy Holcomb, Steve Dieringer, Marsha Curles, Penny Neighbors, and Ann Miller during the preparation of the manuscript for publication, and extend our gratitude to the Institute of International Studies at the University of South Carolina for support of that assistance.

Descriptive, Explanatory, and Prescriptive Analysis in International Relations Research: An Overview

This book is designed to fulfill two basic objectives: (1) to illustrate and introduce various approaches to the study of international phenomena and (2) to present an overview of the essential substantive features of contemporary international relations. Each of these goals may be examined separately.

APPROACHES TO THE STUDY OF INTERNATIONAL RELATIONS

How do scholars study international relations? Unfortunately, there is no simple answer to this question. The field of international relations is torn between differing conceptions of what the study of international relations should encompass and how the investigation of world affairs should be undertaken. To some scholars this study entails the mere recounting of the history we have suffered through in recent decades; to others it is encompassed by critical evaluations of American foreign policy; while to a third group it involves the generation of scientific theories of international behavior that describe relationships between variables and link cause to effect.

The approach of this text, however, assumes that the study of international relations may be most meaningfully conceived as combining all three elements through the making of descriptions, explanations, and prescriptions about those events and processes that affect and are affected by behavior transcending national boundaries. We do not claim that our image of the field is definitive, and we know full well that it oversimplifies the tasks involved in conducting international relations research. While some will undoubtedly object to what we have included or excluded, or both, we feel that our definition captures the salient and essential features of international relations research. We will employ this view of the study of international relations throughout the remainder of the book.

DESCRIPTION

The investigation of any subject necessarily involves at the outset a description of its distinguishing characteristics. Before one can purport to explain the conduct of nations, one must first describe what is meant by international conduct—that is, what separates and distinguishes it from other forms of human behavior—and must construct an image of the basic patterns that define that conduct. Some construct of the dimensionality of international behavior must be devised.

The development of a mental image with which to describe international relations is dependant upon the analyst's process of observing those phenomena. Observations of international relations must be converted into descriptions of what is observed. In formal study, observation involves more than "seeing" something; it also involves recording what is seen in descriptive statements so that communication about the subject can commence. Thus, when we talk about description in the study of international relations, we are concerned with two acts—observing and communicating what is observed by forming descriptive definitions.

The use of the term "see" in this context might seem rather misleading. Very few people are able to see international events as they occur. Much of what constitutes international state action takes place in secret, and the individual observer has no means of ascertaining what events will be worth recording because transnational implications will not become apparent until after the fact. Moreover, while researchers strive for objectivity in making observations, their observations are inaccurate. Because observation in this case is a subjective exercise entailing selection and interpretation of information and because it is influenced by sense perceptions and psychological predispositions, it is incapable of exactly reproducing reality. What we observe about international politics is a second-order representation of reality, and the world as we see it is inevitably different from the world as it really is. Consequently, the descriptions of international phenomena in the literature resulting from this observational process necessarily distort the world as it really is and are incapable of achieving full representational accuracy.

The "seeing" component of observation and description, then, raises a series of difficult definitional and methodological issues. These issues have been dealt with systematically by the philosopher in general and the epistemologist in particular. The philosophical problems involved in the empirical study of politics are exceedingly complex, and indeed many of the controversies over method remain unresolved. Our purpose is not to rehash these arguments but to attack the issues at a much more superficial level. We hope this approach will enable the student to understand enough about the problems discussed in this book to recognize their existence and their limiting effects. We will leave the more complicated epistemological problems to other scholars.

At a practical level, scholarly description of international politics necessitates asking, "What can we look at?" Although the answer varies from scholar to scholar and depends on the phenomena being studied, some common objects of observation can be identified. First, governmental action or the action of other actors involved in a particular event can be studied. Examples are Democratic Party platform statements on foreign policy. Usually we must depend on written documents because rarely can we directly observe these participants in action. Second, we can examine the public and private positions of those involved, primarily through their written statements and occasionally through personal interviews. Third, we can look at the publications of organs that record activities relating to foreign affairs. These organs range from the hundreds of newspapers circulating throughout the world to international organizations that seek to monitor the actions of states, like the United Nations. Fourth, we often turn to experts whose detailed knowledge of specific events or processes is respected enough to generate confidence in their views of the events.

These four classes represent different kinds of optical lenses through which we see and describe the world of international politics. The first is closest to the foreign-policy activities of a state because it represents direct information, while the last is farthest removed because we are blindly dependent upon the expert. This is not to say that documents are the best sources. Documents usually represent a statement of momentary significance whose meaning can be assessed only in the context of other documents and events. If they are offered for public consumption, they may not be very accurate or revealing indicators of the intentions and motivations of those actors. Moreover, certain foreign-policy actions are not documented—for example, the activities of the Central Intelligence Agency.

The second and third classes of views also represent partial pictures of reality. The public and private statements of the people involved in international events and processes will be biased by their desire to defend their actions. Nor can we trust such institutionalized reporting organs as newspapers or statistical bureaus and international organizations. Unconscious human error alone introduces considerable distortion, which, when added to the particular biases of institutions, makes these pictures of reality even less reliable.

But observation is more than seeing, even when our view is seriously limited by our lenses or the things we look at. It also involves communicating what is seen. The traditional method of reporting observations is to examine documents, memoirs, news reports, and expert opinions and intuitively produce a new concept—new either because new facts have been accumulated or because old facts have been assembled in a new way. The aim of the traditional method is to find meaning within the views presented by these four classes of sources in order to describe a particular event, a series of events, or a process.

A different approach has developed as part of the methodology of the social sciences. This approach takes the four classes of sources and transforms them into data. The process of making data by systematic treatment of the sources ensures that all scholars receive the same picture. To be sure, the data might give a distorted picture of reality, but at least every scholar has the same picture, distorted or not. As a result of the nature of these operations, information generated by data-making procedures tends to be more compartmentalized than evidence generated by traditional impressionistic methods. This compartmentalization constitutes both the strength and the weakness of social science methodology because it helps to insure common reporting of observations but also of necessity presents a fragmented description.

EXPLANATION

We have called description the act of observing and reporting the occurrence of events or patterns of events; explanation is the process of making sense out of that occurrence. We make sense out of things by analyzing why and how particular events have taken place or considering their consequences in terms of future events.

The type of explanation one makes is determined by a number of factors, including the scholar's theoretical interests and needs, his intuitive sense of what is important, and what the descriptions themselves will permit. But the point to emphasize is that there are many types of explanations, and their relative worth depends on which type best suits the purposes of the question under investigation. Any event can be explained in many ways: Our own concerns and preferences will largely determine which explanation is most appealing.

Generally, social scientists employ a specific notion of explaining the how and why of an event. Some scholars are interested primarily in discovering causes. Others are satisfied merely with showing that one set of events usually occurs coincidentally with other events or conditions, thus employing statistical or intuitive correlational analysis; some employ deductive explanations to show that a conclusion logically follows from a given premise; and some try to explain phenomena functionally by showing how one set of actions serves to perform essential tasks for the operation of another set of actions. A number of writers base their explanations on the intentions of the actors responsible for events, assuming that the causes of actions can be found in the images held by the actors. In addition, some scholars prefer what might be termed historical-sociological explanations that seek reasons for an event in evolutionary sources.

Each of these types of explanations has its own merits and limitations, but we will not discuss them here. What should be underscored is that the problem of sufficient explanation in social science is a subject of much dispute. A great deal of debate surrounds the very idea of explanation, with some arguing that the search for necessary cause is hopeless. But our concern in this book will not be whether causal explanation is preferable to some other type. Rather, we are interested in discovering how different scholars seek to explain the observations they report.

It might be noted that differentiation between the traditional approach to description and the social science approach is closely related to methods and styles of explanation. Because the traditional approach seeks to assemble pieces of evidence to present a relatively complete picture of a particular set of phenomena, description and explanation tend to be closely linked. The classic example is the traditional historical approach of considering events and processes in a time sequence. This time sequence itself is granted a certain explanatory function. The traditional approach, reporting events almost directly from the natural setting, intuitively assigns meaning and weight to various observations almost as an inevitable part of the observing process itself.

The obvious danger in linking explanation and description too closely is that the former may determine the latter and therefore affect its accuracy. The self-fulfilling prophecy operates in scholarship as well as in other facets of life. Most scholars show a propensity to perceive selectively, so that every new bit of information corroborates previous perceptions. Given our infinite capacity to bias phenomena that are already imperfectly viewed, we should be receptive to the possibility that new data may disconfirm our theories. We should, therefore, be wary of tying explanations too closely to what has been selectively observed.

If the weakness in the traditional approach is the danger of having the explanation bias the observations, its strength lies in the minimal constraints it places on man's infinite capacity to make sense out of his universe. While hidden assumptions often impede evaluation of speculative scholarship, they also frequently allow for the inferential leap to discover heretofore hidden relationships.

The social science approach to explanation also has strengths and weaknesses. Data-making from the observations is clearly separated from the search for explanations of the observations, and therefore the danger of biasing is minimized. But the danger is not eliminated, because a researcher might have a preconceived notion that in part will direct his collection of data. But the methods used in collecting the data are so open that others can either check the existing data for bias or reassemble the same data to derive new descriptions inductively.

Other strengths in this approach are the various techniques of suggesting different explanations and use of experimental methods for checking the validity of these explanations. In the first category, statistics are used to determine inductively whether particular relationships exist among various data. In addition, theories tested in other social science areas such as psychology are used to suggest relationships in the subject being described—foreign-policy decisions, for example. In the second category, a well-respected body of rules and procedures is available to determine the amount of confidence that should be placed in any explanation of a given set of observations.

The social science approach to explanation in international politics, however, has serious limitations. First, the raw data are so fragmented and compartmentalized that often little theoretical sense can be made out of them. Often, the accusation that the explanations of the social scientist in the field of international politics are trivial is related to the problems one encounters in making sense out of bits of information that made more sense before being separated into parts. Second, the requirements of data called for by many explanations are just impossible to meet. An explanation that maintains, for example, that the paranoia of leaders leads to war calls for data that are not available. Finally, requirements of the experimental method are also frequently too stringent. Testing a particular explanation requires a large number of relevant occurrences, but these occurrences might actually be relatively infrequent. How does one evaluate a particular explanation of a single event if the explanation cannot be tested for similar events?

Given the strengths and weaknesses inherent in almost every approach to explanation, we have tried to include in this book a survey of the variety of approaches that have been taken to the explanation of phenomena in international relations. We are not interested in proving to the student that one particular approach is *the* right approach. Rather, we want to show the large variety of approaches taken so that he can decide which approach is most suited to the phenomena under study.

PRESCRIPTION

Some might argue that (1) prescription is not a bona fide part of the study of international relations and (2) the scholar does not have a legitimate role as an advocate of particular foreign policies or particular types of international processes such as disarmament. While such an argument would have some support in the scholarly community, we see no reason why such a far-ranging debate is relevant to this study. First, despite the common contention that scholars should not recommend policies or advocate particular conditions, almost all do, including those most committed to social science methodology. Second, prescription and the evaluation of policies should not be avoided, since the consequences of international events have a profound impact on our daily lives. Therefore, it is worthwhile to judge the value of international events and processes, and we will analyze how various scholars approach this task.

In this context, the term "prescription" means the evaluation of international relations and the recommendation or determination, from that evaluation, of ways to sustain or change existing conditions. A student might concentrate his prescriptions at various levels; he might advocate a different foreign policy for a particular country, or he might suggest that certain processes in the international environment be changed. Another differentiation is between those who make general evaluations about a particular policy, event, or process and those who suggest specific alternative actions. The former prescribe by implication; the latter, by explicit direction.

Another aspect of prescription concerns the over-all style of scholars.

Some tend to interweave their descriptions, explanations, and prescriptions in such a way as to make them indistinguishable. While such a style is often more interesting and persuasive than one that attempts to maintain meticulous distinctions between the three types of activities, it generates many of the dangers found in traditional methods. In addition, a more complex biasing results: observing by explanation and prescription, as well as explaining by prescription. Some mixture and confusion of the three activities may be unavoidable, but it seems preferable to attempt to maintain systematically the distinction among the three.

We have attempted to include a variety of prescriptive discussions throughout this book and hope to convince you that the most valuable type of prescription is systematic and seeks to identify the values and assumptions underlying the study. We will show that prescription is a substantial part of existing literature on international relations.

SUMMARY ON APPROACHES

The above discussion should have familiarized you with methods currently used in the field. Our threefold distinction—description, explanation, and prescription—serves as a theme throughout the book. We have attempted to denote in each chapter what types of descriptions, explanations, and prescriptions are performed in each reading. The concluding chapter compares and contrasts various approaches to each of these three activities. The three activities will be more clearly defined if you ask yourself as you read each article:

1. Does the author basically attempt to describe his observations, to develop his explanations, or to present his prescriptions?

2. What is the style, form, or procedure employed in performing each of these activities?

AN OVERVIEW OF THE ESSENTIAL FEATURES OF CONTEMPORARY INTERNATIONAL RELATIONS

We have presented here a cursory overview of the essential investigative tasks inherent in the study of international relations. In addition, this book will attempt to provide an introduction to the salient substantive characteristics of contemporary international relations. To this end, readings have been grouped into three chapters to correspond to three levels of analysis by which international phenomena may be differentiated: foreign policy, international interactions, and the international system. Because some researchers tend to distinguish sharply between foreign policy and international relations, and moreover tend to emphasize one component rather than the other, we have organized the subsequent material in order to provide as balanced a picture as possible by dividing the field into three levels: (1) foreign-policy actors (Chapter 2); (2) interactions among actors (Chapter 3); and (3) the international system (Chapter 4). This three-part division constitutes one appealing and conventional approach to meaningfully categorizing components of an extremely complex subject for analytic purposes. Thus, this organizational framework allows us to slice up the totality of phenomena related to international relations and to focus selectively on particular aspects of those phenomena while ignoring, or "holding constant," the other aspects or factors.

The following chapter examines what is viewed as foreign policy by most scholars. Foreign policy deals essentially with two factors: (1) the nature of national actors and (2) the characteristics of the behavior such actors initiate that are directed to their external environment and cross national boundaries. Included under the generic term "foreign-policy analysis" are a cluster of related considerations, such as the impact that the wealth of the country, the type of policy-making process of the state, or the personalities of governmental officials responsible for formulating external policy exert on the type of behavior the state transmits toward foreign targets. Hence, when a scholar seeks to analyze foreign policy, he focuses his attention on factors related to why states behave the way they do in the international arena and seeks to determine which of those factors are responsible for producing foreign-policy actions. In so doing, the foreign-policy analyst concentrates his inquiry on the domestic and external determinants of the foreign-policy behavior of nations. Foreign-policy analysis, therefore, seeks to describe the attributes of nations and the characteristics of the foreign-policy behavior of national actors and to uncover the empirical relationship that exists between the two (i.e., national attributes and foreign-policy behavior). Analysis conducted at this level may seek to describe, explain, or prescribe foreign policy from this focus, and the readings in Chapter 2 are designed to illustrate analytic efforts designed to achieve each of these investigative goals.

Chapter 3 concentrates on the interactions between states taking place at the private and public levels. That is, interaction analysis shifts focus from the foreign-policy outputs of states to analyses that seek to describe, explain, and evaluate *behavior exchanged* between two or more national actors in the international system. Here the object of inquiry is the nature of transaction flows between states, whether initiated by subnational groups such as private citizens traveling abroad or by official policy-makers.

Chapter 4 addresses analyses dealing with the international system as a whole. It looks at the complex set of interactions among all states in the globe and attempts to treat those interactive patterns as a political system. Systemic properties include those features of past foreign-policy exchanges of states that serve to define the nature of the international environment, such as its legal culture, the polarity attributes of its alliance network, the degree to which the nations constituting its membership are stratified and differentiated between rich and poor, the extent to which its membership is economically and politically interdependent, and the degree to which supranational actors such as the United Nations possess capabilities of exerting influence over the policies of states. Analyses couched at this level tend to investigate such questions as the historical conditions that have contributed to the maintenance of the state system (particularly in the face of threats of widespread warfare and empire building) or the consequences of secular trends such as the growth of the number of intergovernmental organizations in the system.

Organizationally, then, the book is structured substantively to move from the simple to the more complex by starting with the nature of the primary actor in international relations, the nation-state, then moving to patterns of interaction among actors, and finally concluding with a discussion of the properties of the global system. The first level concerns how particular states or types of states behave—that is, the behavior of national *actors* in international relations. The second level deals with *interaction* between two or more states because it focuses on the kinds of enduring relationships national actors maintain with respect to one another and assumes that a nation's behavior is dependent on whom it is interacting with and the type of behavior of which it is a recipient. The third level considers the international system, seeking to treat the totality of events and processes that make up the pattern of behavior among all members of the global system.

While this threefold distinction serves to organize the book by categorizing various components of international behavior, the astute reader will note that the distinctions between the three levels are not totally clear. Nations maintain foreign policies not only with respect to other nations but also with respect to the international system as a whole. Similarly, the foreign-policy behavior of a particular state not only has meaning in and of itself but has important implications for, and affects the nature of, the global system of which it is a part. Moreover, a systemic property such as the nature of the international legal culture may be viewed as the product of the foreign policies of separate states and interactions among states. Hence, the levels-of-analysis distinction employed to divide the substantive chapters describe overlapping features of international relations. Yet, though the components overlap, one of the three alone would provide a sufficiently broad base to describe international relations. Faced with the necessity of looking at actors, interactions, and the international system, we have found it convenient sometimes to include certain relevant aspects of one level in the chapter discussing a different level. Similarly, our decision to start the examination of international relations by looking at the actor first is also somewhat arbitrary. Many books reverse the order. Nevertheless, as long as the reader remains attentive to the high degree of interdependence between actors, interactions, and the system, this nonexclusive typology should facilitate understanding of the factors that influence international conduct.

In order to meet the methodological objectives of the book with this organizational structure, an introduction in each substantive chapter is presented that discusses the readings in terms of the three types of analyses identified above. A concluding chapter compares the various readings with respect to the posture they assume toward the conduct of descriptive, explanatory, and prescriptive analysis, in order to develop some salient methodological points while suggesting ways in which the student might be better able to understand how international relations can be analyzed.

2

The Analysis of Foreign Policy

When we speak of foreign policy, we speak in the most general sense of the behavior that may be observed in a state's relations with other states and global actors. The analysis of foreign policy is thus composed of efforts to understand the ways states behave in the world arena and the reasons they take the actions they do. Foreign-policy analyses attempt, therefore, to describe and explain the contribution that various factors make to precipitating certain kinds of foreign-policy behavior, as well as to prescribe the kinds of behaviors the analyst thinks states ought to adopt.

In attempting to conduct foreign-policy analysis, scholars focus on myriad aspects of that behavior from a variety of perspectives. This is because many components of the behavior crossing national boundaries are amenable to description and explanation. While it is difficult to classify the various types of foreign-policy analysis with a meaningful category system, one way of differentiating the different types of that analysis is in terms of the kinds of factors the analyst regards as particularly potent in determining or causing the observed behavior. From this perspective, foreign policy may be analyzed in terms of (1) psychological and idiosyncratic factors related to the decision-making of governmental officials responsible for the formulation and conduct of foreign policy; (2) the internal characteristics of nation-states, including the attributes of the domestic political system within which foreign policy is made and executed; (3) the economic and military factors bearing on the conduct of external behavior; and (4) the international context of foreign-policy formation, including the situational and circumstantial condition in which the nation finds itself in its relations with others at the time of foreign-policy initiation. While certainly not exhaustive or mutually exclusive, these four categories serve to differentiate the major perspectives from which foreign policy tends to be analyzed. Let us briefly examine each of these types of foreign-policy research before turning to some examples from the international relations literature.

Psychological and idiosyncratic factors. When the analyst concentrates his attention on the individual foreign-policy decision-maker, he acknowledges that, ultimately, the behavior of nations is a product of the behavior of discrete individuals, and that the individual person is the primary actor in international relations. That is to say, "nations" are not actors, but people are; and thus, unless we are willing to reify and personify the state, we must investigate the behavior of those who act on behalf of the state if we are to study realistically the foreign conduct of nations. The unit of observation, then, becomes those responsible for making foreign policy, under the assumption that the behavior of those actors is most important in accounting for the national behavior of the societies of which they are a part. From this perspective foreign-policy analysis consists of studying the actions of a collectivity (i.e., the nation) by investigating the characteristics of the people composing it.

The analysis of foreign policy from the perspective of the decision-maker, with its emphasis on the fact that politics is produced by people, enjoys a long and reputable tradition in scholarly inquiry. Inquiry began from the assumption that foreign-policy decision is an ideal problem-solving activity, an assumption underlying the work begun with Herbert A. Simon (147) and continuing through the debate between Edward C. Banfield (11) and Simon (148), the work of Richard M. Cyert and James G. March (36), and the investigative efforts of Charles E. Lindblom (91) and David Braybrooke and Lindblom (20). These studies maintain two basic views of decision-making, the first as a rational problem-solving activity and the second as a product of interaction among social, psychological, and environmental factors in the process of policy formation. Particular attention has been paid to the contrast between, on the one hand, what Braybrooke and Lindblom (20) termed "synoptic" (maximizing) approaches pictured in the traditional writings and, on the other, the disjointed incrementalism (satisficing) approaches that actually take place. The differences between these approaches are relevant to the study of foreign policy because most analysis in the field continues to assume that foreign-policy decision-making *is* or *should be* rationalistic and value-maximizing rather than the behavior it usually is. In recent years, a movement to counter the traditional approach has grown; the extension of this movement culminated in a well-known essay by Richard C. Snyder, H. W. Bruck, and Burton Sapin (156), "Decision-Making as an Approach to the Study of International Politics." Condensed and refined later in a much briefer work by James A. Robinson and Snyder (126), the new framework is primarily a checklist of factors to consider when analyzing foreign-policy decision-making. Although the framework has been explicitly applied—by Glenn D. Paige (113)—only to the case of the United States's decision to intervene in Korea, it has been generally recognized as a valuable contribution to the study of foreign-policy decision-making. If nothing else, the impact of the work of Simon as well as Snyder, Bruck, and Sapin has been to suggest the need for looking at psychological and organizational factors in foreign-policy decision-making even though the attempts to do so are still rare.

In recent years, social scientists have examined psychological and organizational factors in foreign-policy decision-making. Two psychologists, Ross Stagner (159) and Herbert Kelman (82), as well as a political scientist, Sidney Verba (164), have offered a framework for considering psychological factors in foreign-policy decision-making. Two recent books on foreign policy, Joseph de Rivera (37) and Jan F. Triska and David Finley (163), are particularly important. The former, written by a social psychologist, explicitly applies organizational and psychological concepts to case materials on American foreign-policy decisions; the latter, written by two experts on the Soviet Union, examines both the organizational environment and the psychological predispositions of foreign-policy decision-makers in the Soviet Union. These works, together with Graham Allison's study on the Cuban missile crisis, which appears in this chapter, represent attempts to develop explanations of foreign-policy decisions.

Despite these extensive writings, however, until very recently little concern has been given to the systematic description, explanation, and prescription of foreign policy from the perspective of the decision-maker. Instead, description, explanation, and prescription have been thoroughly confused in the bulk of the literature. Most writers have implicitly assumed that foreign-policy decision-making is and can conform to a rational process, rather than viewing the process of making foreign-policy decisions as a product of the interaction of psychological, personality, and organizational forces within the domestic and international environments. These studies try to reconstruct the foreign policies of a state by examining its goals, values, objectives, and choices of strategy through an impressionistic survey of its statements and actions. Examples are Henry A. Kissinger (86) and Charles O. Lerche, Jr. (90), which assume that leaders do indeed seek to devise policies according to means-ends, cost-benefit analysis in order to maximize the probability of achieving goals. Frequently, it may be submitted, leaders fail to undertake policy calculations in these terms. Moreover, instead of checking various types of data for support of their interpretations, scholars are prone to let an examination of the logical consistency of policy statements suffice for disciplined inquiry. This is dangerous when the fragmentated nature of policy choice is considered, a consideration that suggests that policy-makers themselves rarely see their actions as part of an integrated or logically consistent plan. In addition, students of foreign-policy decision-making often succumb to the temptation to judge whether the images they attribute to policy-makers correspond to their own images of the international environment, on the assumption that the student's image is necessarily the more accurate one and can be used as a yardstick to estimate the appropriateness of the policy-maker's perceptions. Because this type of discussion is so prevalent in the literature and serves as a basis for innumerable prescriptive studies, we have included an essay by Hans J. Morgenthau as an example of this approach.

Internal characteristics of nation-states. From another perspective, many analysts attempt to study foreign policy by examining the internal characteristics of a nation—from its domestic political and social structure to its foreign predicament—in terms of the relation of those characteristics to its external behavior. The assumption here is that such factors as a nation's size, wealth, and type of political system (e.g., totalitarian vis-à-vis democratic) go far in determining the kind of behavior the nation will tend to initiate toward others in the international system. As intuitively pleasing and attractive as this focus is, most of the literature that employs it is weak. This is because there has been, until recently, a paucity of work attempting to attack the problem by developing and applying a theoretical framework as a basis of comparison. Most of the previous work has been in the form of case studies, which tell us what happened at a particular time, in a particular place, and under particular conditions, but which do not provide us with generalizations to enable us to discover the impact that various internal factors exert on foreign-policy output behavior. Most work is case specific. While case studies occasionally have theoretical significance— as, for example, Bernard C. Cohen (31)—they fail to enable us to make generalizations across a large number of cases. Even books with avowedly comparative orientations, such as Joseph E. Black and Kenneth W. Thompson (15) and Roy C. Macridis (94), are only collections of essays focusing on one at a time, with little or no integration around a single theoretical framework.

In order to circumvent this deficiency in research, a number of investigators began to search for an investigative strategy for linking internal factors to foreign conduct propensities. This effort was led by James N. Rosenau and the Inter-University Comparative Foreign Policy study group. As its name suggests, this collective research enterprise concluded that, if foreign-policy research were to proceed beyond historical narrative and journalistic anecdote, analysts would have to confront foreign-policy phenomena in accordance with the accepted norms of scientific method; moreover, it was recognized that it is the method of comparison in particular that affords the foreign-policy researcher with something approaching the classical experiment and thereby provides the means by which such general knowledge may be obtained. Consequently, beginning in the mid-1960's, foreign-policy research shifted to a cross-national comparative perspective, and the "comparative study of foreign policy" research orientation was born. Exemplary of this genre of research are the works of Rosenau, particularly his *Domestic Sources of Foreign Policy* (130), *The Scientific Study of Foreign Policy* (132), and *Linkage Politics* (131); others include the edited works of R. Barry Farrell (45), Jonathan Wilkenfeld (171), and Charles W. Kegley, *et al.* (80), and books that attempt to develop a basis for the comparative study of foreign policy (e.g. David O. Wilkinson, 172, and Wolfram F. Hanrieder, 61).

A major difficulty that comparative studies of foreign policy faced was the lack of adequate data with which theories about that behavior could be tested. A recent breakthrough occurred with the advent of the events data research movement in the late 1960's; this movement was predicated on the assumption that the foreign-policy *event* was an appropriate behavioral unit for measuring foreign-policy behavior, and that data regarding the event/interactions of countries could be acquired through systematic coding of the behavior of nations reported in the mass media. For discussions of the theoretical and conceptual underpinnings of this movement, the reader

movements is now voluminous, as recent texts by Patrick J. McGowan and Howard B. Shapiro (99) and Rosenau (132) clearly indicate. It is safe to regard these developments as constituting somewhat of a major research breakthrough. Wilkenfeld's contribution in this chapter (p. 96) represents an early classic comparative study of foreign policy with quantitative data and is included to illustrate how empirical data may be probed in order to derive knowledge about the relation between the amount of conflict experienced domestically and the amount of conflict initiated abroad, on a cross-national basis.

Many aspects of the linkage between internal conditions and foreign behavior have been investigated. These range from investigations of the role of bureaucratic politics in foreign policy–making (e.g., William O. Chittick, 27, Richard A. Brody, 22, and Allison in Chapter 2 of this volume) to the relation of public opinion and foreign performance (e.g., Rosenau, 132, and Gabriel A. Almond, 5) and include also studies of the effects of crisis on foreign policy (e.g., Charles F. Hermann, 64), and analyses of interest-group influences on national conduct (e.g., Lester W. Milbrath, 102). Moreover, many students of comparative foreign policy have begun to investigate how the national attributes of states, such as their relative size, influence foreign behavior; here, the work of Maurice A. East (41) is exemplary.

Another focus in comparative foreign-policy research has been the description and classification of that behavior. Many taxonomies have been devised to classify the types of foreign policy a state may demonstrate. Both the great-power or small-power distinction and the status quo or revisionist distinction are popular with historians like A. J. P. Taylor (160) and with some political scientists—see especially A. F. K. Organski's (109) classification of satisfied and dissatisfied states. Several writers have set out to develop empirical measurements of various types of foreign relations between states. A review of event data and quantitative efforts is provided by Kegley, Stephen A. Salmore, and David Rosen (81) and illustrated by Chittick (27). A sample of the existing work appears in Table 1, which indicates the scholar, the dimension of foreign policy being measured, and the types of data used in the study. Interested students should examine these works in listed order to gain understanding of the kind and variety of systematic description on foreign policy that might be done.

Economic and military factors. Traditionally, scholars have attempted to explain the nature of international politics by looking at the power possessed by the states that make up the international system. This approach to explanation has implicitly assumed that relative economic strength and military capability have a substantial bearing on a state's conduct of its foreign affairs. Since power is usually conceived as the ability of a state to (1) achieve its objectives, (2) force its adversaries to do what they would not otherwise do, (3) prevail in conflict, or (4) influence others to agree with its purposes, it was natural to assume that economic and military capability was the most crucial factor determining the power of states.

They were considered the most effective means by which one state was able to coerce another state to act in a manner the first state desired. Hence, this conception of power suggested an economic and military ordering of states in the world that would often enable the more powerful to get the less powerful to conform to the former's wishes.

The power politics school of thought has sought to explain how states influence each other's behavior by identifying the various elements of national power that contribute to the state's capacity to control the behavior of others. This has involved intuitive speculation about the relative impact of economic and military aspects of power. Table 2 illustrates how some international relations scholars have identified and categorized what they consider to be the salient elements of power that contribute to the way nations influence each other.

More and more students of international politics, including some of those in Table 2, have come to recognize the limitations of these capability attributes as explanations of a nation's influence in the international system. While it is obvious that some nations are more powerful than others (they are able to get what they want from others in the international system), it has become questionable whether these indicators provide a good predictor of which nations possess that power. States that are more "powerful" according to these indicators frequently are unable to achieve their objectives when dealing with weaker states: Prominent examples are the failures of the United States to get its way with Cuba and of the Soviet Union to influence Tito's Yugoslavia. Hence, the so-called sources, or determinants, of power often have failed to predict the successful exercise of influence.

Part of the problem with the power approach to international politics has been the failure to distinguish capability analysis (the sources of power) from the uses to which those sources can be put. If the elements of power are to be used to explain international control and influence, then an empirical analysis of the relationship between the possession of the sources of power and the ability to exert influence needs to be undertaken. To assume *a priori* that economic and military capability enables nations to control other nations is not warranted unless that relationship has been tested first. Empirical investigation might reveal other indicators of power that are more explanatory and predictive. Already, some preliminary work suggests that the way nations influence each other depends upon such things as a nation's willingness to employ its resources to coerce, its willingness to make sacrifices or risk destruction to achieve its ultimate ends, and its adversaries' images of its objectives and capabilities. These findings suggest that the mere possession of capabilities does not explain states' behavior.

Therefore, it is unsafe to equate the determinants, or elements, of power with power. One reason scholars have tended to do so is that the concept of power is elusive and ambiguous. It is difficult to define empirically, for it must be discussed in relative terms: Power over whom? Relative to whom? It makes little sense to speak of a nation's power unless it can be shown to be related to one's ability to alter another's behavior in order to align it with one's own interests.

While substantial literature, both empirical and analytical, describes and discusses the dimensions of economic and military capability, the literature attempting to relate this capability to foreign policy is extremely weak. As we have indicated, the most common approach has been to employ the concept of national power when discussing economic and military capability. As indicated in Table 2, each scholar has mixed economic and military factors with noneconomic and nonmilitary ones as bases of national power. Although the inventories all suggest that national power is more than the capacity to fight a war, these writers do not systematically describe the relationships between economic and military capabilities and other capabilities. Hence, the implication remains that the ability to wage war is synonymous with power and the ability to wield influence. While the relationship between economic and military capabilities, on the one hand, and the general ability to influence states, on the other, remains unclear, more and more scholars are questioning whether the notion of power defined as economic-military capability is at all useful in explaining how or why states influence each other.

Some attempts in the field explicitly approach the problem of the relationship between economic and military capability and foreign policy. Empirical work has been undertaken by Rudolph J. Rummel (134), Bruce M. Russett, et al. (139), and Jack Sawyer (140) that employs various methods of correlation statistics to search for relationships between economic, military, and some foreign-policy variables. In addition, there are the more traditional attempts to relate economic and military factors to foreign policy. The impact of military capability on domestic politics and indirectly on foreign policy is examined in Glenn H. Snyder and William L. Baldwin (9). Albert O. Hirschman (67) has examined the role of foreign trade in political relationships among states. Foreign aid as a tool of foreign policy is discussed from various viewpoints in Robert A. Goldwin (53). It is illustrated by Wittkopf's contribution to this chapter. Charles Wolf (174) has examined economic and military factors as they pertain to guerrilla warfare.

Most of the work on economic and military factors deals with what might be called the dimensions of economic and military conditions within states. Data on economic variables may be obtained from the *United Nations Statistical Yearbooks* and the *Statesman's Year Books,* as well as from Russett, et al. (139), and A. S. Banks and R. B. Textor (12). Information on military capability can be acquired from *The Military Balance,* compiled and published yearly by the Institute for Strategic Studies in London. There are many studies on the dynamics of economic conditions, some of which are relevant to foreign policy. Examples are W. W. Rostow (133), Max F. Millikan and Donald L. Blackmer (103), Robert L. Heilbroner (63), Irving Louis Horowitz (69), and John Kenneth Galbraith (49). Also abundant is literature dealing with the history and dynamics of military factors. Basic studies are Klaus Knorr (88), Kissinger (85), Herman Kahn (75), and Quincy Wright (176).

International context. Finally, but not exhaustively, a number of scholars have focused on the international context, or setting, of a nation as an explanatory variable in foreign-policy analysis. This focus assumes

TABLE 2 Sources of National Power

Crabb(1)	Hartmann(2)	Kulski(3)	Lerche and Said(4)	Morgenthau(5)
geography	geographic element	size, location topography	geographic position	geography
economic resources	economic element	economic resources and raw materials	resource endowment	national resources
technological resources		technological resources	educational and technical level	
military forces	military element	military potential	military power	military preparedness
population	demographic element	population characteristics	population and manpower	population
national character	historical-psychological-sociological element			national character
			national morale	national morale
	organizational-administrative element	quality of national leaders and elites	political economic and social structure	quality of government
ideology				
		industrial capacity	industrial and agricultural productive capacity	industrial capability
			international strategic position	
				quality of diplomacy
		land, maritime, and air transportation capacity		

(1) Cecil V. Crabb, Jr., **American Foreign Policy in the Nuclear Age** (New York: Harper & Row, 1965), p. 7.

(2) Frederick H. Hartmann, **The Relations of Nations** (New York: Macmillan, 1967), p. 44.

(3) W. W. Kulski, **International Politics in a Revolutionary Age** (Philadelphia: Lippincott, 1968), pp. 98-101.

(4) Charles O. Lerche, Jr., and Abdul A. Said, **Concepts of International Politics** (Englewood Cliffs, N.J.: Prentice-Hall, 1963), p. 59.

(5) Hans J. Morgenthau, **Politics Among Nations** (New York: Knopf, 1961), pp. 110-149.

as Identified by Various Scholars

Organski (6)	Palmer and Perkins(7)	Stoessinger(8)	U.S. Army(9)	Van Dyke(10)
geography	geography	geography	geographic component	geographic base
resources	natural resources	natural resources	economic component	economic system
economic development	technology	economic and industrial development		scientific and inventive potentialities
			military component	armed establishment
population	population	population		demographic base
		national character	sociological component	
national morale	morale	national morale		
political development	leadership	government; national leadership	political component	governmental organization and administration (wisdom of leadership)
	ideology	ideology		ideas
				productive capacity
				stragegic position
				transportation and communications
				intelligence

(6) A.F.K. Organski, **World Politics,** 2nd ed. (New York; Knopf, 1968), p. 124.

(7) Norman D. Palmer and Howard C. Perkins, **International Relations: The World Community in Transition** (Boston: Houghton-Mifflin, 1957), pp. 35-91.

(8) John G. Stoessinger, **The Might of Nations: World Politics in our Time,** 3rd ed (New York: Random House, 1969) pp. 15-27.

(9) U.S. Army War College, **Power Analysis of the Nation-State,** Discussion Topic 2-B, Carlisle Barracks, Pa., 1960, p. 2.

(10) Vernon Van Dyke, **International Politics,** 2nd ed. (New York: Appleton-Century-Crofts, 1966), pp. 199-200.

that the international circumstances and situations a nation experiences at any given time serves to determine the nature of its foreign conduct, rather than the conditions that prevail in the nation itself. While the traditional literature on foreign policy is voluminous, as is illustrated by the historical work of Taylor (161), that literature possesses much folklore that has yet to be subjected to disciplined inquiry through scientific investigative procedures. Much needs to be done from a systematic analytic focus. Exemplary of work on this dimension of foreign policy that demonstrates what might be done is that of Herman (64) on international crises and Singer and Small on systemic sources of foreign policy.

The foregoing literature review of approaches to the analysis of foreign policy suggests that, although we have made appreciable progress, we still have far to go before acquiring precise knowledge about the sources of foreign policy. Many areas of research remain neglected, and methodological sophistication, while growing, needs further development. Nevertheless, the success of much recent research of the type proposed by J. David Singer in this book suggests that, as the discipline continues to mature, the result will prove worth the effort. For current information on developments, and prospects for developments, in the field of foreign-policy analysis, it is worthwhile to consult the *Sage International Yearbook of Foreign Policy Studies,* edited by McGowan (98), and the new journal *International Interactions,* edited by Azar.

Our categorization of the varieties of foreign-policy research leaves much to be desired. It is neither exhaustive nor fully descriptive of all analytic perspectives on the foreign behavior of nations. In order to avoid the impression that the majority of work on the determinants of foreign policy has been an effort to describe and explain that behavior systematically, it should be noted that much of the discussion of this subject continues to be intuitive or traditional. Particularly prominent has been the discussion of the "political realist" school of thought. Indeed, Kenneth Thompson, himself a leading advocate of the realist position, has suggested that most of the scholarly dialogue in the last twenty-five years has consisted of an implicit debate between Hans Morgenthau and his critics. It is therefore important to point out the intellectual background of the realists. Reacting critically to what they assumed to be America's and the other Western democracies' failures to cope with Hitler, the "realist" school—characterized by the writing of Morgenthau (106) and George F. Kennan (83) in the 1940's and 1950's—tended to overemphasize the impact of the international context on foreign policy. Disliking the way in which domestic politics and the popularization of foreign policy affected foreign policy, they argued that a true understanding of national interest was based on the awareness of immutable interests and conditions in the international environment. Because the realists have confused their prescriptive analysis (domestic politics should not interfere with foreign policy) with their descriptive analysis (the international context determines foreign policy), they have tended to adopt a monocausal approach by emphasizing power and the international system in their foreign-policy analysis.

In closing, it should be emphasized that descriptive analysis of foreign policy must be both multicausal and multileveled. The student must not only look for general relationships among foreign-policy behavior and various foreign-policy determinants; he must also attempt to apply his general ideas about determinants and patterns to specific foreign-policy cases. By attempting to analyze foreign policy at both levels, he can develop and test better theories.

In order to illustrate some of the points raised in the preceding discussion of foreign-policy analysis, as well as to provide samples of existing literature in the field, what follows are several reading selections in modern foreign-policy studies. When reading these articles, the student should ask not only what information about foreign-policy behavior the author is providing, but also what investigative procedure the auther employed to reach his conclusions. With respect to this latter objective, it is especially instructive to compare the readings for the analytic techniques used to describe, explain, and prescribe foreign policy, because the differences identified should provide insights into some of the methodological points raised below.

SELECTED READINGS

The process of descriptive analysis covers a large variety of investigative techniques and styles for converting observations into statements identifying the distinguishing characteristics of phenomena. Aspects of foreign-policy behavior invite myriad descriptive approaches, ranging from purely verbal statements based on sense impresssions to statistical approaches descriptively summarizing enormous amounts of information in terms of generalizations. Our first reading selection illustrates the use of one such descriptive methodology—content analysis—to analyze an important but often overlooked component of foreign policy, the images held by members of the foreign-policy elite responsible for making decisions.

In this particular study, Ole R. Holsti sought to delineate the images and attitudes held by one such influential foreign policy–maker, John Foster Dulles, who, as Secretary of State during the Eisenhower Administration, had authority to make crucial foreign-policy decisions at the height of the Cold War. In order to do this, Holsti utilized content analysis, which is a technique for systematically classifying and counting words and themes contained in speeches or written material. By subjecting a large number of Dulles's policy statements and writings to rigorous comparative analysis through quantitative procedures, Holsti was able to discern and profile Dulles's attitudes as they were reflected in those statements and thereby generate a reliable description of the dimensions of his images and perceptions of the world. The description of Dulles's belief system that emerged from this approach to data collection provided Holsti with an empirical foundation from which to postulate some hypotheses regarding the sources

of that belief system as well as the consequences of those beliefs for the
kinds of relations the United States maintained with the Soviet Union.
Thus, Holsti was able to move from empirical description of beliefs to explanations of Dulles's beliefs in terms of the relationship between attitudes
and overt behavior. The product of the analysis is a classic example of how
systematic observation and descriptive techniques may be employed to
study what has traditionally been regarded as not amenable to measurement—namely, the beliefs people hold about the world in which they live.
Holsti's article demonstrates that, while we cannot get inside a decision-
marker's head in order to discern his thoughts and feelings, we can indirectly tap and analyze his beliefs by subjecting policy articulations as
revealed in public utterances to disciplined scrutiny. Thus, beliefs, while
not observable directly, can be estimated and inferred from public statements, under the assumption that such statements reflect and reveal the
attitudes of policy-makers. This is important analytically because, if we are
to study national conduct, we must consider as a salient variable accounting
for that conduct the beliefs people hold about the world in which they live.
No theory of international relations can purport to be adequate without
taking cognizance of the attitudinal dimension.

THE BELIEF SYSTEM AND NATIONAL
IMAGES: A CASE STUDY

Ole R. Holsti

I. THE BELIEF SYSTEM AND NATIONAL IMAGES

Even a cursory survey of the relevant literature reveals that in recent years
—particularly in the decade and a half since the end of World War II—
students of international politics have taken a growing interest in psycho-
attitudinal approaches to the study of the international system. It has
been proposed, in fact, that psychology belongs at the "core" of the discipline (Wright, 1955, p. 506). Two related problems within this area have
become particular foci of attention.

  1. A number of studies have shown that the relationship between "belief system," perceptions, and decision making is a vital one (Rokeach,
1960; Smith et al., 1956; Snyder et al., 1954).[1] A decision maker acts upon
his "image" of the situation rather than upon "objective" reality, and it
has been demonstrated that the belief system—its structure as well as its

Ole R. Holsti, "The Belief System and National Images: A Case Study," The Journal
of Conflict Resolution, VI, 3 (1962), pp. 244-52. Copyright, 1962, by the University of Michigan. Reprinted by permission of the author and publisher.

Holsti is a professor of political science at the University of British Columbia.

content—plays an integral role in the cognitive process (Boulding, 1956; Festinger, 1957; Ray, 1961).

2. Within the broader scope of the belief-system-perception-decision-making relationship there has been a heightened concern for the problem of stereotyped national images as a significant factor in the dynamics of the international system (Bauer, 1961; Boulding, 1959; Osgood, 1959b; Wheeler, 1960; Wright, 1957). Kenneth Boulding, for example, has written that, "The national image, however, is the last great stronghold of unsophistication. . . . Nations are divided into 'good' and 'bad'—the enemy is all bad, one's own nation is of spotless virtue" (Boulding, 1959, p. 130).

The relationship of national images to international conflict is clear: decision makers act upon their definition of the situation and their images of states--others as well as their own. These images are in turn dependent upon the decision-makers' belief system, and these may or may not be accurate representations of "reality." Thus it has been suggested that international conflict frequently is not between states, but rather between distorted images of states (Wright, 1957, p. 266).

The purpose of this paper is to report the findings of a case study dealing with the relationship between the belief system, national images, and decision making. The study centers upon one decision maker of unquestioned influence, John Foster Dulles, and the connection between his belief system and his perceptions of the Soviet Union.

The analytical framework for this study can be stated briefly. The belief system, composed of a number of "images" of the past, present, and future, includes "all the accumulated, organized knowledge that the organism has about itself and the world" (Miller et al., 1960, p. 16). It may be thought of as the set of lenses through which information concerning the physical and social environment is received. It orients the individual to his environment, defining it for him and identifying for him its salient characteristics. National images may be denoted as subpart of the belief system. Like the belief system itself, these are "models" which order for the observer what will otherwise be an unmanageable amount of information (Bauer, 1961).

In addition to organizing perceptions into a meaningful guide for behavior, the belief system has the function of the establishment of goals and the ordering of preferences. Thus it actually has a dual connection with decision making. The direct relationship is found in the aspect of the belief system which tells us "what ought to be," acting as a direct guide in the establishment of goals. The indirect link—the role that the belief system plays in the process of "scanning, selecting, filtering, linking, reordering, organizing, and reporting," (McClelland, 1962, p. 456)—arises from the tendency of the individual to assimilate new perceptions to familiar ones, and to distort what is seen in such a way as to minimize the clash with previous expectations (Bronfenbrenner, 1961; Ray, 1961; Rokeach, 1960). Like the blind men, each describing the elephant on the basis of the part he touches, different individuals may describe the same object or situation in terms of what they have been conditioned to see. This may be particularly true in a crisis situation: "Controversial issues tend to be polarized not only because commitments have been made but also because certain perceptions are actively excluded from consciousness if they do not fit the chosen world image" (Rapoport, 1960, p. 258). These relationships are presented in Figure 1.

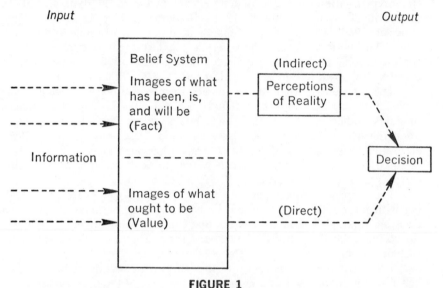

FIGURE 1
The dual relationship between belief system and decision making

The belief system and its component images are, however, dynamic rather than static; they are in continual interaction with new information. The impact of this information depends upon the degree to which the structure of the belief system is "open" or "closed." According to Rokeach,

> At the closed extreme, it is new information that must be tampered with—by narrowing it out, altering it, or constraining it within isolated bounds. In this way, the belief-disbelief system is left intact. At the open extreme, it is the other way around: New information is assimilated *as is* . . . thereby producing "genuine" (as contrasted with "party-line") changes in the whole belief-disbelief system [Rokeach, 1960, p. 50].

Thus while national images perform an important function in the cognitive process, they may also become dysfunctional. Unless they coincide in some way with commonly perceived reality, decisions based on these images are not likely to fulfill expectations. Erroneous images may also prove to have a distorting effect by encouraging the reinterpretation of information that does not fit the image; this is most probable with rigid "models" such as "totalitarian communism" or "monopolistic capitalism" which exclude the very types of information that might lead to a modification of the models themselves (Bauer, 1961; Wheeler, 1960).

II. JOHN FOSTER DULLES AND THE SOVIET UNION

The selection of John Foster Dulles as the central figure for my study fulfilled a number of historical and research requirements for the testing of hypotheses concerning the relationship between the belief system and perceptions of other nations. He was acknowledged as a decision maker of first-rate importance, and he held office during a period of dramatic changes in Soviet elites, capabilities, and tactics. In addition, he left voluminous public pronouncements and writings on both the Soviet Union and on the theoretical aspects of international politics, thus facilitating a reconstruction of salient aspects of both his belief system and his perceptions of the Soviet Union.

The sources used in this study included all of Dulles' publicly available statements concerning the Soviet Union during the 1953-1959 period, derived from a content analysis of 434 documents, including Congressional testimony, press conferences, and addresses.[2] These statements were transcribed, masked, and quantified according to the "evaluative assertion analysis" technique devised by Charles E. Osgood and his associates (Osgood *et al.,* 1956; Osgood, 1959a).[3]

All of Dulles' statements concerning the Soviet Union were translated into 3,584 "evaluative assertions" and placed into one of four categories:

1. *Soviet Policy:* assessed on a friendship-hostility continuum (2,246 statements).
2. *Soviet Capabilities:* assessed on a strength-weakness continuum (732 statements).
3. *Soviet Success:* assessed on a satisfaction-frustration continuum (290 statements).
4. *General Evaluation of the Soviet Union:* assessed on a good-bad continuum (316 statements).

The resulting figures, when aggregated into time periods, provide a record of the way in which Dulles' perceptions of each dimension varied. From this record inferences can be made of the perceived relationship between the dimensions.

Dulles' image of the Soviet Union was built on the trinity of atheism, totalitarianism, and communism, capped by a deep belief that no enduring social order could be erected upon such foundations.[4] He had written in 1950, for example, that: "Soviet Communism starts with an atheistic, Godless premise. Everything else flows from that premise" (Dulles, 1950, p. 8). Upon these characteristics—the negation of values at or near the core of his belief system—he superimposed three dichotomies.

1. The "good" Russian people versus the "bad" Soviet leaders.[5]
2. The "good" Russian national interest versus "bad" international communism.[6]
3. The "good" Russian state versus the "bad" Communist Party.[7]

That image of the Soviet Union—which has been called the "inherent bad faith of the Communists" model (Kissinger, 1962, p. 201)—was sustained in large part by his heavy reliance on the study of classical Marxist writings, particularly those of Lenin, to find the keys to all Soviet policies (Dulles, 1958b).

In order to test the general hypothesis that information concerning the Soviet Union tended to be perceived and interpreted in a manner consistent with the belief system, the analysis was focused upon the relationship Dulles perceived between Soviet hostility and Soviet success, capabilities, and general evaluation of the Soviet Union. Specifically, it was hypothesized that Dulles' image of the Soviet Union would be preserved by associating decreases in perceived hostility with:

1. Increasing Soviet frustration in the conduct of its foreign policy.
2. Decreasing Soviet capabilities.
3. No significant change in the general evaluation of the Soviet Union.

Similarly, it was hypothesized that increasing Soviet hostility would be correlated with success and strength.

The results derived through the content analysis of Dulles' statements bear out the validity of the hypotheses. These strongly suggest that he attributed decreasing Soviet hostility to the necessity of adversity rather than to any genuine change of character.

In a short paper it is impossible to include all of the evidence and illustrative material found in the full-length study from which this paper is derived. A few examples may, however, illuminate the perceived relationship presented in Table 1.

The 1955-1956 period, beginning with the signing of the Austrian State Treaty and ending with the dual crises in Egypt and Hungary, is of particular interest. As shown in Fig. 2, Dulles clearly perceived Soviet hostility to be declining. At the same time, he regarded that decline to be symptomatic of a regime whose foreign policy had been an abysmal failure and whose declining strength was forcing Soviet decision makers to seek a respite in the Cold War. That he felt there was a causal connection between these factors can be suggested by numerous statements made during the period.[8]

The process of how Soviet actions were reinterpreted so as to preserve the model of "the inherent bad faith of the Communists" can also be illustrated by specific examples. Dulles clearly attributed Soviet actions which led up to the Geneva "Summit" Conference—notably the signing of the Austrian State Treaty—to factors other than good faith. He proclaimed that a thaw in the Cold War had come about because, "the policy of the Soviet Union with reference to Western Europe has failed" (U.S. Senate, 1955, p. 15), subsequently adding that, "it has been their [Soviet] system that is on the point of collapsing" (U.S. House of Representatives, 1955, p. 10).

A year later, when questioned about the Soviet plan to reduce their armed forces by 1,200,000 men, he quickly invoked the theme of the bad faith of the Soviet leadership. After several rounds of questions, in which each reply increasingly deprecated the value of the Soviet move in lowering world tensions, he was asked, "Isn't it a fair conclusion from what you have said this morning that you would prefer to have the Soviet Union keep these

TABLE 1

Period	Hostility	Success	Capabilities	General evaluation
1953: Jan.-June	+2.01	−1.06	+0.33	−2.81
July-Dec.	+1.82	−0.40	−0.30	−2.92
1954: Jan.-June	+2.45	+0.46	+2.00	−2.69
July-Dec.	+1.85	−0.25	+1.93	−3.00
1955: Jan.-June	+0.74	−1.81	−0.80	−2.83
July-Dec.	+0.96	−1.91	−0.20	−2.33
1956: Jan.-June	+1.05	−1.68	+0.37	−2.91
July-Dec.	+1.72	−2.11	−0.22	−3.00
1957: Jan.-June	+1.71	−2.10	−0.28	−2.79
July-Dec.	+2.09	−1.01	+0.60	−2.93
1958- Jan.-June 1959	+2.03	+0.02	+1.47	−2.86
July-Feb.	+2.10	−1.20	+1.71	−2.90

Correlations*

	N	r	P
Hostility—Success (Friendship— Failure):			
6 Month Periods (Table Above)	12	+0.71	0.01
12 Month Periods	6	+0.94	0.01
3 Month Periods	25	+0.58	0.01
Hostility—Strength (Friendship— Weakness):			
6 Month Periods (Table Above)	12	+0.76	0.01
12 Month Periods	6	+0.94	0.01
3 Month Periods	25	+0.55	0.01
Hostility—Bad (Friendship— Good):			
6 Month Periods (Table Above)	12	+0.03	n.s.
12 Month Periods	6	+0.10	n.s.
3 Month Periods	25	+0.10	n.s.

*Correlations, based on rank ordering of variables, were computed using Spearman's formula:

$$r = 1 - \frac{6 \Sigma D^2}{N(N^2 - 1)}$$

(McNemar, 1955, p. 208).

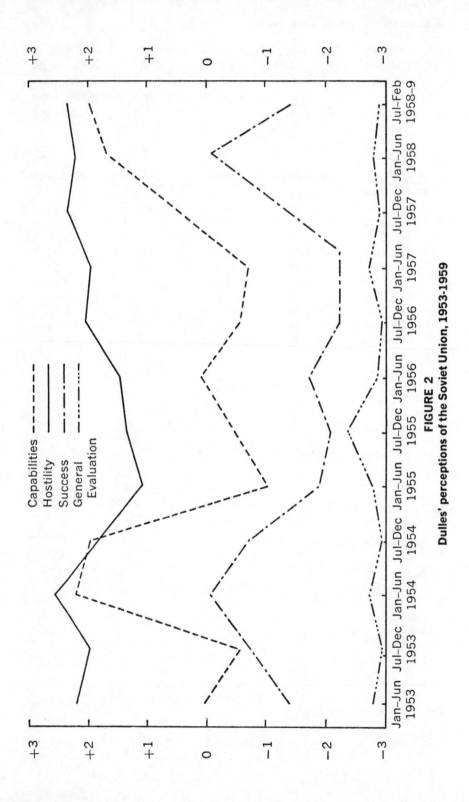

FIGURE 2
Dulles' perceptions of the Soviet Union, 1953-1959

men in their armed forces?" He replied, "Well, it's a fair conclusion that I would rather have them standing around doing guard duty than making atomic bombs." In any case, he claimed, the reduction was forced by industrial and agricultural weakness: "I think, however, that what is happening can be explained primarily by economic factors rather than by a shift in foreign policy intentions" (Dulles, 1956, pp. 884-5).

There is strong evidence, then, that Dulles "interpreted the very data which would lead one to change one's model in such a way as to preserve that model" (Bauer, 1961, p. 227). Contrary information (a general decrease in Soviet hostility, specific nonhostile acts) were reinterpreted in a manner which did not do violence to the original image. In the case of the Soviet manpower cuts, these were attributed to necessity (particularly economic weakness), and bad faith (the assumption that the released men would be put to work on more lethal weapons). In the case of the Austrian State Treaty, he explained the Soviet agreement in terms of frustration (the failure of its policy in Europe), and weakness (the system was on the point of collapse).

The extent to which Dulles' image of the Soviet Union affected American decision making during the period cannot be stated with certainty. There is considerable evidence, however, that he was the primary, if not the sole architect of American policy vis-à-vis the Soviet bloc (Adams, 1961; Morgenthau, 1961; Davis, 1961). Moreover, as Sidney Verba has pointed out, the more ambiguous the cognitive and evaluative aspects of a decision-making situation, and the less a group context is used in decision making, the more likely are personality variables to assert themselves (Verba, 1961, pp. 102-3). Both the ambiguity of information concerning Soviet intentions and Dulles' *modus operandi* appear to have increased the importance of his image of the Soviet Union.[9]

III. CONCLUSION

These findings have somewhat sobering implications for the general problem of resolving international conflict. They suggest the faliacy of thinking that peaceful settlement of outstanding international issues is simply a problem of devising "good plans." Clearly as long as decision makers on either side of the Cold War adhere to rigid images of the other party, there is little likelihood that even genuine "bids" (North *et al.*, 1960, p. 357) to decrease tensions will have the desired effect. Like Dulles, the Soviet decision makers possess a relatively all-encompassing set of lenses through which they perceive their environment. Owing to their image of "monopoly capitalism," they are also pre-conditioned to view the actions of the West within a framework of "inherent bad faith."

To the extent that each side undeviatingly interprets new information, even friendly bids, in a manner calculated to preserve the original image, the two-nation system is a closed one with small prospect for achieving even a desired reduction of tensions. If decreasing hostility is assumed to arise from weakness and frustration, and the other party is defined as inherently evil, there is little cause to reciprocate. Rather, there is every reason to press further, believing that added pressure will at least insure the continued good conduct of the adversary, and perhaps even cause its collapse. As a result, perceptions of low hostility are self-liquidating and perceptions of high hostility are self-fulfilling. The former, being associated with weakness and frustration, do not invite reciprocation; the latter, assumed to derive from strength and success, are likely to result in reactions which will increase rather than decrease tensions.

There is also another danger: to assume that the decreasing hostility of an adversary is caused by weakness (rather than, for example, the sense of confidence that often attends growing strength), may be to invite a wholly unrealistic sense of complacency about the other state's capabilities.

In such a closed system—dominated by what has been called the "mirror image"—misperceptions and erroneous interpretations of the other party's intentions feed back into the system, confirming the original error (Ray, 1961).[10] Figure 3 depicts such a system.

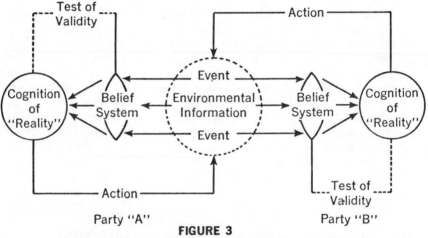

FIGURE 3
The indirect relationship between belief system and action
(Source: Ray, 1961, p. 21)

If this accurately represents the interaction between two hostile states, it appears that the probability of making effective bids to break the cycle would depend upon at least two variables:

1. The degree to which the decision makers on both sides approach the "open" end of Rokeach's scale of personality types (Rokeach, 1960).

2. The degree to which the social systems approach the "pluralistic" end of the pluralistic-monolithic continuum. The closer the systems come to the monolithic end, the more they appear to require the institutionalization of an "external enemy" in order to maintain internal cohesion (North, 1962, p. 41; Wheeler, 1960).

The testing of these and other hypotheses concerning the function of belief systems in international politics must, however, await further research. Certainly this looms as a high priority task given the current state of the international system. As Charles E. Osgood has so cogently said,

> Surely, it would be tragedy, a cause for cosmic irony, if two of the most civilized nations on this earth were to drive each other to their mutual destruction because of their mutually threatening conceptions of each other—without ever testing the validity of those conceptions [Osgood, 1959b, p. 318].

This is no idle warning. It has been shown empirically in this paper that the characteristics of the reciprocal mirror image operated between the two most powerful nations in the international system during a crucial decade of world history.

NOTES

[1]Although in the literature the terms "belief system" (Rokeach, 1960, pp. 18-9), "image" (Boulding, 1956, pp. 5-6) and "frame of reference" (Snyder et al., 1954, p. 101) have frequently been used synonymously, in this paper "belief system" will denote the complete world view, whereas "image" will denote some subpart of the belief system.

[2]The author has corresponded with a number of Dulles' close associates. They almost unanimously stated that Dulles' public assessments of various characteristics of the Soviet regime were identical with his private beliefs.

[3]The method involves the translation of all statements into one of two common sentence structures: 1. Attitude Object$_1$ (AO$_1$)/Verbal Connector (c)/Common-meaning Evaluator (cm); 2. Attitude Object$_1$ (AO$_1$)/Verbal Connector (c)/Attitude Object$_2$ (AO$_2$). For example, the sentence, "The Soviet Union is hostile, opposing American national interests," is translated to read: 1. The Soviet Union/is/hostile (form 1); 2. The Soviet Union/opposes/American national interests (form 2).

The value of AO$_1$'s are computed on the basis of values assigned to the cm's, c's and AO$_2$'s. These range from $+3$ to -3, depending upon their direction and intensity.

[4]"Dulles was an American Puritan very difficult for me (Albrecht von Kessel), a Lutheran, to understand. This partly led him to the conviction that Bolshevism was a product of the devil and that God would wear out the Bolsheviks in the long run, whereas many consider it a perversion of Russian qualities" (Drummond and Colbentz, 1960, p. 15).

[5]"There is no dispute at all between the United States and the peoples of Russia. If only the Government of Russia was interested in looking out for the welfare of Russia, the people of Russia, we would have a state of non-tension right away" (Dulles, 1958a, p. 734).

[6]"The time may come—I believe it will come—when Russians of stature will patriotically put first their national security and the welfare of their people. They will be unwilling to have that security and that welfare subordinated to the worldwide ambitions of international communism" (Dulles, 1955b, p. 329).

[7]"The ultimate fact in the Soviet Union is the supreme authority of the Soviet Communist Party. . . . That fact has very important consequences, for the State and the Party have distinctive goals and they have different instruments for getting those goals. . . . Most of Russia's historic goals have been achieved. . . . But the big, unattained goals are those of the Soviet Communist Party" (Dulles, 1948, pp. 271-2).

[8]"It is that (United States) policy, and the failure of the Soviet Union to disrupt it, and the strains to which the Soviet Union has itself been subjected which undoubtedly require a radical change of tactics on the part of the Soviet Union" (Dulles, 1955a, p. 914).

"Today the necessity for (Soviet) virtue has been created by a stalwart thwarting of efforts to subvert our character. If we want to see that virtue continue, I suggest that it may be prudent to continue what produced it" (Dulles, 1955c, p. 8).

"The fact is, (the Soviets) have failed, and they have got to devise new policies. . . . Those policies have gradually ceased to produce any results for them. . . . The result is, they have got to review their whole creed, from A to Z" (U.S. Senate, 1956, p. 190).

[9]"Nor was the Secretary of State, in either his thinking or his decisions, much affected by what the Department of State knew and did. Dulles devised the foreign policies of the United States by drawing upon his own knowledge, experience and insight, and the Department of State merely implemented these policies" (Morgenthau, 1961, p. 305).

"He was a man of supreme confidence within himself. . . . He simply did not pay any attention to staff or to experts or anything else. Maybe in a very subconscious way he did catalogue some of the information given him but he did not, as was characteristic of Acheson and several others of the Secretaries of State with whom I have worked, take the very best he could get out of his staff" (Anon., 1961).

[10]"Herein lies the terrible danger of the distorted mirror image, for it is characteristic of such images that they are self-confirming; that is, each party, often against its own wishes, is increasingly driven to behave in a manner which fulfills the expectations of the other. . . . Seen from this perspective, the primary danger of the Soviet-American mirror image is that it impels each nation to act in a manner which confirms and enhances the fear of the other to the point that even deliberate efforts to reverse the process are reinterpreted as evidence of confirmation" (Bronfenbrenner, 1961, p. 51).

REFERENCES

Adams, Sherman. *Firsthand Report*. New York: Harper, 1961.

Anonymous. "Letter to Author by an Associate of Mr. Dulles." August 25, 1961.

Bauer, Raymond A. "Problems of Perception and the Relations Between the United States and the Soviet Union," *The Journal of Conflict Resolution* 5 (1961): 223-29.

Boulding, Kenneth E. *The Image*. Ann Arbor: University of Michigan Press, 1956.

———. "National Images and International Systems," *The Journal of Conflict Resolution* 3 (1959): 120-31.

Bronfenbrenner, Urie. "The Mirror Image in Soviet-American Relations: A Social Psychologist's Report," *The Journal of Social Issues* 17 (1961): 45-56.

Davis, S. R. "Recent Policy Making in the United States Government." In D. G. Brennan (ed.). *Arms Control, Disarmament, and National Security*. New York: Braziller, 1961.

Drummond, R. and Coblentz, G. *Duel at the Brink*. Garden City: Doubleday, 1960.

Dulles, John F. "Not War, Not Peace," *Vital Speeches* 14 (1948): 270-73.

———. *War and Peace*. New York: Macmillan, 1950.

———. "Transcript of News Conference, May 24, 1955," *Department of State Bulletin* 32 (1955): 914. (a)

———. "Our Foreign Policies in Asia," *Department of State Bulletin* 32 (1955): 327-32. (b)

———. "Tenth Anniversary of the U.N.," *Department of State Bulletin* 33 (1955): 6-10. (c)

———. "Transcript of News Conference, May 15, 1956," *Department of State Bulletin* 34 (1956): 880-86.

———. "Interview," *Department of State Bulletin* 39 (1958): 733-39. (a)

———. "Reply to Bertrand Russell," *Department of State Bulletin* 38 (1958): 290-93. (b)

Festinger, Leon. *A Theory of Cognitive Dissonance*. Evanston, Ill.: Row, 1957.

Kissinger, H. *The Necessity of Choice*. Garden City: Doubleday, 1962.

McClelland, Charles A. "General Systems and the Social Sciences," *Etc.: A Review of General Semantics* 18 (1962): 449-68.

McNemar, Q. *Psychological Statistics*. New York: Wiley, 1955.

Miller, G. A., Galanter, E., and Pribram, K. H. *Plans and the Structure of Behavior*. New York: Holt, 1960.

Morgenthau, Hans J. "John Foster Dulles." In N. A. Grabner (ed.). *An Uncertain Tradition*. New York: McGraw, 1961.

North, Robert C. "Some Informal Notes on Conflict and Integration." Unpublished manuscript, 1962.

North, Robert C., Koch, Howard, and Zinnes, Dina. "The Integrative Functions of Conflict," *The Journal of Conflict Resolution* 4 (1960): 353-74.

Osgood, C. E. "The Representational Model." In I. Pool (ed.). *Trends in Content Analysis.* Urbana, Ill.: University of Illinois Press, 1959. (a)

————. "Suggestions for Winning the Real War with Communism," *The Journal of Conflict Resolution* 3 (1959): 311-25. (b)

Osgood, C. E., Saporta, S., and Nunnally, J. C. "Evaluative Assertion Analysis," *Litera* 3 (1956): 47-102.

Rapoport, A. *Fights, Games, and Debates.* Ann Arbor: University of Michigan Press, 1960.

Ray, J. C. "The Indirect Relationship Between Belief System and Action in Soviet-American Interaction." Unpublished M.A. Thesis: Stanford University, 1961.

Rokeach, M. *The Open and Closed Mind.* New York: Basic Books, 1960.

Smith, M. B., Bruner, J. S., and White, R. W. *Opinions and Personality.* New York: Wiley, 1956.

Snyder, R. C., Bruck, H. W., and Sapin, B. *Decision-making as an Approach to the Society of International Politics.* Princeton: Princeton University Press, 1954.

U.S. House of Representatives. Committee on Appropriations. *Hearings.* (June 10, 1955), Washington, 1955.

U.S. Senate. Committee on Foreign Relations. *Hearings.* (May 5, 1955), Washington, 1955.

————. *Hearings.* (February 24, 1956), Washington, 1956.

Verba, Sidney. "Assumptions of Rationality and Non-Rationality in Models of the International System," *World Politics* 14 (1961): 93-117.

Wheeler, H. "The Role of Myth System in American-Soviet Relations," *The Journal of Conflict Resolution* 4 (1960): 179-84.

Wright, Quincy. *The Study of International Relations.* New York: Appleton, 1955.

————. "Design for a Research Project on International Conflict and the Factors Causing Their Aggravation or Amelioration," *Western Political Quarterly* 10 (1957): 263-75.

The preceding article illustrates how an ostensibly intractable problem—the description of a person's belief system—may be approached in a meaningful analytic manner. Substantively, Holsti's study does much to inform us about the connection between policy-makers' images of their external environment, on the one hand, and their actual conduct, on the other. Holsti's systematic observational and descriptive procedures enable him to identify four dimensions of the Secretary of State's attitude toward the U.S.S.R. He found that over time Dulles consistently perceived a relationship between Soviet hostility-friendship and Soviet strength. When the Soviets were perceived as becoming more friendly, they were also perceived as becoming weaker. Holsti asserts that Dulles's predisposition to see a casual connection between Soviet friendship and Soviet weakness is evident of an "inherent bad faith model" stemming from Dulles's personality. Dulles is found to have a rigid, stereotyped image of the Soviet Union (evil, hostile, and aggressive), and his strong psychological need for image maintenance led him to reject any information that conflicted with his pre-existing belief that the Soviets could not be trusted. Friendly initiatives from the Soviets were therefore interpreted by Dulles to be attempts at deception rather than efforts at tension reduction. By implication, the study suggests that the hostility of the Cold War may be the product not of real conflicts of interests between countries but of images held by foreign-policy decision-makers.

In interpreting an analytic article of this sort, several methodological points are especially relevant and need to be identified. First, it may be argued that the systematic nature of the study's approach to description enhances the plausibility of its conclusions. Because this study is based on empirical evidence generated by systematic and replicable observational techniques, we can have more confidence in it than we would in a study that reached the same conclusions by the mere assertion of opinion about Dulles's beliefs. Holsti makes explicit the basis for his conclusions by clearly identifying what it is he is looking at (i.e., Dulles's speeches) and how he classified and treated the information contained in those sources (i.e., content analysis). One scholar (John E. Mueller, 107: pp. 217–18) has lucidly summarized the advantages of this approach to descriptive analysis in these terms:

> When properly performed, content analysis has an important advantage over more impressionistic modes of investigation: it is systematic. In non-systematic research, a single utterance, editorial, or anecdote may be glibly seized to represent an entire personality, political movement, or historical era. If Bismarck said once that he expected the next war to start with some damn foolishness in the Balkans, the content analyst argues, how many times did he say it would start with some damn foolishness in Scandinavia, or in the Baltic; and how many times did he refuse to speculate? The answer to this quite proper question can only be ascertained when one tediously examines *all* of Bismarck's sage pronouncements about the next war. To be sure, since Bismarck was accompanied constantly neither by a Boswell nor a tape-recorder, all his utterances on the subject are not preserved; nevertheless, one who wishes to comment on Bismarck's presence must at least make a systematic effort to examine all the records that are available.

Hence, because Holsti has undertaken the tedious task of probing a large quantity of Dulles's statements before arriving at any descriptive generalizations about the Secretary of State's beliefs, our confidence in the generalizations are increased; we are able to estimate the extent to which the generalizations adequately sample and represent the attitudes Dulles held. This avoids the risk of mistaking a single utterance for a person's entire belief system. The conclusions drawn are all the more convincing because we are able to know whether the analyst has allowed his a priori opinions about his subject to structure his observations and predetermine the descriptions he makes.

At the same time, however, we should not assume that the conclusions Holsti draws are necessarily valid. The accuracy of the descriptions made may be questioned in at least two respects. On the one hand, the descriptions can be no more valid than the evidence on which they are based. Working from Dulles's statements, Holsti generalizes about the Secretary of State's perceptions. We should entertain the possibility that foreign-

policy decision-makers might not reveal their true feelings and perceptions in statements made for public consumption. Thus, some doubt must always remain about any observational procedure that infers perceptions from an individual's statements. The descriptive generalizations that are presented must therefore be regarded as no more accurate or objective than the data on which they are based; a rigorous and systematic methodology is no guarantee of validity, no matter how sophisticated. On the other hand, we should test the validity of the findings by their applicability to other decision-makers and international situations. Since Holsti has conducted a case or idiographic study of one individual, we have no a priori way of knowing whether his findings regarding the relationship of beliefs to behavior are accurate or descriptive of the relationship as it applies to other decision-makers. A case study is incapable of demonstrating a general law, and hence we must regard findings that emerge from case studies as merely suggestive of the types of processes that are operative across many cases.

One last point about this reading is that it also presents a series of prescriptions. Rather than focusing on U.S. foreign policy per se, Holsti discusses the general implications for the international system of decision-makers holding cognitive bad-faith models. His prescriptions, therefore, are directed at all foreign-policy decision-makers and suggest that the maintenance of images based on suspicion and closed to new events is ultimately dysfunctional. The prescription is based on Holsti's commitment to the cause of international peace, since he assumes that, when decision-makers act on the kinds of images maintained by Dulles, conflict and war will result. This draws our attention to the indissoluble link that obtains between descriptive and prescriptive analyses. The descriptions we arrive at invariably have implications for the kind of behavior that ought to be pursued. Consequently, advice regarding the way states should behave must be based, to some extent, on empirical descriptions both of the kinds of behaviors states have undertaken in the past and of the products of those behaviors. Prescriptions are always made by reference, implicit or explicit, to conditions as they exist. Thus, every description has value implications, and every prescription is grounded on, or tied to, descriptions of the world as it is presumed to be.

A deficiency of current foreign-policy research has been the paucity of theoretical works that attempt to describe the nature of foreign-policy phenomena and the forces shaping those phenomena. Before one can begin an analysis of foreign policy, one must decide what is meant by those phenomena and determine the boundaries separating them from other forms of behavior. That is, analysis requires the construction of a paradigm of—or way of thinking about—a subject before an effort is made to explain it. Because foreign policy is a complex and amorphous form of behavior, its analysis invites a large number of ways of defining its distinguishing characteristics and differentiating it from similar aspects of social behavior. For this purpose, what is needed is a conceptual framework for investigating foreign-policy behavior. When we speak of conceptualization, we speak ultimately of how we organize our perceptions about a subject in order to make it comprehensible. A conceptual framework, therefore, is a heuristic device that slices up reality in a set of categories so that our observations about that reality can be structured. It tells us what to look at and informs us what attributes of it are most worthy of attention. Few such conceptual frameworks exist at the moment. A notable early work was that of Snyder, Bruck, and Sapin (156), which attempted to formulate a framework for analyzing foreign-policy decisions; more accurately, it sought to isolate the factors bearing on the behavior of decision-makers in foreign-policy situations. This framework served to stimulate a number of scholars to construct alternate ways of differentiating variables that influence external conduct to facilitate research. An example of one such follow-up work is that of Michael Brecher, Blema Steinberg, and Janice Stein (21).

Since the mid-1960's, partly as a consequence of the behavioral revolution in political science and partly as a result of the advent of comparative studies of foreign policy, the number of conceptual frameworks for the descriptive analysis of foreign policy have proliferated at an expanding rate. To some, the construction of conceptual frameworks may appear as a growth industry, given the number of scholars who have attempted to provide a cogent and meaningful way of looking at foreign policy from a comparative perspective. One of the first of these recent efforts, however, remains the most persuasive, judging by the frequency with which it is cited in the literature. This is the conceptual framework elaborated by James Rosenau, a portion of which is reprinted in Chapter 2. In his classic essay, Rosenau sought to identify the factors that were most potent, under various conditions, in affecting the behavior of nations beyond their borders. This framework—which he termed a "pretheory," to underscore its role of ordering perceptions so as to facilitate theorizing about the subject—spurred the development of comparative studies of foreign policy by demonstrating how the investigator might think about foreign policy in terms of the antecedent circumstances and national conditions that precipitate that behavior. As such, it made an important contribution to the systematic description of foreign policy, because it sought to identify the principal factors shaping foreign policy that could be studied on a cross-national basis. What follows is a portion of that much longer essay that explains Rosenau's own pretheory of foreign policy; while the original version elaborates in detail the methodological and epistemological ingredients of any pretheoretic framework of foreign policy, the material presented here outlines an approach to foreign policy that continues to influence and indeed dominate the thinking of a whole generation of foreign-policy analysts.

A PRE-THEORY OF FOREIGN POLICY

James N. Rosenau

Two basic shortcomings, one philosophical and the other conceptual, would appear to be holding back the development of foreign policy theory.[1] Let us look first at the philosophical shortcoming. If theoretical development in a field is to flourish, empirical materials which have been similarly processed must be available. It is no more possible to construct models of human behavior out of raw data than it is to erect a building out of fallen trees and unbaked clay. The trees must be sawed and the clay must be baked, and the resulting lumber and bricks must be the same size, shape, and color if a sturdy and coherent building is to be erected. Note that the design and function of the structure are not determined by the fact that materials comprising it have been similarly processed. The same bricks and lumber can be used to build houses or factories, large structures or small ones, modern buildings or traditional ones. So it is with the construction and use of social theories. There must be, as it were, pre-theory which renders the raw materials comparable and ready for theorizing. The materials may serve as the basis for all kinds of theories—abstract or empirical, single- or multi-country, pure or applied—but until they have been similarly processed, theorizing is not likely to occur, or, if it does, the results are not likely to be very useful.

Unlike economics, sociology, and other areas of political science, the field of foreign policy research has not subjected its materials to this preliminary processing. Instead, . . . each country and each international situation in which it participates is normally treated as unique and nonrecurrent, with the result that most available studies do not treat foreign policy phenomena in a comparable way. Thus it is that the same data pertaining to the external behavior of the Soviet Union are interpreted by one observer as illustrative of Khrushchev's flexibility, by another as reflective of pent-up consumer demands, and by still another as indicative of the Sino-Soviet conflict. To recur to the analogy of physical materials, it is as if one person cut up the fallen trees for firewood, another used them as the subject of a painting, and still another had them sawed for use in the building of a frame house.

It must be emphasized that the preliminary processing of foreign

James N. Rosenau, "Pre-theories and Theories of Foreign Policy," in R. Barry Farrell, ed., *Approaches to Comparative and International Politics* (Evanston, Ill.: Northwestern University Press, 1966), pp. 27-92. The article reprinted here encompasses only a small segment (pp. 39-52) of the original essay, which discusses in detail the nature of pretheories in the construction of comparative theories of foreign policy. The abridged version is reprinted by permission of the author and publisher.

Rosenau is a professor of transnational studies at the University of Southern California.

policy materials involves considerably more than methodological tidiness. We are not referring here to techniques of gathering and handling data, albeit there is much that could be said about the need for standardization in this respect. Nor do we have in mind the desirability of orienting foreign policy research toward the use of quantified materials and operationalized concepts, albeit again good arguments could be advanced on behalf of such procedures. Rather, the preliminary processing to which foreign policy materials must be subjected is of a much more basic order. It involves the need to develop an explicit conception of where causation is located in international affairs. Should foreign policy researchers proceed on the assumption that identifiable human beings are the causative agents? Or should they treat political roles, governmental structures, societal processes, or international systems as the source of external behavior? And if they presume that causation is located in all these sources, to what extent and under what circumstances is each source more or less causal than the others? Few researchers in the field process their materials in terms of some kind of explicit answer to these questions. Most of them, in other words, are not aware of the philosophy of foreign policy analysis they employ, or, more broadly, they are unaware of their pre-theories of foreign policy.[2]

To be sure, foreign policy researchers are not so unsophisticated as to fail to recognize that causation can be attributed to a variety of actors and entities. For years now it has been commonplace to avoid single-cause deterministic explanations and to assert the legitimacy of explaining the same event in a variety of ways. Rather than serving to discipline research, however, this greater sophistication has in some ways supplied a license for undisciplined inquiry. Now it is equally commonplace to assume that one's obligations as a researcher are discharged by articulating the premise that external behavior results from a combination of many factors, both external and internal, *without* indicating how the various factors combine under different circumstances. Having rejected single-cause explanations, in other words, most foreign policy researchers seem to feel they are therefore free *not* to be consistent in their manner of ascribing causation. Deterministic theories have philosophical roots, much foreign policy research seems to say, so that in abandoning the theories it is also necessary to give up the practice of locating one's work in a pre-theoretical context. Thus, as previously indicated, rare is the observer who is troubled by the discrepancy between his attribution of causation to De Gaulle's personal qualities and not to Khrushchev's. On the contrary, many apparently believe that such discrepancies are the mark of flexibility in research and the surest sign of having avoided deterministic modes of thought.

Nothing could be further from the truth. The development and employment of a pre-theory of foreign policy does not, as noted below, necessarily lead to determinism or even to greater rigidity. It merely provides a basis for comparison in the examination of the external behavior of various countries in various situations and, to repeat, there can be no real flourishing of theory until the materials of the field are processed—i.e., rendered comparable—through the use of pre-theories of foreign policy.

Perhaps the best way to indicate exactly what a pre-theory of foreign policy involves is by outlining the main ingredients of any pre-theory and then indicating how the author has integrated these ingredients into his own particular pre-theory. Although the statement is subject to modification and elaboration, it does not seem unreasonable to assert that all pre-theories of foreign policy are either five-dimensional or translatable into five dimensions. That is, all foreign policy analysts either explain the external behavior of societies in terms of five sets of variables, or they proceed in such a way that their explanations can be recast in terms of the five sets.[3] Listed in order of increasing temporal and spatial distance from the external behaviors for which they serve as sources, the five sets are what we shall call the idiosyncratic, role, governmental, societal, and systemic variables.

The first set encompasses the idiosyncrasies of the decision-makers who determine and implement the foreign policies of a nation. Idiosyncratic variables include all those aspects of a decision-maker—his values, talents, and prior experiences—that distinguish his foreign policy choices or behavior from those of every other decision-maker. John Foster Dulles' religious values, De Gaulle's vision of a glorious France, and Khrushchev's political skills are frequently mentioned examples of idiosyncratic variables. The second set of variables pertains to the external behavior of officials that is generated by the roles they occupy and that would be likely to occur irrespective of the idiosyncrasies of the role occupants. Regardless of who he is, for example, the U.S. ambassador to the United Nations is likely to defend American and Western positions in the Security Council and General Assembly. Governmental variables refer to those aspects of a government's structure that limit or enhance the foreign policy choices made by decision-makers. The impact of executive-legislative relations on American foreign policy exemplifies the operation of governmental variables. The fourth cluster of variables consists of those nongovernmental aspects of a society which influence its external behavior. The major value orientations of a society, its degree of national unity, and the extent of its industrialization are but a few of the societal variables which can contribute to the contents of a nation's external aspirations and policies. As for systemic variables, these include any nonhuman aspects of a society's external environment or any actions occurring abroad that condition or otherwise influence the choices made by its officials. Geographical "realities" and ideological challenges from potential aggressors are obvious examples of systemic variables which can shape the decisions and actions of foreign policy officials.

But these are only the ingredients of a pre-theory of foreign policy. To formulate the pre-theory itself one has to assess their *relative potencies*. That is, one has to decide which set of variables contributes most to external behavior, which ranks next in influence, and so on through all the sets. There is no need to specify exactly how large a slice of the pie is accounted for by each set of variables. Such precise specifications are characteristics of theories and not of the general framework within which data are organized. At this pre-theoretical level it is sufficient merely to have an idea of the relative potencies of the main sources of external behavior.

Note that constructing a pre-theory of foreign policy is not a matter of choosing to employ only one set of variables. We are not talking about levels of analysis but, in effect, about philosophies of analysis with respect to one particular level,[4] that of national societies. We assume that at this level behavior is shaped by individual, role, governmental, societal, and systemic factors and that the task is thus one of choosing how to treat each set of variables relative to the others. Many choices are possible. One hundred and twenty pre-theories can be constructed out of the 120 possible ways in which the five sets of variables can be ranked. Some analysts may prefer to use one or another of the rankings to analyze the external behavior of all societies at all times. Others may work out more complex pre-theories in which various rankings are applied to different societies under different circumstances.[5] Whatever the degree of complexity, however, the analyst employs a pre-theory of foreign policy when he attaches relative potencies to the main sources of external behavior.

Attaching causal priorities to the various sets of variables is extremely difficult. Most of us would rather treat causation as idiographic than work out a consistent pre-theory to account for the relative strength of each variable under different types of conditions. One way to overcome this tendency and compel oneself to differentiate the variables is that of engaging in the exercise of mentally manipulating the variables in actual situations. Consider, for example, the U.S.-sponsored invasion of Cuba's Bay of Pigs in April 1961. To what extent was that external behavior a function of the idiosyncratic characteristics of John F. Kennedy (to cite, for purposes of simplicity, only one of the actors who made the invasion decision)? Were his youth, his commitments to action, his affiliation with the Democratic party, his self-confidence, his close election victory—and so on through an endless list—relevant to the launching of the invasion and, if so, to what extent? Would any President have undertaken to oust the Castro regime upon assuming office in 1961? If so, how much potency should be attributed to such role-derived variables? Suppose everything else about the circumstances of April 1961 were unchanged except that Warren Harding or Richard Nixon occupied the White House; would the invasion have occurred? Or hold everything constant but the form of government. Stretch the imagination and conceive of the U.S. as having a cabinet system of government with Kennedy as prime minister; would the action toward Cuba have been any different? Did legislative pressure derived from a decentralized policy-making system generate an impulse to "do something" about Castro, and, if so, to what extent did these governmental variables contribute to the external behavior? Similarly, in order to pre-theorize about the potency of the societal variables, assume once more a presidential form of government. Place Kennedy in office a few months after a narrow election victory, and imagine the Cuban situation as arising in 1921, 1931, or 1951; would the America of the roaring twenties, the depression, or the McCarthy era have "permitted," "encouraged," or otherwise become involved in a refugee-mounted invasion? If the United States were a closed, authoritarian society rather than an open, democratic one, to what extent would the action toward Cuba have been different? Lastly, hold the idiosyncratic, role, governmental, and societal variables constant in the imagination, and posit Cuba as 9,000 rather than 90 miles off the Florida coast; would the invasion have nevertheless been launched? If it is estimated that no effort would have been made to span such a distance, does this mean that systemic variables should always be treated as overriding, or is their potency diminished under certain conditions?

The formulation of a pre-theory of foreign policy can be further simulated by expanding this mental exercise to include other countries and other situations. Instead of Kennedy, the presidency, and the U.S. of 1961 undertaking action toward Cuba, engage in a similar process of holding variables constant with respect to the action taken by Khrushchev, the monolithic Russian decision-making structure, and the U.S.S.R. of 1956 toward the uprising in Hungary. Or apply the exercise to the actions directed at the Suez Canal by Eden, the cabinet system, and the England of 1956. Or take still another situation, that of the attack on Goa carried out by the charismatic Nehru and the modernizing India of 1961. In all four cases a more powerful nation initiated military action against a less powerful neighbor that had come to represent values antagonistic to the interests of the attacker. Are we therefore to conclude that the external behavior of the U.S., Russia, England, and India stemmed from the same combination of external and internal sources? Should the fact that the attacked society was geographically near the attacking society in all four instances be interpreted as indicating that systemic variables are always relatively more potent than any other type? Or is it reasonable to attribute greater causation to idiosyncratic factors in one instance and to social factors in another? If so, what is the rationale for subjecting these seemingly similar situations to different kinds of analysis?

Reflection about questions similar to those raised in the two previous paragraphs has led this observer to a crude pre-theory of foreign policy in which the relative potencies of the five sets of variables are assessed in terms of distinctions between large and small countries, between developed and underdeveloped economies, and between open and closed political systems. As can be seen in Table 1 these three continua give rise to eight types of countries and eight different rankings of relative potency. There is no need here to elaborate at length on the reasoning underlying each ranking.[6] The point is not to demonstrate the validity of the ranking but rather to indicate what the construction of a pre-theory of foreign policy involves and why it is a necessary prerequisite to the development of theory. Indeed, given the present undeveloped state of the field, the rankings can be neither proved nor disproved. They reflect the author's way of organizing materials for close inspection and not the inspections themselves. To be theoretical in nature, the rankings would have to specify *how much* more potent each set of variables is than those below it on each scale, and the variables themselves would have to be causally linked to specific forms of external behavior.

To be sure, as in all things, it is possible to have poor and unsound pre-theories of foreign policy as well as wise and insightful ones. The author's pre-theory may well exaggerate the potency of some variables and underrate others, in which case the theories which his pre-theory generates or supports will in the long run be less productive and enlightening than those based on pre-theories which more closely approximate empirical reality. Yet, to repeat, this pre-theory is not much more than an orientation and is not at present subject to verification.

One suspects that many foreign policy analysts would reject this pre-theory, not because they conceive of different rankings or even different sets of variables but rather because the very idea of explicating a pre-theory strikes them as premature or even impossible. Those committed to the single-country, historical approach to foreign affairs would no doubt object that developing a pre-theory is a fruitless endeavor, since every situation is different from every other and no pre-theory can possibly be so coherent as to account for the infinite variation that marks international life. Other analysts, including some who are more social-scientific in their orientation, reject the possibility of pre-theorizing on the grounds that the same events can be explained in several ways and that therefore the problem of determining the relative potencies of different sets of variables can never be satisfactorily solved.[7]

The fact is, however, that one cannot avoid having a pre-theory of foreign policy whenever one takes on the task of tracing causation. Even the most historical-minded analyst makes the initial assumption that events derive from an underlying order, that every external behavior of every society stems from some source and is therefore, at least theoretically, explicable. To assume otherwise—to view the external behaviors of societies as random and impulsive, as occurring for no reason, and as therefore unknowable—is to render analysis useless and to condemn the analyst to perpetual failure. Since we cannot avoid the presumption of an underlying order, neither can we avoid having some conception of its nature. Yet causation is not self-revealing. The underlying order does not simply manifest itself for the diligent analyst who gathers every scrap of evidence and then takes a long, hard look at what he has accumulated. Inevitably he must organize the evidence in terms of some frame of reference, crude and premature as it may seem. There may be infinite variety in international life, but analysts are not so infinitely flexible. They cannot, and they do not, ignore their prior knowledge about foreign affairs and start over, so to speak, each time they undertake to analyze an external behavior. Furthermore, even if one were to assume that each international situation is different from every other situation, it is still necessary to have some basis for recognizing and explaining the differences. Similarly, even if one assumes that the same event is subject to a variety of interpretations, depending on the perspective of the observer, it is nevertheless necessary to adopt a particular perspective if any interpretation is to be made.

While it is thus impossible to avoid possession of a pre-theory of foreign policy, it is quite easy to avoid awareness of one's pre-theory and to proceed as if one started over with each situation. Explicating one's conception of the order that underlies the external behavior of societies can

Table 1

An Abbreviated Presentation of the Author's Pre-Theory of Foreign Policy, in Which Five Sets of Variables Underlying the External Behavior of Societies Are Ranked According to Their Relative Potencies in Eight Types of Societies

Geography and physical resources	Large Country				Small Country			
State of the economy	Developed		Underdeveloped		Developed		Underdeveloped	
State of the polity	Open	Closed	Open	Closed	Open	Closed	Open	Closed
Rankings of the variables	Role Societal Governmental Systemic Idiosyncratic	Role Idiosyncratic Governmental Systemic Societal	Idiosyncratic Role Societal Systemic Governmental	Idiosyncratic Role Governmental Systemic Societal	Role Systemic Societal Governmental Idiosyncratic	Role Systemic Idiosyncratic Governmental Societal	Idiosyncratic Systemic Role Societal Governmental	Idiosyncratic Systemic Role Governmental Societal
Illustrative examples	U.S.	U.S.S.R.	India	Red China	Holland	Czecho-slovakia	Kenya	Ghana

be an excruciating process. As in psychoanalysis, bringing heretofore implicit and examined assumptions into focus may compel one to face considerations which one has long sought to ignore. Some of the assumptions may seem utterly ridiculous when exposed to explicit and careful perusal. Others may seem unworkable in the light of new knowledge. Still others may involve mutually exclusive premises, so that to recognize them would be to undermine one's previous work and to obscure one's present line of inquiry.

Nor are matters greatly simplified by emotional readiness to live with the results of explication. There still remains the intellectually taxing task of identifying the variables which one regards as major sources of external behavior and of then coming to some conclusion about their relative potencies under varying circumstances. Such a task can be very difficult indeed. Long-standing habits of thought are involved, and the analyst may have become so accustomed to them that for him the habits are part of ongoing reality and not of his way of perceiving reality. In addition, if these habits provide no experience in pre-theorizing about the processes of causation, it will not be easy to tease out variable and assess their potencies. For example, while it is relatively simple to observe that a De Gaulle is less restrained in foreign policy than a Khrushchev, many analysts—especially those who insist that every situation is unique and that therefore they do not possess a pre-theory of foreign policy—would have a hard time discerning that the observation stems from their pre-theoretical premise that idiosyncratic variables have greater potency in France than in the Soviet Union.

Great as the obstacles to explication may be, however, they are not insurmountable. Patience and continual introspection can eventually bring implicit and unexamined premises to the surface. The first efforts may result in crude formulations, but the more one explicates, the more elaborate does one's pre-theory become.

But, it may be asked, if the purpose of all this soul-searching and anguish is that of facilitating the devolopment of general theory, how will the self-conscious employment of pre-theories of foreign policy allow the field to move beyond its present position? As previously implied, the answer lies in the assumption that the widespread use of explicit pre-theories will result in the accumulation of materials that are sufficiently processed to provide a basis for comparing the external behavior of societies. If most researchers were to gather and present their data in the context of their views about the extent to which individuals, roles, governments, societies, and international systems serve as causal agents in foreign affairs, then even though these views might represent a variety of pre-theories, it should be possible to discern patterns and draw contrasts among diverse types of policies and situations. Theoretical development is not in any way dependent on the emergence of a consensus with respect to the most desirable pre-theory of foreign policy. Comparison and theorizing can ensue as long as each researcher makes clear what variables he considers central to causation and the relative potencies he ascribes to them. For even if one analyst ascribes the greatest potency to idiosyncratic variables, while another views them as having relatively little potency and still another regards them as important, they will have all provided data justifying their respective assumptions, and in so doing they will have given the theoretician the materials he needs to fashion if-then propositions and to move to ever higher levels of generalization.

NOTES

1. A third shortcoming, so closely intertwined with the other two that its relevance is manifest throughout the ensuing discussion and requires only brief identification here, is of an organizational nature: Namely, the discipline of political science is at present organized in such a way that the external behavior of national political systems does not fall within the purview of scholars who are interested in the construction of general theories. Neither of the two groups of model builders who might be expected to theorize about foreign policy—those in comparative politics and those in international politics—is drawn by conceptual necessity to find a theoretical home for the external behavior of societies. Students of comparative politics focus primarily on national political systems and the interaction processes that occur *within* them. Once a pattern of interaction moves outside a national system, therefore, the comparative politics specialist tends to lose interest in it. Of primary concern to students of international politics, on the other hand, are the processes of interaction that occur *among* national systems. Consequently the international politics specialist tends to take internal influences on external behavior for granted and to become interested in the patterns generated by national systems only after they have crossed over into the international realm. Foreign policy phenomena, in short, are the unwanted stepchildren of political systems. They serve as outputs for one type of system and as inputs for another, but they do not constitute actions which both begin and culminate in any system that is of interest to present-day political theorists. Hence, notwithstanding their intense relevance to students of practical policy-making problems, foreign policy phenomena have been neglected by theoreticians and relegated to the residual category of systems theory known as "boundary problems."
   The one exception to this pattern is, of course, those theoreticians for whom the boundary between national and international systems is the core of their concern, i.e., those who specialize in the processes of supranational integration. It is perhaps significant that the most promising theory in this area is presently being developed by a sociologist, Amitai Etzioni, whose training and experience do not confine him to the traditional boundaries of the discipline of political science.
2. Briefly, by pre-theory is meant both an early step toward explanation of specific empirical events and a general orientation toward all events, a point of view or philosophy about the way the world is. Ideally pre-theories would be limited to the former meaning, but this requires that a field be in general agreement about the "proper" orientation toward its subject matter, a situation which the field of foreign policy research is far from even approximating.
3. For approaches which assert the utility of employing two and six sets of variables, see, respectively, J. David Singer, "The Levels-of-Analysis Problem in International Relations," *World Politics*, XIV: 1, October 1961, pp. 77–92; and Robert C. North *et al.*, *Content Analysis* (Evanston, Ill.: Northwestern University Press, 1963), pp. 5–7.
4. A level of analysis is distinguished by the units in terms of which behavior is explained, whereas a philosophy of analysis pertains to how the units are interrelated at a given level. The same behavior, therefore, can be analyzed both at

several levels and in several ways at the same level. Consider the act of blushing. This can be explained both physiologically and psychologically, but S-R and Lewinian psychologists would offer different explanations of what caused the blush (as there might, for all the author knows, be sharp differences among the physiologists). Likewise, a presidential speech at the United Nations can be explained both physiologically and politically, but some political scientists might see the behavior as the last act in a sequence fostered by a loose bipolar system and others would treat it as derived from the requirements of an oncoming election campaign. An even better example of different philosophies of analysis in the foreign policy field is provided by the role accorded to motivational variables by students of decision-making on the one hand and by "realists" on the other. Both groups attempt to explain the external behavior of societies, but the former give high priority to the motives of officials while the latter consider the examination of motives to be "both futile and deceptive." Confirm, respectively Snyder, Bruck, and Sapin, *Decision-Making as an Approach to the Study of International Politics* (Princeton, N.J.: Organizational Behavior Section, Foreign Policy Analysis Series, No. 3, 1954), pp. 92–117, and Hans J. Morgenthau, *Politics Among Nations*, 3d ed. (New York: Knopf, 1960), p. 6.

5. Ultimately, of course, the number of pre-theories will dwindle. A large number seems plausible at present because of the undevelopd state of the field. So little systematic knowledge about the sources of external behavior is currently available that fault cannot be found with any pre-theory on the grounds that it is discrepant with observed phenomena. However, as pre-theories make theorizing possible, and as theories then facilitate more systematic observation and more incisive comprehension of how international behavior is generated, consensuses will develop about the nature of empirical reality. Accordingly, those pre-theories which prove to be most "unreal" will be abandoned. Whether the number will ever dwindle down to a single pre-theory espoused by all analysts seems doubtful. Or at least many decades will have to elapse before the mysteries of international life are fathomed to the point where widespread agreement exists on the dynamics of external behavior. More likely is a long-run future in which knowledge of empirical reality becomes sufficiently extensive to reduce the field to several major schools of thought.

6. Suffice it to note that the potency of a systemic variable is considered to vary inversely with the size of a country (there being greater resources available to larger countries and thus lesser dependence on the international system than is the case with smaller countries), that the potency of an idiosyncratic factor is assumed to be greater in less developed economies (there being fewer of the restraints which bureaucracy and large-scale organization impose in more developed economies), that for the same reason a role variable is accorded greater potency in more developed economies, that a societal variable is considered to be more potent in open polities than in closed ones (there being a lesser need for officials in the latter to heed nongovernmental demands than in the former), and that for the same reason governmental variables are more potent than societal variables in closed polities than in open ones.

7. A succinct illustration of this viewpoint is provided by the following: "All governments seek success in foreign policy. . . . But the determination or desperation with which they do so is due to their position in the balance of rising and declining energies and power that is a primary given, *not capable of satisfactory explanation,* of the politics of international systems. It is possible to explain particular expansionist drives as the result of a desire to escape from internal tensions; but it is also possible to impute the intensification of internal tensions and controls to the fact that a nation is committed to an expansionist policy in the first place. *The relative significance of internal and external determinants is as insoluble as is the question whether economic or*

political ones are more important" (George Liska, "Continuity and Change in International Systems," *World Politics*, XVI: 1, October 1963, p. 126, italics added). . . . This line of reasoning assumes that there is only one "right" solution to every analytic problem, and it thus does not allow for the possibility that different observers, employing different perspectives (i.e., pre-theories), will arrive at different solutions to the same problem. In this sense the question of the relative importance of economic and political determinants is not as insoluble as Liska believes. The former determinants take on greater importance from the perspective of the economist, whereas greater significance attaches to the latter from the perspective of the political scientist.

In interpreting Rosenau's article, it is important to keep in mind his primary objective: providing a basis for analyzing foreign policy by identifying the major factors bearing on it that are given to comparison. While this goal is designed to facilitate the construction of explanations of foreign policy, it is essentially a descriptive exercise, because it describes what it is about foreign-policy phenomena we might try to account for, and how. That is, it tells us about the nature of foreign policy and its causes through a description of the major components underlying it. As Rosenau took care to note,

. . . by pre-theory is meant both an early step toward explanation of specific empirical events and a general orientation toward all events, a point of view or philosophy about the way the world is. Ideally pre-theories would be limited to the former meaning, but this requires that a field be in general agreement about the "proper" orientation toward its subject matter, a situation which the field of foreign policy research is far from even approximating.

Hence, Rosenau's influential contribution to the field is both descriptive, in the sense that it suggests a posture the analyst might assume in observing the factors affecting foreign policy, and explanatory, in the sense that it suggests in a postulational manner the relative potencies that those factors exert, under specified conditions, in molding external conduct. Unlike the previous selection by Holsti, which described the behavior and beliefs observed about a discrete individual, Rosenau's effort described the variables presumed to condition the behavior of nations in general. Thus, Rosenau's conceptual framework is descriptive of the environment in which foreign policy is conducted, and it is designed to facilitate crossnational generalizations about the determinants of foreign behavior. The differences between the two studies show that, although descriptive analyses of foreign policy may be undertaken from varied perspectives (i.e., description of concrete events or actors as opposed to description of abstract processes) and for contrasting purposes (i.e., profiling a brief system vis-à-vis enhancing the prospects for nomothetic theory building), they nevertheless share a common interest in systematic analysis.

The preceding studies of foreign policy illustrated two modes of descriptive analysis. Once the investigator has devised a description of the phenomenon he seeks to investigate, he then must provide an explanation of that description. For instance, Holsti's study of Dulles's belief system encourages us to ask questions about the sources of those beliefs, whereas Rosenau's conceptual description motivates us to test some of his hypotheses regarding the determinants of national external behavior. Description precedes explanation.

A number of analytical styles are noticeable in the literature attempting to explain the nature of foreign policy. What follows are three examples of studies of foreign policy that are primarily explanatory. The first is a case study of a particular foreign-policy event, the Cuban Missile Crisis, in which alternate theoretical explanations of the behavior of individuals directly involved in that event are devised; the second is also a case study that seeks to test contending interpretations of American foreign-aid allocative behavior with a set of quantitative empirical data; and the third is a cross-national comparative study that seeks to develop an explanation of foreign conflict behavior that holds for virtually all states in the global system. Let's look at each of these explanatory analyses separately.

Graham T. Allison attempts, in "Conceptual Models and the Cuban Missile Crisis," to develop explanations of American decision-making during the Cuban Missile Crisis in 1962. Starting with the generic question "Why did U.S. foreign policy–makers act the way they did in response to the threats they perceived to exist in Cuba in 1962?" Allison seeks to provide a series of answers in terms of various factors operative in the foreign policy–making establishment, under the reasonable assumption that how a nation organizes itself to make foreign-policy decisions is important in understanding the decisions that are made. In conducting this analysis, he first constructs various descriptions of the events associated with the Cuban Missile Crisis; then he devises alternate explanations of the behavior he observes in the descriptive analysis. The result of this juxtaposed set of explanations is to demonstrate vividly how various conceptual models, or competing sets of explanations, equally plausible, might be made and justified, given the available evidence. *The reading selection thus illustrates that, in social science, complete explanation of a particular event is rarely obtainable, yet several reasonable explanations can be offered, with varying degrees of completeness.*

CONCEPTUAL MODELS AND THE CUBAN MISSILE CRISIS

Graham T. Allison

The Cuban missile crisis is a seminal event. For thirteen days of October 1962, there was a higher probability that more human lives would end suddenly than ever before in history. Had the worst occurred, the death of 100 million Americans, over 100 million Russians, and millions of Europeans as well would make previous natural calamities and inhumanities appear insignificant. Given the probability of disaster—which President Kennedy estimated as "between 1 out of 3 and even"—our escape seems awesome.[1] . . .

This study proceeds from the premise that marked improvement in our understanding of such events depends critically on more self-consciousness about what observers bring to the analysis. What each analyst sees and judges to be important is a function not only of the evidence about what happened but also of the "conceptual lenses" through which he looks at the evidence. The principal purpose of this essay is to explore some of the fundamental assumptions and categories employed by analysts in thinking about problems of governmental behavior, especially in foreign and military affairs.

The general argument can be summarized in three propositions:

1. Analysts think about problems of foreign and military policy in terms of largely implicit conceptual models that have significant consequences for the content of their thought.[2]

* * *

2. Most analysts explain (and predict) the behavior of national governments in terms of various forms of one basic conceptual model, here entitled the Rational Policy Model (Model I).[3]

* * *

Graham T. Allison, "Conceptual Models and the Cuban Missile Crisis," *The American Political Science Review*, LXIII, 3 (September, 1969): 689-718. (Abridged.) Footnotes have been renumbered. Copyright, 1969, the American Political Science Association. Reprinted by permission of the author and publisher.

A longer version of this paper was presented at the Annual Meeting of the American Political Science Association, September, 1968 (reproduced by the Rand Corporation, P-3919). The paper is part of a larger study, scheduled for publication in 1969 under the title *Bureaucracy and Policy: Conceptual Models and the Cuban Missile Crisis*. For support in various stages of this work I am indebted to the Institute of Politics in the John F. Kennedy School of Government and the Center for International Affairs, both at Harvard University, the Rand Corporation, and the Council on Foreign Relations. For critical stimulation and advice I am especially grateful to Richard E. Neustadt, Thomas C. Schelling, Andrew W. Marshall, and Elisabeth K. Allison.

Allison is a professor of government at Harvard University.

3. Two "alternative" conceptual models, here labeled an Organizational Process Model (Model II) and a Bureaucratic Politics Model (Model III) provide a base for improved explanation and predicition.

* * *

How do analysts attempt to explain the Soviet emplacement of missiles in Cuba? The most widely cited explanation of this occurrence has been produced by two RAND Sovietologists, Arnold Horelick and Myron Rush.[4] They conclude that "the introduction of strategic missiles into Cuba was motivated chiefly by the Soviet leaders' desire to overcome . . . the existing large margin of U.S. strategic superiority."[5] How do they reach this conclusion? In Sherlock Holmes style, they seize several salient characteristics of this action and use these features as criteria against which to test alternative hypotheses about Soviet objectives. For example, the size of the Soviet deployment, and the simultaneous emplacement of more expensive, more visible intermediate range missiles as well as medium range missiles, it is argued, exclude an explanation of the action in terms of Cuban defense—since that objective could have been secured with a much smaller number of medium range missiles alone. Their explanation presents an argument for one objective that permits interpretation of the details of Soviet behavior as a value-maximizing choice.

How do analysts account for the coming of the First World War? According to Hans Morgenthau, "the first World War had its origin exclusively in the fear of a disturbance of the European balance of power."[6] In the period preceding World War I, the Triple Alliance precariously balanced the Triple Entente. If either power combination could gain a decisive advantage in the Balkans, it would achieve a decisive advantage in the balance of power. "It was this fear," Morgenthau asserts, "that motivated Austria in July 1914 to settle its accounts with Serbia once and for all, and that induced Germany to support Austria unconditionally. It was the same fear that brought Russia to the support of Serbia, and France to the support of Russia."[7] How is Morgenthau able to resolve this problem so confidently? By imposing on the data a "rational outline."[8] The value of this method, according to Morgenthau, is that "it provides for rational discipline in action and creates astounding continuity in foreign policy which makes American, British, or Russian foreign policy appear as an intelligent, rational continuum . . . regardless of the different motives, preferences, and intellectual and moral qualities of successive statesmen."[9]

* * *

What is striking about these examples from the literature of foreign policy and international relations are the similarities among analysts of various styles when they are called upon to produce explanations. Each assumes that what must be explained is an action, i.e., the realization of some purpose or intention. Each assumes that the actor is the national government. Each assumes that the action is chosen as a calculated response to a strategic problem. For each, explanation consists of showing what goal the government was pursuing in committing the act and how this action was a reasonable choice, given the nation's objectives. This set of assumptions characterizes the rational policy model . . .

Most contemporary analysts (as well as laymen) proceed predominantly—albeit most often implicitly—in terms of this model when attempting to explain happenings in foreign affairs. Indeed, that occurrences in foreign affairs are the *acts* of *nations* seems so fundamental to thinking about such problems that this underlying model has rarely been recognized: to explain an occurrence in foreign policy simply means to show how the government could have rationally chosen that action.

* * *

RATIONAL POLICY PARADIGM

* * *

Happenings in foreign affairs are conceived as actions chosen by the nation or national government, governments select the action that will maximize strategic goals and objectives. These "solutions" to strategic problems are the fundamental categories in terms of which the analyst perceives what is to be explained.

This paradigm leads analysts to rely on the following pattern of inference: if a nation performed a particular action, that nation must have had ends towards which the action constituted an optimal means. The rational policy model's explanatory power stems from this inference pattern. Puzzlement is relieved by revealing the purposive pattern within which the occurrence can be located as a value-maximizing means.

General Propositions

The disgrace of political science is the infrequency with which propositions of any generality are formulated and tested. "Paradigmatic analysis" argues for explicitness about the terms in which analysis proceeds, and seriousness about the logic of explanation. Simply to illustrate the kind of propositions on which analysts who employ this model rely, the formulation includes several.

The basic assumption of value-maximizing behavior produces propositions central to most explanations. The general principle can be formulated as follows: the likelihood of any particular action results from a combination of the nation's (1) relevant values and objectives, (2) perceived alternative courses of action, (3) estimates of various sets of consequences (which will follow from each alternative), and (4) net valuation of each set of consequences. This yields two propositions.

A. An increase in the cost of an alternative, i.e., a reduction in the value of the set of consequences which will follow from that action, or a reduction in the probability of attaining fixed consequences, reduces the likelihood of that alternative being chosen.

B. A decrease in the costs of an alternative, i.e., an increase in the value of the set of consequences which will follow from that alternative, or an increase in the probability of attaining fixed consequences, increases the likelihood of that action being chosen.[10]

Specific Propositions

A. *Deterrence.* The likelihood of any particular attack results from the factors specified in the general proposition. Combined with factual assertions, this general proposition yields the propositions of the sub-theory of deterrence.

(1) A stable nuclear balance reduces the likelihood of nuclear attack. This proposition is derived from the general proposition plus the asserted fact that a second-strike capability affects the potential attacker's calculations by increasing the likelihood and the costs of one particular set of consequences which might follow from attack—namely, retaliation.

(2) A stable nuclear balance increases the probability of limited war. This proposition is derived from the general proposition plus the asserted fact that though increasing the costs of a nuclear exchange, a stable nuclear balance nevertheless produces a more significant reduction in the probability that such consequences would be chosen in response to a limited war. Thus this set of consequences weighs less heavily in the calculus.

B. *Soviet Force Posture.* The Soviet Union chooses its force posture (i.e., its weapons and their deployment) as a value-maximizing means of implementing Soviet strategic objectives and military doctrine. A proposition of this sort underlies Secretary of Defense Laird's inference from the fact of 200 SS-9s (large intercontinental missiles) to the assertion that, "the Soviets are going for a first-strike capability, and there's no question about it."[11]

* * *

THE U.S. BLOCKADE OF CUBA: A FIRST CUT[12]

The U.S. response to the Soviet Union's emplacement of missiles in Cuba must be understood in strategic terms as simple value-maximizing escalation. American nuclear superiority could be counted on to paralyze Soviet nuclear power; Soviet transgression of the nuclear threshold in response to an American use of lower levels of violence would be wildly irrational since it would mean virtual destruction of the Soviet Communist system and Russian nation. American local superiority was overwhelming: it could be initiated at a low level while threatening with high credibility an ascending sequence of steps short of the nuclear threshold. All that was required was for the United States to bring to bear its strategic and local superiority in such a way that American determination to see the missiles removed would be demonstrated, while at the same time allowing Moscow time and room to retreat without humiliation. The naval blackade—euphemistically named a "quarantine" in order to circumvent the niceties of international law—did just that.

The U.S. government's selection of the blockade followed this logic. Apprised of the presence of Soviet missiles in Cuba, the President assembled an Executive Committee (ExCom) of the National Security Council and directed them to "set aside all other tasks to make a prompt and intense survey of the dangers and all possible courses of action."[13] This group functioned as "fifteen individuals on our own, representing the President and not different departments."[14] As one of the participants recalls, "The remarkable aspect of those meetings was a sense of complete equality."[15] Most of the time during the week that followed was spent canvassing all the possible tracks and weighing the arguments for and against each. Six major categories of action were considered.

1. Do nothing. U.S. vulnerability to Soviet missiles was no new thing. Since the U.S. already lived under the gun of missiles based in Russia, a Soviet capability to strike from Cuba too made little real difference. The real danger stemmed from the possibility of U.S. over-reaction. The U.S. should announce the Soviet action in a calm, casual manner thereby deflating whatever political capital Khrushchev hoped to make of the missiles.

This argument fails on two counts. First, it grossly underestimates the military importance of the Soviet move. Not only would the Soviet Union's missile capability be doubled and the U.S. early warning system outflanked. The Soviet Union would have an opportunity to reverse the strategic balance by further installations, and indeed, in the longer run, to invest in cheaper, shorter-range rather than more expensive longer-range missiles. Second, the political importance of this move was undeniable. The Soviet Union's act challenged the American President's most solemn warning. If the U.S. failed to respond, no American commitment would be credible.

2. Diplomatic pressures. Several forms were considered: an appeal to the U.S. or O.A.S. for an inspection team, a secret approach to Khrushchev, and a direct approach to Khrushchev, perhaps at a summit meeting. The United States would demand that the missiles be removed, but the final settlement might include neutralization of Cuba, U.S. withdrawal from the Guantanamo base, and withdrawal of U.S. Jupiter missiles from Turkey or Italy.

Each form of the diplomatic approach had its own drawbacks. To arraign the Soviet Union before the U.N. Security Council held little promise since the Russians could veto any proposed action. While the diplomats argued, the missiles would become operational. To send a secret emissary to Khrushchev demanding that the missiles be withdrawn would be to pose untenable alternatives. On the one hand, this would invite Khrushchev to seize the diplomatic initiative, perhaps committing himself to strategic retaliation in response to an attack on Cuba. On the other hand, this would tender an ultimatum that no great power could accept. To confront Khrushchev at a summit would guarantee demands for U.S. concessions, and the analogy between U.S. missiles in Turkey and Russian missiles in Cuba could not be erased.

But why not trade U.S. Jupiters in Turkey and Italy, which the President had previously ordered withdrawn, for the missiles in Cuba? The U.S. had chosen to withdraw these missiles in order to replace them with superior, less vulnerable Mediterranean Polaris submarines. But the middle of the crisis was no time for concessions. The offer of such a deal might suggest to the Soviets that the West would yield and thus tempt them to demand more. It would certainly confirm European suspicions about American willingness to sacrifice European interests when the chips were down. Finally, the basic issue should be kept clear. As the President stated in reply to Bertrand Russell, "I think your attention might well be directed to the burglars rather than to those who have caught the burglars."[16]

3. A secret approach to Castro. The crisis provided an opportunity to separate Cuba and Soviet Communism by offering Castro the alternatives, "split or fall." But Soviet troops transported, constructed, guarded, and controlled the missiles. Their removal would thus depend on a Soviet decision.

4. Invasion. The United States could take this occasion not only to remove the missiles but also to rid itself of Castro. A Navy exercise had long been scheduled in which Marines, ferried from Florida in naval vessels, would liberate the imaginary island of Vieques.[17] Why not simply shift the point of disembarkment? (The Pentagon's foresight in planning this operation would be an appropriate antidote to the CIA's Bay of Pigs!)

Preparations were made for an invasion, but as a last resort. American troops would be forced to confront 20,000 Soviets in the first Cold War case of direct contact between the troops of the super powers. Such brinksmanship courted nuclear disaster, practically guaranteeing an equivalent Soviet move against Berlin.

5. Surgical air strike. The missile sites should be removed by a clean, swift conventional attack. This was the effective counter-action which the attempted deception deserved. A surgical strike would remove the missiles and thus eliminate both the danger that the missiles might become operational and the fear that the Soviets would discover the American discovery and act first.

The initial attractiveness of this alternative was dulled by several difficulties. First, could the strike really be "surgical"? The Air Force could not guarantee destruction of all the missiles.[18] Some might be fired during the attack; some might not have been identified. In order to assure destruction of Soviet and Cuban means of retaliating, what was required was not a surgical but rather a massive attack—of at least 500 sorties. Second, a surprise air attack would of course kill Russians at the missile sites. Pressures on the Soviet Union to retaliate would be so strong that an attack on Berlin or Turkey was highly probable. Third, the key problem with this program was that of advance warning. Could the President of the

United States, with his memory of Pearl Harbor and his vision of future U.S. responsibility, order a "Pearl Harbor in reverse"? For 175 years, unannounced Sunday morning attacks had been an anathema to our tradition.[19]

6. Blockade. Indirect military action in the form of a blockade became more attractive as the ExCom dissected the other alternatives. An embargo on military shipments to Cuba enforced by a naval blockade was not without flaws, however. Could the U.S. blockade Cuba without inviting Soviet reprisal in Berlin? The likely solution to joint blockades would be the lifting of both blockades, restoring the new *status quo,* and allowing the Soviets additional time to complete the missiles. Second, the possible consequences of the blockade resembled the drawbacks which disqualified the air strike. If Soviet ships did not stop, the United States would be forced to fire the first shot, inviting retaliation. Third, a blockade would deny the traditional freedom of the seas demanded by several of our close allies and might be held illegal, in violation of the U.N. Charter and international law, unless the United States could obtain a two-thirds vote in the O.A.S. Finally, how could a blockade be related to the problem, namely, some 75 missiles on the island of Cuba, approaching operational readiness daily? A blockade offered the Soviets a spectrum of delaying tactics with which to buy time to complete the missile installations. Was a *fait accompli* not required?

In spite of these enormous difficulties the blockade had comparative advantages: (1) It was a middle course between inaction and attack, aggressive enough to communicate firmness of intention, but nevertheless not so precipitous as a strike. (2) It placed on Khrushchev the burden of choice concerning the next step. He could avoid a direct military clash by keeping his ships away. His was the last clear chance. (3) No possible military confrontation could be more acceptable to the U.S. than a naval engagement in the Caribbean. (4) This move permitted the U.S., by flexing its conventional muscle, to exploit the threat of subsequent non-nuclear steps in each of which the U.S. would have significant superiority.

Particular arguments about advantages and disadvantages were powerful. The explanation of the American choice of the blockade lies in a more general principle, however. As President Kennedy stated in drawing the moral of the crisis:

> Above all, while defending our own vital interests, nuclear powers must avert those confrontations which bring an adversary to a choice of either a humiliating retreat or a nuclear war. To adopt that kind of course in the nuclear age would be evidence only of the bankruptcy of our policy—of a collective death wish for the world.[20]

The blockade was the United States' only real option.

MODEL II: ORGANIZATIONAL PROCESS

For some purposes, governmental behavior can be usefully summarized as action chosen by a unitary, rational decisionmaker: centrally controlled, completely informed, and value maximizing. But this simplification must not be allowed to conceal the fact that a "government" consists of a conglomerate of semi-feudal, loosely allied organizations, each with a substantial life of its own. Government leaders do sit formally, and to some extent in fact, on top of this conglomerate. But governments perceive problems through organizational sensors. Governments define alternatives and estimate consequences as organizations process information. Governments act as these organizations enact routines. Government behavior can therefore be understood according to a second conceptual model, less as deliberate choices of leaders and more as *outputs* of large organizations functioning according to standard patterns of behavior.

To be responsive to a broad spectrum of problems, governments consist of large organizations among which primary responsibility for particular areas is divided. Each organization attends to a special set of problems and acts in quasi-independence on these problems. But few important problems fall exclusively within the domain of a single organization. Thus government behavior relevant to any important problem reflects the independent output of several organizations, partially coordinated by government leaders. Government leaders can substantially disturb, but not substantially control, the behavior of these organizations.

To perform complex routines, the behavior of large numbers of individuals must be coordinated. Coordination requires standard operating procedures: rules according to which things are done. Assured capability for reliable performance of action that depends upon the behavior of hundreds of persons requires established "programs." Indeed, if the eleven members of a football team are to perform adequately on any particular down, each player must not "do what he thinks needs to be done" or "do what the quarterback tells him to do." Rather, each player must perform the maneuvers specified by a previously established play which the quarterback has simply called in this situation.

At any given time, a government consists of *existing* organizations, each with a *fixed* set of standard operating procedures and programs. The behavior of these organizations—and consequently of the government —relevant to an issue in any particular instance is, therefore, determined primarily by routines established in these organizations prior to that instance. But organizations do change. Learning occurs gradually, over time. Dramatic organizational change occurs in response to major crises. Both learning and change are influenced by existing organizational capabilities.

* * *

ORGANIZATIONAL PROCESS PARADIGM

* * *

The happenings of international politics are, in three critical senses, outputs of organizational processes. First, the actual occurrences are organizational outputs.

Government leaders can trim the edges of this output and exercise some choice in combining outputs. But the mass of behavior is determined by previously established procedures. Second, existing organizational routines for employing present physical capabilities constitute the effective options open to government leaders confronted with any problem.

The fact that fixed programs (equipment, men, and routines which exist at the particular time) exhaust the range of buttons that leaders can push is not always perceived by these leaders. But in every case it is critical for an understanding of what is actually done. Third, organizational outputs structure the situation within the narrow constraints of which leaders must contribute their "decision" concerning an issue. Outputs raise the problem, provide the information, and make the initial moves that color the face of the issue that is turned to the leaders. As Theodore Sorensen has observed: "Presidents rarely, if ever, make decisions—particularly in foreign affairs—in the sense of writing their conclusions on a clean slate . . . The basic decisions, which confine their choices, have all too often been previously made."[21] If one understands the structure of the situation and the face of the issue—which are determined by the organizational outputs—the formal choice of the leaders is frequently anti-climactic.

* * *

General Propositions

A number of general propositions have been stated above. In order to illustrate clearly the type of proposition employed by Model II analysts, this section formulates several more precisely.

A. *Organizational Action.* Activity according to SOPs and programs does not constitute far-sighted, flexible adaptation to "the issue" (as it is conceived by the analyst). Detail and nuance of actions by organizations are determined predominantly by organizational routines, not government leaders' directions.

1. SOPs constitute routines for dealing with *standard* situations. Routines allow large numbers of ordinary individuals to deal with numerous instances, day after day, without considerable thought, by responding to basic stimuli. But this regularized capability for adequate performance

is purchased at the price of standardization. If the SOPs are appropriate, average performance, i.e., performance averaged over the range of cases, is better than it would be if each instance were approached individually (given fixed talent, timing, and resource constraints). But specific instances, particularly critical instances that typically do not have "standard" characteristics, are often handled sluggishly or inappropriately.

2. A program, i.e., a complex action chosen from a short list of programs in a repertoire, is rarely tailored to the specific situation in which it is executed. Rather, the program is (at best) the most appropriate of the programs in a previously developed repertoire.

3. Since repertoires are developed by parochial organizations for standard scenarios defined by that organization, programs available for dealing with a particular situation are often ill-suited.

B. *Limited Flexibility and Incremental Change.* Major lines of organizational action are straight, i.e., behavior at one time is marginally different from that behavior at $t - 1$. Simpleminded predictions work best: Behavior at $t + 1$ will be marginally different from behavior at the present time.

1. Organizational budgets change incrementally—both with respect to totals and with respect to intra-organizational splits. Though organizations could divide the money available each year by carving up the pie anew (in the light of changes in objectives or environment), in practice, organizations take last year's budget as a base and adjust incrementally. Predictions that require large budgetary shifts in a single year between organizations or between units within an organization should be hedged.

2. Once undertaken, an organizational investment is not dropped at the point where "objective" costs outweigh benefits. Organizational stakes in adopted projects carry them quite beyond the loss point.

C. *Administrative Feasibility.* Adequate explanation, analysis, and prediction must include administrative feasibility as a major dimension. A considerable gap separates what leaders choose (or might rationally have chosen) and what organizations implement.

1. Organizations are blunt instruments. Projects that require several organizations to act with high degrees of precision and coordination are not likely to succeed.

2. Projects that demand that existing organizational units depart from their accustomed functions and perform previously unprogrammed tasks are rarely accomplished in their designed form.

3. Government leaders can expect that each organization will do its "part" in terms of what the organization knows how to do.

4. Government leaders can expect incomplete and distorted information from each organization concerning its part of the problem.

5. Where an assigned piece of a problem is contrary to the existing goals of an organization, resistance to implementation of that piece will be encountered.

Specific Propositions

1. *Deterrence.* The probability of nuclear attack is less sensitive to balance and imbalance, or stability and instability (as these concepts are employed by Model I strategists) than it is to a number of organizational factors. Except for the special case in which the Soviet Union acquires a credible capability to destroy the U.S. with a disarming blow, U.S. superiority or inferiority affects the probability of a nuclear attack less than do a number of organizational factors.

First, if a nuclear attack occurs, it will result from organizational activity: the firing of rockets by members of a missile group. The enemy's *control system,* i.e., physical mechanisms and standard procedures which determine who can launch rockets when, is critical. Second, the enemy's programs for bringing his strategic forces to *alert status* determine probabilities of accidental firing and momentum. At the outbreak of World War I, if the Russian Tsar had understood the organizational processes which his order of full mobilization triggered, he would have realized that he had chosen war. Third, organizational repertoires fix the range of effective choice open to enemy leaders. The menu available to Tsar Nicholas in 1914 has two entrees: full mobilization and no mobilization. Partial mobilization was not an organizational option. Fourth, since organizational routines set the chessboard, the training and deployment of troops and nuclear weapons is crucial. Given that the outbreak of hostilities in Berlin is more probable than most scenarios for nuclear war, facts about deployment, training, and tactical nuclear equipment of Soviet troops stationed in East Germany—which will influence the face of the issue seen by Soviet leaders at the outbreak of hostilities and the manner in which choice is implemented—are as critical as the question of "balance."

2. *Soviet Force Posture.* Soviet force posture, i.e., the fact that certain weapons rather than others are procured and deployed, is determined by organizational factors such as the goals and procedures of existing military services and the goals and processes of research and design labs, within budgetary constraints that emerge from the government leader's choices. The frailty of the Soviet Air Force within the Soviet military establishment seems to have been a crucial element in the Soviet failure to acquire a large bomber force in the 1950s (thereby faulting American intelligence predictions of a "bomber gap"). The fact that missiles were controlled until 1960 in the Soviet Union by the Soviet Ground Forces, whose goals and procedures reflected no interest in an intercontinental mission, was not irrelevant to the slow Soviet buildup of ICBMs (thereby faulting U.S. intelligence predictions of a "missile gap"). These organizational factors (Soviet Ground Forces' control of missiles and that service's fixation with European scenarios) make the Soviet deployment of so many MRBMs that European targets could be destroyed three times over, more understandable. Recent weapon developments, e.g., the testing of a Fractional Orbital Bombardment System (FOBS) and multiple warheads for the SS-9, very likely reflect the activity and in-

terests of a cluster of Soviet research and development organizations, rather than a decision by Soviet leaders to acquire a first strike weapon system. Careful attention to the organizational components of the Soviet military establishment (Strategic Rocket Forces, Navy, Air Force, Ground Forces, and National Air Defense), the missions and weapons systems to which each component is wedded (an independent weapon system assists survival as an independent service), and existing budgetary splits (which probably are relatively stable in the Soviet Union as they tend to be everywhere) offer potential improvements in medium and longer term predictions.

THE U.S. BLOCKADE OF CUBA: A SECOND CUT

Organizational Intelligence. At 7:00 P.M. on October 22, 1962, President Kennedy disclosed the American discovery of the presence of Soviet strategic missiles in Cuba, declared a "strict quarantine on all offensive military equipment under shipment to Cuba," and demanded that "Chairman Khrushchev halt and eliminate this clandestine, reckless, and provocative threat to world peace."[22] This decision was reached at the pinnacle of the U.S. Government after a critical week of deliberation. What initiated that precious week were photographs of Soviet missile sites in Cuba taken on October 14. These pictures might not have been taken until a week later. In that case, the President speculated, "I don't think probably we would have chosen as prudently as we finally did."[23] U.S. leaders might have received this information three weeks earlier—if a U-2 had flown over San Cristobal in the last week of September.[24] What determined the context in which American leaders came to choose the blockade was the discovery of missiles on October 14.

There has been considerable debate over alleged American "intelligence failures" in the Cuban missile crisis.[25] But what both critics and defenders have neglected is the fact that the discovery took place on October 14, rather than three weeks earlier or a week later, as a consequence of the established routines and procedures of the organizations which constitute the U.S. intelligence community. These organizations were neither more nor less successful than they had been the previous month or were to be in the months to follow.[26]

The notorious "September estimate," approved by the United States Intelligence Board (USIB) on September 19, concluded that the Soviet Union would not introduce offensive missiles into Cuba.[27] No U-2 flight was directed over the western end of Cuba (after September 5) before October 4.[28] No U-2 flew over the western end of Cuba until the flight that discovered the Soviet missiles on October 14.[29] Can these "failures" be accounted for in organizational terms?

On September 19 when USIB met to consider the question of Cuba, the "system" contained the following information: (1) shipping intelligence had noted the arrival in Cuba of two large-hatch Soviet lumber ships, which were riding high in the water; (2) refugee reports of countless sightings of missiles, but also a report that Castro's private pilot, after a night of drinking in Havana, had boasted: "We will fight to the death and perhaps we can win because we have everything, including atomic weapons"; (3) a sighting by a CIA agent of the rear profile of a strategic missile; (4) U-2 photos produced by flights of August 29, September 5 and 17 showing the construction of a number of SAM sites and other defensive missiles.[30] Not all of this information was on the desk of the estimators, however. Shipping intelligence experts noted the fact that large-hatch ships were riding high in the water and spelled out the inference: the ships must be carrying "space consuming" cargo.[31] These facts were carefully included in the catalogue of intelligence concerning shipping. For experts sensitive to the Soviets' shortage of ships, however, these facts carried no special signal. The refugee report of Castro's private pilot's remark had been received at Opa Locka, Florida, along with vast reams of inaccurate reports generated by the refugee community. This report and a thousand others had to be checked and compared before being sent to Washington. The two weeks required for initial processing could have been shortened by a large increase in resources, but the yield of this source was already quite marginal. The CIA agent's sighting of the rear profile of a strategic missile had occurred on September 12; transmission time from agent sighting to arrival in Washington typically took 9 to 12 days. Shortening this transmission time would impose severe cost in terms of danger to sub-agents, agents, and communication networks.

On the information available, the intelligence chiefs who predicted that the Soviet Union would not introduce offensive missiles into Cuba made a reasonable and defensible judgment.[32] Moreover, in the light of the fact that these organizations were gathering intelligence not only about Cuba but about potential occurrences in all parts of the world, the informational base available to the estimators involved nothing out of the ordinary. Nor, from an organizational perspective, is there anything startling about the gradual accumulation of evidence that led to the formulation of the hypothesis that the Soviets were installing missiles in Cuba and the decision on October 4 to direct a special flight over western Cuba.

The ten-day delay between that decision and the flight is another organizational story.[33] At the October 4 meeting, the Defense Department took the opportunity to raise an issue important to its concerns. Given the increased danger that a U-2 would be downed, it would be better if the pilot were an officer in uniform rather than a CIA agent. Thus the Air Force should assume responsibility for U-2 flights over Cuba. To the contrary, the CIA argued that this was an intelligence operation and thus within the CIA's jurisdiction. Moreover, CIA U-2's had been modified in certain ways which gave them advantages over Air Force U-2's in averting Soviet SAM's. Five days passed while the State Department pressed for less risky alternatives such as drones and the Air Force (in Department of Defense guise) and CIA engaged in territorial disputes. On October 9 a flight plan over San Cristobal was approved by COMOR, but to the CIA's dismay, Air Force pilots rather than CIA agents would take charge of the mission. At this point details become sketchy, but several members of the intelligence community have speculated that an Air Force pilot in an Air Force U-2 attempted a high altitude overflight on October 9 that "flamed out," i.e., lost power, and thus had to descend in order to restart its engine. A second round between Air Force and CIA followed, as a result of which Air Force pilots were trained to fly CIA U-2's. A successful overflight took place on October 14.

This ten-day delay constitutes some form of "failure." In the face of well-founded suspicions concerning offensive Soviet missiles in Cuba that posed a critical threat to the United States' most vital interest, squabbling between organizations whose job it is to produce this information seems entirely inappropriate. But for each of these organizations, the question involved the issue: *"Whose* job was it to be?" Moreover, the issue was not simply, which organization would control U-2 flights over Cuba, but rather the broader issue of ownership of U-2 intelligence activities—a very long standing territorial dispute. Thus though this delay was in one sense a "failure," it was also a nearly inevitable consequence of two facts: many jobs do not fall neatly into precisely defined organizational jurisdictions; and vigorous organizations are imperialistic.

Organizational Options. Deliberations of leaders in ExCom meetings produced broad outlines of alternatives. Details of these alternatives and blueprints for their implementation had to be specified by the organizations that would perform these tasks. These organizational outputs answered the question: What, specifically, *could* be done?

Discussion in the ExCom quickly narrowed the live options to two: an air strike and a blockade. The choice of the blockade instead of the air strike turned on two points: (1) the argument from morality and tradition that the United States could not perpetrate a "Pearl Harbor in reverse"; (2) the belief that a "surgical" air strike was impossible.[34] Whether the United States *might* strike first was a question not of capability but of morality. Whether the United States *could* perform the surgical strike was a factual question concerning capabilities. The majority of the members of the ExCom, including the President, initially preferred the air strike.[35] What effectively foreclosed this option, however, was the fact that the air strike they wanted could not be chosen with high confidence of success.[36] After having tentatively chosen the course of prudence —given that the surgical air strike was not an option—Kennedy reconsidered. On Sunday morning, October 21, he called the Air Force experts to a special meeting in his living quarters where he probed once more for the option of a *"surgical"* air strike.[37] General Walter C. Sweeny, Commander of Tactical Air Forces, asserted again that the Air Force could guarantee no higher than ninety percent effectiveness in a surgical air strike.[38] That "fact" was false.

The air strike alternative provides a classic case of military estimates. One of the alternatives outlined by the ExCom was named "air strike." Specification of the details of this alternative was delegated to the Air Force. Starting from an existing plan for massive U.S. military action against Cuba (prepared for contingencies like a response to a Soviet Berlin grab), Air Force estimators produced an attack to guarantee success.[39] This plan called for extensive bombardment of all missile sites, storage depots, airports, and, in deference to the Navy, the artillery batteries opposite the naval base at Guantanamo.[40] Members of the ExCom repeatedly expressed bewilderment at military estimates of the number of sorties required, likely casualties, and collateral damage. But the "surgical" air strike that the political leaders had in mind was never carefully examined during the first week of the crisis. Rather, this option was simply excluded on the grounds that since the Soviet MRBM's in Cuba were classified "mobile" in U.S. manuals, extensive bombing was required. During the second week of the crisis, careful examination revealed that the missiles were mobile, in the sense that small houses are mobile: that is, they could be moved and reassembled in 6 days. After the missiles were reclassified "movable" and detailed plans for surgical air strikes specified, this action was added to the list of live options for the end of the second week.

Organizational Implementation. Ex-Com members separated several types of blockade: offensive weapons only, all armaments, and all strategic goods including POL (petroleum, oil, and lubricants). But the *"details"* of the operation were left to the Navy. Before the President announced the blockade on Monday evening, the first stage of the Navy's blueprint was in motion, and a problem loomed on the horizon.[41] The Navy had a detailed plan for the blockade. The President had several less precise but equally determined notions concerning what should be done, when, and how. For the Navy the issue was one of effective implementation of the Navy's blockade—without the meddling and interference of political leaders. For the President, the problem was to pace and manage events in such a way that the Soviet leaders would have time to see, think, and blink.

A careful reading of available sources uncovers an instructive incident. On Tuesday the British Ambassador, Ormsby-Gore, after having attended a briefing on the details of the blockade, suggested to the President that the plan for intercepting Soviet ships far out of reach of Cuban jets did not facilitate Khrushchev's hard decision.[42] Why not make the interception much closer to Cuba and thus give the Russian leader more time? According to the public account and the recollection of a number of individuals involved, Kennedy "agreed immediately, called McNamara, and over emotional Navy protest, issued the appropriate instructions."[43] As Sorensen records, "in a sharp clash with the Navy, he made certain his will prevailed."[44] The Navy's plan for the blockade was thus changed by drawing the blockade much closer to Cuba.

A serious organizational orientation makes one suspicious of this account. More careful examination of the available evidence confirms these suspicions, though alternative accounts must be somewhat speculative. According to the public chronology, a quarantine drawn close to Cuba became effective on Wednesday morning, the first Soviet ship was contacted on Thursday morning, and the first boarding of a ship occurred on Friday. According to the statement by the Department of Defense, boarding of the *Marcula* by a party from the *John R. Pierce* "took place at 7:50 A.M., E.D.T., 180 miles northeast of Nassau."[45] The *Marcula* had been trailed since about 10:30 the previous evening.[46] Simple calculations suggest that the *Pierce* must have been stationed along the Navy's original arc which extended 500 miles out to sea from Cape Magsi, Cuba's eastern most tip.[47] The blockade line was *not* moved as the President ordered, and the accounts report.

What happened is not entirely clear. One can be certain, however, that Soviet ships passed through the line along which American destroyers had posted themselves before the official "first contact" with the Soviet ship. On October 26 a Soviet tanker arrived in Havana and was honored by a dockside rally for "running the blockade." Photographs of this vessel show the name *Vinnitsa* on the side of the vessel in Cyrillic letters.[48] But according to the official U.S. position, the first tanker to pass through the blockade was the *Bucharest,* which was hailed by the Navy on the morning of October 25. Again simple mathematical calculation excludes the possibility that the *Bucharest* and the *Vinnitsa* were the same ship. It seems probable that the Navy's resistance to the President's order that the blockade be drawn in closer to Cuba forced him to allow one or several Soviet ships to pass through the blockade after it was officially operative.[49]

This attempt to leash the Navy's blockade had a price. On Wednesday morning, October 24, what the President had been awaiting occurred. The 18 dry cargo ships heading towards the quarantine stopped dead in the water. This was the occasion of Dean Rusk's remark, "We are eyeball to eyeball and I think the other fellow just blinked."[50] But the Navy had another interpretation. The ships had simply stopped to pick up Soviet submarine escorts. The President became quite concerned lest the Navy— already riled because of Presidential meddling in its affairs—blunder into an incident. Sensing the President's fears, McNamara became suspicious of the Navy's procedures and routines for making the first interception. Calling on the Chief of Naval Operations in the Navy's inner sanctum, the Navy Flag Plot, McNamara put his questions harshly.[51] Who would make the first interception? Were Russian-speaking officials on board? How would submarines be dealt with? At one point McNamara asked Anderson what he would do if a Soviet ship's captain refused to answer questions about his cargo. Picking up the Manual of Navy Regulations the Navy man waved it in McNamara's face and shouted, "It's all in there." To which McNamara replied, "I don't give a damn what John Paul Jones would have done; I want to know what you are going to do, now." [52] The encounter ended on Anderson's remark: "Now, Mr. Secretary, if you and your Deputy will go back to your office the Navy will run the blockade."[53]

MODEL III: BUREAUCRATIC POLITICS

The leaders who sit on top of organizations are not a monolithic group. Rather, each is, in his own right, a player in a central, competitive game. The name of the game is bureaucratic politics: bargaining along regularized channels among players positioned hierarchically within the government. Government behavior can thus be understood according to a third conceptual model not as organizational outputs, but as outcomes of bargaining games. In contrast with Model I, the bureaucratic politics model sees no unitary actor but rather many actors as players, who focus not on a single strategic issue but on many diverse intra-national problems as well, in terms of no consistent set of strategic objectives but rather according to various conceptions of national, organizational, and personal goals, making government decisions not by rational choice but by the pulling and hauling that is politics.

The apparatus of each national government constitutes a complex arena for the intra-national game. Political leaders at the top of this apparatus plus the men who occupy positions on top of the critical organizations form the circle of central players. Ascendancy to this circle assures some independent standing. The necessary decentralization of decisions required for action on the broad range of foreign policy problems guarantees that each player has considerable discretion. Thus power is shared.

* * *

Men share power. Men differ concerning what must be done. The differences matter. This milieu necessitates that policy be resolved by politics. What the nation does is sometimes the result of the triumph of one group over others. More often, however, different groups pulling in different directions yield a resultant distinct from what anyone intended. What moves the chess pieces is not simply the reasons which support a course of action, nor the routines of organizations which enact an alternative, but the power and skill of proponents and opponents of the action in question.

This characterization captures the thrust of the bureaucratic politics orientation. If problems of foreign policy arose as discreet issues, and decisions were determined one game at a time, this account would suffice. But most "issues," e.g., Vietnam or the proliferation of nuclear weapons, emerge piecemeal, over time, one lump in one context, a second in another. Hundreds of issues compete for players' attention every day. Each player is forced to fix upon his issues for that day, fight them on their own terms, and rush on to the next. Thus the character of emerging issues and the pace at which the game is played converge to yield government "decisions" and "actions" as collages. Choices by one player, outcomes of minor games, outcomes of central games, and "foul-ups"—these pieces, when stuck to the same canvas, constitute government behavior relevant to an issue.

The concept of national security policy as political outcome contradicts both public imagery and academic orthodoxy. Issues vital to national security, it is said, are too important to be settled by political games. They must be "above" politics. To accuse someone of "playing politics with national security" is a most serious charge. What public conviction demands, the academic penchant for intellectual elegance reinforces. Internal politics is messy; moreover, according to prevailing doctrine, politicking lacks intellectual content. As such, it constitutes gossip for journalists rather than a subject for serious investigation. Occasional memoirs, anecdotes in historical accounts, and several detailed case studies to the contrary, most of the literature of foreign policy avoids bureaucratic politics. The gap between academic literature and the experience of participants in government is nowhere wider than at this point.

BUREAUCRATIC POLITICS PARADIGM[54]

* * *

Individuals become players in the national security policy game by occupying a critical position in an administration. . . .

Positions define what players both may and must do. The advantages and handicaps with which each player can enter and play in various games stem from his position. So does a cluster of obligations for the performance of certain tasks. The two sides of this coin are illustrated by the position of the modern Secretary of State. First, in form and usually in fact, he is the primary repository of political judgment on the political-military issues that are the stuff of contemporary foreign policy; consequently, he is a senior personal advisor to the President. Second, he is the colleague of the President's other senior advisers on the problems of foreign policy, the Secretaries of Defense and Treasury, and the Special Assistant for National Security Affairs. Third, he is the ranking U.S. diplomat for serious negotiation. Fourth, he serves as an Administration voice to Congress, the country, and the world. Finally, he is "Mr. State Department" or "Mr. Foreign Office," "leader of officials, spokesman for their causes, guardian of their interests, judge of their disputes, superintendent of their work, master of their careers."[55] But he is not first one, and then the other. All of these obligations are his simultaneously. His performance in one affects his credit and power in the others. The perspective stemming from the daily work which he must oversee—the cable traffic by which his department maintains relations with other foreign offices—conflicts with the President's requirement that he serve as a generalist and coordinator of contrasting perspectives. The necessity that he be close to the President restricts the extent to which, and the force with which, he can front for his department. When he defers to the Secretary of Defense rather than fighting for his department's position—as he often must—he strains the loyalty of his officialdom. The Secretary's resolution of these conflicts depends not only upon the position, but also upon the player who occupies the position.

For players are also people. Men's metabolisms differ. The core of the bureaucratic politics mix is personality. How each man manages to stand the heat in his kitchen, each player's basic operating style, and the complementarity or contradiction among personalities and styles in the inner circles are irreducible pieces of the policy blend. Moreover, each person comes to his position with baggage in tow, including sensitivities to certain issues, commitments to various programs, and personal standing and debts with groups in the society.

B. *Parochial Priorities, Perceptions and Issues.* Answers to the questions: "What is the issue?" and "What must be done?" are colored by the position from which the questions are considered. For the factors which encourage organizational parochialism also influence the players who occupy positions on top of (or within) these organizations. To motivate members of his organization, a player must be sensitive to the organization's orientation. The games into which the player can enter and the advantages with which he plays enhance these pressures. Thus propensities of perception stemming from position permit reliable prediction about a player's stances in many cases. But these propensities are filtered through the baggage which players bring to positions. Sensitivity to both the pressures and the baggage is thus required for many predictions.

* * *

"Solutions" to strategic problems are not derived by detached analysts focusing coolly on *the* problem. Instead, deadlines and events raise issues in games, and demand decisions of busy players in contexts that influence the face the issue wears. The problems for the players are both narrower and broader than *the* strategic problem. For each player focuses not on the total strategic problem but rather on the decision that must be made now. But each decision has critical consequences not only for the strategic problem but for each player's organizational, reputational, and personal stakes. Thus the gap between the problems the player was solving and the problem upon which the analyst focuses is often very wide.

. . . Bargaining games do not proceed randomly. Action-channels, i.e., regularized ways of producing action concerning types of issues, structure the game by pre-selecting the major players, determining their points of entrance into the game, and distributing particular advantages and disadvantages for each game. . . . Weapon procurement decisions are made within the annual budgeting process; embassies' demands for action cables are answered according to routines of consultation and clearance from State to Defense and White House; . . . crisis responses are debated among White House, State, Defense, CIA, and Ad Hoc players; major political speeches, especially by the President but also by other Chiefs, are cleared through established channels.

. . . Government decisions are made and government actions emerge neither as the calculated choice of a unified group, nor as a formal summary of leaders' preferences. Rather the context of shared power but separate judgments concerning important choices, determines that politics is the mechanism of choice. Note the *environment* in which the game is played: inordinate uncertainty about what must be done, the necessity that something be done, and crucial consequences of whatever is done. These features force responsible men to become active players. The *pace of the game—* hundreds of issues, numerous games, and multiple channels—compels players to fight to "get other's attention," to make them "see the facts," to assure that they "take the time to think seriously about the broader issue." The *structure of the game*—power shared by individuals with separate responsibilities—validates each player's feeling that "others don't see my problem," and "others must be persuaded to look at the issue from a less parochial perspective." The *rules of the game*—he who hesitates loses his chance to play at that point, and he who is uncertain about his recommendation is overpowered by others who are sure—pressures players to come down on one side of a 51-49 issue and play. The *rewards of the game*—effectiveness, i.e., impact on outcomes, as the immediate measure of performance—encourages hard play. Thus, most players come to fight to "make the government do what is right." The strategies and tactics employed are quite similar to those formalized by theorists of international relations.

. . . Important government decisions or actions emerge as collages composed of individual acts, outcomes of minor and major games, and foul-ups. Outcomes which could never have been chosen by an actor and would never have emerged from bargaining in a single game over the issue are fabricated piece by piece. Understanding of the outcome requires that it be disaggregated.

. . . If a nation performed an action, that action was the *outcome* of bargaining among individuals and groups within the government. That outcome included *results* achieved by groups committed to a decision or action, *resultants* which emerged from bargaining among groups with quite different positions and *foul-ups*. Model III's explanatory power is achieved by revealing the pulling and hauling of various players, with different perceptions and priorities, focusing on separate problems, which yielded the outcomes that constitute the action in question.

General Propositions

1. *Action and Intention.* Action does not presuppose intention. The sum of behavior of representatives of a government relevant to an issue was rarely intended by any individual or group. Rather separate individuals with different intentions contributed pieces which compose an outcome distinct from what anyone would have chosen.

2. *Where you stand depends on where you sit.*[56] Horizontally, the diverse demands upon each player shape his priorities, perceptions, and issues. For large classes of issues, e.g., budgets and procurement decisions, the stance of a particular player can be predicted with high reliability from information concerning his seat. In the notorious B-36 controversy, no one was surprised by Admiral Radford's testimony that "the B-36 under any theory of war, is a bad gamble with national security," as opposed to Air Force Secretary Symington's claim that "a B-36 with an A-bomb can destroy distant objectives which might require ground armies years to take."[57]

3. *Chiefs and Indians.* The aphorism "where you stand depends on where you sit" has vertical as well as horizontal application. Vertically, the

demands upon the President, Chiefs, Staffers, and Indians are quite distinct.

The foreign policy issues with which the President can deal are limited primarily by his crowded schedule: the necessity of dealing first with what comes next. His problem is to probe the special face worn by issues that come to his attention, to preserve his leeway until time has clarified the uncertainties, and to assess the relevant risks.

Foreign policy Chiefs deal most often with the hottest issue *de jour*, though they can get the attention of the President and other members of the government for other issues which they judge important. What they cannot guarantee is that "the President will pay the price" or that "the others will get on board." They must build a coalition of the relevant powers that be. They must "give the President confidence" in the right course of action.

Most problems are framed, alternatives specified, and proposals pushed, however, by Indians. Indians fight with Indians of other departments; for example, struggles between International Security Affairs of the Department of Defense and Political-Military of the State Department are a microcosm of the action at higher levels. But the Indian's major problem is how to get the *attention* of Chiefs, how to get an issue decided, how to get the government "to do what is right."

In policy making then, the issue looking *down* is options: how to preserve my leeway until time clarifies uncertainties. The issue looking *sideways* is commitment: how to get others committed to my coalition. The issue looking *upwards* is confidence: how to give the boss confidence in doing what must be done. To paraphrase one of Neustadt's assertions which can be applied down the length of the ladder, the essence of a responsible official's task is to induce others to see that what needs to be done is what their own appraisal of their own responsibilities requires them to do in their own interests.

Specific Propositions

1. *Deterrence.* The probability of nuclear attack depends primarily on the probability of attack emerging as an outcome of the bureaucratic politics of the attacking government. First, which players can decide to launch an attack? Whether the effective power over action is controlled by an individual, a minor game, or the central game is critical. Second, though Model I's confidence in nuclear deterrence stems from an assertion that, in the end, governments will not commit suicide, Model III recalls historical precendents. Admiral Yamamoto, who designed the Japanese attack on Pearl Harbor, estimated accurately: "In the first six months to a year of war against the U.S. and England I will run wild, and I will show you an uninterrupted succession of victories; I must also tell you that, should the war be prolonged for two or three years, I have no confidence in our ultimate victory."[58] But Japan attacked. Thus, three questions might be considered. One: could any member of the government solve his problem by attack? What patterns of bargaining could yield attack as an outcome? The major difference between a stable balance of terror and a questionable balance may simply be that in the first case most members of

the government appreciate fully the consequences of attack and are thus on guard against the emergence of this outcome. Two: what stream of outcomes might lead to an attack? At what point in that stream is the potential attacker's politics? If members of the U.S. government had been sensitive to the stream of decisions from which the Japanese attack on Pearl Harbor emerged, they would have been aware of a considerable probability of that attack. Three: how might miscalculation and confusion generate foul-ups that yield attack as an outcome? For example, in a crisis or after the beginning of conventional war, what happens to the information available to, and the effective power of, members of the central game.

THE U.S. BLOCKADE OF CUBA: A THIRD CUT

The Politics of Discovery. A series of overlapping bargaining games determined both the *date* of the discovery of the Soviet missiles and the *impact* of this discovery on the Administration. An explanation of the politics of the discovery is consequently a considerable piece of the explanation of the U.S. blockade.

Cuba was the Kennedy Administration's "political Achilles' heel."[59] The months preceding the crisis were also months before the Congressional elections, and the Republican Senatorial and Congressional Campaign Committee had announced that Cuba would be "the dominant issue of the 1962 campaign."[60] What the administration billed as a "more positive and indirect approach of isolating Castro from developing, democratic Latin America," Senators Keating, Goldwater, Capehart, Thurmond, and others attacked as a "do-nothing" policy.[61] In statements on the floor of the House and Senate, campaign speeches across the country, and interviews and articles carried by national news media, Cuba—particularly the Soviet program of increased arms aid—served as a stick for stirring the domestic political scene.[62]

These attacks drew blood. Prudence demanded a vigorous reaction. The President decided to meet the issue head-on. The Administration mounted a forceful campaign of denial designed to discredit critics' claims. The President himself manned the front line of this offensive, though almost all Administration officials participated. In his news conference on August 19, President Kennedy attacked as "irresponsible" calls for an invasion of Cuba, stressing rather "the totality of our obligations" and promising to "watch what happens in Cuba with the closest attention."[63] On September 4, he issued a strong statement denying any provocative Soviet action in Cuba.[64] On September 13 he lashed out at "loose talk" calling for an invasion of Cuba.[65] The day before the flight of the U-2 which discovered the missiles, he campaigned in Capehart's Indiana against those "self-appointed generals and admirals who want to send someone else's sons to war."[66]

On Sunday, October 14, just as a U-2 was taking the first pictures of Soviet missiles, McGeorge Bundy was asserting:

> I *know* that there is no present evidence, and I think that
> there is no present likelihood that the Cuban government and
> the Soviet government would, in combination, attempt to install
> a major offensive capability.[67]

In this campaign to puncture the critics' charges, the Administration
discovered that the public needed positive slogans. Thus, Kennedy fell into a
tenuous semantic distinction between "offensive" and "defensive" weapons.
This distinction originated in his September 4 statement that there was no
evidence of "offensive ground to ground missiles" and warned "were it to
be otherwise, the gravest issues would arise."[68] His September 13 statement turned on this distinction between "defensive" and "offensive"
weapons and announced a firm commitment to action if the Soviet Union
attempted to introduce the latter into Cuba.[69] Congressional committees
elicited from administration officials testimony which read this distinction
and the President's commitment into the *Congressional Record*.[70]

What the President least wanted to hear, the CIA was most hesitant
to say plainly. On August 22 John McCone met privately with the President
and voiced suspicions that the Soviets were preparing to introduce offensive
missiles into Cuba.[71] Kennedy heard this as what it was: the suspicion of
a hawk. McCone left Washington for a month's honeymoon on the Riviera.
Fretting at Cap Ferrat, he bombarded his deputy, General Marshall Carter,
with telegrams, but Carter, knowing that McCone had informed the
President of his suspicions and received a cold reception, was reluctant
to distribute these telegrams outside the CIA.[72] On September 9 a
U-2 "on loan" to the Chinese Nationalists was downed over mainland
China.[73] The Committee on Overhead Reconnaissance (COMOR) convened on September 10 with a sense of urgency.[74] Loss of another U-2
might incite world opinion to demand cancellation of U-2 flights. The
President's campaign against those who asserted that the Soviets were
acting provocatively in Cuba had begun. To risk downing a U-2 over Cuba
was to risk chopping off the limb on which the President was sitting. That
meeting decided to shy away from the western end of Cuba (where
SAMs were becoming operational) and modify the flight pattern of the
U-2s in order to reduce the probability that a U-2 would be lost.[75]
USIB's unanimous approval of the September estimate reflects similar
sensitivities. On September 13 the President had asserted that there were
no Soviet offensive missiles in Cuba and committed his Administration to
act if offensive missiles were discovered. Before Congressional committees,
Administration officials were denying that there was any evidence whatever
of offensive missiles in Cuba. The implications of a National Intelligence
estimate which concluded that the Soviets were introducing offensive missiles into Cuba were not lost on the men who constituted America's highest
intelligence assembly.

The October 4 COMOR decision to direct a flight over the western
end of Cuba in effect "overturned" the September estimate, but without
officially raising that issue. The decision represented McCone's victory for
which he had lobbied with the President before the September 10 decision,

in telegrams before the September 19 estimate, and in person after his return to Washington. Though the politics of the intelligence community is closely guarded, several pieces of the story can be told.[76] By September 27, Colonel Wright and others in DIA believed that the Soviet Union was placing missiles in the San Cristobal area.[77] This area was marked suspicious by the CIA on September 29 and certified top priority on October 3. By October 4 McCone had the evidence required to raise the issue officially. The members of COMOR heard McCone's argument, but were reluctant to make the hard decision he demanded. The significant probability that a U-2 would be downed made overflight of western Cuba a matter of real concern.[78]

The Politics of Issues. The U-2 photographs presented incontrovertible evidence of Soviet offensive missiles in Cuba. This revelation fell upon politicized players in a complex context. As one high official recalled, Khrushchev had caught us "with our pants down." What each of the central participants saw, and what each did to cover both his own and the Administration's nakedness, created the spectrum of issues and answers.

At approximately 9:00 A.M., Tuesday morning, October 16, Mc-George Bundy went to the President's living quarters with the message: "Mr. President, there is now hard photographic evidence that the Russians have offensive missiles in Cuba."[79] Much has been made of Kennedy's "expression of surprise,"[80] but "surprise" fails to capture the character of his initial reaction. Rather, it was one of startled anger, most adequately conveyed by the exclamation: "He can't do that to *me!*"[81] In terms of the President's attention and priorities at that moment, Khrushchev had chosen the most unhelpful act of all. Kennedy had staked his full Presidential authority on the assertion that the Soviets would not place offensive weapons in Cuba. Moreover, Khrushchev had assured the President through the most direct and personal channels that he was aware of the President's domestic political problem and that nothing would be done to exacerbate this problem. The Chairman had *lied* to the President. Kennedy's initial reaction entailed action. The missiles must be removed.[82] The alternatives of "doing nothing" or "taking a diplomatic approach" could not have been less relevant to *his* problem.

These two tracks—doing nothing and taking a diplomatic approach—were the solutions advocated by two of his principal advisors. For Secretary of Defense McNamara, the missiles raised the spectre of nuclear war. He first framed the issue as a straightforward strategic problem. To understand the issue, one had to grasp two obvious but difficult points. First, the missiles represented an inevitable occurrence: narrowing of the missile gap. It simply happened sooner rather than later. Second, the United States could accept this occurrence since its consequences were minor: "seven-to-one missile 'superiority,' one-to-one missile 'equality,' one-to-seven missile 'inferiority'—the three postures are identical." McNamara's statement of this argument at the first meeting of the ExCom was summed up in the phrase, "a missile is a missile."[83] "It makes no great difference," he maintained, "whether you are killed by a missile from the Soviet Union or Cuba."[84] The implication was clear. The United States should not initiate a crisis with the Soviet Union, risking a significant probability of nuclear war over an occurrence which had such small strategic implications.

The perceptions of McGeorge Bundy, the President's Assistant for National Security Affairs, are the most difficult of all to reconstruct. There is no question that he initially argued for a diplomatic track.[85] But was Bundy laboring under his acknowledged burden of responsibility in Cuba I? Or was he playing the role of devil's advocate in order to make the President probe his own initial reaction and consider other options?

The President's brother, Robert Kennedy, saw most clearly the political wall against which Khrushchev had backed the President. But he, like McNamara, saw the prospect of nuclear doom. Was Khrushchev going to force the President to an insane act? At the first meeting of the ExCom, he scribbled a note, "Now I know how Tojo felt when he was planning Pearl Harbor."[86] From the outset he searched for an alternative that would prevent the air strike.

The initial reaction of Theodore Sorensen, the President's Special Counsel and "alter ego," fell somewhere between that of the President and his brother. Like the President, Sorensen felt the poignancy of betrayal. If the President had been the architect of the policy which the missiles punctured, Sorensen was the draftsman. Khrushchev's deceitful move demanded a strong counter-move. But like Robert Kennedy, Sorensen feared lest the shock and disgrace lead to disaster.

To the Joint Chiefs of Staff the issue was clear. *Now* was the time to do the job for which they had prepared contingency plans. Cuba I had been badly done; Cuba II would not be. The missiles provided the *occasion* to deal with the issue: cleansing the Western Hemisphere of Castro's Communism. As the President recalled on the day the crisis ended, "An invasion would have been a mistake—a wrong use of our power. But the military are mad. They wanted to do this. It's lucky for us that we have McNamara over there."[87]

McCone's perceptions flowed from his confirmed prediction. As the Cassandra of the incident, he argued forcefully that the Soviets had installed the missiles in a daring political probe which the United States must meet with force. The time for an air strike was now.[88]

The Politics of Choice. The process by which the blockade emerged is a story of the most subtle and intricate probing, pulling, and hauling; leading, guiding, and spurring. Reconstruction of this process can only be tentative. Initially the President and most of his advisers wanted the clean, surgical air strike. On the first day of the crisis when informing Stevenson of the missiles, the President mentioned only two alternatives: "I suppose the alternatives are to go in by air and wipe them out, or to take other steps to render them inoperable."[89] At the end of the week a sizeable minority still favored an air strike. As Robert Kennedy recalled: "The fourteen people involved were very significant. . . . If six of them had been President of the U.S., I think that the world might have been blown up."[90] What prevented the air strike was a fortuitous coincidence of a number of factors—the absence of any one of which might have permitted that option to prevail.

First, McNamara's vision of holocaust set him firmly against the air strike. His initial attempt to frame the issue in strategic terms struck Kennedy as particularly inappropriate. Once McNamara realized that the name of the game was a strong response, however, he and his deputy Gilpatric chose the blockade as a fallback. When the Secretary of Defense—whose department had the action, whose reputation in the Cabinet was unequaled, in whom the President demonstrated full confidence —marshalled the arguments for the blockade and refused to be moved, the blockade became a formidable alternative.

Second, Robert Kennedy—the President's closest confidant—was unwilling to see his brother become a "Tojo." His arguments against the air strike on moral grounds struck a chord in the President. Moreover, once his brother had stated these arguments so forcefully, the President could not have chosen his initially preferred course without, in effect, agreeing to become what RFK had condemned.

The President learned of the missiles on Tuesday morning. On Wednesday morning, in order to mask our discovery from the Russians, the President flew to Connecticut to keep a campaign commitment, leaving RFK as the unofficial chairman of the group. By the time the President returned on Wednesday evening, a critical third piece had been added to the picture. McNamara had presented his argument for the blockade. Robert Kennedy and Sorensen had joined McNamara. A powerful coalition of the advisers in whom the President had the greatest confidence, and with whom his style was most compatible, had emerged.

Fourth, the coalition that had formed behind the President's initial preference gave him reason to pause. *Who* supported the air strike—the Chiefs, McCone, Rusk, Nitze, and Acheson—as much as *how* they supported it, counted. Fifth, a piece of inaccurate information, which no one probed, permitted the blockade advocates to fuel (potential) uncertainties in the President's mind. When the President returned to Washington Wednesday evening, RFK and Sorensen met him at the airport. Sorensen gave the President a four-page memorandum outlining the areas of agreement and disagreement. The strongest argument was that the air strike simply could not be surgical.[91] After a day of prodding and questioning, the Air Force had asserted that it could not guarantee the success of a surgical air strike limited to the missiles alone.

Thursday evening, the President convened the ExCom at the White House. He declared his tentative choice of the blockade and directed that preparations be made to put it into effect by Monday morning.[92] Though he raised a question about the possibility of a surgical air strike subsequently, he seems to have accepted the experts' opinion that this was no live option.[93] (Acceptance of this estimate suggests that he may have learned the lesson of the Bay of Pigs—"Never rely on experts"—less well than he supposed.)[94] But this information was incorrect. That no one probed this estimate during the first week of the crisis poses an interesting question for further investigation.

A coalition, including the President, thus emerged from the President's initial decision that something had to be done; McNamara, Robert Kennedy, and Sorensen's resistance to the air strike; incompatibility between the President and the air strike advocates; and an inaccurate piece of information.[95]

CONCLUSION

This essay has obviously bitten off more than it has chewed. For further developments and synthesis of these arguments the reader is referred to the larger study.[96] In spite of the limits of space, however, it would be inappropriate to stop without spelling out several implications of the argument and addressing the question of relations among the models and extensions of them to activity beyond explanation.

At a minimum, the intended implications of the argument presented here are four. First, formulation of alternative frames of reference and demonstration that different analysts, relying predominantly on different models, produce quite different explanations should encourage the analyst's self-consciousness about the nets he employs. The effect of these "spectacles" in sensitizing him to particular aspects of what is going on—framing the puzzle in one way rather than another, encouraging him to examine the problem in terms of certain categories rather than others, directing him to particular kinds of evidence, and relieving puzzlement by one procedure rather than another—must be recognized and explored.

Second, the argument implies a position on the problem of "the state of the art." While accepting the commonplace characterization of the present condition of foreign policy analysis—personalistic, non-cumulative, and sometimes insightful—this essay rejects both the counsel of despair's justification of this condition as a consequence of the character of the enterprise, and the "new frontiersmen's" demand for *a priori* theorizing on the frontiers and *ad hoc* appropriation of "new techniques."[97] What is required as a first step is non-casual examination of the present product: inspection of existing explanations, articulation of the conceptual models employed in producing them, formulation of the propositions relied upon, specification of the logic of the various intellectual enterprises, and reflection on the questions being asked. Though it is difficult to overemphasize the need for more systematic processing of more data, these preliminary matters of formulating questions with clarity and sensitivity to categories and assumptions so that fruitful acquisition of large quantities of data is possible are still a major hurdle in considering most important problems.

NOTES

[1]Theodore Sorensen, *Kennedy* (New York, 1965), p. 705.

[2]In attempting to understand problems of foreign affairs, analysts engage in a number of related, but logically separable enterprises: (a) description, (b) explanation, (c) prediction, (d) evaluation, and (e) recommendation. This essay focuses primarily on explanation (and by implication, prediction).

[3]Earlier drafts of this argument have aroused heated arguments concerning proper names for these models. To choose names from ordinary language is to court confusion, as well as familiarity. Perhaps it is best to think of these models as I, II, and III.

[4]Arnold Horelick and Myron Rush, *Strategic Power and Soviet Foreign Policy* (Chicago, 1965). Based on A. Horelick, "The Cuban Missile Crisis: An Analysis of Soviet Calculations and Behavior," *World Politics* (April, 1964).

[5]Horelick and Rush, *Strategic Power and Soviet Foreign Policy*, p. 154.

[6]Hans Morgenthau, *Politics Among Nations* (3rd ed.; New York, 1960), p. 191.

[7]*Ibid.*, p. 192

[8]*Ibid.*, p. 5.

[9]*Ibid.*, pp. 5-6.

[10]This model is an analogue of the theory of the rational entrepreneur which has been developed extensively in economic theories of the firm and the consumer. These two propositions specify the "substitution effect." Refinement of this model and specification of additional general propositions by translating from the economic theory is straight forward.

[11]*New York Times*, March 22, 1969.

[12]As stated in the introduction, this "case snapshot" presents, without editorial commentary, a Model I analyst's explanation of the U.S. blockade. The purpose is to illustrate a strong, characteristic rational policy model account. This account is (roughly) consistent with prevailing explanations of these events.

[13]Theodore Sorensen, *op. cit.*, p. 675.

[14]*Ibid.*, p. 679.

[15]*Ibid.*, p. 679.

[16]Elie Abel, *The Missile Crisis* (New York, 1966), p. 144.

[17]*Ibid.*, p. 102.

[18]Sorensen, *op. cit.*, p. 684.

[19]*Ibid.*, p. 685. Though this was the formulation of the argument, the facts are not strictly accurate. Our tradition against surprise attack was rather younger than 175 years. For example President Theodore Roosevelt applauded Japan's attack on Russia in 1904.

[20]*New York Times*, June, 1963.

[21]Theodore Sorensen, "You Get to Walk to Work," *New York Times Magazine*, March 19, 1967.

[22]U. S. Department of State, *Bulletin*, XLVII, pp. 715-720.

[23]Schlesinger, *op. cit.*, p. 803.

[24]Theodore Sorensen, *Kennedy*, p. 675.

[25]See U.S. Congress, Senate, Committee on Armed Services, Preparedness Investigation Subcommittee, *Interim Report on Cuban Military Build-up*. 88th Congress, 1st Session, 1963, p. 2; Hanson Baldwin, "Growing Risks of Bureaucratic Intelligence," *The Reporter* (August 15, 1963), 48-50; Roberta Wohlstetter, "Cuba and Pearl Harbor," *Foreign Affairs* (July, 1965), 706.

[26]U.S. Congress, House of Representatives, Committee on Appropriations, Subcommittee on Department of Defense Appropriations, *Hearings*, 88th Congress, 1st Session, 1963, 25 ff.

[27]R. Hilsman, *To Move a Nation* (New York, 1967), pp. 172-173.

[28]Department of Defense Appropriations, *Hearings*, p. 67.

[29]*Ibid.*, pp. 66-67.

[30]For (1) Hilsman, *op. cit.*, p. 186; (2) Abel, *op. cit.*, p. 24; (3) Department of Defense Appropriations, *Hearings*, p. 64; Abel, *op. cit.*, p. 24; (4) Department of Defense Appropriations, *Hearings*, pp. 1-30.

[31]The facts here are not entirely clear. This assertion is based on information from (1) "Department of Defense Briefing by the Honorable R. S. McNamara, Secretary of

Defense, State Department Auditorium, 5:00 P.M., February 6, 1963." A verbatim transcript of a presentation actually made by General Carroll's assistant, John Hughes; and (2) Hilsman's statement, *op. cit.*, p. 186. But see R. Wohlstetter's interpretation, "Cuba and Pearl Harbor," 700.

[32]See Hilsman, *op. cit.*, pp. 172-174.

[33]Abel, *op. cit.*, pp. 26 ff; Weintal and Bartlett, *Facing the Brink* (New York, 1967), pp. 62 ff; *Cuban Military Build-up;* J. Daniel and J. Hubbell, *Strike in the West* (New York, 1963), pp. 15 ff.

[34]Schlesinger, *op. cit.*, p. 804.

[35]Sorensen, *Kennedy*, p. 684.

[36]*Ibid.*, pp. 684 ff.

[37]*Ibid.*, pp. 694-697.

[38]*Ibid.*, p. 697; Abel. *op. cit.*, pp. 100-101.

[39]Sorensen, *Kennedy*, p. 669.

[40]Hilsman, *op. cit.*, p. 204.

[41]See Abel, *op. cit.*, pp. 97 ff.

[42]Schlesinger, *op. cit.*, p. 818.

[43]*Ibid.*

[44]Sorensen, *Kennedy*, p. 710.

[45]*New York Times*, October 27, 1962.

[46]Abel, *op. cit.*, p. 171.

[47]For the location of the original arc see Abel, *op. cit.*, p. 141.

[48]*Facts on File*, Vol. XXII, 1962, p. 376, published by Facts on File, Inc., New York, yearly.

[49]This hypothesis would account for the mystery surrounding Kennedy's explosion at the leak of the stopping of the *Bucharest*. See Hilsman, *op. cit.*, p. 45.

[50]Abel, *op. cit.*, p. 153.

[51]See *ibid.*, pp. 154 ff.

[52]*Ibid.*, p. 156.

[53]*Ibid.*

[54]This paradigm relies upon the small group of analysts who have begun to fill the gap. My primary source is the model implicit in the work of Richard E. Neustadt, though his concentration on presidential action has been generalized to a concern with policy as the outcome of political bargaining among a number of independent players, the President amounting to no more than a "superpower" among many lesser but considerable powers. As Warner Schilling argues, the substantive problems are of such inordinate difficulty that uncertainties and differences with regard to goals, alternatives, and consequences are inevitable. This necessitates what Roger Hilsman describes as the process of conflict and consensus building. The techniques employed in the process often resemble those used in legislative assemblies, though Samuel Huntington's characterization of the process as "legislative" overemphasizes the equality of participants as opposed to the hierarchy which structures the game. Moreover, whereas for Huntington, foreign policy (in contrast to military policy) is set by the executive, this paradigm maintains that the activities which he describes as legislative are characteristic of the process by which foreign policy is made.

[55]Richard E. Neustadt, Testimony, United States Senate, Committee on Government Operations, Subcommittee on National Security Staffing, *Administration of National Security*, March 26, 1963, pp. 82-83.

[56]This aphorism was stated first, I think, by Don K. Price.

[57]Paul Y. Hammond, "Super Carriers and B-36 Bombers." in Harold Stein (ed.), *American Civil-Military Decisions* (Birmingham, 1962).

[58]Roberta Wohlstetter, *Pearl Harbor* (Stanford).

[59]Sorensen, *Kennedy*, p. 670.

[60]*Ibid.*

[61]*Ibid.* pp. 670 ff.

[62]*New York Times*, August, September, 1962.

[63]*New York Times*, August 20, 1962.

[64]*New York Times*, September 5, 1962.

[65]*New York Times*, September 14, 1962.

[66]*New York Times,* October 14, 1962.

[67]Cited by Abel, *op. cit.,* p. 13.

[68]*New York Times,* September 5, 1962.

[69]*New York Times,* September 14, 1962.

[70]Senate Foreign Relations Committee; Senate Armed Services Committee; House Committee on Appropriation; House Select Committee on Export Control.

[71]Abel, *op. cit.,* pp. 17-18. According to McCone, he told Kennedy, "The only construction I can put on the material going into Cuba is that the Russians are preparing to introduce offensive missiles." See also Weintal and Bartlett, *op. cit.,* pp. 60-71.

[72]Abel, *op. cit.,* p. 23.

[73]*New York Times,* September 10, 1962.

[74]See Abel, *op. cit.,* pp. 25-26; and Hilsman, *op. cit.,* p. 174.

[75]Department of Defense Appropriation, *Hearings,* 69.

[76]A basic, but somewhat contradictory, account of parts of this story emerges in the Department of Defense Appropriations, *Hearings,* 1-70.

[77]Department of Defense Appropriations, *Hearings,* 71.

[78]The details of the 10 days between the October 4 decision and the October 14 flight must be held in abeyance.

[79]Abel, *op. cit.,* p. 44.

[80]*Ibid.,* pp. 44 ff.

[81]See Richard Neustadt, "Afterword," *Presidential Power* (New York, 1964).

[82]Sorensen, *Kennedy,* p. 676; Schlesinger. *op. cit.,* p. 801.

[83]Hilsman, *op. cit.,* p. 195.

[84]*Ibid.*

[85]Weintal and Bartlett, *op. cit.,* p. 67; Abel, *op. cit.,* p. 53.

[86]Schlesinger, *op. cit.,* p. 803.

[87]*Ibid.,* p. 831.

[88]Abel, *op. cit.,* p. 186.

[89]*Ibid.,* p. 49.

[90]Interview, quoted by Ronald Steel, *New York Review of Books,* March 13, 1969, p. 22.

[91]Sorensen, *Kennedy,* p. 686.

[92]*Ibid.,* p. 691.

[93]*Ibid.,* pp. 691-692.

[94]Schlesinger, *op. cit.,* p. 296.

[95]Space will not permit an account of the path from this coalition to the formal government decision on Saturday and action on Monday.

[96]*Bureaucracy and Policy* (forthcoming, 1969).

[97]Thus my position is quite distinct from both poles in the recent "great debate" about international relations. While many "traditionalists" of the sort Kaplan attacks adopt the first posture and many "scientists" of the sort attacked by Bull adopt the second, this third posture is relatively neutral with respect to whatever is in substantive dispute. See Hedly Bull, "International Theory: The Case for a Classical Approach," *World Politics* (April, 1966); and Morton Kaplan, "The New Great Debate: Traditionalism vs. Science in International Relations," *World Politics* (October, 1966).

As Allison notes in the preface to his study, one of his purposes is to sensitize the reader to the problems involved in analyzing foreign policy and in making the transition from description to explanation. His article clearly illustrates how the categories we employ to describe phenomena serve to structure how we interpret those phenomena; it also shows how the observations and descriptions we make tend to determine the explanations we construct. How one interprets and explains the decisions Americans made during that crisis is contingent partly on how those decisions are described. It should be obvious from Allison's treatment that we can perceive different aspects of the same events, and the way we choose to organize our perceptions about those events structures the meaning we attach to them. If nothing else, Allison's study shows us that the adage "What you see is what you get" is meaningful epistemologically; how we think about social phenomena is influenced by what we happen to look at and consider important. Thus, the adequacy of any explanation depends, in part, on the accuracy of the observations one makes.

To illustrate several additional methodological points about the Allison study, let us briefly contrast it with one of the preceding reading selections, Holsti's study of Dulles's belief system. The Allison and Holsti works can be compared on at least two dimensions. First, Allison's is deductive, while Holsti's is inductive. The former begins with a set of models of foreign-policy decision-making behavior and shows how various facts can be used to substantiate theoretical propositions in the models. The latter begins with a set of systematic observations of Dulles's statements about the Soviet Union and shows how those observations form patterns. Ultimately, Holsti generalizes from those observed patterns to their implications for international conflict.

A second contrast lies in the authors' use of data. Allison approaches data in a traditional way by using public documents, journalistic accounts, and personal memoirs as factual evidence. As with most traditional uses of data, one can question the criteria employed by Allison to select the significant facts. One should remember, however, that his purpose is not to find the one correct definitive interpretation but to provide alternative and competitive interpretations. In contrast, Holsti is more concerned with making systematic observation and therefore utilizes content analysis to generate data from Dulles's statements specifically for this purpose. Neither approach is more correct, for one must judge appropriateness of a research technique by the purposes the study is designed to perform.

Allison's effort to apply theoretical models in his explanation of the Cuban Missile Crisis is not alone in the field of foreign-policy analysis. A number of scholars have attempted to apply a specific theoretical framework to a foreign-policy decision. These include Allen S. Whiting's (169) study of the decision of Mainland China to become involved in the Korean conflict, as well as Paige's application of the Synder, Bruck, and Sapin (156) analytic scheme to the American decision to intervene in that same war.

The application of a general theoretical scheme to a particular foreign-policy decision represents one common type of study focusing on external behavior that one encounters in the literature. Another type of analysis, which is found less frequently but which will undoubtedly become increasingly important in the next decade of research, is represented by the essay that follows, by Eugene Wittkopf. That essay takes a set of foreign-policy decisions by one actor, the United States, with respect to a large number of foreign targets and seeks to discern the factors that led the United States to behave the way it did toward those targets. Written especially for this book to illustrate the use of quantitative and statistical techniques of politi-

cal analysis, Wittkopf's study shows how a specific aspect of foreign-policy behavior—the giving of foreign aid—might be predicted and explained by a particular variable.

CONTAINMENT VERSUS UNDERDEVELOPMENT IN THE DISTRIBUTION OF UNITED STATES FOREIGN AID: AN INTRODUCTION TO THE USE OF CROSSNATIONAL AGGREGATE DATA ANALYSIS IN THE STUDY OF FOREIGN POLICY[1]

Eugene R. Wittkopf

I. INTRODUCTION

For the last two decades there has been increasing debate at both the academic and policy-making levels on foreign aid as a tool of American foreign policy. Academicians have struggled with such issues as United States motives in using aid, the consequence of aid policy on the domestic and foreign policies of the recipient countries, and the role of aid in the cold war. Debate at the policy-making levels has taken place within the administrations of the last five Presidents as well as in public forums such as Congress and political campaigns. Despite this attention, however, there have been few attempts to systematically state and empirically study the diverse questions which relate to foreign aid.[2]

This paper suggests how crossnational aggregate data analysis might be used to study one aspect of foreign aid: how the United States distributes its foreign aid. It should be stated at the outset that the purpose is to demonstrate an approach rather than to present a definitive study of the whole foreign aid allocation process. Hence, we will look at the distribution of United States foreign aid in the year 1964 to test two propositions that might be used to explain the allocation of foreign aid: (1) greater amounts of foreign aid tend to be distributed to the poorer developing countries, which "need it most," and (2) greater amounts of foreign aid

---

Wittkopf is an assistant professor of international relations at the University of Florida.

tend to be distributed to developing countries in close proximity to, or on the periphery of, the Communist world.[3]

These two propositions are selected because they represent two major interpretations of United States motives for giving foreign aid.[4] The second proposition clearly implies a political-security motivation—the "containment of Communism"—while the first implies a more altruistic motivation: assisting the underdeveloped world in achieving a modicum of economic and social well-being.

In order to empirically study these two propositions, it is necessary to perform two tasks. The first is to measure the central variables mentioned in the propositions, which are foreign aid, underdevelopment, and containment. The second task is to analyze the data collected on these two variables using several statistical tests. The following pages illustrate how these two tasks might be performed.

II. MEASURING FOREIGN AID, UNDERDEVELOPMENT, AND CONTAINMENT

A. Foreign Aid

The foreign aid data used is total net disbursement in millions of U.S. dollars of official economic assistance in 1964 flowing from the United States to developing countries independent by the end of that year.[5] Seventy-one developing nations were recipients of net disbursements in 1964.[6] These recipients, listed in Table 1, constitute the *observations* on the foreign aid variable analyzed below. It should be emphasized that only economic assistance, and not military assistance, is included in the foreign aid definition.

B. Underdevelopment

Gross Domestic Product (GDP) per capita in 1963 is used as the measure of developing countries' need for foreign aid.[7] We will also treat the variable as an approximate indicator of the level of social and economic development of developing countries. The choice of 1963 per capita income figures in our study of 1964 aid distributions is based on an implicit assumption that the need for aid in some way "causes" the aid received, and that the lag between "cause" and "effect" is one year. By taking data on our two variables from different years, we are introducing temporal sequence into our theory of foreign aid behavior.

Lack of data frequently restricts the scope of aggregate data analyses, and some variation in the number of observations in the subsequent analyses will be attributable to this fact. More important, it is also true that the variables we can measure quantitatively often are only imperfect indicators of the underlying concepts we wish to describe and explain, and that actual data values frequently vary considerably in quality. This is

TABLE 1
Names and Abbreviations of the Seventy-one Independent Developing
Nations Receiving Net Foreign Economic Assistance
from the United States in 1964

Abbreviation		Nation	Abbreviation		Nation
1	AFGH	Afghanistan	37	KORS	Korea (South)
2	ALGE	Algeria	38	LAOS	Laos
3	ARGE	Argentina	39	LIBE	Liberia
4	BOLI	Bolivia	40	LIBY	Libya
5	BRAZ	Brazil	41	MADA	Madagascar
6	BURM	Burma	42	MLWI	Malawi
7	CAMB	Cambodia	43	MALA	Malaysia
8	CAME	Cameroon	44	MALI	Mali
9	CENT	Central African Republic	45	MORO	Morocco
10	CEYL	Ceylon	46	NEPA	Nepal
11	CHAD	Chad	47	NICA	Nicaragua
12	CHIL	Chile	48	NEGE	Niger
13	COLO	Colombia	49	NGRA	Nigeria
14	CONK	Congo (Kinshasa)	50	PAKI	Pakistan
15	COST	Costa Rica	51	PANA	Panama
16	CYPR	Cyprus	52	PARA	Paraguay
17	DAHO	Dahomey	53	PERU	Peru
18	DOMI	Dominican Republic	54	PHIL	Philippines
19	ECUA	Ecuador	55	SENE	Senegal
20	EL S	El Salvador	56	SIER	Sierra Leone
21	ETHI	Ethiopia	57	SOMA	Somalia
22	GABO	Gabon	58	SUDA	Sudan
23	GHAN	Ghana	59	TAIW	Taiwan (China)
24	GREE	Greece	60	TANZ	Tanzania
25	GUAT	Guatemala	61	THAI	Thailand
26	GUIN	Guinea	62	TOGO	Togo
27	HAIT	Haiti	63	TRIN	Trinidad and Tobago
28	HOND	Honduras	64	TUNI	Tunisia
29	INDI	India	65	TURK	Turkey
30	INDO	Indonesia	66	UGAN	Uganda
31	IRAQ	Iraq	67	UAR	United Arab Republic
32	ISRA	Israel	68	UPPE	Upper Volta
33	IVOR	Ivory Coast	69	VITS	Vietnam (South)
34	JAMA	Jamaica	70	YEME	Yemen
35	JORD	Jordan	71	YUGO	Yugoslavia
36	KENY	Kenya			

certainly true with per capita GDP. Although we cannot adequately deal with all of the questions and problems here, the researcher and reader alike should at least be aware of measurement problems that may inhere in the data analyzed.[8]

Among the principal problems is the fact that national accounts statistics are designed principally as a measure of economic activity entering the monetary or exchange economy. However, much of the economic activity of developing economies, such as subsistence agriculture, remains outside the exchange economy. Yet the extent and reliability of imputations of the monetary value of goods and services produced in the subsistence sector are difficult to trace. Further, for purposes of cross-national comparisons it is necessary to convert national accounts data reported in local currencies into a single monetary unit. Both the choice of base currency (U.S. dollars versus Iraqi Dinars) and the exchange rate (based on the value of goods and services entering international trade) used for the conversion will have important consequences for the final dollar estimate of economic activity. Typically, therefore, analysts refer to per capita income measures expressed in a single currency as reflecting more the relative *rank* of countries than actual disparities in income between and among them.

Given the goal of achieving higher levels of economic development avowed by leaders of developing nations, there is little problem in interpreting per capita GDP as measuring the need for foreign aid if we assume that, in general, nations poorest in these terms have been least successful in bringing the fruits of economic progress to their inhabitants. We should remember, however, that the variable in no way describes the *distribution* of wealth *within* each nation.

It is also reasonable to assume that countries richer in per capita terms are more likely to be nearer the point of ensuring their own self-sustained economic growth. However, some kind of composite index which would account for such additional indicators as communication flows, energy consumption, educational achievement, and nutritional standards would perhaps more fully describe development levels.

On the other hand, there is at least some empirical evidence to suggest that alternative measures of development do correlate highly with per capita income measures.[9] Moreover, per capita income is perhaps the most frequently used and easily interpreted single measure of levels of development. As Black has pointed out (referring to per capita GNP):

> The principal merit in using GNP per capita for comparative purposes is that, by reducing the production of goods and services to monetary values, an all-inclusive common denominator is achieved. Furthermore, economic growth is usually expressed in terms of per capita GNP, and the goals and progress of national development plans are established and measured in terms of GNP trends.[10]

C. Proximity to the Communist world

Proximity to the Communist world will be measured by asking whether or not each of the recipients of U.S. foreign aid border physically on the Soviet Union, Communist China, North Vietnam, North Korea, or the eastern European Communist nations, and by then placing each recipient into one of two mutually exclusive classes based on the response.

Bordering on the Communist world was interpreted quite literally. Thus Pakistan, separated from the Soviet Union by a small projection of Afghanistan and from China by the disputed states of Jammu and Kashmir, was considered as not bordering on the Communist states. Nationalist China (Taiwan) was treated similarly since it is separated from mainland China by the Formosa Straits.

The particular coding scheme used here has the virtue of operational clarity and ease, and of being tied to the traditional concept of containment in American foreign policy (as it has been modified over time). We must recognize, however, that an alternative measurement criterion—such as one based on some specified number of air miles from a Communist border or capital—would probably affect the results of our statistical analyses, though in what direction and to what extent remains an empirical question.[11] It should also be emphasized that while we shall retain the term "proximity," what we really mean is *contiguity*.

III. THE FINDINGS

A. Underdevelopment and foreign aid

The first proposition we wish to examine is that greater amounts of foreign aid tend to be distributed to the poorer developing countries—those that need it most. The simplest way to assess this proposition is with a scatter diagram, as shown in Figure 1, which depicts graphically the relationship between aid and underdevelopment as represented by all of the foreign aid recipients. Each point in the graph represents at least one developing country (identified according to the abbreviation given in Table 1) positioned simultaneously according to the amount of foreign aid it received from the United States and its per capita GDP.

We can note that in certain portions of the diagram—particularly the band of countries running from Pakistan and South Vietnam through Turkey, Chile, Greece, and Cyprus—there appears to be strong support for our proposition, since there is an inverse relationship between the amount of aid these countries receive from the United States and their per capita wealth. However, the overall picture is considerably more mixed. In particular, the large concentration of poorer African States in the lower left portion of the graph (twenty countries are represented by the nine data points) violates our expectations, since our proposition implies that these countries would be placed considerably higher on the total aid scale.

A more exacting summary of the overall relationship between the

FIGURE 1

Scatter Diagram of Total Aid Received from the United States in 1964 and Per Capita Gross Domestic Product of Recipient Nations in 1963

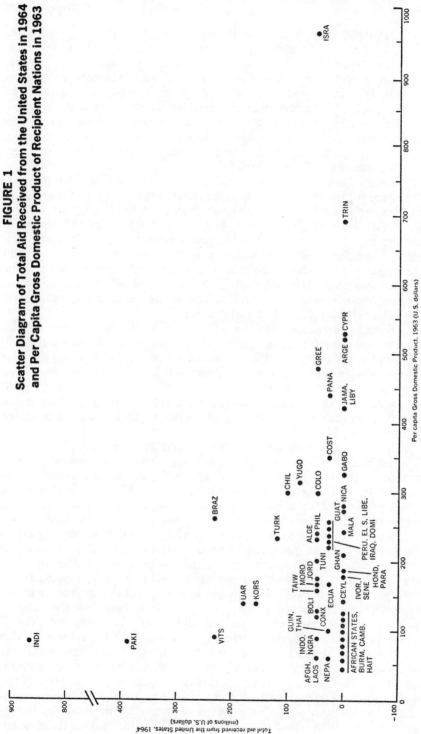

two variables, than is possible through visual inspection alone, can be made by the use of correlation and regression analysis. These techniques were developed by statisticians for measuring the association between two (or more) variables.[12] The Pearson Product-Moment correlation, r, describes the degree and direction of the relationship between two "interval-scale" variables; that is, variables which are measured in uniform units such as dollars for both total aid and per capita GDP. The value of the coefficient can range between plus and minus one, indicating, respectively, a perfectly positive or a perfectly negative (inverse) relationship between the variables correlated.

Regression analysis, while similar to correlation, is a more powerful tool since it provides a measure of the *slope* in the data points represented by two variables. That is, if we treat changes in the foreign aid variable (the dependent variable) as "depending on" or "responding to" changes in the per capita wealth of underdeveloped countries (the independent variable), regression analysis provides an estimate of the average change in the dependent variable associated with every unit increase in the independent variable. This estimate is known as a regression coefficient. The technique also provides an estimate of the dependent variable when the value of the independent variable is zero.

Because the proposition we wish to assess implies an inverse relationship between foreign aid and underdevelopment—the more the aid, the less the per capita GDP—we would expect to find a strong negative correlation between the two variables and a large negative regression coefficient. In fact, however, the correlation is negative but very small, $-.10$ (N = 70, i.e. based on seventy foreign aid recipients). This regression equation summarizes the relationship between the two variables shown graphically in Figure 1:

$$\text{total aid} = 60.02 - .07 \, (\text{GDP/capita})$$

The equation tells us that on the average there is a decrease of $.07 million in the total aid receipts of developing countries associated with every dollar increase in their per capita wealth. With this equation, one could predict, within a given degree of error, the aid a nation receives from the United States by knowing that country's per capita GDP.

Again we can note that the relationship indicated by the regression coefficient is in the predicted direction, but how should we regard the result? Techniques developed by statisticians for assessing what they call the "statistical significance" of correlation and regression coefficients can help provide an answer. We can assess the statistical significance of the regression coefficient using the F test, which is based on the ratio of sums of squares derived in the calculation of the coefficient. The F value for the above regression coefficient is .71, while the critical F value for this case (the F value we must achieve in order to conclude that the relationship between the variables analyzed should be regarded as meaningful on the basis of their *statistical* association) is approximately 4.00.[13] Because the calculated F value is less than 4.00, we can conclude that the relationship between the two variables described by the regression coefficient is *not* statistically significant, that is, that the relationship could very well be due to chance. Similarly, with a correlation based on seventy observations (N = 70), the statistically significant value of r is approximately .232. Because the calculated correlation between total aid and per capita GDP of −.10 is less than this critical value, we can conclude that the correlation coefficient may also reflect a chance association between the two variables.

Substantively, therefore, our correlation and regression analyses, supplemented by the use of statistical significance, *fail* to support the proposition that the United States has tended to distribute its foreign aid to those developing countries which need it most as measured by their per capita wealth.[14]

B. Proximity to the Communist world and foreign aid

The second proposition we wish to examine is that there is a relationship between foreign aid and the geographical position of the developing countries relative to the Communist world. While we are still using the interval-scale variable of foreign aid, our second variable is a nominal scale variable, that is, it is measured by two or more classes or categories. Proximity to the Communist world as discussed earlier will be measured by whether or not the particular country is contiguous with a Communist nation. Hence, there are two classes in this variable—contiguous or non-contiguous with the Communist world—and the variable is said to be dichotomous.

When dealing with an interval-scale variable and a nominal variable, one of the methods is to transform the interval-scale variable into a nominal scale variable. In this case, we create classes of foreign aid recipients so as to make the foreign aid variable comparable to the dichotomous variable measuring proximity to the Communist world. This was done by assigning all developing countries receiving U.S. foreign aid to two mutually exclusive classes: (1) less than or equal to the average amount of total aid ($45.1 million) disbursed to all seventy-one aid recipients, or (2) greater than the average amount of aid.

After transforming the aid variable and classifying the recipient countries into whether or not they border on the Communist world, the data could be displayed in a two-by-two contingency table. Such tables are useful because they organize data so that hypothesized relationships can be evaluated. If the hypothesis were true that the United States was primarily motivated by the fear of Communist takeovers in countries bordering the Communist world. the contingency table might look like Table 2. However, the real world is complex, and social scientists cannot expect to find completely clearcut relationships between variables. Table 3 displays the actual results that were found between the two variables. Notice that the cells with zeroes in them in Table 2 now contain some entries. Rather than assume that no relationship exists between the two variables, however, statistics can help us to decide whether or not and to what degree one exists even though the findings are ambiguous.

TABLE 2
Hypothetical Data Assuming United States Distributes Aid
only on the Motivation of Fear of Communist
Takeover in Bordering Countries

Location of countries	U.S. total aid, 1964		Total
	Less than or equal to mean	Greater than mean	
Not border on Communist country	61	0	61
Border on Communist country	0	10	10
Total	61	10	

One of the more prevalent statistical tests in the chi-square measure, which is used to test the hypothesis that two (or more) variables cross-classified in a contingency table are independent—that is, have no relationship between them. Based on the row and column marginal totals in the table (indicated by dash marks in Table 3), expected frequencies are cal-

TABLE 3
Chi-square Test of the Relationship between the
Proximity of Foreign Aid Recipient Nations to
the Communist World and the Distribution
of United States Total Aid in 1964
(Cell entries are percentages; N in parentheses)

Location of countries	U.S. total aid, 1964		Total
	Less than or equal to mean	Greater than mean	
Not border on Communist country	90.2 (55)	9.8 (6)	85.9 (61)
Border on Communist country	50.0 (5)	50.0 (5)	14.1 (10)
Total	84.5 (60)	15.5 (11)	100.0 (71)

$X^2 = 10.59$ $\lambda a = 0.0$

culated for each cell in the table and then compared with the actual number of observations to determine the chi-square value. This value is then compared to the chi-square values in a table of significant or critical chi-square values in order to determine whether the association between the two variables could be considered a chance occurrence.

For Table 2 the critical value of chi-square[15] is 3.84. Because the calculated chi-square of 10.59 is greater than this critical value, we can reject the null hypothesis that the relationship between the two variables is a chance association. In other words, the analysis tells us that the distribution of U.S. total aid is quite probably *not* independent of the location of developing nations vis-à-vis the Communist world.

Also reported in Table 2 is λa. In contrast to X^2, which measures *any* deviation from a random distribution, λa, is more clearly a measure of *predictive* association. That is, lambda measures, in percentage terms, the degree to which values of the dependent variable (total aid) can be predicted on the basis of knowledge of the values of the independent variable (bordering on the Communist world). The fact that in this case λa is zero reflects the sensitivity of X^2 to the concentration of the observations in the upper left-hand cell of the contingency table and is for this reason a useful complement to the latter measure.[16]

We might also wonder how much information we lost by transforming the foreign aid variable from an interval to a nominal scale. Fortunately, there are tests which allow us to measure the relationship between a nominal and interval measure. One such method is the analysis of variance. In a sense, this technique is more powerful than chi-square, for it describes the relationship between an interval-scale and a dichotomous variable and thus does not require collapsing the foreign aid variable into a dichotomous variable according to some arbitrary criterion.[17]

Analysis of variance is used to test the hypothesis that the means of the interval-scale variable classified according to the dichotomous variable are both centered around the same "grand" mean. For our purposes, this is equivalent to asking whether any of the variability in the interval-scale variable, total aid, can be attributed to the categorized variable, proximity to the Communist world. Though a test for differences in means, the term "analysis of variance" derives from the fact that the tests themselves are based on an examination of the between and within group variances.[18] The F statistic is again used here to test the null hypothesis that the means are equal.

The results of the analysis-of-variance test are shown in Table 4. As in the case of the regression analysis, the critical value of F (at the .05 confidence level) is approximately 4.00. Because the calculated F value of 12.68 is greater than 4.00, we can reject the null hypothesis and instead accept the alternative, that variability about the mean total aid received by developing countries can be attributed to the variable measuring proximity to the Communist world. Like the chi-square analysis, these results thus support the proposition that greater amounts of foreign aid tend to be distributed to developing countries situated in close proximity to the Communist world.

TABLE 4
Analysis of Variance Test of the Relationship between the
Proximity of Foreign Aid Recipient Nations to the
Communist World and the Distribution of
United States Total Aid in 1964

(Millions of U.S. dollars)

Location of countries	U.S. total aid, 1964			
	N	**Mean**	**Variance**	**Total received**
Not border on Communist country	61	26.6	3509.9	1622.0
Border on Communist country	10	157.8	66058.0	1578.0
Total	71	45.1	13614.7	3200.0

F = 12.68

IV. SUMMARY AND CONCLUSION

A variety of statistical analyses have been demonstrated in the paper as a means of suggesting their utility in cross-national aggregate data analysis. The particular focus of attention has been the distribution of United States foreign aid in 1964 and how the distributional patterns discerned have been related to the characteristics of recipient developing nations, which have been treated as the units of analysis.

Our statistical results, although limited in scope, have been provocative. The analyses have shown that:

1) Developing countries' need for foreign aid as measured by their per capita wealth is of virtually no utility in describing United States aid patterns.

2) Geographic proximity of developing countries to the Communist world is a useful concept in explaining the distribution of United States economic assistance. Because proximity to the Communist world is closely related to the idea of a containment foreign policy, the analysis thus suggests that the United States has pursued this policy objective through its distribution of foreign aid.

Clearly these results are only suggestive. However, if we treat these conclusions as empirically-generated theoretical propositions subject to further analysis, several alternative lines of inquiry are suggested. Having already discerned a pattern that suggests a strong association between the aid receipts of developing countries and their proximity to the Communist world, but very little relationship between aid and recipient countries' wealth, the focal point of our substantive concern might well be whether the geographic factor should be considered important in and of itself or whether it is simply an historical artifact attributable to the fact that the least developed and poorest developing nations "just happen" to also border on the Communist world. The size of developing countries, whether operationalized in terms of population size or size of the economy, would also be considered as a possible "artifact" relating to the geographic factor. Multiple regression analysis, conceptually similar to the simple regression discussed earlier but involving more than one variable predicting to foreign aid distribution, is particularly suited to an analysis of these questions, since each of the regression coefficients in multiple regression can be interpreted as measuring the relationship between its corresponding independent variable and the dependent variable after controlling for the effects of all other variables in the model.

In addition, analysis could be directed to the question of the stability of the relationship between aid and underdevelopment and containment. That is, analysis using the techniques discussed in the paper applied to the variables extended both forward and backward in time could be used to ascertain whether our conclusions regarding U.S. aid patterns in 1964 are applicable throughout a longer time span.

Similarly, since the distribution of foreign aid is clearly a multi-factor phenomena, alternative models of the allocation process that would include an examination of additional variables tapping attributes of the recipient countries' society, polity and external relations—such as absorbtive capacity, the extent of democratization, and whether they receive aid from the Soviet Union— would be a useful complementary line of inquiry.

Finally, we might well seek an answer to the question whether patterns similar to or dissimilar from those ascertained for the United States hold for the distribution of foreign aid by other donor countries.[19]

NOTES

[1]The research reported in this paper is part of a larger study entitled *The Distribution of Foreign Aid in Comparative Perspective: An Empirical Study of the Flow of Foreign Economic Assistance.* I wish to express my appreciation to the International Relations Program of Syracuse University for its generous financial support of the project.

[2]A useful survey of many of the practical difficulties associated with the analysis of foreign aid is David A. Baldwin, "Analytical Notes on Foreign Aid and Politics," *Background,* Vol. 10, No. 1, pp. 66-90. An attempt to deal with certain aspects of aid questions of interest to the foreign policy analyst is Masakatsu Kato, "A Model of U.S. Foreign Aid Allocation: An Application of a Rational Decision-Making Scheme," in John E. Mueller, ed., *Approaches to Measurement in International Relations* (New York: Appleton-Century-Crofts, 1969), pp. 198-215. Studies which deal with the domestic side of aid questions are Michael K. O'Leary, *The Politics of American Foreign Aid* (New York: Atherton, 1967) and H. Field Haviland, "Foreign Aid and the Policy Process: 1957," *American Political Science Review* LII (September 1958), 689-724. An excellent survey of much of the work done by economists on aid questions is Raymond F. Mikesell, *The Economics of Foreign Aid* (Chicago: Aldine, 1968).

[3]The phrase "need it most" has been set in quotation marks to indicate that per capita wealth, as need is measured in this paper, is but one measure of developing countries' need for

foreign aid. As Mason has pointed out, foreign aid for development inevitably turns on questions of the foreign exchange developing countries require in order to import the goods necessary to promote economic growth. An alternative measure of need might therefore be one which taps developing countries' ability or inability to generate foreign exchange holdings. Edward S. Mason, *Foreign Aid and Foreign Policy* (New York: Harper and Row, 1964), p. 10.

[4]In addition to Mason cited *ibid.,* other studies which discuss both the developmental and political rationales for foreign aid are Edward C. Banfield, *American Foreign Aid Doctrines* (Washington, D. C.: American Enterprise Institute for Public Policy Research, 1963); Lloyd D. Black, *The Strategy of Foreign Aid* (Princeton, N.J.: Van Nostrand, 1968); Herbert Feis, *Foreign Aid and Foreign Policy* (New York: Dell, 1966); Robert A. Goldwin, ed., *Why Foreign Aid?* (Chicago: Rand McNally, 1963); Jacob J. Kaplan, *The Challenge of Foreign Aid* (New York: Praeger, 1967); George Liska, *The New Statecraft: Foreign Aid in American Foreign Policy* (Chicago: The University of Chicago Press, 1960); John D. Montgomery, *Foreign Aid in International Politics* (Englewood Cliffs, N.J.: Prentice-Hall, 1967); Joan M. Nelson, *Aid, Influence, and Foreign Policy* (New York: Macmillan, 1968); John Pincus, *Trade, Aid and Development* (New York: McGraw-Hill, 1967); and Andrew F. Westwood, *Foreign Aid in a Foreign Policy Framework* (Washington, D. C.: The Brookings Institution, 1966).

[5]The aid data were drawn from Organization for Economic Co-operation and Development, *Geographical Distribution of Financial Flows to Less Developed Countries 1960-1964* (Paris: O.E.C.D., 1966). Total aid is defined as the sum of grants ("gifts in money or in kind, for which no repayment is required"); net official loans ("loans extended by governments and official agencies in currencies other than that of the recipient country" less amortization payments by the recipient country to the donor on previous loans and related items); loans repayable in recipients' currencies (net); and transfers of resources through sales for recipients' currencies (principally food aid as distributed under the aegis of Public Law 480), *ibid.,* pp. xi-xii.

Monies included in the definition of total aid are disbursements conducted under the Foreign Assistance Acts of the United States, the Social Progress Trust Fund, the Peace Corps, Public Law 480, and the Export-Import Bank. Thus no distinctions are drawn according to agencies, and we are in effect treating the aid data analyzed as the output of an aggregate decisional unit.

[6]Six developing countries making net repayments of aid to the United States in 1964 are excluded from the analysis. Further, attention has been restricted to those developing countries which actually received some (net) total aid from the United States in 1964. This means that we are restricting the scope of the two propositions under study, applying them not to the entire underdeveloped world which could be considered candidates for foreign aid, but only to those developing nations in which the United States has in fact manifested an interest through its distribution of foreign aid.

[7]Estimates of Gross Domestic Product (GDP) at current factor cost expressed in U.S. dollars were drawn from United Nations, *Yearbook of National Accounts Statistics 1968,* Vol. II (New York: U.N., 1969), pp. 54-59. These data were converted into per capita GDP using the population estimates of developing countries drawn from Organization for Economic Co-operation and Development, *National Accounts Statistics of Less Developed Countries 1950-1966* (Paris: O.E.C.D., 1968), pp. 14-17. The reader is referred to the original United Nations source for a broad indication of the quality of both the local currency GDP estimates and the exchange rates employed for conversion of the data into U.S. dollars.

GDP differs from Gross National Product (GNP) by a quantity known as net factor income from abroad. GDP is thus a geographically based national accounts measure rather than one based on nationality. GDP at factor cost is derived by subtracting from GDP indirect taxes net of subsidies. Although the data analyzed is GDP at current factor cost, we will refer to it simply as GDP.

[8]Useful discussions of the problems related to crossnational comparisons using national accounts data, including those touched on here, can be found in Everett E. Hagen, "Some Facts About Income Levels and Economic Growth," *The Review of Economics and Statistics* 42 (February 1960), 62-67; Bruce M. Russett, et al., *World Handbook of Political and Social Indicators* (New Haven: Yale University Press, 1964), pp. 149-51; and Goran Ohlin, "Aggregate Comparisons: Problems and Prospects of Quantitative Analysis Based on National

Accounts," in Charles L. Taylor, ed., *Aggregate Data Analysis: Political and Social Indicators in Cross-National Research* (Paris: Mouton, 1968), pp. 79-86.

[9]Russett, *World Handbook of Political and Social Indicators*, p. 261 and ff.

[10]Black, *The Strategy of Foreign Aid*, pp. 24-25.

[11]It is important to note, however, that if an alternative operationalization were to include Pakistan and Taiwan in the proximity group, the result would probably be an even stronger relationship between aid and proximity to the Communist world than that discussed later, since both of these countries received relatively large amounts of United States aid in 1964.

[12]Important assumptions regarding the data being analyzed underlie the use of correlation and regression analyses. For our purposes we shall proceed as though these assumptions are not violated. For an explication of these assumptions as well as the computational procedures involved see Linton C. Freeman, *Elementary Applied Statistics* (New York: Wiley, 1965), pp. 89-106; Hubert M. Blalock, Jr., *Social Statistics* (New York: McGraw-Hill, 1960), pp. 274-92; and William L. Hays, *Statistics for Psychologists* (New York: Holt, Rinehart, & Winston, 1963), pp. 490-538.

[13]The 5 percent confidence limit has been used to assess the statistical significance of both F and r. In effect, this is a measure of the risk of making the wrong decision we are willing to tolerate. As used here, we would say that there is only a 5 percent chance that our conclusion regarding the relationship between aid and underdevelopment is incorrect. For a short but useful discussion of some of the issues involved in the unresolved debate on the appropriateness of statistical significance tests, including cases where random sampling has not been employed, as is frequently true in crossnational aggregate data analysis, see Edward R. Tufte, "Improving Data Analysis in Political Science," *World Politics* 21 (July 1969), 643-44.

[14]The reader is cautioned to note that tne aid and per capita wealth variables are measured in dissimilar units. The former is measured in millions of dollars, the latter simply in dollars. Although this is a reasonable way to operationalize the proposition we wish to examine, it is also reasonable to assume that the size of developing countries may likewise be important in explaining the amount of aid which they receive. An alternative way to analyze the relationship between aid and wealth, therefore, is to correlate aid received and GDP without dividing the latter variable by population. The correlation, r, between these two variables is .86, and the regression coefficient is +0.02 (N = 70). Both are statistically significant. These results thus indicate the importance of the size factor implicit in the GDP variable. Note also that the sign of both measures is positive. To the extent that the size of developing countries' economies is an indication of their need for foreign aid, these results also fail to support the proposition that the United States has distributed its aid to those developing countries which need it most. In fact, the relationship is not even in the direction predicted by our proposition.

[15]At the 5 percent confidence level.

[16]See Freeman,. *Elementary Applied Statistics*, pp. 71-78, 215-226 for chi-square and lambda computational procedures.

In part the choice of the mean as the measure of central tendency used to partition the aid recipients into mutually exclusive classes affects the distribution of cell entries in the contingency table. Because of the large amount of aid received by India ($862 million), the mean aid received by all countries is quite high. The result is that most countries, sixty of them, received actual amounts of aid less than this mean value. Another measure of central tendency, the median value of aid received by developing countries, might therefore have been used to classify the aid recipients into two classes. However, technical considerations involving the calculation of expected frequencies for the chi-square test argue against using the median as the partitioning criterion.

[17]For an elaboration of the computational procedures and important assumptions underlying analysis of variance see Blalock, *Social Statistics*, pp. 242-52.

[18]Variance is· a measure of the variability or dispersion of data values about the mean value for a given variable. Variance is the square of the standard deviation for that variable, the latter being a more commonly used measure of dispersion.

[19] Many of the research questions raised in the preceeding paragraphs have been examined in Eugene R. Wittkopf, *Western Bilateral Aid Allocations: A Comparative Study of Recipient State Attributes and Aid Received* (Beverly Hills, Calif.: Sage Publications, 1972).

In some respects, Wittkopf's study, like Allison's, is a case study, in that it focuses its attention on the behavior of a particular national action. Yet, it is cross-national in the sense that the generalizations Wittkopf discovers about the allocative behavior of the United States are based on a comparative examination of the recipients of that behavior. Consequently, our confidence in Wittkopf's findings is enhanced by the fact that they are based on a large number of observations. Another salient contrast between the Wittkopf and Allison articles is that the former uses systematic observation/descriptive techniques, quantitative procedures, and a hypothesis-testing format, whereas the latter employs narrative descriptive techniques and verbal analysis.

Moreover, the reader should note how Wittkopf used different statistical techniques in constructing his explanations; particularly important in this context is the fact that, when different statistical techniques were applied to the problem, subtle differences obtained in the results. Note also how the different techniques were able to tell us different things, and the differences in his two explanatory variables in their power to explain different aid patterns. Certainly other techniques might have been employed as profitably, but we purposely requested the author to restrict his analysis to a few of the simpler techniques for demonstration purposes. What his demonstration indicates is that investigation should employ a variety of analytic procedures to guard against the danger that the results are artifactual or dependent upon the procedure used. When two or more methods produce the same findings, then our confidence in the validity of the study is increased.

Wittkopf's study is probably best considered an exercise in both description and explanation.

He systematically observed and measured the variables under consideration and has used his findings to generate theoretical explanations of the motivations for U.S. aid donations. The reader should be aware that this study also contains implicit prescriptions, since it suggests differences between reasons the United States gives for offering aid and its actual motivations.

Another type of explanatory analysis is that which looks not only at a set of foreign-policy decisions but also at a large number of states simultaneously. The purpose of such analysis is to uncover patterns, or regularities, of behavior and to discover generalizations about the association among variables. Because there is so much information involved in this kind of comparative study, sophisticated statistical techniques are often required. Statistical techniques aid the researcher in reducing large quantities of data into statements descriptive of similarities and differences in units of behavior, and the generalizations that emerge from such statistical analysis of empirical data are "covering laws" presumed to hold across time and place. While scholarship that employs statistical procedures is more difficult for the beginning student to read, the statistical treatment of a large body of data makes the findings that result more substantial and easier to interpret. The general approach used by the scholar in this way is called "cross-national research" because it attempts to develop and test propositions applicable to a large number of nations. The findings are therefore not specific to a particular country or unique to a particular span of history. The number of such studies using this approach is increasing, and the investigation that follows is exemplary. Written by Jonathan Wilkenfeld, "Domestic and Foreign Conflict Behavior of Nations" is a specially revised comparative foreign-policy study by the author of a work that appeared previously in the Journal of Peace Research. *Wilkenfeld uses a specific statistical technique called "factor analysis" to study the relationship between domestic instability and foreign conflict behavior. Hence, he is looking at conditions within nations as a determinant of a particular kind of foreign-policy behavior, namely, international hostility.*

Certain aspects of this reading need discussion. First, Wilkenfeld is examining a theory that has been suggested by some writers (Frankel and Rosecrance) and systematically studied by others (Rummel and Tanter). Hence, he is making a cumulative contribution to the existing scholarly literature by refining the work of Rummel and Tanter. Note the difference between the hypothesis of the latter and Wilkenfeld's reformulation. Second, Wilkenfeld uses factor analysis, a statistical technique with which you are probably unfamiliar, and which you need not completely understand to comprehend the reading. Factor analysis is merely a technique for taking a large number of variables and determining a small number of dimensions around which the variables cluster. Hence, he describes three types of political regimes—"personalist," "centrist," and "polyarchic"— by finding three dimensions among a large number of variables on politics through factor analysis. Although you may have difficulty in understanding everything in the reading, the above comments should allow you to understand Wilkenfeld's approach and basic findings.

DOMESTIC AND FOREIGN CONFLICT BEHAVIOR OF NATIONS*

Jonathan Wilkenfeld

1. INTRODUCTION

One of the most intriguing questions recently raised in the literature of international relations concerns the relationship between the domestic and foreign conflict behavior of nations. In an article written in 1963, Rudolph J. Rummel reported the results of a factor analytic study of 77 nations. One of the major findings was that 'foreign conflict behavior is generally completely unrelated to domestic conflict behavior' (Rummel, [7] 1963, p. 24).

This initial result was further substantiated in two succeeding studies. In a second study, utilizing slightly different methods of analysis, Rummel found there was 'a positive association, *albeit small,* between domestic conflict behavior and the more belligerent forms of foreign conflict behavior on the part of a country' (italics mine) (Rummel, [8], 1963, pp. 101-102). Subsequently, Raymond Tanter, in a study which essentially replicated the original Rummel study for a later period, concluded 'there is a *small* relationship between 1958-60 domestic and foreign conflict behavior which increases with a time lag' (italics mine) (Tanter, 1966, pp. 61-62). The significant aspect of these latter two studies is that although a relationship was found between internal and external conflict behavior, this relationship was found to be small in both cases.

These findings, and particularly those of the first Rummel study, appear to run counter to well-accepted notions as to the internal and external behavior patterns of nations. Specifically, the most widely held notion is that a nation experiencing internal disorders will tend to engage in external conflict behavior in order to divert the attention of the population from internal problems. This is the notion of uniting a divided people behind the banner of a common cause. For example, Joseph Frankel has stated:

> One of the most significant relationships within the environment is the interaction between domestic and foreign af-

---

This is a specially revised version by Jonathan Wilkenfeld, "Domestic and Foreign Conflict Behavior of Nations," *Journal of Peace Research* 1 (1968): 56-59. Permission to print this version was granted by the International Peace Research Institute, Oslo, who holds the copyright.

*I wish to thank Professor Dina A. Zinnes for her valuable suggestions during the preparation of this study, and Douglas Van Houweling for his assistance in the preparation of the computer programs involved. I also wish to thank Professor Rudolph J. Rummel for his helpful comments on an earlier draft.

Wilkenfeld is an assistant professor in the Department of Government and Politics at the University of Maryland.

fairs. On the basis of relative security and isolation from foreign affairs, it has been customary for British and American thinkers and statesmen to believe that the two domains are separate, and that domestic affairs prevail. Very different is the tradition of the continental countries where such separation has never taken place. (Frankel, 1964, p. 54)

This position is further supported by Richard Rosecrance in his systemic study of world politics. He found:

There tends to be a correlation between international instability and the domestic insecurity of elites. This correlation does not hold in all instances. War may occur in the absence of internal instability; internal friction may occur in the absence of war. In many of the chaotic international patterns of modern times, however, the two factors were associated. (Rosecrance, 1963, pp. 304-305)

Finally, in this regard, F. H. Denton has written the following:

Civil wars preceding and contributing to international wars and international wars causing internal instability and contributing to civil wars both are intuitively satisfying hypotheses. (Denton, 1965, p. 20)

Thus, there would appear to be some contradiction here between the Rummel and Tanter findings and those of such writers as Frankel, Rosecrance, and Denton. This conflict, however, may be more apparent than real. It is not proposed that the mere fact that contradictory examples exist constitutes a negation of the conclusions of the Rummel and Tanter studies. Rather, it is suggested that Rummel's arrival at this conclusion was facilitated by the fact that he did not (nor was it his intention to) differentiate between the nations under consideration. Rummel's approach, therefore, in the interests of reaching generalized conclusions, may have tended to obscure any trends in the opposite direction of his conclusions. It is these trends, which were not of primary importance to Rummel and Tanter, which are of particular interest in the present study.

The purpose of the present study is the re-evaluation of Rummel's data in an effort to both retain and properly identify any relationships which had previously been obscured, due to the method used by Rummel to analyze his data. The method adopted in the present study is the rearrangement of the nations under consideration into groups, according to type of nation, in an effort to determine whether type of nation has any bearing on the relationship between internal and external conflict behavior.

2. DATA AND STUDY DESIGN

The study proposed above suggests the following hypotheses:

(1) Within certain groups of nations, classified according to type of nation, there tends to be a relationship between internal (domestic) conflict behavior and external (foreign) conflict behavior.

TABLE 1

Personalist	Loadings	Polyarchic	Loadings
Guatemala	.78	Norway	—.92
El Salvador	.68	Ireland	—.92
Panama	.68	W. Germany	—.92
Peru	.68	Sweden	—.92
Honduras	.67	Australia	—.92
Argentina	.66	Netherlands	—.91
Korea Rep.	.65	Denmark	—.91
Nicaragua	.64	New Zealand	—.91
Ecuador	.59	Finland	—.90
Lebanon	.59	Switzerland	—.87
Paraguay	.58	Italy	—.86
Iraq	.57	UK	—.86
Haiti	.53	US	—.86
Thailand	.50	Canada	—.85
Indonesia	.35	Belgium	—.84
		Costa Rica	—.81
Centrist		Uruguay	—.81
Bulgaria	.90	Japan	—.79
Albania	.89	Greece	—.77
E. Germany	.88	Israel	—.75
Hungary	.86	France	—.75
Mongolia	.86	Chile	—.74
Czechoslovakia	.86	Dom. Rep.	—.74
N. Korea	.85	Philippines	—.73
USSR	.85	Turkey	—.72
Rumania	.84	Colombia	—.66
Poland	.83	Mexico	—.65
Yugoslavia	.82	Venezuela	—.63
Spain	.80	India	—.62
Portugal	.77	Brazil	—.62
China	.76	Bolivia	—.57
Cuba	.69	S. Africa	—.55
Afghanistan	.64	Ceylon	—.50
Saudi Arabia	.63		
UAR	.62		
Liberia	.58		
Jordan	.58		
Nepal	.53		
Ethiopia	.52		
Iran	.48		
Pakistan	.48		
Cambodia	.47		
Burma	.41		

(2) Within certain groups of nations, classified according to type of nation, there is a tendency for internal (domestic) and external (foreign) conflict behavior to co-occur, or for the occurrence of one to be followed in time by the occurrence of the other.

The two hypotheses stated here are parallel to two stages in the research proposed. Hypothesis 1 merely infers that there is in fact a relationship, depending upon type of nation, between certain types of internal and external conflict behavior. Hypothesis 2 goes a good deal beyond this, in that it postulates a temporal relationship between elements of internal and external conflict behavior, again depending upon the type of nation under discussion and the nature of the conflict behavior.

Nations were classified into types according to the findings of Banks and Gregg (1965), who performed a Q-factor analysis of the political variables of *A Cross-Polity Survey* (Banks and Textor, 1963).[1] It is presently proposed that these groupings, with some modifications, be adopted for purposes of re-evaluating the data collected for the original Rummel and Tanter studies. The final groupings and the loadings for each nation are presented in Table 1.

The specific data used in the present study were collected and compiled using the Dimensionality of Nations Project data. Specifically, Rummel and Tanter collected extensive data on measures of domestic and foreign conflict behavior for all nations in the system for the period 1955-1960 (Rummel, [7], 1963; Tanter, 1966). In separate studies, both writers begin with nine measures of domestic conflict behavior, and these are grouped, by means of a factor analysis, into three domestic conflict dimensions. Similarly, thirteen measures of foreign conflict behavior are factored into three foreign conflict dimensions (see Table 2).[2]

TABLE 2
Factor analysis of domestic conflict measures

Turmoil		Revolutionary		Subversive	
Anti-government		Revolutions	(.85)	Guerrilla	
demonstrations	(.85)	Number killed—		warfare	(.90)
Riots	(.79)	domestic	(.75)	Assassinations	(.66)
Major government		Purges	(.71)		
crises	(.60)	General strikes	(.60)		

Factor analysis of foreign conflict measures

War		Diplomatic		Belligerency	
Number killed—		Expulsions or		Severance of	
foreign	(.87)	recalls—		diplomatic	
Wars	(.85)	ambassadors	(.66)	relations	(.82)
Accusations	(.70)	Expulsions or		Negative	
Threats	(.65)	recalls—		sanctions	(.64)
Military actions	(.65)	lesser		Anti-foreign	
Protests	(.62)	officials	(.60)	demonstrations	(.63)
Mobilizations	(.60)	Troop movements	(.59)		

For the measures of domestic conflict behavior, Rummel labeled the first dimension 'turmoil', designating a non-organizational spontaneous conflict behavior dimension. Those measures with the highest loadings on this dimension are anti-government demonstrations, riots, and major government crises. The second dimension, designated 'revolutionary', represents overt organized conflict behavior, and contains revolutions, number of domestic killed, purges, and general strikes. Finally, a 'subversive' dimension was identified, designating covert organized conflict behavior, and composed of guerrilla warfare and assassinations.[3]

Three dimensions of foreign conflict behavior were also identified in the factor analysis. The first was designated 'war', and was composed of number of foreign killed, wars, accusations, threats, military actions, protests, and mobilizations. The second dimension was 'diplomatic', and constituted a non-military form of foreign conflict behavior. It included expulsions and recalls of ambassadors, expulsions and recalls of lesser officials, and troop movements. Finally, a dimension designated 'belligerency' was identified, representing an actively hostile mood. It included severance of diplomatic relations, negative sanctions, and anti-foreign demonstrations.

Stage 1

At this point it was determined to analyze the data in two slightly different forms, corresponding to tests of the two hypotheses suggested above. These two steps will be referred to hereafter as stages 1 and 2. In the nature of a pretest of hypothesis 1, it was determined that a test would be performed using the factor scores which emerged from the factor analysis performed by Rummel. The factor scores are the values each nation has on each of the dimensions extracted. These scores for each dimension were calculated by Rummel by adding together the standard scores for those measures on the particular dimension which had a correlation greater than or equal to .50 and no correlation greater than or equal to .40 on another dimension. Therefore, the factor may be thought of as a composite of those measures which are most strongly associated with that dimension (Rummel, [8], pp. 15-16).[5] The calculations performed in the present study were the correlations between the factor scores of all nine possible pairs of three domestic and three foreign conflict behavior dimensions. The results of this analysis are presented in Table 3.

Although a more extensive treatment of these results will be presented later, a quick glance at Table 3 will indicate that some interesting findings emerge. For the personalist group, composed primarily of Latin American nations, it is clear that any type of internal conflict behavior appears to be related to the 'diplomatic' external conflict dimension. For the centrist group, composed primarily of socialist nations, the important relationships are those between 'turmoil' and 'diplomatic', 'turmoil' and 'belligerency', and 'revolutionary' and 'war'. Finally, for the polyarchic group, consisting for the most part of economically developed, western nations, the relationships which emerge are between 'turmoil' and 'war' and 'revolutionary' and 'belligerency'.

TABLE 3
Factor score analysis

Domestic conflict dimension	Foreign conflict dimension	Personalist[a]	Centrist[b]	Polyarchic[c]
TURMOIL	—WAR	—.29	.28	.39*
TURMOIL	—DIPLOMATIC	.66***	.40*	—.02
TURMOIL	—BELLIGERENCY	.10	.43*	.27
REVOLUTIONARY	—WAR	—.20	.55***	—.09
REVOLUTIONARY	—DIPLOMATIC	.49	.21	—.10
REVOLUTIONARY	—BELLIGERENCY	—.27	.33	.45**
SUBVERSIVE	—WAR	—.16	—.08	—.08
SUBVERSIVE	—DIPLOMATIC	.55*	—.04	—.10
SUBVERSIVE	—BELLIGERENCY	—.19	—.12	.08

[a] N=15
[b] N=26
[c] N=33

*p < .05
**p < .01
***p < .005

A preliminary conclusion seems to be warranted on the basis of the above results. It appears to be the case that the grouping of nations in the manner attempted here does in fact isolate relationships which were present but nevertheless obscured in both the Rummel and Tanter analyses. This may be seen from the fact that pairs of dimensions for which relationships were found between internal and external conflict behavior, do not repeat themselves across all other groups. Thus, for the centrist group, in the case of 'revolutionary' and 'war', a high correlation was obtained. However, low negative correlations for this pair were obtained for the other two groups. When the nations were taken together, it is easily seen how this important relationship was obscured.

Further analysis of these findings will await the explanation of the next stage of research, since it will be more meaningful at that point. The above results may be viewed as those of a preliminary and exploratory study. The main function of this initial stage was to determine whether, by breaking down the nations studied by Rummel and Tanter into groups, any relationship was found. Having determined this, we now feel justified in going one step further, both in the data used and the methods of analysis to further develop the theoretical implications of the results. It is to this stage which we now turn.

Stage 2

While stage 1 proposed a correlation analysis of the *factor scores* which emerged from the Rummel study of the years 1955-1957, stage 2, which specifically tests hypothesis 2, proposes the use of raw scores. In addition to this change, stage 2 also increases the data by incorporating the data collected by Tanter (1966). This provides a six year period of analysis, from 1955 to 1960. Although the factor scores were available only in an aggregate form for a three year period, the raw scores were available on a year-ly basis for the entire six year period.

The raw score assigned to each nation for each year for a particular factor was arrived at by summing the frequency of that particular measure for a given year. However, scaling was performed in the case of some of the measures, in order to reduce the problem of outliers.[6]

The use of yearly data in this stage facilitated the specific testing of hypothesis 2. Thus, it was now possible to investigate the possibility of time lags as a factor in the relation between the occurrence of internal conflict behavior and the occurrence of external conflict behavior. The data were tested not only in order to determine whether there was a relation-ship between the two for the same year, but also in an effort to determine whether one and two year time lags were appropriate in certain cases. Fur-thermore, time lags of one and two years both from the occurrence of in-ternal to the occurrence of external, *and vice versa,* were attempted. This possibility was suggested by Denton, in the passage quoted earlier (1963). As will be noted from Tables 5, 6 , and 7, negative lags (—1 and —2) in-dicate that the lag was from foreign conflict in year n to domestic conflict in year n + 1 or n + 2. Similarly, positive lags (+1 and +2) indicate lags from internal in year n to external in year n + 1 and n + 2. A zero lag in-dicates the analysis in which both occurred in the same year. The case of the zero lag is roughly equivalent to the analysis performed in stage 1 of this study.

Finally, a specific statistical method was employed in order to deal with a large number of cases for each correlation. For example, for the polyarchic group, composed of 33 nations, when investigating the occur-rence of both internal and external conflict behavior in the same year, not only 1955 internal to 1955 external were taken, but also 1956—1956 . . . 1960—1960. Thus, rather than having only 33 cases for one year, we now have 198 cases for six years. This method contributed greatly to the significance levels of the results obtained, as well as to their reliability.

The results of both stages are presented in Tables 3, 4, 5, and 6. They will be discussed according to group, i.e. personalist, centrist, and polyarchic.

(a) Personalist group. The personalist group is composed of 15 nations. Table 1 indicates that this group is composed primarily of Latin American nations (10 out of 15). To a large degree, the nations which make up this group are dictatorships of one sort or another, but differ from the centrist group of dictatorships in degree of centralization.

With regard to the results obtained from stage 1, as reported in column 1 of Table 3, the only significant correlations (p < .05) were obtained be-tween 'turmoil' and 'diplomatic' (.66), 'revolutionary' and 'diplomatic' (.49), and 'subversive' and 'diplomatic' (.55). Table 4 indicates that for stage 2, comparing internal and external conflict behavior for the same year (lag = 0), which is roughly comparable to what was done in stage 1, these three relationships held, while the significance levels increased (p < .01). Furthermore, almost without exception, for each of these three cases, the significance levels as well as the correlations for the other possible lags were lower than those for lag = 0.

In terms of the original hypothesis, then, for the personalist group, the occurrence of all types of internal conflict behavior tends to be accompanied by the co-occurrence of external conflict behavior of the 'diplomatic' type. With reference to Table 2, indicating the components of these dimensions, any type of internal conflict behavior is accompanied by expulsions or recalls of ambassadors and lesser officials, as well as troop movements.

TABLE 4
Personalist [a]

	lag = —2 [b]	lag = —1 [c]	lag = 0 [d]	lag = +1 [c]	lag = +2 [b]
TUR—WAR	.22	.15	.14	—.05	.01
TUR—DIP	—.01	.23*	.29**	.22	.16
TUR—BEL	.17	.25*	.20	.21	.40***
REV—WAR	.23	.00	.13	—.05	—.16
REV—DIP	.12	.15	.29**	.23*	.22
REV—BEL	.29*	.18	.14	.18	.31*
SUB—WAR ...	.33*	.28*	.24*	.14	—.01
SUB—DIP	.05	.34***	.49***	.11	—.04
SUB—BEL	.38***	.37***	.34***	.31**	.40***

[a] Negative lags indicate the occurrence of external before internal and positive lags indicate the occurrence of internal before external. Lag = 0 designates the measurement of both internal and external for the same year.

[b] N = 60   *p < .05
[c] N = 75   **p < .01
[d] N = 90   ***p < .005

There are other important relations of note in the personalist group. 'Turmoil' and 'belligerency' have a correlation of .40 (p < .005) for a two year time lag between the internal and the external. In other words, the occurrence of internal conflict behavior of the type classified as 'turmoil', i.e., anti-government demonstrations, riots, and major government crises, tends to be associated with the occurrence of external conflict behavior of the type classified as 'belligerency', i.e., severance of diplomatic relations, negative sanctions, and anti-foreign demonstrations, two years later. On the other hand, 'war' and 'subversive' have a correlation of .33 (p < .05) for lag = —2. In other words, the occurrence of external conflict behavior of type 'war', i.e., foreign killed, wars, mobilizations, accusations, threats, military actions, and protests, tends to be accompanied by the occurrence of internal conflict behavior of type 'subversive', i.e., guerrilla warfare and assassinations, two years later.

In those cases where 'belligerency' is involved, a rather interesting relationship emerges. Particularly for 'revolutionary'—'belligerency' and 'subversive'—'belligerency', it is difficult to determine exactly what is taking place. It appears that the internal and external conflict behavior patterns involved here are mutually reinforcing in some way. Since the 'belligerency' dimension includes severance of diplomatic relations, negative sanctions, and anti-foreign demonstrations, the answer may lie in the nature of these factors and their interaction with these particular nations. At this stage of the research, we cannot give an adequate explanation for this phenomenon.

(b) Centrist group. The centrist group is composed of 26 nations. Twelve of the 26 were socialist during the years under consideration, while an additional 4 are Middle Eastern. The nations exhibit both dictatorial and highly centralized patterns of leadership.

To a certain extent, the results obtained in stage 2 (Table 5) confirm those of stage 1. That is, in stage 2 there continues to be a relationship, for lag = 0, between 'turmoil' and 'belligerency' and 'revolutionary' and 'war'.

TABLE 5
Centrist [a]

	lag = —2 [b]	lag = —1 [c]	lag = 0 [d]	lag = 1 [c]	lag = +2 [b]
TUR—WAR	.04	.08	.10	.13	.10
TUR—DIP	—.11	.06	.13	.19*	.08
TUR—BEL	.07	.16	.26***	.18*	.06
REV—WAR	—.04	.06	.21**	.21*	.34***
REV—DIP	—.11	—.10	.07	.20*	.13
REV—BEL	—.07	..11	.24***	.24**	.30***
SUB—WAR	—.06	—.07	—.04	.01	.05
SUB—DIP	—.05	—.03.	—.07	.02	.02
SUB—BEL	—.02	—.01	.10	.08	.25**

[a] Negative lags indicate the occurrence of external before internal, and positive lags indicate the occurrence of internal before external. Lag = 0 designates the measurement of both internal and external for the same year.
[b] N = 104   *p < .05
[c] N = 130   **p < .01
[d] N = 156   ***p < .005

Of far greater import, however, in analyzing the results obtained for the centrist group are the correlations obtained when time lags were used. Thus, in terms of hypothesis 2, for the centrist group, it appears never to be the case that the occurrence of external conflict behavior of any sort will be accompanied by the occurrence of internal conflict behavior of any sort in a later period. Furthermore, in only one case—that of 'turmoil', i.e., anti-government demonstrations, riots, and major government crises, and 'belligerency', i.e., severance of diplomatic relations, negative sanctions, and anti-foreign demonstrations—does the occurrence of internal conflict behavior and external conflict behavior in the same period appear to be the most likely possibility.

On the other hand, Table 5 clearly shows that in all cases in which 'revolutionary' internal conflict behavior is involved—i.e., revolutions, number killed in domestic violence, purges, and general strikes—all types of foreign conflict behavior tend to occur given a one or two year time lag. In terms of hypothesis 2, then, for the centrist group, internal conflict behavior of the 'revolutionary' type tends to be accompanied by the occurrence of all types of external conflict behavior after a lag of either one or two years.

If in fact we can isolate what appears to be a trend in the centrist group, from the occurrence of internal conflict behavior to the occurrence of external conflict behavior, how can we account for the fact that in some cases a two year lag occurs, while in others a one year lag occurs, while in still others no time lag at all is apparent? If for the moment we restrict ourselves to the cases involving 'revolutionary' internal conflict behavior, certain possibilities begin to appear. A centrist nation experiencing internal conflict behavior of the 'revolutionary' type certainly cannot respond in full force and immediately with external conflict behavior. Thus, although an initial response appears to be made in the cases of 'revolutionary'—'war' and 'revolutionary'—'belligerency', it is really only two years later that the nation is in a position, in a sense, to act out its internal problems externally. During the two year period, although some response is made, it may be postulated that the main attention of the leadership is focused upon the task of quelling domestic unrest. Only after this has been accomplished to some degree may the regime attempt to divert the attention of the population from its domestic problems. In this sense, we may have isolated some relevant findings with regard to the ability of a centrist nation to respond to internal stress.

The contention that within the centrist group external conflict behavior is a tool in the hands of the leadership for diverting attention from internal disorders is further substantiated by the results obtained for the -1 and -2 lags. Since it is apparently never the case that external conflict behavior can lead to domestic unrest, the use of foreign conflict behavior as an 'attention-diverter' can never endanger the regime in terms of its corresponding effect on domestic factors, as it did in the case of the personalist group and as will be seen to be the case in the polyarchic group. If foreign conflict behavior apparently never leads to domestic conflict behavior, then it may be engaged in without the fear of domestic repercussions.

(c) Polyarchic group. This group is composed of 33 nations. It will be noted from Table 1 that virtually all of the nations correlating above .80 with this group are economically developed, western nations. Furthermore, those nations with low loadings (below .80) usually exhibit at least one of the above characteristics.

In neither stage 1 nor stage 2 does a clear pattern of relations between internal and external conflict behavior emerge here. In stage 1, two significant correlations were obtained, 'turmoil'—'war' .39 ($p < .45$), and 'revolutionary'—'belligerency' .45 ($p < .41$). The results of stage 2 indicate confirmation for the case of 'turmoil', i.e., anti-government demonstrations, riots, and major government crises, and 'war', i.e., number of foreign killed, wars, accusations, threats, military actions, protests, and mobilizations. The relationship between 'revolutionary' and 'belligerency' was not confirmed in stage 2.

However, here again it is the case that several new relationships and trends emerge from the analysis. First of all, the results from stage 2

TABLE 6
Polyarchic[a]

	lag = −2[b]	lag = −1[c]	lag = 0[d]	lag = +1[c]	lag = +2[b]
TUR—WAR	.30***	.29***	.36***	.26***	.42***
TUR—DIP	.20*	.15*	.23***	.10	.10
TUR—BEL	.29***	.18*	.30***	.19*	.20*
REV—WAR	−.04	−.01	.03	.00	.04
REV—DIP	−.03	.03	−.01	−.04	−.06
REV—BEL·......	.00	.08	.16*	.06	.13
SUB—WAR	.02	.18*	.12	.17*	.14
SUB—DIP	−.08	.02	.05	.00	.01
SUB—BEL	.07	.16*	.16*	.09	−.01

[a] Negative lags indicate the occurrence of external before internal, and positive lags indicate the occurrence of internal before external. Lag ″ 0 designates the measurement of both internal and external for the same year.

[b] N = 132   *p < .05
[c] N = 165   **p < .01
[d] N = 198   ***p < .005

indicate that for the polyarchic group, the domestic conflict behavior dimensions 'revolutionary', i.e., revolutions, number killed in domestic violence, purges, and general strikes, and 'subversive', i.e., guerrilla warfare and assassinations, never precede or follow the occurrence of any form of external conflict behavior. This appears to be a characteristic of only the polyarchic nations.

Furthermore, the domestic conflict behavior dimension 'turmoil' appears to be related to all types of foreign conflict behavior. Here again, as was the case with certain pairs of conflict dimensions for the personalist group, a relationship of mutual reinforcement between the internal and the external appears to be indicated. Polyarchic nations experiencing anti-government demonstrations, riots, and major government crises appear to engage in all types of external conflict behavior, and vice versa. As stated earlier, no ready answer is available to deal with this phenomenon, except to suggest that the answer may lie in the nature of the components of the 'turmoil' dimension and their particular relevance to the type of nation characterized as polyarchic.

3. CONCLUSION

The results obtained in the analysis performed here indicate confirmation of both hypotheses 1 and 2. Thus, not only was a relationship between internal and external conflict behavior found, but the indication is that in some cases a time lag is involved. This statement should now be qualified by indicating the degree of interaction between the two key variables, i.e., type of nation and dimension of conflict. Clearly, as we shift our attention from the personalist, to the centrist, and finally to the polyarchic group, the particular dimensions of conflict behavior which are related change. Indeed, there is no one particular relationship between any pair of internal and external conflict dimensions which holds for all groups equally well.

In the section devoted to the centrist group, we have already examined some possible explanations for the outstanding characteristic of this group, i.e., that a significant relationship is virtually never found when external conflict behavior occurs before internal. In this connection, it was felt that in centrist type nations, in which centralized control of most aspects of life is the primary characteristic, the leadership does not have to concern itself with internal repercussions of external acts.

In the personalist and polyarchic groups, the pattern of relationships is less clearcut. Here we find some significant relationships for virtually every time lag, from internal to external and from external to internal. Perhaps even more significant was the finding that in several cases in both groups, there appears to be a pattern of mutual reinforcement, in which for a certain pair of internal and external conflict measures, internal appears to precede external while at the same time external appears to precede internal. This is of course in sharp contrast to the type of finding for the centrist group.

These findings may lead us to some interesting conclusions regarding the types of nations with which we are dealing and their basic decision-making processes. On the one hand, we have highly centralized nations, in which decisions concerning foreign conflict behavior are in some cases generated by the types of internal conflict behavior it is experiencing, but in which these external conflict decisions are made in relative isolation from possible internal reactions. On the other hand, in the polyarchic nations, and to a lesser extent in the personalist nations, neither internal nor external actions are taken in isolation from each other.

An additional factor analytic study by Gregg and Banks (1965) may help us gain some insights into the phenomena isolated in the present study. In that study, the same variables which were used in the Q-factor analysis were employed, but here the 68 *Cross Polity Survey* variables were grouped. The first factor, which accounted for 24.6 per cent of the variance, was labeled 'Access'. Gregg and Banks note that in the 'Access' factor, the following dichotomies are apparent, based on high positive versus low negative loadings: Hierarchical as opposed to competitive bargaining processes; consolidated as opposed to distributed authority and force; executive and single party politics as opposed to legislative and group politics; totalitarian restrictions as opposed to institutionalized openness of political channels (1965, p. 607). Table 7 presents the factor loadings of the various areal groupings on this factor. As we would expect, given the nature of the variables concerned, and with particular reference to the types of dichotomies noted above, the East European areal group has the highest negative loading on this factor, followed by the Asian and North

African-Middle Eastern areal groups. Virtually all the nations loading on the centrist group fall into these areal groupings. On the other hand, the Advanced Western areal group and the Latin American areal group load positively on this factor. These groups are similar in makeup to the polyarchic and personalist groups, respectively.

TABLE 7
Distribution of areal groupings on Access factor

Areal group	Loading
Advanced Western areal group	.45
Latin American areal group	.21
African areal group	—.05
North African, Middle Eastern areal group	—.06
Asian areal group	—.16
East European areal group	—.58

We are left with the task of relating the areal group loadings on the 'Access' factor to the relationships between types of conflict behavior noted in the present study. Table 8 presents data on the instances in which two groups have significant correlations on the same pair of internal and external conflict measures for the same time lag. While the personalist and polyarchic groups overlap on seven correlations, each overlaps with the centrist group on only three. This might indicate a certain relationship between the way in which personalist and polyarchic nations react to internal and external conflict behavior. These findings are in line with the results obtained by Gregg and Banks on the 'Access' factor, i.e., that along this factor the personalist-polyarchic and centrist nations are at opposite poles.

TABLE 8
Overlapping correlations

Personalist— Polyarchic		Centrist— Personalist		Centrist— Polyarchic	
TUR—DIP	lag = −1	REV—DIP	lag = +1	TUR—BEL	lag = 0
TUR—BEL	lag = −1	REV—BEL	lag = +2	REV—BEL	lag = 0
SUB—WAR	lag = −1	SUB—BEL	lag = +2	TUR—BEL	lag = +1
SUB—BEL	lag = −1				
TUR—DIP	lag = 0				
SUB—BEL	lag = 0				
TUR—BEL	lag = +2				

Building upon the base provided by the findings obtained here, one area clearly indicated as potentially fruitful for further research is the investigation of the behavior of particular nations involved as participants in particular international conflict situations. Specifically, the confirmation of hypotheses 1 and 2 for certain groups and certain dimensions should give us additional information upon which to judge the behavior of nations. What is being proposed here is that nations in the international system do not behave solely on the basis of the givens of the international situation. Depending upon the type of nation, we must look beyond the international sphere to the internal situation in the participating nation, to determine that nation's reactions.

What we are in essence suggesting here is a new look at the notion of 'rational' behavior on the part of a nation engaged in conflict. It would appear that the idea of a nation making a correct or an incorrect choice, given the international situation, must be expanded to include the whole sphere of internal politics. Only when we possess all the facts which contribute to a particular response on the part of a nation may we make judgments pertaining to the correctness or rationality of the choice. The hypotheses proposed and tested in this study may contribute to formulating a more comprehensive theory of international conflict.

NOTES

[1]This technique of factor analysis results in the grouping of nations according to similarities across certain political variables. The actual groupings which emerged from this factor analysis were labeled polyarchic, elitist, centrist, personalist, and traditional.

[2]Tanter's factor analysis, based on the data from 1958 to 1960, identified slightly different dimensions. For purposes of the present study, it was decided to use only those factors identified in the Rummel analysis.

[3]The "turmoil" and "revolutionary" dimensions account for 39.0 per cent and 37.6 per cent of the common variance, respectively. The "subversive" dimension accounts for only 23.4 per cent. Clearly, the first two may be considered the most important dimensions of domestic conflict behavior (Rummel, (8), 1963, pp. 11-13).

[4]The "war" dimension accounted for 46.2 per cent of the common variance, and clearly was the most important foreign conflict dimension. "Belligerency" accounted for 29.1 per cent while "diplomatic" accounted for 24.6 per cent of the common variance (Rummel, (8), 1963, pp. 13-14).

[5]The factor scores for each nation on the six dimensions are reported by Rummel (1963 (8), pp. 44-45).

[6]The table below lists all the factors used and indicates whether or not scaling was employed.

Domestic conflicts measures

Class 1	Class 2	Class 3
Assassinations	General strikes	Number killed in domestic violence
Guerrilla wars	Purges	
Major government crises	Riots	
Revolutions	Demonstrations	

Foreign conflict measures

Class 1	Class 2	Class 3
Severance of diplomatic relations	Anti-foreign demonstrations	Accusations
Expulsions or recalls— ambassadors	Negative sanctions	Number killed in foreign violence
Military actions	Protests	
Wars	Expulsions or recalls— lesser officials	
Troop movements	Threats	
Mobilizations		

Class 1—data unchanged

Class 2—data transformed by grouping according to geometric progression:

Raw data	Group value
0	0
1	1
2—3	2
4—7	3
8—15	4
16—32	5
33—64	6

Class 3—data transformed according to the following:

$$\log_{10}(\text{number} + 1)$$

The next step was the combination of the raw scores on particular factors into the appropriate dimensions. For example, in the case of the "war" dimension, military actions, wars, and mobilizations for a particular nation were summed directly. Protests and threats were transformed by grouping according to geometric progression, and then added to the total. The values for accusations and number of foreign killed were converted to $\log_{10}$ (accusations + 1) and $\log_{10}$ (killed + 1), and then added to the total. What emerged from this process was a raw score for each nation on each of the six dimensions, for each of the six years studied.

REFERENCES

[1] Banks, Arthur S. and Gregg, Phillip M. 'Grouping Political Systems: Q-Factor Analysis of *A Cross-Polity Survey'*, *The American Behavioral Scientist*, 9, (November 1965), pp. 3-6.

[2] Banks, Arthur S. and Textor, Robert B. *A Cross Polity Survey*. (Cambridge: M. I. T. Press, 1963)

[3] Denton, F. H. 'Some Regularities in International Conflict, 1820-1949   (The RAND Corporation, 1965)

[4] Frankel, Joseph. *International Relations*. (New York: Oxford University Press, 1964)

[5] Gregg, Phillip M. and Banks, Arthur S. 'Dimensions of Political System: Factor Analysis of *A Cross-Polity Survey'*, *The American Political Science Review*, 59, (September 1965), pp. 602-614.

[6] Rosecrance, Richard N. *Action and Reaction in World Politics*. (Boston: Little, Brown, and Co., 1963)

[7] Rummel, Rudolph J. 'Dimensions of Conflict Behavior Within and Between Nations', *General Systems*, 8, (1963), pp. 1-50.

[8] Rummel, Rudolph J. 'Testing Some Possible Predictors of Conflict Behavior Within and Between Nations', *Peace Research Society Papers*, (1963)

[9] Tanter, Raymond, 'Dimensions of Conflict Behavior Within and Between Nations, 1958-60', *The Journal of Conflict Resolution*, 10, (March 1966), pp. 41-64.

This explanatory article differs from the two preceding ones, first, because it attempts to explain a general phenomenon, conflict behavior, rather than the behavior of a particular actor (e.g., the foreign-aid donorship of the United States), and, second, because it attempts to develop generalizations that hold up across virtually all nations in the world. Wilkenfeld's nomothetic findings that there is a relationship between domestic instability and foreign-policy hostility, if one takes into account type of political regime and time-lags between domestic instability and foreign-policy behavior, applies not just to the United States but to the seventy-four nations studied.

It should be pointed out that the Allison and Wittkopf approaches do not preclude generalizations that hold up across a large number of nations. One could apply Allison's framework to other foreign-policy decisions by other nations, while Wittkopf's study could be expanded to include all the aid-giving countries in order to determine whether the motivations behind U.S. aid policy are similar to those behind the policies of the Soviet Union, France, and so on. Although the Allison and Wittkopf selections are not comparative, they represent approaches that could be made comparative in the future.

Our introduction identified several possible categories of determinants of foreign policy: the international context, domestic politics, the decision-makers, and economic and military factors. In this discussion of the scholarly literature, we noted that most theorists tend to ignore some factors and concentrate on others in attempting to explain foreign-policy behavior. The former looks only at the international context—the economic development and the geographical location of the recipient states. The latter ignores the international context, economic and military factors, and the decision-making variables, while devoting all its attention to domestic factors as determinants of foreign-policy behavior.

Although the Allison study deals with most of the relevant variables that affected a particular set of foreign policy decisions, it confronts substantial observation problems as well as difficulties in providing succinct explanations. Given the intensive nature of his study, the casual links Allison has attempted to examine demand data on the behavior and perceptions of decision-makers and the social-psychological interactions among decision-makers at a variety of points in America. Similarly, the vast number of complex interrelated variables involved in an event as momentous as the Cuban Missile Crisis renders the explicit statement of relationships among variables exceedingly difficult.

Comparison of the Allison study with the Wittkopf and Wilkenfeld readings clearly illustrates a basic dilemma facing those interested in foreign-policy analysis. Intensive studies that focus on a specific event or a particular foreign policy differ from extensive studies that attempt to develop general explanations. This applies not only to differences in relevant data but also to the style, content, and even purposes of the work. When one performs intensive studies, one is looking for specific explanations that may or may not be generalizable. In contrast, those who do extensive studies that are comparative in nature are willing to "trade off" specific knowledge about particular events and processes for generalized knowledge. Although each can contribute to the other, the two approaches represent different styles, content, data, and purposes. Rather than indicate which is preferable, we might note that the requirement of being explicit and systematic applies for both, and, given the present state of the literature on foreign-policy analysis, both approaches appear to be useful.

From the preceding discussion and reading selections, the reader may get the impression that foreign-policy analysis is dominated by studies that are primarily descriptive or explanatory in focus. Such an impression is probably inaccurate. Because the foreign policy of a state attempts to represent the diverse interests of that state in a very complex world, there is always controversy over the appropriateness of specific foreign-policy decisions. Consequently, much of the literature is prescriptive, designed to advocate particular policy options over others. Indeed, it would probably not be an exaggeration to suggest that most of the attention of foreign-policy analysts, broadly defined, is concentrated on efforts to evaluate, critique, and prescribe current foreign policy in a variety of ways.

In turning from descriptive and explanatory analysis to prescriptive analysis, we may note that the latter is conducted in numerous modes, ranging from the polemic found on the editorial page of the daily newspaper to rigorous normative investigations seeking to assess foreign-policy actions by clear value criteria. The two prescriptive articles that follow illustrate two contrasting styles of prescriptive analysis. The first is a general critique of the goals and methods employed by American policy-makers with respect to the Vietnam conflict. It is one of literally hundreds of such essays found in various books (e.g., Robert W. Gregg and Kegley, 54) and journal articles (see Foreign Affairs *or* Foreign Policy *for examples of this genre of research). The second is a systematic attempt to state evaluative criteria explicitly and then apply those criteria in assessing decision options. There are very few works in the literature similar to it, although the approach represents one that can be usefully emulated by foreign-policy researchers interested in pursuing systematic normative inquiry. It sets a model for such inquiry because it uses empirical data to support a proposed foreign-policy course of action. Let us look at these prescriptive investigations separately.*

The first prescriptive reading is exemplary of the logical critique associated with traditional techniques of political analysis. Hans Morgenthau is one of the most creative and prolific scholars in the field of international politics and foreign policy and the leading exponent of the "political realist" school of thought. One of the most vocal and cogent critics of American involvement in Vietnam, Morgenthau, in this article, castigates American policy in Southeast Asia during the Johnson Administration. When reading this essay, note how description, explanation, and prescription are combined throughout his account and critique of American policy. The student should take special care to distinguish and note: (1) Morgenthau's view of the world, (2) his assumptions about the views of those responsible for the making of American foreign policy, (3) his criticisms of these assumptions, and (4) the kinds of different assumptions and different policy actions he prescribes.

THE INTELLECTUAL, POLITICAL, AND MORAL ROOTS OF U.S. FAILURE IN VIETNAM

Hans J. Morgenthau

I. THE AMERICAN NATIONAL INTEREST IN ASIA

The United States has one basic interest in Asia: maintenance or, if need be, restoration of a viable balance of power. Thus the United States has pursued in Asia the same basic interest it has tried to realize in Europe since the beginning of its history. For in both Europe and Asia the United States has consistently opposed the power which threatened to make itself the master of the continent and in consequence would be in a position to threaten the security of the United States across the ocean.

As far as Europe is concerned, this interest has always existed even though it was not always recognized for what it was. It has remained throughout the persistent rationale of our European policies. The active interest of the United States in Asia dates only from the turn of the century. Its first expression is the Open Door policy with regard to China. At the outset, this policy had exclusively a commercial purpose: it sought to maintain freedom of competition for all interested parties in the semi-colonial exploitation of China. But very soon it took on a political and military connotation as well. For the United States recognized that any great power, European or Asian, which added the enormous power potential of China to its own would thereby make itself the master of its own continent, if not of the world. Thus the policy of the Open Door for China transformed itself organically into a policy of the balance of power for Asia, of which the independence of China was the corner-stone.

It is for this reason that the United States opposed from the very beginning Japan's attempts at creating an Asian empire, primarily at China's expense. That opposition started out ineffectually in the form of the Stimson Doctrine, that is, the refusal to recognize territorial changes realized by force. Yet from the late 1930's onward, ever more stringent actions implemented that verbal expression of this country's opposition until in the fall of 1941 it confronted Japan with the choice between giving up any further territorial expansion or going to war with the United States.

Hans J. Morgenthau, "The Intellectual, Political, and Moral Roots of U.S. Failure in Vietnam," a paper prepared for the Annual Meeting of the American Political Science Association, Washington, D.C., Sept. 2-7, 1968. (Abridged.) Copyright, the American Political Science Association. Reprinted by permission of the author and the American Political Science Association.

Morgenthau is currently Albert A. Michelson Distinguished Professor of Political Science at the University of Chicago.

1. The United States, China, and Vietnam

During and immediately after the Second World War, the United States tried to make China into a counter-weight to Japan, thus restoring the Asian balance of power. In anticipation and furtherance of this development, the United States endowed China both legally and politically with the status of a great power. When the Communists defeated Chiang Kai-shek and took over China in 1949, they also destroyed the foundations of our Asian policy. Suddenly, China, instead of serving as a counter-weight to a power inimical to the United States, became the ally of one of them. Japan, disarmed and occupied, could not serve as a counter-weight to the emergent power of China. That function could be performed by only one power, the United States itself.

The policies through which the United States has implemented this function, it seems to me, have been decisively determined by the Chinese intervention in the Korean War. Before that intervention, the United States moved towards recognition of the Communist government of China and away from complete military and political identification with Chiang Kai-shek's regime on Taiwan. The policy which the United States then intended to pursue vis-à-vis China was clearly formulated in the famous and often misquoted speech which the then Secretary of State Dean Acheson gave at the National Press Club in Washington on January 12, 1950. That speech did not envisage a unilateral military commitment of the United States on the mainland of Asia. Acheson identified the island chain adjacent to the Asian mainland from Japan to the Philippines as the outer limits of America's military presence.

China's intervention in the Korean War radically transformed the Asian policies of the United States. The United States responded to that intervention with two policies: the policy of isolating China and the policy of peripheral military containment.

The policy of isolating China originally sought the downfall of the Communist government. It was organically connected with the recognition of the Chiang Kai-shek government as the legitimate government of China and with the expectation of its return to the mainland. The policy of peripheral military containment derives from two assumptions: that China threatens its neighbors primarily with local military expansion, and that the United States is capable of bringing to bear sufficient local military force to contain an expansionist China.

Even if one were to hold that these two assumptions are empirically correct—which, as we shall see, they are not—our military involvement in Vietnam could be justified in terms of our traditional national interest in Asia only by making the additional assumption that a Viet Cong victory in South Vietnam or the unification of North and South Vietnam under the Hanoi government would be tantamount to an expansion of Chinese power threatening the balance of power in Asia. While this was indeed the original position the U.S. government and its supporters took in justifying our military involvement in Vietnam, the speciousness of the argument, never valid to begin with, has been rendered obvious by subsequent events.

These events have shown that the Viet Cong are not a mere instrument of foreign aggression perpetrated by the government of North Vietnam, and that the latter is not a mere agent of the government of China. In other words, these events have demonstrated, what should have been obvious from the whole history of Chinese-Vietnamese relations and from the character of the national Communism of Vietnam, North and South, that Vietnamese nationalism, even under Communist auspices, far from being an instrument of Chinese expansion, is a natural obstacle to it. Thus by combating the national Communism of Vietnam, not only have we not served our traditional national interest in Asia, but we have actually acted counter to it. For if we had been successful in what we have been trying to do in Vietnam, we would have created a vacuum at the borders of China which either we would have had to fill in virtual permanence or into which an expansionist China would have been able to move.

2. The Impairment of the American National Interest

The damage which our military involvement in Vietnam has inflicted upon the national interest of the United States is not limited to Vietnam itself. It encompasses the overall position of the United States among the nations. This position has been impaired in three different respects.

The United States has lost much of that moral attractiveness which throughout its history set it apart from other nations. The actions which the United States has performed in Vietnam appear to be morally as deficient as the actions traditionally associated with other nations. Yet what the world takes for granted when it contemplates the actions of other nations, it did not expect of the United States. What the world once acclaimed as the unique virtues of America, it now sees replaced by the vices common to all. Hence its disillusionment, resentment, and mistrust—reactions no less damaging to the interests of the United States for being imponderable. For as in times past the admiration of the world for the United States as a model worthy of emulation permeated all attitudes and actions other nations took with regard to the United States, so now these negative reactions similarly permeate these attitudes and actions.

More specifically, the character of the war fought by the United States in Vietnam has disheartened its friends and encouraged its enemies. This war is widely regarded to be unwinnable militarily, aimless politically, and dubious morally. Many watch with amazement the most powerful nation on earth waging a war it is neither able to win nor liquidate. They have come to doubt not American power and determination, but American wisdom.

In consequence, American prestige throughout the world has sunk to the lowest level in living memory. Our friends cannot help but hesitate to follow an American leadership which has shown itself so incompetent in Vietnam. More particularly, they can have no desire to be saved from Communism in the destructive manner in which we are trying to save South Vietnam. Our enemies, on the other hand, are not being deterred from instigating or supporting "wars of national liberation" in view of the inconclusive manner in which we are waging the war in Vietnam, and of our weakened overall position because of that war. Furthermore, while we are fascinated by the specter of Communism in South Vietnam, concentrating our attention and material and human resources upon this trouble spot to the detriment of other, more vital national interests, the Soviet Union, unobtrusively and effectively, has expanded its political, military, and economic power into the vacuums left by British and French withdrawals and our preoccupation with Vietnam, such as Africa, the Middle East, the Indian Ocean, and South Asia.

Nothing has illustrated more vividly the disarray of our national priorities and the resulting weakness, if not impotence of our foreign policy than the conjunction of the Tet offensive with the Pueblo affair. With our mobile conventional forces fully committed in Vietnam, we were unable to forestall that offensive, and we were also unable to defend our interests vis-à-vis North Korea. Immediately after these events occurred, I was at a dinner party in New Delhi at which an Indian Cabinet minister, influential diplomats and leading intellectuals were present. There was no dissent when the host declared that this demonstration of American impotence was the third great event in the modern decline of the West in Asia. It followed the defeat of Russia by Japan in 1905, and the defeat of France, Great Britian, and the Netherlands by Japan in the Second World War. While there was sympathy for the folly of a nation so strong and well-intentioned, there was also a note of triumphant solidarity of Asians against the West in what was said at that party.

II. THE ROOTS OF FAILURE IN VIETNAM

What accounts for the failure of a nation so amply endowed with human and material resources? The roots of that failure are to be looked for in three areas: intellectual understanding, political judgment, and moral standards.

1. Defects of Intellectual Understanding

Failures of intellectual understanding have led us into four far-reaching errors: the mechanistic approach to politics, reasoning by historic analogy, belief in the transferability of Western political institutions to Asia, confidence in the unlimited perfectibility of governments.

a. *The Mechanistic Approach to Politics.* I have argued elsewhere at length against the pseudo-science of politics which endeavors to reduce the political sphere to an interplay of quantitative factors and which ends up by banishing politics altogether. This new political science seeks the pervasive rationalization of politics for the practical purpose of increasing the reliability of prediction and thereby removing uncertainty from political action. Yet this practical purpose differs from the traditional orientation toward practice characteristic of pre-modern political science. The latter endeavored to maximize rationality and success through the rational manipulation of the objective factors of politics; the former attempts to eradicate obstacles to pervasive rationalization that are inherent in the objective character of politics by overwhelming them with theoretical devices. The new theories, insofar as they are new in more than terminology, are in truth not so much theories as dogmas. They do not so much try to reflect reality as it actually is, as to superimpose upon a recalcitrant reality a theoretical scheme that satisfies the desire for thorough rationalization. Their practicality is specious since it substitutes what is desirable for what is possible.

What characterizes the most spectacular contemporary theories of politics is the attempt to use the tools of modern economic analysis in a modified form in order to understand their subject matter. Their mainstay is quantification. The use of terms such as "systems analysis," "feedback," "input," and "output" (to mention only a few common and easily accessible ones) is revealing; for these concepts were first developed by economic theory. Even more revealing is the mode of thought that dominates many of the contemporary theories of politics. Whether they deal with the strategy of conflict or diplomatic bargaining or nuclear escalation, they visualize international conflict as a special case of social conflict in general (which is correct if one does not neglect the paramount distinctive factor that the parties to international conflict are sovereign nations with a monopoly of organized force), whose paradigm is economic conflict (which, as we shall see, is incorrect). In such a theoretical scheme, nations confront each other not as living historic entities with all their complexities but as rational abstractions, after the model of "economic man," playing games of military and diplomatic chess according to a rational calculus that exists nowhere but in the theoretician's mind.

It is widely recognized by economists that this rationalistic, quantitative approach is of limited applicability even to economics; for even here it neglects psychological forces that interfere with the smooth operation of the rational calculus. Its applicability is established by the nature of the central concept of economics: wealth. Conversely, its inapplicability to politics is established by the nature of the central concept of politics: power. Wealth is a measurable quantity that an individual aspires to, competes or fights for, controls, possesses, or loses. Power is a quality of interpersonal relations that can be experienced, evaluated, guessed at, but that is not susceptible to quantification. What can be quantified are certain elements that go into the making of power, individual or collective, and it is a common error to equate such a quantifiable element of power with power as such. It is certainly possible and necessary to determine how many votes a politician controls, how many divisions or nuclear warheads a government disposes of; but if I want to know how much power this politician or that government has, I must leave the adding machine and the computer for historic and necessarily qualitative judgment.

Modern theorists of politics are repelled by history; for history is the realm of the accidental, the contingent, the unpredictable. They are instead fascinated by the rational model of the natural sciences, which appears to be free of these blemishes that stand in the way of the thorough rationalization of politics. I tried to show more than twenty years ago that this model of the natural sciences harks back to a Newtonian universe that the contemporary natural sciences have left far behind. This rational model is a utopia that reflects the desires of theoreticians but not the real physical world, dominated as that world is by the principle of indeterminacy, and predictable as it is, at least as microcosmos, only by way of statistical probability.

I have also tried to show that politics, domestic and international, is susceptible to a radically different kind of understanding from that which is appropriate to the world of nature. When we try to understand politics, we are dealing, it is true, with men in the aggregate, but with men per se, that is, as spiritual and moral beings, whose actions and reactions can be rationalized and quantitatively understood only on the lowest level of their existence. Thus what the contemporary theories of politics endeavor to exorcise as deficiencies in view of an ideal, pervasively rational theory is in truth but the ineradicable qualities of the subject matter itself. A theory that does not take them into account transforms itself into a dogma, a kind of metaphysics, regardless in what empirical or mathematical garb it is clothed.

This dogmatic outlook of modern political science has greatly contributed to our failure in Vietnam. It has prevented us from understanding the true nature of the issues we were facing and, more particularly, their complexity and imponderable qualities. Thus we reduced what was actually a national and social revolution dominated by a national Communism to the simplicity of foreign aggression under the auspices of Chinese Communism. In resisting foreign aggression, success or failure can easily be ascertained by the standard of the relative geographic position of the contesting armies; thus we resisted foreign aggression in Korea by holding the 38th Parallel. No such standard is available when one is engaged in a counter-revolution, as we have been in Vietnam, against a genuine popular revolution. Success in such a case is to be achieved by a combination of military and political measures, culminating in giving satisfaction to the revolutionary aspirations; it is to be determined by a qualitative political judgment, which is bound to be tentative and precarious while the struggle is going on.

The prevailing dogmatic presuppositions have precluded us from making such qualitative judgments. These presuppositions compel us to search for quantitative measurements which will determine the success or failure of our enterprise. Thus we have been reduced to making the "body count" the main measure of our achievements. I shall not dwell upon the self-evident fictitious character of this quantitative measurement, especially in the conditions of a jungle war of movement, which invariably has favored our side, but shall only raise the question what would the "body count" prove for our success or failure, provided it were technically feasible? It would prove only that the number of enemies killed is larger than our losses. Given the actual and potential reserves of manpower of which the enemy disposes, this measurement would be irrelevant even in conventional warfare since it leaves out of account all strategic and tactical considerations. It is doubly irrelevant for the kind of counter-revolutionary warfare we have been engaged in in Vietnam.

It could not escape the attention of the more thoughtful actors and observers that what determines the success or failure of a counter-revolutionary war is not the number of enemies killed but the conditions of life and the state of mind of those who stay alive. That is what we mean by "pacification" as the ultimate goal of our efforts. The answer to the question as to whether a man or a village has been "pacified" in the sense of not only being protected from enemy action but also of having been weaned away from the revolutionary movement is a matter of political judgment. Yet having been disabused of such "inexact" intellectual operations, we have sought the answer in quantitative computation. We isolated a number of quantitative criteria, such as whether or not the village chief sleeps in the village, according to which we distinguish different degrees of pacification. We fed these factors into a computer that could determine at a glance to what extent that village had been pacified.

However, this mechanistic, quantitative operation cannot tell us where the loyalties of the villagers lie, which side they will choose when the chips are down, and in whose hands effective political and administrative control rests. But these are the questions to which the policy-maker needs answers, and only qualitative political judgment can try to answer them. The computer can provide only the illusion of an answer. This is not to say that the computerization of quantitative criteria is worthless in itself. It has its proper place as one datum among others upon which a political judgment must be based. What makes it an intellectual error is its substitution for a qualitative political judgment. The inevitable consequence of this intellectual error is the failure of political judgment. In Vietnam, this failure has manifested itself in the consistent illusion of military and political success, derived from the delusion that the "body count" and the quantitative criteria of physical control are the determinants of that success.

b. *Reasoning by Historic Analogy.* The mechanistic approach to politics is duplicated, perhaps less crudely and simplistically, by the approach to history that has dominated official thinking on Vietnam: reasoning by analogy without awareness of the unique character of historic events. When we try to draw lessons from history, it is indeed inevitable that we reason by analogy; for we have nothing else to go on but past events similar to those we must deal with in the present. Yet this is only half the story. While the historic events are similar in certain respects insofar as they are the typical manifestations of basic social and psychological forces, they are in other respects unique events which in that way happened only once. The typicality of historic events enables us to understand history as an unfolding objective process which has a rational meaning. The uniqueness of historic events precludes us from drawing unambiguous lessons from historic experience. What is required of the circumspect observer who consults history as a teacher for action, then, is a sharp distinction between what is typical and what is unique in two historic situations. If the typical elements of the two situations coincide and are relevant to the issue at hand, the lesson of the past can indeed be applied to the present.

It is characteristic of the official mode of thought to be oblivious of that distinction. It takes the coincidence and relevance of the typical elements in the historic and the present situation for granted. Thus it equates without investigation Nazism and Communism because they are both totalitarian; Vietnam in 1968 and Czechoslovakia in 1938 because they are both threatened with a totalitarian takeover; retreat from Vietnam and appeasement preceding the Second World War because both constitute territorial concessions to totalitarianism. These equations serve the purpose of justifying policies which, since they would have been appropriate to the historic situation, must be also appropriate to the contemporary one.

These unqualified analogies obliterate the unique elements in the historic situations that are being compared. The policies recommended for the present may or may not be justified, but they cannot be justified through the invocation of these analogies. However, while that invocation is without intellectual value, it performs an important political function. It makes it appear that today's policy makers have learned the lesson history teaches. We are being assured that President Johnson has not made and will not make Neville Chamberlain's mistake. But that assurance does not cover the possibility that Mr. Johnson, thinking in false historic analogies, has not made, and will not make, other mistakes, perhaps worse than that of which Mr. Chamberlain stands accused.

c. *Transferability of Western Political Institutions.* An analogy of a different kind is responsible for the almost universal insistence upon free elections as the way out of the political impasse in Vietnam. That insistence derives from the assumption that free elections are able to perform in Vietnam, and for that matter anywhere else, the same functions for the distribution of political power they perform in Western democracies. However, the very essence of Chinese political culture, of which Vietnam forms a part, militates against the correctness of that assumption.

Elections in the Western sense have two roots: a political pluralism which allows different individuals, philosophies, and policies to compete for political power on the basis of equality, and a political individualism which allows the individual citizen to choose among these competitors. These two interconnected concepts are completely alien to Chinese political culture. That culture postulates an objective order from the compliance with which the government derives its legitimacy, that is, its right to govern. That order allows the citizen no choice among political competitors but demands his obedience to the legitimate government, which can claim that obedience as long as it governs in accord with the objective order. When it visibly ceases to do so, having lost the "mandate of heaven," the citizen is absolved of the duty to obey and can and must transfer his allegiance to another government representative of the objective order.

It ought to be obvious that in such a cultural context elections perform a function utterly different from that performed in a relativistic and individualistic society of the West. In a country such as Vietnam elections are in the nature of a plebiscite in support of the government rather than of a choice among several competitors for the powers of the government. This is obviously so in North Vietnam and the part of South Vietnam controlled by the Viet Cong. But it is also so in the part of South Vietnam controlled by the Saigon government; for the freedom of choice among different parties and individuals which obviously exists there is strictly limited to parties and individuals who have essentially the same outlook and agree on basic policies.

Considering the present situation in Vietnam in which two governments are controlling different parts of the country, both claiming legitimacy for the whole country, elections are likely to confirm the status quo without resolving the conflict. That is to say, people will vote for that government that happens to control them: the Viet Cong will receive the votes of those whom they control, and the people controlled by the Saigon government will vote for it. That will be so for both philosophic and practical reasons. For an individual living under the control of the Saigon government, who would vote for the Viet Cong, and an individual controlled by the Viet Cong, who would vote for the Saigon government, would take very considerable risks for his livelihood, freedom, and life. Thus elections are not likely to settle the fundamental issue over which the war is being fought: shall South Vietnam be governed by a Communist or non-Communist government? That issue can be decided only by a political settlement which reflects the actual distribution of military and political power between the Communist and non-Communist factions.

d. *Perfectibility of Governments.* Finally, another ethnocentrism, projected from the American experience onto the Vietnam scene, has led us into an intellectual error. That is the assumption that the defects of a government are susceptible to remedial efforts. Imbued with this belief in the unlimited perfectibility of governments, we have been urging a succession of South Vietnamese governments to institute land reforms, to stamp out corruption, and in particular to shift the main burden of the war from the American armed forces to the South Vietnamese army. While these urgings have been well-nigh universal, amounting to a veritable consensus among supporters and critics of the war, they have been fruitless. It could not have been otherwise.

One does not need to be a Marxist in order to realize that individual and collective interests set limits to the ability of governments to reform themselves. That is as true of the government of the United States as it is of all governments past and present. The stringency of these limits may change from country to country and from one historic situation to another. But in view of the interests of its members and supporters, no government can do by way of reforms everything it ought to do on rational grounds. The limits within which a government is able to reform itself are particularly narrow when that government has been imposed upon a hostile or indifferent population by a foreign power and can keep itself in office only through the instrumentality of a large foreign army of occupation. A government's ability to reform itself is first of all predicated upon its willingness to do so. That willingness, in turn, depends upon incentives of a moral, political, or material nature, not only for the leaders but the main body of the administration as well. But what incentives for reform can motivate a government, which is led by officers who fought with the French against their own people and, hence, are regarded by the latter as traitors, which is in the main supported by the upper bourgeoisie and absentee landowners, which can govern only by leave of a foreign power, and which is infiltrated by large numbers of Viet Cong? Why should such a government, for instance, institute land reforms since its principal supporters derive their economic and political power from the unequal distribution of land? Why should a South Vietnamese soldier risk his life in a war which is ever more intensely and widely experienced by the people of South Vietnam as being waged by a foreign power on Vietnamese soil for foreign purposes? How can a government thus constituted be expected to stamp out corruption, which in a country such as South Vietnam is not a deviation from the norm but is bound to be the norm itself? For a government so precariously and in all likelihood temporarily placed as that of South Vietnam, can only have two main incentives: to insure the survival of its members and to draw as much material gain as possible from an advantageous situation which is not likely to last. For such a government, corruption is not a vice but a necessity. To expect such a government to rid itself of corruption is tantamount to expecting that it act against its very nature.

2. Defects of Political Judgments

Errors in the way of thinking about foreign policy lead of necessity to wrong political judgments. There are, however, wrong political judgments which are not so occasioned but can result from a variety of factors. Three such misjudgments have had a deleterious effect upon our policies in Vietnam. They concern the nature of Communism, of revolution, and of limited war.

a. *The Nature of Communism*. It is one of the great ironies of history that we have tended to take Communism as a political ideology more seriously than have the major Communist governments. For Stalin and his successors in particular, Communism was first of all an ideological means to the traditional ends of imperial Russia. By contrast, we have tended to take the Communist postulates and prophecies at their face value and in consequence have been unable to divorce our political judgments from the assumption of the monolithic, conspiratorial character of Communism. Thus we have been unable to judge Vietnamese Communism on its own national merits, as an indigenous phenomenon due to the peculiar circumstances of time and place. Instead, Vietnamese Communism has appeared to us as a special instance of a general phenomenon which is not by accident the same regardless of time and place. For it has been created by a worldwide conspiracy whose headquarters are assumed to be in Moscow or Peking or both and whose aim is to communize the world. In this view, what happens in Vietnam is just an episode in that world-wide struggle between Communism and the "free world" and consequently the outcome of the Vietnamese War has worldwide significance.

b. *The Nature of Revolution.* The misjudgment of revolution fits organically into this—largely fictitious—picture of the political world. Revolution, too, must not be understood on its own terms but must be traced to a conspiracy of foreign origin imposed upon an unwilling people. That concept of revolution is in good measure responsible for the fiasco of the Bay of Pigs. We thought of Castro as a dictator imposed by the Communist conspiracy of Moscow upon the unwilling Cubans, who, at the sight of a thousand anti-Castro refugees, would rise *en masse* against their oppressor. Similarly, the revolution in South Vietnam must be traced to a foreign conspiracy located in Hanoi, and, at one remove, in Moscow and Peking. What looks like revolution, then, is really foreign aggression, and the revolution can be suppressed by thwarting that aggression.

What is inadmissible to us is the recognition that in large parts of the world there exists today an objective revolutionary situation. This revolutionary situation would exist even if Communism had never been heard of, and is in good measure a response to the Western teachings and examples of national self-determination and radical social reform. That these national and social revolutions are largely identified with Communism is primarily the result of the West's failure to identify with them morally and to support them materially. The Vietnamese revolution is a case in point. In Vietnam as elsewhere, particularly in Latin America, the Communist and anti-American orientation of revolutionary movements is directly related to the American misunderstanding of the nature both of Communism and of revolution.

c. *The Nature of Limited War.* While our misjudgments of Communism and revolution are organically related, our reliance upon limited war to combat them is a spectacular *non sequitur.* For if we are combating in Vietnam foreign aggression inspired and supported by the centers of world communism, more particularly Peking, and if we are serious about getting rid of the trouble then we must strike at the source of the trouble and not only at one of its outward manifestations. But for perfectly good reasons we shy away from a direct military confrontation with China, let alone the Soviet Union. Thus the means we have been employing in Vietnam are divorced from our conception of the nature of the conflict. While we conceive of the conflict as a particular manifestation of a worldwide struggle, we try to win that struggle through victory in a localized war.

That discrepancy also determines the nature of the localized war we are fighting. Not only are we fighting North Vietnam in order to suppress a South Vietnamese revolution inspired and supported by either China or the Soviet Union or both, but we also impose limitations upon this war against North Vietnam in order to avoid a direct military confrontation with either the Soviet Union or China or both. But these limitations are at the very least a factor which makes military victory more difficult to attain. Thus our political misjudgments have put us into the doubly paradoxical situation in which we respond to what we consider to be the worldwide challenge of Communist revolution with a local war which is itself subject to limitations making a military victory more difficult, if not impossible, to attain. Thus in consequence we are engaged in a war which we can neither win on the battlefield without risking a direct military confrontation with the two major Communist powers, nor liquidate without giving the lie to the political assumptions upon which our involvement in Vietnam is based.

What accounts, not for these intellectual errors and political judgments themselves, but for their persistence in the face of unmistakable evidence to the contrary? For what is extraordinary and disquieting is not that we can commit intellectual errors and make wrong political judgments but that intelligent and honest men, drawing upon the best expert advice and ample sources of information, are unable to renounce a course of action which should have been recognized as unpromising and potentially disastrous from the very outset and is now so recognized by almost all concerned. The issue we are here facing is neither intellectual nor political but moral. Defects of moral standards are responsible for this persistence in a losing undertaking.

3. Defects of Moral Standards

a. *The Dilemma of the Democratic Conduct of Foreign Policy.* The conduct of foreign policy under democratic conditions inevitably puts the moral stamina of the makers of policy to the test. A democratic government must accomplish two tasks. On the one hand, it must pursue foreign policies which maximize the chance for success. On the other, it must secure the approval of its people for these foreign policies as well as the domestic ones designed to support them. The necessity to perform these two tasks simultaneously faces a democratic government with a dilemma; for the conditions under which popular support can be obtained for a foreign policy are not necessarily identical with the conditions under which a foreign policy can be successfully pursued. A popular foreign policy is not necessarily a good foreign policy. As Tocqueville put it, with special reference to the United States: "Foreign politics demand scarcely any of those qualities which are peculiar to a democracy; they require, on the contrary, the perfect use of almost all those in which it is deficient."

Faced with this dilemma between a sound foreign policy and an unsound one supported by public opinion, a government is naturally tempted to sacrifice the sound policy upon the altar of public opinion, abdicating leadership and exchanging short-lived political advantage for the permanent interest of the country. This temptation will become well-nigh irresistible if the government has persuaded itself that the foreign policy it pursues is sound because it has popular support. The policy maker who points to the latest public opinion poll as proof of the soundness of his policy is no longer even aware of the existence of the dilemma. He escapes it by identifying standards of foreign policy with what appear to be the preferences of the people. He is no longer called upon to make a moral choice since his frame of reference precludes it. His unawareness of the existential dilemma and of the moral choice it requires is worse than yielding to the temptation to make the wrong choice. We are here in the presence not of moral corruption, which still presupposes the awareness of moral standards, but of moral decay: "What the crowd wants," to quote Mr. Justice Holmes, becomes the ultimate standard by which the soundness of a policy is judged.

Since, however, what the crowd wants is in good measure determined by what the government and the molders of public opinion which are at its service suggest it ought to want, the government is here caught in a vicious circle of its own making. It molds public opinion in support of a foreign policy upon which it has decided, and then invokes public opinion in justification of that policy. "The competition of the market," to quote Mr. Justice Holmes again, from which the truth is supposed to emerge, is here replaced by a quasi-monopoly, which does not allow the truth, that is, the correct policy, to be discovered through the free interplay of diverse opinions and divergent interests. Rather the truth is assumed to be exclusively owned by a government supported by public opinion. The issue is thus settled before it is really joined.

In such a situation, the dissenter fulfills no function useful for the government. Quite to the contrary, he becomes the disturber of a pre-established consensus, endowed with the attributes of truth and virtue. He must be silenced, and if he does not allow himself to be silenced, he must at least be discredited. Having thus pre-established the correctness of its policies, the government has morally incapacitated itself to put the correctness of its policies in question. Thus the simple-minded persistence in error, which has been characteristic of our policies in Vietnam, results from the government's destruction of the dynamics of pluralistic debate through which errors can be corrected and wrong policies set right. It is quite in character that the Administration has changed its policies, however more in appearance than in substance, since the continuation of its futile efforts on an escalating scale would have required a reallocation of resources threatening its domestic support.

b. *Bureaucratic Conformism.* This tendency, common to all democratic governments, to compromise the quality of foreign policy for the sake of popular support is strengthened by the tendency, common to all bureaucracies, to support and execute government policies regardless of their own views of the merits. Within broad limits, this is as it should be. For no government could function if subordinate officials were to substitute their own views for those of the government with regard to the merits of the policy to be put into practice. However, from time to time, a government will embark upon policies which raise basic political and moral issues, such as our involvement in Vietnam. In such a case, the public official charged with the execution of a policy with which he fundamentally disagrees on political, military, or moral grounds is faced with a dilemma. By opposing policies which he deems to be detrimental to the national interest, he risks jeopardizing his public career. By supporting and executing such a foreign policy, he will remain a team worker in good standing at the sacrifice of his convictions and of the national interest.

As the government faced with a choice between a sound foreign policy and popular support is likely to sacrifice the former for the sake of the latter, so the public official having to choose between his career and his convictions is likely to choose the former over the latter. Human nature being what it is, powerfully supported by the specific intensity of America's conformism, these choices are not surprising. What is surprising and disquieting is the virtual absence of an exception to the rule of conformity. In talking to high government officials, I have time and again been startled, and sometimes confounded, by the contrast between their public positions and private convictions. This contrast, I should add, concerned not only subjective estimates of the political and military situation but hard facts and figures ascertainable by objective calculations.

While many high-ranking officials who are opposed to our policies in Vietnam have resigned their positions since 1965, not one of them has justified his resignation with his opposition to these policies. If some of the more illustrious of them had made their opposition to these policies a matter of public record, they might well have rendered a great service to the national interest. But they would have risked the premature termination of their public careers, and none of them was evidently willing to face that dire prospect. As in the case of the government discussed above, the issue of a moral choice did not even seem to have arisen. Here again, the issue was settled before it could have been raised, and it was settled in favor of private concerns and to the detriment of the national interest. Here again, what is ominous is not so much that moral judgment has been corrupted as that it has disappeared.

The preceding article illustrates a classic prescriptive study of foreign-policy decision-making. Because Morgenthau writes clearly and organizes his material well, one is able to discern easily what he assumes to be the correct view of the world, and what he believes to be the image of the world held by those responsible for American policy formulation. To some extent, his criticism rests on a perceived divergence between the two views.

Some students of foreign policy have been critical of this type of analysis for several reasons. First, no basis is provided for determining whether his reading of history is any more accurate than any other. His observations and subsequent descriptions of the assumptions of American policy-makers are based only on his personal judgment of what is significant. There are no criteria by which to estimate the realism of his interpretation because there are no means of judging whether the policy statements and actions he found significant are representative of American thinking. Second, there is no way of knowing whether the assumptions of American policy-makers discovered by Morgenthau were, in fact, the ones that guided the course of American action in Vietnam. The same foreign-policy responses could conceivably have been derived from quite different assumptions. Third, Morgenthau implicitly assumes that his observations about American motivations serve as an adequate explanation of American policy, without considering the extent to which foreign-policy behavior may be explained by factors other than the motivations of the foreign-policy elites. Furthermore, he combines prescription with description and explanation. The assumptions of American policy-makers are equated with the mistakes of these policy-makers, so that his inevitable and only solution for realizing a better foreign policy for America is for it to stop doing what it is doing. This prescription is axiomatic if one first accepts as correct Morgenthau's image of reality and his image of the assumptions guiding American decision-makers. In short, Morgenthau's prescription rests on his assuming that decision-makers can be faulted for failing to maintain and act on the same assumptions that Morgenthau himself has about American foreign policy.

These criticisms of Morgenthau's approach suggest that studies of foreign-policy decision-making behavior, even if they are prescriptive, require more systematic investigation that distinguishes between description, explanation, and prescription. However much one may be sympathetic to the views expressed by Morgenthau, one must question the analytic means by which he reached them. By citing other policy statements and noting other foreign-policy acts, a different investigator could come to quite contradictory conclusions. Hence, this technique leaves us with mere opinion rather than reliable knowledge.

By way of contrast to the prescriptive mode of inquiry adopted by Morgenthau, we provide a brief example of prescriptive analysis based on quantitative data. Unlike the Morgenthau contribution, which seeks to evaluate normatively the policies of a particular country with respect to a specific foreign target, the author of the second selection addresses himself to a problem of general concern to the world community: the control of population growth rates. As this book went to press, in late 1974, 1,100 delegates from 141 countries gathered in Bucharest for the U.N. Population Conference to consider ways of remedying the soaring population that is straining declining world food reserve. The problem is grave. The world's population is growing at a rate of 2 per cent annually, and experts estimate that, if the rate continues, the present population of 3.9 billion will double by the year 2009. With 200,000 more people born each day, nations are forced to devise a solution if catastrophic famine is to be avoided. Consequently, population control is a major ethical and pragmatic problem affecting the entire world. Oscar Harkavy contends that economic aid should be a central component of any international strategy to control the growth of population. Basing his arguments on some observed relationships between economic growth and population growth, Harkavy submits that developed states should use their foreign policies to promote economic development. While his prescription is controversial, it does rely on statistical analysis, and in this respect it is a different approach to a given problem from the one pursued by Morgenthau, which rests on logical deductions from qualitative historical interpretations.

A PRESCRIPTION FOR INTERNATIONAL ASSISTANCE TO POPULATION PROGRAMS IN THE DEVELOPING WORLD

Oscar Harkavy

Banality is probably the greatest risk in making the case for international assistance to population programs in the developing world. That excessive population growth is a deterrent to development has been asserted many times and in many ways. Its cogency has been dulled by repetition. There is also a risk of appearing to protest too much. One is a little embarrassed to assert that the motives for international assistance to birth control efforts are humanitarian and that they are neither genocidal, neocolonial, nor part of the game of international power politics. Those who have been in population work for any length of time are inclined to assume general agreement on the need to cope with population growth and to get on to the difficult business of devising strategies for increasing the effectiveness of population assistance. However, Drs. Hall and Taylor note . . . that "the abrupt rise of population programs, from their original minor status to their present importance in international assistance . . . [has] produced some tensions and misunderstandings." Thus there is need to re-examine and restate the case for attention to population problems by international assistance agencies.

Ernst Michanek, Director-General of the Swedish International Development Agency, expresses the common point of view of the donor community.

> We who plan for a larger food production know that the next billion of people will add to the starving majority of mankind. We who finance educational activities know that the growth of training facilities will be surpassed by the growth of the number of children, so that illiteracy will actually increase. We who support industrial undertakings know quite well that the rate of unemployment in the developing countries is bound to increase, as the school leavers of tomorrow are flooding the labor market. We who earmark funds for housing and sewage projects know that the influx of people will increase the slum areas, increase the poverty, the overcrowding, the promiscuity and delinquency in many areas, primarily in the less developed countries. We know that this will be so,

Oscar Harkavy, "The Rationale for International Assistance to Population Programs in the Developing World," *International Journal of Health Services*, **3, 4** (1973). Reprinted by permission of the author and publisher.

Harkavy is a demographer and developmental economist associated with the Ford Foundation.

unless at the same time Governments undertake to tackle decisively the population problem.[1]

Because it would be inappropriate for a representative of only one of the players in the population game to speak on behalf of the others, I shall not attempt a systematic survey of the motives of the other donors; the attitudes and activities of the Ford Foundation are overrepresented in what follows.

As a basis for considering a rationale for population work in the context of development assistance, one should go back a step and make explicit the rationale for providing assistance to the developing world. In a recent self-examination, we in the Ford Foundation's International Division asked ourselves "What should be the Foundation's objectives in developing countries, what underlying values should they reflect, and how should they relate to the values and objectives of the developing countries themselves?" [2] Recognizing that these are complicated questions that defy simple answers, we asserted that there is a basis for common action with developing countries where we share at least three beliefs: active efforts to improve human conditions are better than resignation; material well-being is a good thing; and all of mankind should be accorded basic equality of status and regard. The idea of "development" as a rationally guided effort toward better human condtions, material and otherwise, follows naturally from these values.

This concept of development puts major emphasis on improvement of human conditions. Within this context the control of fertility must be considered not only as it affects national economic development, i.e. as it helps increase gross national product per capita, but also as it affects the welfare of the individual family. This focus on individual family welfare is a powerful, and I believe unassailable, rationale for population work, whether in the industrialized or the developing world. If population assistance makes it possible for an increasing number of couples to exercise freedom of choice over their family size, this in itself justifies substantial effort and expenditure by donor agencies.

Of direct relevance to the family welfare goal of population assistance is the re-emergence of enthusiasm on the part of the donor agencies for the integration of family planning within broader maternal and child health services or within comprehensive health and nutrition services. Some assistance agencies have been criticized for de-emphasizing health at the same time as they increased their attention to birth control. This may be corrected in the coming years as the leaders of assistance agencies appreciate that health delivery systems can be extremely effective carriers of family planning services. If donor agencies are prepared to allocate sufficiently large parts of their budgets to the development of health networks and, more importantly, if host countries are prepared to devote increasing proportions of their financial resources and administrative energy to the development of health networks, the outcomes can only be positive in terms of family health and welfare. This is particularly true as long as the most effective birth control methods are "doctor dependent." All too often, however, decreeing that birth control will be provided as "just another service" by overburdened health workers means that little family planning will get done. It is no mean challenge to the management of health systems to be sure that the contraceptive supplies, services, and information are not neglected if family planning is made a part of the over-all effort to provide other preventive and curative health services.

Of course, consideration of private benefits and costs of population growth is not the entire justification for international assistance in population work. Achieving adequate food, adequate job opportunities, adequate education, and the other traditional goals of economic development are continually frustrated by the growth of population. The Commission on International Development chaired by the late Lester Pearson of Canada has summed up succinctly some of the major difficulties created by very rapid population growth in the developing world:

> 1. Expenditures for education, health, housing, water supply, and so forth increase sharply and create severe budgetary strains.
> 2. The quality of the next generation, on which the prospects for development crucially rest, is jeopardized. There is a strong inverse correlation between child health and family size. Rapid growth of the child population also delays educational development.
> 3. Considerable resources are devoted to the support of a large dependent population which would otherwise be available to raise standards and increase capital formation.
> 4. Aid requirements are larger when population rises fast, and the possibility of future financial independence smaller than if fertility is declining.
> 5. The distribution of income is unequal, and population growth tends to make it more so by raising land values and rents while depressing wages. As ownership, too, is usually very unequally distributed, the bulk of the population may fail to participate in whatever improvement occurs.
> 6. Severe urban problems arise, partly from natural increase and partly from migration from the country into the cities. Urban populations tend to double in fifteen to eighteen years. Housing already presents almost insoluble problems in many developing countries. . . . The rapid growth of population adds to the already severe unemployment problem in developing countries.[3]

I submit that people of good will who are genuinely concerned with fostering improvement in the levels of living of the populations of poor countries must concede the validity of the points enumerated by the Pearson Commission. Assistance agencies must not fall into the trap, however, of twisting these arguments and appearing to claim that control of population growth is *all* that is necessary to achieve economic development. Thus, while he does not deny the potential contribution of population control to development, Simon Kuznets argues that "it may well be that social feasibility is more important than the simpler relations of numbers to resources, natural or reproducible. . . . The capacity of societies to change their institutions and beliefs in order to make more effective use of natural resources is the most important key to development." [4]

While it was a brave statement at the time, hindsight indicates that it was most unfortunate for President Johnson to have proclaimed on the occasion of the 20th anniversay of the United Nations on June 25, 1965, "Let us act on the fact that less than $5 invested in population control is worth $100 invested in economic growth." [5] This and similar declarations have been misinterpreted to suggest that birth control can be offered as a cheap substitute for conventional assistance. But no international assistance agency follows this strategy. Even the Agency for International Development (AID), which has increased greatly the dollar magnitude of its population assistance, still provides only a small fraction of its resources for this purpose. In 1972, for example, the $125 million allocated by AID for population work was 7.8 per cent of the $1.6 billion it provided in economic assistance in that year. It is estimated that not more than 2 per cent of total overseas economic assistance by all agencies goes into population work.

According to Pradervand, in a paper presented at the African Population Conference, emphasis on population control is regarded by some as a diversion from the "much more fundamental factors on which it might be objectively more profitable to act with a view to attaining real development . . . such variables as the structures of production, international trade, political administrative structures, and so on." [6] Also in this paper, Pradervand, a member of the American Friends Service Committee, criticized donor agencies' interest in population and called instead for comprehensive programs of social and economic reform emphasizing rejection of the heritage of colonial domination. This position was supported by a distinguished group of Francophone Africans. Even while attacking the macroeconomic development rationale for fertility control, Pradervand endorsed the microfamilial benefits of family planning: "Family planning can be an effective means to fight against sterility, enhance the quality of health and the socio-economic conditions of mothers and children, and to liberate women."

It is understandable that there should be Third World suspicion of rich, ex-colonialist countries that seem to offer birth control as a substitute for basic social and economic reform, but against this suspicion one can only assert a conviction that control of population growth can only help, and not hinder, the process of development and the spread of the benefits of such development to an increasing proportion of the population.

However, there are those who ask whether the soft, humanitarian, "every-child-a-wanted-child" family planning approach offers any real hope of coping with population growth in the developing world. Kingsley Davis's critique of this position is the pre-eminent example, He is at one with Pradervand and his colleagues in calling for basic social restructuring. His objective, however, is to provide alternatives to familial satisfactions: reducing the economic utilities of children and altering the status of women so that their prestige and social meaning no longer stem from the number of children they bear.[7] It is extraordinarily difficult, however, for assistance agencies to be in the forefront of such efforts. It is difficult enough for outsiders to provide effective assistance in the design and implementation of family planning programs. It is an even more difficult and more delicate matter to urge host countries to adopt measures beyond family planning that seek deliberately to change the socio-economic environment. Given little research and experimentation in this area, we cannot yet prescribe ethically acceptable, economically and politically feasible policy measures that will bring down the birth rate. The appropriate role of assistance agencies, therefore, is to help develop a nation's own competence to understand and analyze its population problems and to recognize how they affect and are affected by their strategies of national development. This requires nurture of intellectual resources that seek to identify the determinants of fertility and understand the interrelations of population policy with other areas of social and economic policy.

Those who criticize the assistance agencies for focusing on birth control instead of concerning themselves with broad restructuring should be heartened by a new theme sounded by the leadership of these agencies. In his address to the Board of Governors of the World Bank Group, Robert McNamara declared:

> It is possible to design policies with the explicit goal of improving the conditions of life of the poorest 40 per cent of the populations in the developing countries—and that this can be done without unacceptable penalties to the concomitant goal of national growth. . . .
>
> When the highly privileged are few and the desperately poor are many—and when the gap between them is worsening rather than improving—it is only a question of time before a decisive choice must be made between the political costs of reform and the political risks of rebellion.[8]

McNamara goes on to urge attack on unemployment, rural and urban public works, construction of low-cost housing, reforestation, highway maintenance, and similar low-skill, labor-intensive, and economically useful projects, as well as "institutional reforms to redistribute economic power . . . land reform, corporate reform, tax reform, credit and banking reform."

This new emphasis on greater equity, even at the expense of lessened growth in gross national product per capita, is significant for those who are concerned with reduction of population growth. Staff of the Overseas Development Council have examined the experience of Taiwan and Korea in the sixties in comparison with that of the Philippines, Mexico, and Brazil.[9] All of these countries have achieved substantial economic growth rates as measured by gross national product, ranging from 10 per cent annually in Taiwan to an impressive 6 per cent per year in the Philippines and Brazil. But special attention is called to the ratio of income controlled by the top 20 per cent of income recipents to the bottom 20 per cent as indicated in Table 1. Thus, there was strong movement toward increased equality of income distribution in Taiwan and Korea, but not in the other countries. Unemployment and underemployment were substantially reduced in the former, not in the latter. Associated with these economic changes were changes in rates of population growth. As shown in Table 1, there was a dramatic drop in the growth rates in Taiwan and Korea, but little

Table 1

Comparison of economic and population growth rates of the Philippines, Taiwan, Mexico, Brazil, and Korea[a]

Indicator	Philippines	Taiwan	Mexico	Brazil	Korea
Per capita income (1960)	$ 169	$ 176	$ 441	$ 268	$ 138
(1969)	208	334	606	348	242
GNP growth rates in 1960s	6%	10%	7%	6%	9%
Ratio of income controlled by top 20% of income recipients to bottom 20%	12:1 (1956) 16:1 (1965)	15:1 (1953) 5:1 (1969)	10:1 (1950) 16:1 (1969)	22:1 (1960) 25:1 (1970)	5:1
Income improvement of poorest 20% over past 20 years	Negligible	200%	Negligible	Negligible	Over 100%
Population growth rates	2.4% (1952) 3.0% (1963) 3.4% (1970)	3.8% (1951) 3.0% (1963) 2.2% (1970)	3.5% (1955) 3.4% (1963) 3.4% (1970)	3.0% (1960) 2.9% (1970)	3.0% (1958) 2.7% (1964) 2.0% (1971)

[a] Source, *A New Development Strategy? Greater Equity, Faster Growth, and Smaller Families.* Overseas Development Council, Development Paper 11, October 1972.

change in the other countries. Of course, nationwide family planning programs had been operating during the 1960s in Taiwan and Korea, while they have just been started in the Philippines, are about to begin in Mexico, and have not yet been approved in Brazil. Furthermore, there are cultural and religious factors that would differentially affect birth rates. Nevertheless, it is consonant with what we know about the determinants of fertility to expect that the rate of population growth will fall as the benefits of modernization are enjoyed by a greater proportion of a nation's population. The provision of safe, effective, and dignified birth control services can only reinforce this process.

NOTES

1. Michanek, E. Quoted in C. Wahren. Sweden: Help from a small developed nation. In *Population: Challenging World Crisis*, edited by B. Berelson. Basic Books, New York, 1969.
2. *The Foundation and the Less Developed Countries: The Decade of the Seventies*, p. 4. The Ford Foundation, New York, 1972.
3. *Partners in Development: Report of the Commission on International Development*, L. B. Pearson, chairman, pp. 57–58. Praeger Publishers, New York, 1969.
4. Kuznets, S. Economic aspects of fertility. In *Fertility and Family Planning: A World View*, edited by S. J. Behrman, L. Corsa, Jr., and R. Freedman, p. 176. University of Michigan Press, Ann Arbor, 1969
5. Johnson, L. B. Address to the United Nations, June 25, 1965.
6. Pradervand, P. The Ideological Premises of Western Research in the Field of Population Policy, pp. 2–8. Paper presented at African Population Conference in Accra, Ghana, December 1971.
7. Davis, K. Population policy: Will current programs succeed? *Science* 158:730–739, 1967.
8. McNamara, R. Address to the Board of Governors of the World Bank Group, September 25, 1972.
9. Hunter, R. E., Grant, J. P., and Rich, W. *A New Development Strategy? Greater Equity, Faster Growth, and Smaller Families.* Overseas Development Council, Development Paper 11, October 1972.

Several aspects of the preceding prescriptive study are noteworthy for international assistance to population programs in the developing from a methodological and research perspective. In examining the rationale world, Harkavy takes care to define precisely the value premises from which he is operating: Development is explicitly defined as a rationally guided effort toward better human conditions, and efforts to investigate population work are defended in terms of the potential it holds for improving the welfare of the individual family. The author also elaborates on his approach by noting that he regards consideration of population problems to be justified on societal grounds as well.

Moreover, the author bases his contentions on more than mere opinion. His basic argument is that fertility reduction is a necessary but not a sufficient condition to achieve improved levels of living in poor countries; birth control, he submits, should not be regarded as a substitute for traditional modes of development assistance or as a divergence from needed social and economic reform. Rather, analysis of available data indicates that, given the relationship obtaining between economic and population growth, development assistance emphasizing equity in income distribution, even at the expense of over-all increases in gross national product, offers the best hope for achieving social justice and reducing fertility in the long run. What is salient about this proposal is not so much the recommendation itself as the manner in which it is devised. The recommendation is grounded on empirically demonstrated descriptions and explanations of the sources of population growth and not on mere assertion. Since the resultant prescriptions are based on explicit evaluative criteria and on verifiable knowledge rather than subjective belief, they are much more convincing. It is hoped that the virtues and benefits of prescriptive analysis conducted on other than logical deductions and speculations are apparent from the foregoing, and that the juxtaposition of this article with the previous one serves to highlight some important differences in the style in which prescriptive inquiries may be conducted.

3

The Analysis of
International Interactions

The previous chapter sought to examine the ways in which scholars analyze the foreign-policy behavior of nations. When we address the problem of analyzing international interactions, we shift our attention from the examination of the causes and consequences of external conduct to the exploration of the behavior flowing between two or more international actors. That is, the analysis of international interactions involves the investigation of behavior initiated by one international actor and directed across borders toward a foreign target. As the term *interaction* implies, its analysis is of *action* taken by an identifiable actor with respect to another actor. At a minimum, this consists of a dyadic unit. Thus, the analysis of international interactions is no longer with a discussion of a state and its behavior *per se*, but with how states, intergovernmental organizations (IGO's), nongovernmental organizations (NGO's), and members of national societies deal with each other. In this chapter, therefore, we will be concerned more with what the actors do to and with each other than with why they behave as they do; the emphasis is consequently on the *relations* and *contact* that international actors maintain with one another.

The analysis of international interactions may take place on various levels. Discussions of international interactions at the governmental level usually focus on the way *states* deal with each other. Intergovernmental organizations are frequently viewed soley as an institutional setting in which the interactions among the states take place, and for good reason. Whether serving as a forum for discussions among states, as the U.N. General Assembly does, or as an instrument through which the will of the states as members of the organization can be realized, 'as the Universal Postal Union does, intergovernmental organizations frequently serve as the setting in which states deal with each other.

Yet, even though much less frequently, intergovernmental organizations serve as actors attempting to shape the behavior of the states. This is as true when the Secretary-General of the United Nations attempts to mediate a dispute between two hostile nations as it is when the permanent staff of an intergovernmental organization seeks to build the consensus among states necessary to solve a particular problem, such as the spread of disease. Hence, although the intergovernmental organization frequently serves as a framework for the interactions among states, it sometimes serves as a force in its own right.

Nevertheless, the state remains the principal actor and accounts for the basic direction of most international interactions. For this reason, our discussion of the nature of international interaction throughout this chapter will focus primarily upon the way states deal with each other. Where appropriate, we will discuss intergovernmental organizations either as an institutional setting or as an actor, and we will consider nongovernmental contact of people across national borders, such as the flow of private citizens in international travel and tourism, as a further form of international exchange. In doing so, however, we will recognize that, for the immediate future, the state continues to be the dominant factor in international intercourse.

Several basic types of interactions characterizing international relations may be identified. In classifying the ways in which states deal with each other, we can distinguish three types of activities. The first and by far the most frequent type of interaction may be characterized as routine, involving the daily flow of events among states. The second might be called "collective problem-solving" because it occurs when two or more states perceive a condition to be unsolvable by independent actions and on which the states are willing to cooperate. The third type of interaction might be called "competitive bargaining" because it involves the efforts of one or more states to have another state agree to something to which that state would not otherwise agree. Routine interactions, ranging from an event in the international environment (for example, the Gold Crisis) to a planned action by one state, often create conditions for collective problem-solving or competitive bargaining. Similarly, the failure to solve a problem cooperatively may lead to competitive bargaining. Hostile states, for example, will frequently skip the collective problem-solving stage.

Although these three classes of interactions are highly interdependent and often very difficult to distinguish, the categories may be used to differentiate the literature dealing with international interactions. Let us examine, briefly, each of these research foci before turning to some examples of international interaction analysis in the descriptive, explanatory, and prescriptive modes.

1. In the first instance, many scholars have focused their attention on the routine interactions occurring among international actors. This attention is warranted when one acknowledges that most of the behavior crossing national borders is relatively peaceful, nondramatic, routinized, and cooperative. The image of international relations conveyed by the mass media, of endemic conflict and interstate violence, is not accurate, for international actors do not spend most of their time and energy in constant conflict with one another. Rather, they spend it in nonviolently dealing with each other, and these dealings are frequently initiated to address

common problems through cooperative enterprises. Typically conducted through foreign-policy bureaucracies by administrative officials, routine interactions are often products of decisions by parties to the interaction to maintain specified patterns of activities. They are called "routine" because the actions they involve are expected by the interacting parties and are considered part of the general pattern of relationships that the sides have developed.

It is important to note that "routine" does not necessarily mean "friendly." Hostile relationships between two states can be routinized just as friendly relationships can be. Communist China's decision during the 1950's and 1960's to avoid almost all contact with the United States was as routinized in the behavior of lower-level Chinese officials as is the decision of the U.S. Government to maintain as much contact as possible with the United Kingdom. Similarly, interactions between India and Pakistan are routinized, even though the two sides are extremely hostile. Although both sides have occasionally attempted to break the routine for bargaining reasons, the great importance attached to such a break indicates conscious awareness of the routinized nature of the interactions.

Although the literature on routine interactions among states is voluminous, few studies exist that seek to construct concepts and test theories with empirical data. Exceptions to this tendency that examine various dimensions of diplomatic activities include Singer and Melvin Small's (150) analysis of patterns of diplomatic representation among states between 1815 and 1940 as an indication of the relative status of states in the system, McClelland's (96) use of quantitative techniques to study routinized hostile behavior, and Dean G. Pruitt's (116) application of the concept of "responsiveness" to routine interactions among states. More representative, however, are studies from the "traditional" perspective focusing on such things as the modern practice of diplomacy, the national and transnational pressures operating on today's national diplomats, and descriptive accounts of the historical evolution of statesmanship behavior; Robert B. Harmon (62) provides an excellent and nearly exhaustive survey of these traditional studies.

2. A number of scholars have concentrated their attention on the kinds of relations international actors develop when they break existing routine interactions in order to create new routines that better serve their mutual aims. This form of interaction, which we may term "collective problem-solving behavior," occurs both bilaterally and multilaterally and consists of cooperative undertakings between and among states to meet common problems. Collective problem-solving behavior, therefore, is the product of a type of interaction in which the participants—whether two states or a hundred—feel that cooperation is necessary to deal with a commonly perceived problem. The problem may range in scope and complexity from an attempt by the United States and Canada to maintain effective border controls to a campaign by most of the nations of the world to contain the spread of a particular disease.

A large proportion of the literature dealing with collective problem-solving interactions concentrates on the role of intergovernmental organizations in providing a setting and arena for cooperative contact among international actors. Less well covered are analyses of the contribution that nongovernmental organizations (NGO's) make to the settlement of disputes and problem-solving. Two texts that examine the activities of a large number of intergovernmental organizations (IGO's) in terms of their problem-solving capacities are Philip E. Jacob and A. L. Atherton (71) and Jack C. Plano and Robert E. Riggs (115), while NGO's tend to be examined singularly in terms of case studies. Generally, there currently exist few works that attempt to develop a theoretical framework in which to analyze comparatively collective problem-solving activities, and consequently the literature is nearly devoid of middle-range theoretical discussions. Most studies deal with specific issue areas, such as James Ridgeway's (124) exploration of global energy issues; many of these studies can be used as case materials to develop theoretical ideas about international cooperation for the solving of problems.

3. A final class of interactions among international actors are principally competitive in nature, dealing with the bargaining efforts of parties to a dispute to resolve the conflict to their own satisfaction. Competitive bargaining behavior and the patterns of activities associated with that behavior constitute a significant segment of what observers have traditionally termed "international politics," and consequently analyses of competitive interaction enjoy a dominant position in the scholarly literature. Such analysis is conducted from a variety of perspectives. Strategic interaction and bargaining have received a good deal of attention in recent years. Always of interest because of its obvious relevance to policy prescriptions, bargaining has been studied along a number of dimensions.

A great amount of effort has come from those who have used game theory concepts, derived from both economics and psychology, to study human behavior in general and bargaining in particular. The pioneering figure in this effort is Thomas C. Schelling, whose book *The Strategy of Conflict* has already become a classic. Others who have used mathematical game theory concepts to study international politics include Howard S. Becker (14) in sociology and Kenneth E. Boulding (17) and Russett (138) in economics. In addition, William H. Riker (125) has applied mathematical concepts derived from game theory to the study of coalition formation. Basic to an introduction to game theory concepts are Snyder (155), Martin Shubik (146), and Anatol Rapoport (118 and 119). For applications of these concepts that are directed at international politics, one might consult Sawyer and Harold Guetzkow (141) and Thomas Schelling (142); empirically oriented studies have been undertaken by Russett (136), Clinton F. Fink (46), and Lloyd Jensen (73 and 74).

Work on the role of norms in shaping bargaining behavior, whether they be formal international laws or tacit norms of behavior among states, is sparse, as William D. Coplin has noted (32). Observations of the World Court activities in bargaining among states can be found in Coplin (34). More general discussions are provided by Michael Barkun (13), Roger Fisher (47), and Coplin (33).

The various capabilities and activities that might be used in bargaining have been extensively examined, though not necessarily in a bargaining framework. War and the use of force have received primary attention. George Quester (117), Morton Halperin (60), and Schelling (143) have handled the question perceptively. Wright (176) remains the classic study of war, while Edward Mead Earle (40) is a good survey of traditional (pre-nuclear) ideas about military strategy. Other aspects of the use of force have received particular treatment, including W. W. Kaufmann (78) on limited war. Armand S. Lall (89) and Fred C. Ikle (70) speak more to the subject of the relationship of force and bargaining strategy in their discussion of negotiating tactics. Arnold Wolfers (175) and George Liska (93) have examined the dynamics of alliances, and Charles Wolf, Jr. (174), has studied the use of foreign aid. Also of importance are the less spectacular and violent bargaining actions; these include diplomatic pro-test studied by Joseph C. McKenna (100) and economic sanctions treated by Johan Galtung (50).

Because of the problems in acquiring the relevant data on bargaining interactions among states (perceptions, attitudes, and strategies), many social scientists have tried to generalize from what they consider relevant situations. As mentioned, these include principles drawn from economics, sociology, mathematical game theory, and psychology. Of particular importance has been the study of bargaining in two-person games. Employed primarily by psychologists to assess the interplay of perceptions, attitudes, and strategies, these experiments are performed to assess how personality and environment interact in competitive situations—for example, Rapoport (119) and Rapoport and Melvin Guyer (120). Although no systematic attempt has yet been made to apply the findings from such experiments to more traditional case analysis, scholars hope that their findings can be made relevant to analysis of particular bargaining situations among states.

Despite the excellent framework provided by Schelling and others, the study of bargaining among states still suffers from a predisposition to examine only those bargaining situations that involve the use of force. Not only does this predisposition limit the attention paid to bargaining that does not lead to war; it also is part of the general failure to develop a com-parative analysis of bargaining behavior. Comparison is one of the best ways to learn about phenomena. Yet, no attempt has been made to develop an explicit framework built on bargaining concepts and models from which comparisons across cases can be made. Atlhough a number of scholars such as McClelland (96) and Russett (136) have looked at conflict situations in quantitative and comparative frameworks, there has been no systematic analysis of cases using bargaining concepts and theories.

While most of the literature on international interactions can be classified according to our tripartite typology of interactions into routine, problem-solving, and competitive classes, it should be noted in closing that a substantial literature exists that is devoted to what might be termed, for lack of a better descriptive label, the "setting of international interactions." Such studies are interested in describing the world's central institutions and processes that influence the way actors exchange behavior across national borders. This literature includes a discussion of the various environmental factors, such as geopolitical conditions (Harold Sprout and Margaret Sprout, 158), the global communications network (Colin Cherry, 26), the attributes of the international legal culture (Adda B. Bozeman, 18), and the international economic system (Charles P. Kindleberger, 84). Since these factors serve to condition and structure the kinds of interactions obtaining between and among international actors, they deserve serious consideration in any effort to explain the nature of intercultural relations.

In order to comprehend more fully the nature of analytic treatments of international interactions, as well as to illustrate some additional methodological points about how scholars study international interactions, a number of readings from the literature have been provided in this chapter. Each reading selection is preceded by a brief introduction and followed by a discussion of its approach.

SELECTED READINGS

One important background characteristic of the international environment is the extent to which individuals interact with each other—on a nonofficial basis—across national borders. While, in the short run, the degree of transactions flowing among members of national societies may have little influence on the types of relations the states themselves maintain with one another, yet, in the long run, the flow of transnational participation may exert a potent impact on the images people hold about those in other countries, and these images may subsequently affect the kinds of behaviors they adopt with respect to their external environment. As such, the level of transnational participation in the global system, defined in terms of the movement—or lack thereof—of private citizens, mail, trade, and communications, is a variable that structures the images people hold of international contact and influences the nature of the international environment itself. If we can accept the assumption that the way people deal with each other is greatly affected by the environment in which they exist, then it would seem that the setting for international relations is an area worth examining.

Our first reading selection is an empirical description of the growth of transnational participation among states—that is, the flow of individuals, groups, and ideas. Written by Robert C. Angell, it addresses itself to the various ways nations may be drawn together and integrated by contact with one another and describes the possible consequences for the expanding scope of activity transcending national boundaries.

THE GROWTH OF TRANSNATIONAL
PARTICIPATION

Robert C. Angell

A fruitful concept is one subsuming data that need to be held together if one is to make valid generalizations. This does not mean that the bundle of data thus held together always has the same consequences. Take the concept of bureaucracy, for instance. There has been much dispute about the effects of what we call bureaucracy, and we now believe that under certain conditions it has one set of effects, under other conditions another set. But few would deny that it is a useful concept because it puts together a cluster of relationships that is central to modern complex societies.

TRANSNATIONAL PARTICIPATION

Transnational participation is a concept that will probably have increasing fruitfulness as communication and transportation draw the world closer together. In trying to isolate the right set of phenomena to be conceptualized, the importance of the idea of crossing national borders is obvious; but it is not at all obvious what set of relationships among persons from different nations needs to be specified. The term participation is designed to draw upon the work of the social psychologists who have found that certain kinds of relationships have much more profound influence on the value-orientations of the actors than others. These relationships are of two sorts: (a) those in which there is necessary collaboration in achieving common objectives, and (b) those in which there is an intimate living together. In the former the participants have a specific, in the latter, a diffuse relationship. In both the interaction is close. If these relationships have been established voluntarily, the result is usually some convergence of the value-orientations of the participants. If, on the other hand, the participants find themselves together involuntarily, the consequence may be hostility and divergence. In either case the effect is profound. Thus, the concept of transnational participation draws together data on relationships across borders that are fateful one way or the other.

This definition of transnational participation excludes much that could be termed transnational experience. The brief and fleeting contacts of the tourist, for instance, are omitted. A fortiori, distance communication through the mass media or via school textbooks is not included. Even international trade is beyond the pale unless the traders are functioning

Robert C. Angell, "The Growth of Transnational Participation," *Journal of Social Issues* 23, 1 (1967): 108-129. Copyright, 1967, by The Society for the Psychological Study of Social Issues. Reprinted by permission of the author and publisher.

Angell is professor emeritus in the Department of Sociology at the University of Michigan.

in some non-contractual grouping. And if they are, it is that grouping, not their trade, that makes them transnational participants.

A concept is developed because it is useful in thinking about a problem—either practical or scientific. Transnational participation is useful for both reasons. It is relevant to the problem of attaining world peace, since it refers to the intimate connection for good or ill of citizens of the units that make war, the nation-states. It is significant scientifically because sociologists are becoming interested in intersystem relations at all levels—interinstitutional as well as intermetropolitan and intersocietal. Participation across system boundaries is therefore a phenomenon in need of conceptualization. Transnational participation can become a subconcept under the broader term, intersystem participation.

From the standpoint of intersystem conflict or cooperation there are two central questions to be asked about any form of intersystem participation: (a) What are the effects on the connected systems? and (b) Is the participation growing or shrinking? I am investigating both of these questions for the transnational case, but I am here presenting material only on the second question. These data are of course, inconclusive for both the practical problem of peace and the theoretical problem of intersystem accommodation without data on the first question, but as trend data they have interest because they describe what is going on in the world.

The six categories of transnational participation that follow are not the fruit of theoretical analysis but are simply those in which existing statistical series are gathered. One category that is important is not represented. This is residence abroad in military service. So far, we have been unable to unearth reliable figures on which trend analysis could be based. Since for several of the categories adequate statistics have only recently been tabulated, the trends are those of the last decade. The time span covered varies, but the figures for different categories are made comparable by computing the rate of increase compounded annually.

PARTICIPATION—BY RENEWING FAMILY TIES

Perhaps the oldest and the simplest form of transnational participation is the visiting of relatives and friends abroad. Human migration must always have been followed by the desire to renew old ties. With the explosion outward of European populations in the nineteenth century and the ability to pay for transportation in the twentieth this form of participation has mushroomed. The only adequate statistics on the subject, however, come from the United States. Fortunately they cover movement in both directions.

The Aviation Department of the Port of New York Authority made a study of all passengers departing for overseas from its international airport (then Idlewild) in 1956-57. The study was repeated in 1963-64. The data are broken down in two ways—by American or foreign residence of the passenger and by European or Bermuda-Latin American destination. We have chosen to utilize data on both American and foreign residents because transnational participation is a two-way street, but have utilized only the Europe-bound trips because we wished to adjust the figures to include those going by ship, and such figures are more reliable for transatlantic than for other voyages.

The adult passengers in a carefully designed sample of all out-bound trips filled out questionnaires about themselves and their trips. They were asked the reasons for their journey and these were coded into eleven categories. One was visiting relatives and friends.

Since roughly two-thirds of all transatlantic flights from the United States originate in New York, we assume that the proportions of all transatlantic air travelers going to or returning from visits to relatives and friends will be much the same as those given by the Port of New York Authority. It is, of course, much more risky to assume that the same proportions hold for transatlantic passengers going by sea. Since, however, there are no data on the reasons for the sea voyages, we make that assumption as better than any other. The number of air and sea passages to Europe are compiled annually by the United States Immigration and Naturalization Service. It is unimportant that the Service distinguishes between Americans and foreigners on the basis of citizenship rather than residence (which was used by the Port of New York Authority).

The proportion of New York transatlantic departures of American residents for the purpose of visiting relatives and friends in 1956-57 was 28%. Of foreign residents returning from visits in the United States it was 15%. In 1963-64 the corresponding figures were 29% and 27%. If these percentages are applied to all air and sea departures from the United States in the two years we get Table 1.

TABLE 1
Transatlantic Travel to Visit Relatives and Friends

| | American Citizens Going to Visit in Europe | | | | Foreign Citizens Returning from Visits in the United States | | | |
| | | | Increase or (Decrease) | | | | Increase or (Decrease) | |
Means	1956-57	1963-64	Number	Per Cent	1956-57	1963-64	Number	Per Cent
By air	93,481	276,790	183,309	196.1	16,291	141,416	125,125	768.1
By sea	66,793	63,453	(3,340)	(5.0)	19,651	36,601	16,950	86.3
Total	160,274	340,243	179,969	112.3	35,952	178,017	142,075	398.1

The 112.3% increase in seven years for American citizens amounts to a yearly rate of increase of 14% (compounded). The greater increase for aliens of 398.1% for the same period yields a rate of increase of 25.8% per year. This rapid rise undoubtedly reflects the fact that the economic recovery of Europe is allowing older Europeans to visit relatives and friends in the United States who migrated before the onset of the Great

Depression. Americans have been able to afford the reverse journey since World War II. Though the numbers visiting in Europe are still almost twice the numbers visiting in the United States, the disproportion is decreasing rapidly. If the trends shown were to continue (which is unlikely) the two movements would balance in the year of 1967. A point that is interesting, but irrelevant for our purposes, is that foreigners continue to use sea travel more than citizens of the United States.

PARTICIPATION—BY CONDUCTING BUSINESS

The second category of transnational participation on which we have data is sojourn abroad for business reasons. These data too are drawn from the two studies of the Port of New York Authority. We have attempted to include only sojourns that involve organic ties with business enterprises or businessmen abroad by omitting those who were coded as traveling to attend a convention or fair or those traveling for business and pleasure combined.

As in the case of visiting relatives and friends abroad we have extrapolated the percentages for both Americans and foreigners leaving the New York International Airport to all those leaving by sea and air from the United States for Europe. These percentages were 19% for Americans and 30% for aliens in 1956-57. In 1963-64 the corresponding figures were 20.4% and 26.6%. Table 2 gives the estimated number of businessmen sojourning abroad in each of the two years.

TABLE 2
Transatlantic Travel for Business Reasons
Other Than Attendance at a Convention or Fair

| | American Citizens Going to Europe | | | | Foreign Citizens Returning from the United States | | | |
| | | | Increase or (Decrease) | | | | Increase or (Decrease) | |
Means	1956-57	1963-64	Number	Per Cent	1956-57	1963-64	Number	Per Cent
By air	63,433	194,719	131,286	207.0	32,582	139,215	106,633	327.3
By sea	45,324	44,636	(688)	(1.5)	39,301	36,059	(3,242)	(8.2)
Total	108,757	239,355	130,598	120.1	71,883	175,274	103,391	143.8

In this case the rates of increase are quite similar in both directions, that for the United States citizens amounting to a compound increase of 11.9% a year and for the foreign citizens one of 13.5%. The volume of travel of the United States citizens is not very much greater than that of the foreigners. This is a little surprising in view of the much greater United States investments in Europe than of European countries in the

United States. Perhaps it is explained, in part, by the employment of foreign nationals as managers by American companies operating abroad.

The term sojourn perhaps aptly describes what is involved in most business trips. The stays are short. The involvement in the other country may be minor. It, therefore, becomes important to ask what are the trends so far as long periods of residence are concerned. Since the duration of actual stay in the case of foreigners returning home and of expected stay in the case of natives is recorded in the Port of New York Authority surveys, we have constructed Table 3 to show the trends in stays of less than and more than one year. Here we note that both types of stays for both United States and foreign citizens are increasing rapidly but that increase is most rapid for long-term stays of foreigners and least for long-term stays of Americans. If we call the long-term stays residence abroad in contrast to sojourn, the rates of increase per year are as follows:

Residence of Americans abroad:	11.6%
Sojourn of Americans abroad:	12.0%
Sojourn of foreigners in the United States:	13.2%
Residence of foreigners in the United States:	25.8%

Although the numbers involved in the residence of foreigners in the United States for business purposes are small, the rate of increase is surprisingly large. It is a curious fact that it is almost identical with the rate of increase of foreigners visiting relatives and friends in this country. It would seem to be true that transatlantic transnational participation is becoming a more balanced process than it has been in the past.

A word of caution is in order about extending the findings on transatlantic visiting and business to the whole globe. Both series would undoubtedly show sharp increases in many parts of the world, but whether the rates would be increasing in all parts of the world as fast as they are across the Atlantic seems doubtful. Per capita income is not increasing as rapidly in most other parts of the world. Nor are there as many ties of relationship and business enterprise.

PARTICIPATION—BY STUDY ABROAD

For our third category of transnational participation—residence abroad for study—we do not have to rely on data from the United States alone, but can turn to the world data set forth in the UNESCO Statistical Yearbook for 1963. Unfortunately the data there are quite incomplete. For many countries the data on foreign students either have not been collected or have not been reported to UNESCO. Table 15, for instance, shows the total number of students in the institutions of the third level (higher education) for 125 countries, but Table 17 which records the number of foreign students, gives data for only 75 countries. And for only 45 of these 75 can good trend data be obtained; that is, a comparison of 1955 with 1961 (or in a few cases 1960).

Before looking at the trends for these 45 countries it is important to indicate to what degree they can be regarded as representative of the world

TABLE 3

Duration of Trips of Transatlantic Travelers for Business Purposes

Duration	American Citizens Going to Europe		Increase		Foreign Citizens Returning from the United States		Increase	
	1956-57	1963-64	Number	Per Cent	1956-57	1963-64	Number	Per Cent
Less than one year	97,881	216,377	118,496	121.1	70,445	168,088	97,643	138.6
More than one year	10,876	22,978	12,102	111.8	1,438	7,186	5,748	399.7
Total	108,757	239,355	130,598	120.1	71,883	175,274	103,391	143.8

trend. First, one can estimate roughly the percentage of all students studying abroad. From Table 15 we learn that in 1961 there were 13,012,996 students in the institutions of higher education of the 125 countries. More than 61% of these were in the 45 countries for which we have trend data. The other 80 countries in the table contributed under 39% of the total.

The most damaging omission from the standpoint of knowing the world picture is the Union of Soviet Socialist Republics. It had 2,639,900 students in its institutions of higher education in 1961, the second largest number for any country. Foreign students are perhaps 1% of this total, or 26,400. Other important omissions are the Chinese Peoples Republic and the Philippines, each with nearly 300,000 students in higher education, and Argentina with nearly 200,000. If the rate of increase in foreign students in these four countries is sharply different from that in the 45 countries for which we have trend data, the latter may be misleading.

Table 4 shows that the increase for the 45 countries over the six-year

TABLE 4
Number of Foreign Students, 15 Countries

			Per Cent Increase	
1955	**1961**	**Increase**	**1955-61**	**Per Year**
107,283	191,359	84,076	78.4	10.0

period is 78.4%. This is a yearly rate of increase of 10.0%. Although we cannot have great confidence in this figure as reflecting the world situation, it probably is based upon some 70% of the students in foreign institutions. Although the 45 countries included in this tabulation have only 61.5% of the students in 125 countries, their institutions tend to be the larger and better known ones and hence more attractive to students wishing to study abroad. We might guess, then, that there are some 270,000 foreign students in all countries.

Though the world figures are the significant ones, it is interesting to compare them with the trends as shown by the departures from New York International Airport expanded to the total sea and air departures for Europe. Using the same techniques described for other forms of transnational participation, we find the compound yearly increase in travel for study and research is 16.6% for Americans leaving for Europe and 18.3% for foreign citizens returning home. These higher rates of increase shown for study abroad on the world level are somewhat surprising since one might have assumed that the United States, as a country long in the business of scholarly exchange, might not show as high rates of increase as more recently participating nations.

Beside data on trends in numbers, the UNESCO Statistical Yearbook gives, in Table 18, data on foreign students by country of origin, in fifteen countries for 1960, 1961 or 1962. Although we cannot derive trends from this table, it does make possible an analysis of the types of relationships that are being established—whether study abroad is mostly confined with ideological blocs, whether it is mostly a matter of students from developed countries going to other developed countries, or whether it is students from underdeveloped countries going to developed countries, and the like. Unfortunately again the fifteen countries are not well distributed over the several types. None of them is a Communist country. Eight of them are Western European, and 10 of them are in the Western camp. The 15 nations are: Australia, Austria, Belgium, France, West Germany, Ireland, Italy, Japan, Mexico, Senegal, Switzerland, Syria, United Arab Republic, United Kingdom, United States. In view of their unrepresentative character we shall supplement the pattern of linkages shown by the recorded data by estimating the pattern of linkages for the countries with large numbers of foreign students not included in the 15, and then combine the two sets of data into an estimated world pattern.

In order to analyze the pattern of transnational participation through study abroad we will classify nations on two bases. One is ideological, the other concerns the degree of development. There are three categories in each: Western, uncommitted and Communist; and developed, semideveloped and underdeveloped. The ideological classification is the conventional one, though some difficult choices had to be made. Finland, Israel and Japan, for instance, were included among the Western nations. Yugoslavia and all the Latin American Countries except Cuba were classified as uncommitted.[1]

The work of Harbison and Myers, *Education, Manpower and Economic Growth* (1964) was drawn upon for the developmental classifications. Gross national product per capita and their Composite Index of Human Resource Development were used as follows:

> *Developed Nations:* at least $400 gross national product per capita and at least 53 or more on the Composite Index.
> These criteria bring in all the Western nations given above except Spain, Portugal, Greece, and Turkey plus the following: Argentina, Uruguay, Soviet Union, Poland, East Germany, Czechoslovakia and Hungary.
> *Semideveloped Nations:* those not qualifying as Developed, but that are above $200 gross national product per capita and above 20 on the Composite Index.
> These criteria bring in the following nations: Mexico, Cuba, Costa Rica, Panama, Colombia, Venezuela, Brazil, Chile, Portugal, Spain, Yugoslavia, Romania, Bulgaria, Albania, Greece, Turkey, Cyprus, Lebanon, South Africa and Malaysia.
> *Underdeveloped Nations:* those not qualifying as either Developed or Semideveloped.

The ideological and developmental classifications yeild a nine-fold table. In such a table there are 45 sorts of linkages including linkages of a country of a particular type with another country of the same type. To simplify matters we have combined cases like the following: the linkage of a Western developed country with an uncommitted semideveloped one, and the linkage of an uncommitted developed country with a Western semideveloped one. This reduces the types of linkage to 36. The situation is most easily expressed in terms of barriers crossed. Table 5 is drawn up in this manner. It will be noted how few linkages there are across the Communist barrier. This, of course, is because only students from Communist countries going to other countries for study could gain entrance into this table, since there is no Communist nation among the 15 comprising it to catch the reverse flow. Hence this table is almost worthless for considering the world situation.

As a basis for estimating the world situation there are two sets of relevant data in the UNESCO volume. Table 17 gives the number of foreign students in 1960 or 1961 for 29 nations in addition to the 45 for which comparisons can be made with 1955. Of these 74, full data are available on 15. An estimate of the numbers in various categories of countries-of-origin for the remaining 59 could be made; however, it hardly seems worth the effort for those having less than 500 foreign students. This cuts out 39. Left are the 20 for which we have established the types of countries from which their foreign students come. This has been done by examining the distributions in the countries that are near them geographically, or like them in either ideology or level of development. It is obvious that there are inadequate analogues for many of them.[2]

The other set of relevant data is contained in the UNESCO Table 15 where the total number of students in 126 countries is given. By applying percentages of foreign students in countries known to be similar in certain respects, the percentage of all their students that are foreign can be estimated. Only 13 further countries were estimated to have more than 500 foreign students.[3] For these 13, distributions have been estimated by the country of origin as in the case of those countries the number of whose foreign students is known. Table 6 gives the linkages for these 33 countries. Whereas Table 5 showed a large proportion studying abroad within the Western orbit, Table 6 shows about one-third studying abroad within the Communist bloc. This is only natural since the Communist countries of study did not appear in Table 5.

Table 7 is a composite of Table 5 and 6. If any reliance can be placed at all on the estimates in Table 6, it would give some inkling of the world picture. Note first that is shows 254,000 students abroad, somewhat less than the 270,000 thought likely on the basis of world enrollments in higher education. Since, however, there are 78 of the 126 nations represented in UNESCO Table 15 that have not been included because they probably have less than 500 foreign students each, the original estimate may be not far from the truth. An average of 200 apiece would bring the total to 270,000.

It is no surprise to find the largest group of students are those linking the uncommitted, underdeveloped countries with the developed, Western countries. Next most important is the group from one Western developed country studying in another. At a much lower level is the Communist interchange of the same kind. If one looks at the columns that show the interchange with uncommitted countries it appears that there is a 7 to 1 advantage in favor of the Western as against the Communist nations.

Review of the data on study abroad indicates that this form of transnational participation is increasing steadily, though not so fast as visiting

TABLE 5
Number of Foreign Students in 15 Countries in Relation to Barriers

	Both Western	Both Uncommitted	Both Communist	One Western, one Uncommit.	One Western, one Communist	One Uncommitted, one Communist	Total
Both developed	46,446			903	2,329		49,678
Both semideveloped		331		14		27	372
Both underdeveloped		7,323					7,323
One developed, one semideveloped	14,232	14		12,489	1,349		28,084
One developed, one underdeveloped	11,656	66		70,578			82,300
One semideveloped, one underdeveloped		1,136		84		4	1,224
Total	72,334	8,870	0	84,068	3,678	31	168,981

TABLE 6

Number of Foreign Students (Estimated) in 33 Countries in Relation to Barriers

	Both Western	Both Uncommitted	Both Communist	One Western, one Uncommit.	One Western, one Communist	One Uncommitted, one Communist	Total
Both developed	4,685	348	15,953	606	846	68	22,515
Both semideveloped	899	835	195	1,282	336	940	4,487
Both underdeveloped	74	6,530	2,494	632		2,787	12,517
One developed, one semideveloped	1,294	2,236	5,341	3,098	614	1,005	13,588
One developed, one underdeveloped	265	1,644	3,190	6,558	58	8,365	20,080
One semideveloped, one underdeveloped	37	5,209	310	5,563	84	837	12,040
Total	7,254	16,794	27,483	17,739	1,955	14,002	85,227

TABLE 7

Number of Foreign Students (Estimated) in 48 Countries in Relation to Barriers

	Both Western	Both Uncommitted	Both Communist	One Western, one Uncommit.	One Western, one Communist	One Uncommitted, one Communist	Total
Both developed	51,131	340	15,953	1,509	3,192	68	72,193
Both semideveloped	899	1,166	195	1,296	336	967	4,859
Both underdeveloped	74	13,853	2,494	632		2,787	19,840
One developed, one semideveloped	15,526	2,250	5,341	15,587	1,963	1,005	41,672
One developed, one underdeveloped	11,921	1,710	3,190	77,136	58	8,365	102,380
One semideveloped, one underdeveloped	37	6,345	310	5,647	84	841	13,264
Total	79,588	25,664	27,483	101,807	5,633	14,033	254,208

relatives and friends, and sojourn for business reasons. Study abroad, however, is linking nations of very different kinds and may well, therefore, have a more profound influence on future relationships in the world.

PARTICIPATION—BY OFFERING TECHNICAL ASSISTANCE

The fourth category of transnational participation is technical assistance. Both bilateral and multilateral assistance are included. For bilateral trends we have only United States data; for multilateral, the data from the United Nations.

The United States has had a succession of agencies in the technical assistance field—the Mutual Security Agency, The Technical Cooperation Administration and the Agency for International Development—but statistics on civilian personnel involved in foreign aid programs have been kept continuously. From 1958 to 1964 the statistics seem to have been gathered in identical categories. Table 8 gives information on American nationals abroad and foreign nationals brought to this country or sent to

TABLE 8
Transnational Participation in the United States
Program of Technical Assistance

	U. S. Nationals Abroad Paid from Regular Program Funds	Foreign Nationals Training		
		In the U.S.	In Third Countries	Total
1958	2926	5596	1746	7342
1961	3485	6915	2093	9008
1964	3431	6511	1703	8214
Increase 1958-64	505	915	(43)	872
% Increase	17.3	16.4	(2.5)	11.9

other countries for training, for the three years—1958, 1961 and 1964—because the former upward trend in personnel has been reversed of recent years. The figures for yearly increases in this situation are meaningless because they represent a combination of two trends. If the recent one persists the mean yearly increase will go to zero or even become negative. It is clear that United States Technical Assistance is not at present a source of increasing transnational participation.

The situation with respect to United Nations Technical Assistance is different. Both the regular programs of technical assistance of the several Specialized Agencies and the Expanded Program financed by the Economic and Social Council (often in cooperation with the Specialized Agencies) are steadily growing. Table 9 gives the figures. It is obvious that the Expanded Program, though growing slowly, is rapidly losing ground to the programs of the Specialized Agencies. This mirrors the fact that the Spe-

TABLE 9

Transnational Participation in the United Nations Technical Assistance Programs

	Experts			Fellowships		
	Expanded Program	Regular Program of Specialized Agencies	Total	Expanded Program	Regular Program of Specialized Agencies	Total
1956	2346	549	2895	2128	1041	3169
1963	2817	1866	4683	2545	3437	5982
Increase 1956-63	471	1317	1788	417	2396	2813
% Increase	20.1	240.0	61.3	19.3	230.2	88.6
Compound Yearly % Increase	2.7	19.1	7.1	2.6	18.6	9.5

cialized Agencies, which originally performed mainly clearing-house functions in the field of technical assistance, have more lately been carrying out field projects. Thus, there is more decentralization of the programs.

The overall rates of increase of the number of experts and of the holders of fellowships for training are modest but significant. It is apparent that even if bilateral technical assistance declines, as that of the United States seems likely to do, the multilateral programs are likely to grow and take over a larger share of the total effort.

PARTICIPATION—BY WORKING FOR INTERNATIONAL ORGANIZATIONS

The fifth sort of transnational participation to be examined is that connected with international nongovernmental organizations. These bring people from different countries together in a multilateral fashion to achieve common objectives. For their study the *Yearbook of International Organizations* published by the Union of International Associations is essential. Here we will analyze the trends as shown in the 1956-57 and 1962-63 editions.

The *Yearbook* includes both intergovernmental and nongovernmental organizations. In the analysis to follow the 177 intergovernmental organizations in the 1962-63 edition are excluded. Such are the units of the United Nations, the official bodies of the European Community, those of the Communist bloc, and technical organizations resulting from treaties like the International Wheat Council. This leaves 1,570 nongovernmental organizations.

Table 10 shows the comparison of 1962-63 with 1956-57 in mere numbers of such organizations, classified according to whether they are regional in name or in fact, whether they have a religious, ideological or ethnic limitation though otherwise potentially worldwide in scope (particularistic), or whether they are potentially worldwide and actually more than regional. The much higher rate of increase for regional organizations is largely due to the great proliferation of groups formed within the Common Market

TABLE 10
Number of International Nongovernmental Organizations

	World-Wide	Particularistic	Regional	Date Insufficient to Classify	Total
1956-57	503	246	191	13	953
1962-63	677	312	555	26	1,570
Increase	174	66	364		617
% Increase	34.6	26.8	190.6		64.7
Compound Yearly % Increase	5.1	4.1	19.5		8.7

after that was established in 1958. Almost two-thirds of the growth in this category is accounted for by the 223 such organizations. But this would have been the fastest growing category in any case. One reason for this may be the resentment by the less developed countries of the dominance of Europeans in world-wide international organizations. Of all the organizations in the 1962-63 *Yearbook,* more than 85% had their headquarters in Europe and more than 75% of their directors and officers were from Europe.

The rate of growth for all types of organization of 8.77% certainly underrepresents the rate at which new people are becoming involved in this form of transnational participation, since the existing organizations are growing at the same time that new ones are being added. Although we cannot obtain any data on individual activity in connection with nongovernmental organizations we can obtain data on how many involvements of countries there are in particular organizations. For this purpose, involvement of Americans in the activities of any nongovernmental organization would count as one involvement for the United States. We have not analyzed this matter for all the organizations but we have done so for a selected group of "globally oriented" ones. These are of three types: those whose aim is to strengthen political ties among nations, those that are in fact participating in a nonpolitical world system, like organizations of meteorologists and those whose main purpose is international understanding. Table 11 gives the number of involvements in such organizations in 1956-57 and 1962-63.

TABLE 11
Number of Country Involvements in Globally Oriented
International Nongovernmental Organizations

	Number of Involvements 1956-57	Number of Involvements 1962-63	Per Cent Increase
12 Organizations 1956-57 edition, not in 1962-63 edition	250		
151 organizations in both editions	4,529	6,534	44.3
33 organizations in 1962-63 edition, not in 1956-57 edition		874	
Total	4,779	7,408	55.0

It is clear from the data presented that, not only is the number of these globally oriented organizations growing, but the number of countries involved in each is doing so. For those existing at the beginning and end of the six-year span the mean yearly increase is 6.3%.

TABLE 12
Coverage of Different Types of Countries by 150 Globally Oriented
International Nongovernmental Organizations

| | With Respect to Ideology | | | |
With Respect to Development	Less in 1962-63 than in 1956-57	Same in 1962-63 as in 1956-57	More in 1962-63 than in 1956-57	Total
Less in 1962-63 than in 1956-57	1	1	0	2
Same in 1962-63 as in 1956-57	3	114	17	134
More in 1962-63 than in 1956-57	0	8	6	14
Total	4	123	23	150

We can show the increasing participation in these organizations in still another way: by analyzing involvement in relation to the barriers discussed in connection with study abroad. The same three classes of ideological position and the same three classes of development are used in reaching the conclusions set for the Table 12. Here we see that only 5 organizations have gone backward in coverage, either ideologically or in terms of the development spectrum; 31 have increased their coverage. From Table 11 we learned that these organizations involved 44% more countries in 1962-63 than in 1956-57. It is evident that the net gain of 26 organizations with broader coverage among 150 organizations (17%) means that about two-fifths of the expansion in involvement carries these organizations across barriers.

Our discussion of nongovernmental organizations can be summed up in three statements: (a) the number of such organizations is growing at almost 9% per year; (b) their involvement of countries is growing at 6.3% per year; and (c) both ideological and developmental barriers are being progressively breached.

PARTICIPATION—BY BEING A MEMBER OF THE U.N.

The last kind of transnational participation to be considered is membership in United Nations secretariats. These consist of the headquarters in New York plus its branches in other parts of the world and the headquarters of the twelve Specialized Agencies and their branches. Members of delegations from member countries to these bodies are not here considered, both for practical and theoretical reasons. Information on the numbers who have served on delegations at different points in time is not easily available. More important, it is doubtful whether such service should be included under the concept of transnational participation. Instructed delegates

TABLE 13
Established Posts in the United Nations and
its Specialized Agencies

	All Established Posts	Established Posts Not Related to Technical Assistance
1956	8,370	7,821
1963	13,165	11,299
Increase	4,795	3,478
% Increase	57.3	45.8
Compound Yearly % Increase	6.7	5.5

hardly participate in the solution of common problems in a way that changes them fundamentally. They tend to interact on a formal level, and they do not live intimately together. It is for the same reason that we have excluded other intergovernmental organizations from consideration while including nongovernmental organizations.

The Annexes to the Official Records of the United Nations General Assembly gives figures each year on the number of established posts in the various agencies of the United Nations system. These are given in Table 13. Since these engaged on the Regular Programs in Technical Assistance as contrasted with the Expanded Program are holders of established posts, and we have shown in Table 9 the growth in United Nations Technical Assistance, we also show here the growth in established posts minus technical assistance personnel. The figures show that the technical assistance work has been growing somewhat faster than the other work of the several agencies, but both rates of increases are modest.

The six sorts of transnational participation that have been examined all show increases. Where we have some inkling of the worldwide situation, as in study abroad, multilateral technical assistance, international nongovernmental organizations and secretariats of the United Nations system, there seems to be a growth rate of between 5% and 10% a year. If this trend countinues for a decade or more the results will almost certainly be important. But whether for good or ill will depend upon knowledge of the effects of the growing participation. Unfortunately, sociologists have carried out few studies of these effects.

NOTES

[1]The Western camp has the following members: United States, Canada, United Kingdom, Ireland, Iceland, Norway, Sweden, Finland, Denmark, West Germany, Netherlands, Belgium, Luxemburg, Switzerland, France, Spain, Portugal, Italy, Austria, Greece, Turkey, Israel, Australia, New Zealand, Japan, Republic of China, South Korea, South Vietnam and Hong Kong. The Communist bloc embraces: Soviet Union, Poland, East Germany, Czecho-

slovakia, Hungary, Rumania, Bulgaria, Albania, Mongolia, Peoples Republic of China, North Vietnam, North Korea and Cuba. All the rest of the nations are classified as uncommitted.

[2]The 20 countries are Morocco, Uganda, Canada, Columbia, Uruguay, Venezuela, Hong Kong, India, Israel, Lebanon, Turkey, Bulgaria, Czechoslovakia, Greece, Netherlands, Poland, Rumania, Spain, Yugoslavia and New Zealand.

[3]The 13 countries are: S. Africa, Cuba, Argentina, Brazil, Peru, Peoples Republic of China, Iran, Philippines, Singapore, West Berlin, East Germany, Sweden and Union of Soviet Socialist Republic.

REFERENCE

Harbison, Frederick H., and Myers, Charles A. *Education, Manpower, and Economic Growth.* New York: McGraw-Hill, 1964.

The foregoing study illustrates the use of systematic observation and descriptive techniques. Rather than merely asserting, on the basis of opinion and impression, that "the world is growing more interdependent," Angell takes care to define operationally what he means by transnational participation (that is, he spells out that interdependence can be measured by observing particular aspects of international contact, such as foreign travel) and demonstrates, on the basis of evidence, that transnational participation is indeed growing. Moreover, because he employs empirical measurement, he is able to tell us precisely how much, at what rate, and in what way the level of systemic participation is expanding. Thus, when the scholar measures his variables, descriptive precision is facilitated.

Note also the nature of Angell's study design. He has conducted an empirical investigation that inductively maps the flows, and changes in those flows, of people across national boundaries. He thus incorporates the time dimension in his descriptive analysis. Rather than measuring the level of international penetration of each society in the world on a cross-national basis by observing the level in each society at a particular period of time, Angell has managed to make his observations at several time-points. In such time-series, or diachronic, analysis, the descriptions that obtain are longitudinal, in the sense that they profile changes over time in the level of transnational participation rather than merely describe the level of transnational participation obtaining at a unique point in history. Trend-line interpretation of the sort presented here makes Angell's findings much more meaningful, given the objectives of his study.

Finally, note that Angell has resisted the temptation to make causal inferences from his descriptions. Intuitively, one is led to suspect that fluctations in the level of transnational participation will have some bearing on the nature of international relations. But Angell makes no attempt at explanation. He has observed the movement of people across national boundaries, but the significance of this flow is not postulated (although he does suggest that it will have some influence on the value-orientations of individuals who participate in transnational activities). Hence, the flows are not related directly to international politics, and one must use one's imagination to guess what the consequences of these interactions might be.

If one type of international interaction involves overt contact between people, a second one involves the kinds of images people hold of each other. On this type we observe the attitudes and perceptions collectivities develop toward nations in their external environment. The perceptual variable is important if we acknowledge that much of the variation in the types of interactions that parties to international interaction develop is a product of how they view one another.

In the article that follows, Urie Bronfenbrenner focuses his attention on a central problem of international politics in the post–World War II era: describing and explaining the interaction between the United States and the Soviet Union during the course of the Cold War. His thesis is that the prolonged conflict between the two superpowers should be viewed less as a product of irreconcilable differences between them than as a consequence of the images they held of each other. More specifically, he sees the conflict as having been exacerbated and intensified by the fact that each side tended to develop distorted and rigid attitudes that were really quite similar. Each party to the adversary relationship perceived itself as peace-loving, virtuous, and cautious and the other, the "enemy," as bellicose, deceptive, and expansionistic. Such an attitudinal relationship between two parties is called a "mirror image." As Arthur Gladstone described the concept:

> Each side believes the other to be bent on aggression and conquest, to be capable of great brutality and evil-doing, to be something less than human and therefore hardly deserving respect or consideration, to be insincere and untrustworthy, etc. To hold this conception of the enemy becomes the moral duty of every citizen, and those who question it are denounced. Each side prepares actively for the anticipated combat, striving to amass the greater military power for the destruction of the enemy. . . . The approaching war is seen as due entirely to the hostile intentions of the enemy.

What follows is Bronfenbrenner's application of the concept of "mirror images" to the analysis of Soviet-American interaction patterns.

THE MIRROR IMAGE
IN SOVIET-AMERICAN RELATIONS

Urie Bronfenbrenner

Let us then briefly examine the common features in the American and Soviet view of each other's societies. For the Russian's image I drew mainly not on official government pronouncements but on what was said to me by Soviet citizens in the course of our conversations. Five major themes stand out.

1. *They* are the aggressors.

The American view: Russia is the warmonger bent on imposing its system on the rest of the world. Witness Czechoslovakia, Berlin, Hungary, and now Cuba and the Congo. The Soviet Union consistently blocks Western proposals for disarmament by refusing necessary inspection controls.

The Soviet view: America is the warmonger bent on imposing its power on the rest of the world and on the Soviet Union itself. Witness American intervention in 1918, Western encirclement after World War II with American troops and bases on every border of the U.S.S.R. (West Germany, Norway, Turkey, Korea, Japan), intransigence over proposals to make Berlin a free city, intervention in Korea, Taiwan, Lebanon, Guatemala, Cuba. America has repeatedly rejected Soviet disarmament proposals while demanding the right to inspect within Soviet territory— finally attempting to take the right by force through deep penetration of Soviet air space.

2. Their government exploits and deludes the people.

The American view: Convinced communists, who form but a small proportion of Russia's population, control the government and exploit the society and its resources in their own interest. To justify their power and expansionist policies they have to perpetuate a war atmosphere and a fear of Western aggression. Russian elections are a travesty since only one party appears on the ballot. The Russian people are kept from knowing the truth through a controlled radio and press and conformity is insured through stringent economic and political sanctions against deviant individuals or groups.

Urie Bronfenbrenner, "The Mirror Image in Soviet-American Relations," *Journal of Social Issues* 27, 1 (1971): 46–51. Copyright, 1971, by the Society for the Psychological Study of Social Issues. Reprinted by permission of the author and publisher.

Bronfenbrenner is a professor of human development, family studies, and psychology at Cornell University.

The Soviet view: A capitalistic-militaristic clique controls the American government, the nation's economic resources, and its media of communication. This group exploits the society and its resources. It is in their economic and political interest to maintain a war atmosphere and engage in militaristic expansion. Voting in America is a farce since candidates for both parties are selected by the same powerful interests leaving nothing to choose between. The American people are kept from knowing the truth through a controlled radio and press and through economic and political sanctions against liberal elements.

3. *The mass of their people are not really sympathetic to the regime.*

The American view: In spite of the propaganda, the Soviet people are not really behind their government. Their praise of the government and the party is largely perfunctory, a necessary concession for getting along. They do not trust their own sources of information and have learned to read between the lines. Most of them would prefer to live under our system of government if they only could.

The Soviet view: Unlike their government, the bulk of the American people want peace. Thus, the majority disapproved of American aggression in Korea, the support of Chiang Kai-shek, and above all, of the sending of U2. But of course they could do nothing since their welfare is completely under the control of the ruling financier-militaristic clique. If the American people were allowed to become acquainted with communism as it exists in the U.S.S.R., they would unquestionably choose it as their form of government. ("You Americans are such a nice people; it is a pity you have such a terrible government.")

4. *They* cannot be trusted.

The American view: The Soviets do not keep promises and they do not mean what they say. Thus while they claim to have discontinued all nuclear testing, they are probably carrying out secret underground explosions in order to gain an advantage over us. Their talk of peace is but a propaganda maneuver. Everything they do is to be viewed with suspicion since it is all part of a single coordinated scheme to further aggressive communist aims.

The Soviet view: The Americans do not keep promises and they do not mean what they say. Thus they insist on inspection only so that they can look at Soviet defenses; they have no real intention of disarming. Everything the Americans do is to be viewed with suspicion (e.g., they take advantage of Soviet hospitality by sending in spies as tourists).

5. *Their* policy verges on madness.

The American view: Soviet demands on such crucial problems as disarmament, Berlin, and unification are completely unrealistic. Disarmament without adequate inspection is meaningless, a "free Berlin" would be equivalent to a Soviet Berlin, and a united Germany without free elections is an impossibility. In pursuit of their irresponsible policies the Soviets do not hesitate to run the risk of war itself. Thus it is only due to the restraint and coordinated action of the Western alliance that Soviet provocations over Berlin did not precipitate World War III.

The Soviet view: The American position on such crucial problems as disarmament, East Germany, and China is completely unrealistic. They demand to know our secrets before they disarm; in Germany they insist on a policy which risks the resurgence of a fascist Reich; and as for China, they try to act as if it did not exist while at the same time supporting an aggressive puppet regime just off the Chinese mainland. And in pursuit of their irresponsible policies, the Americans do not hesitate to run the risk of war itself. Were it not for Soviet prudence and restraint, the sending of U2 deep into Russian territory could easily have precipitated World War III.

It is easy to recognize the gross distortions in the Soviet views summarized above. But is our own outlook competely realistic? Are we correct, for example, in thinking that the mass of the Soviet people would really prefer our way of life and are unenthusiastic about their own? Certainly the tone and tenor of my conversations with Soviet citizens hardly support this belief.

But, you may ask, why is it that other Western observers do not report the enthusiasm and commitment which I encountered?

I asked this very question of newspaper men and embassy officials in Moscow. Their answers were revealing. Thus one reporter replied somewhat dryly, "Sure, I know, but when a communist acts like a communist, it isn't news. If I want to be sure that it will be printed back home, I have to write about what's wrong with the system, not its successes." Others voiced an opinion expressed most clearly by representatives at our embassy. When I reported to them the gist of my Soviet conversations, they were grateful but skeptical: "Professor, you underestimate the effect of the police state. When these people talk to a stranger, especially an American, they *have* to say the right thing."

The argument is persuasive, and comforting to hear. But perhaps these very features should arouse our critical judgment. Indeed, it is instructive to view this argument against the background of its predecessor voiced by the newspaperman. To put it bluntly, what he was saying was that he could be sure of getting published only the material that the *American people wanted to hear*. But notice that the second argument also fulfills this objective, and it does so in a much more satisfactory and sophisticated way. The realization that "Soviet citizens *have* to say the right thing" enables the Western observer not only to discount most of what he hears, but even to interpret it as evidence in direct support of the West's accepted picture of the Soviet Union as a police state.

It should be clear that I am in no sense here suggesting that Western reporters and embassy officials deliberately misrepresent what they know to be the facts. Rather I am but calling attention to the operation, in a specific and critical context, of a phenomenon well known to psychologists—the tendency to assimilate new perceptions to old, and unconsciously to distort what one sees in such a way as to minimize a clash with previous expectations. In recent years, a number of leading social psychologist, notably Heider (1958), Festinger (1957), and Osgood (1960), have emphasized that this "strain toward consistency" is especially powerful in the sphere of social relations—that is, in our perceptions of the motives, attitudes, and actions of other persons or groups. Specifically, we strive to keep our views of other human beings compatible with each other. In the face of complex social reality, such consistency is typically accomplished by obliterating distinctions and organizing the world in terms of artificially simplified frames of reference. One of the simplest of these, and hence one of the most inviting, is the dichotomy of good and bad. Hence we often perceive others, be they individuals, groups, or even whole societies, as simply "good" or "bad." Once this fateful decision is made, the rest is easy, for the "good" person or group can have only desirable social characteristics and the "bad" can have only reprehensible traits. And once such evaluative stability of social perception is established, it is extremely difficult to alter. Contradictory stimuli arouse only anxiety and resistance. When confronted with a desirable characteristic of something already known to be "bad," the observer will either just not "see" it, or will reorganize his perception of it so that it can be perceived as "bad." Finally, this tendency to regress to simple categories of perception is especially strong under conditions of emotional stress and external threat. Witness our readiness in times of war to exalt the virtues of our own side and to see the enemy as thoroughly evil.

Still one other social psychological phenomenon has direct relevance for the present discussion. I refer to a process demonstrated most dramatically and comprehensively in the experiments of Solomon Asch (1956), and known thereby as the "Asch phenomenon." In these experiments, the subject finds himself in a group of six or eight of his peers all of whom are asked to make comparative judgments of certain stimuli presented to them, for example, identifying the longer of two lines. At first the task seems simple enough; the subject hears others make their judgments and then makes his own. In the beginning he is usually in agreement, but then gradually he notices that more and more often his judgments differ from those of the rest of the group. Actually, the experiment is rigged. All the other group members have been instructed to give false responses on a predetermined schedule. In any event, the effect on our subject is dramatic. At first he is puzzled, then upset. Soon he begins to have serious doubts about his own judgment, and in an appreciable number of cases, he begins to "see" the stimuli as they are described by his fellows.

What I am suggesting, of course, is that the Asch phenomenon operates even more forcefully outside the laboratory where the game of social perception is being played for keeps. *Specifically, I am proposing that the mechanisms here described contributed substantially to producing and maintaining serious distortions in the reciprocal images of the Soviet Union and the United States.*

My suggestion springs from more than abstract theoretical inference. I call attention to the possible operation of the Asch phenomenon in the Soviet-American context for a very concrete reason: I had the distressing experience of being its victim. While in the Soviet Union I deliberately sought to minimize association with other Westerners and to spend as much time as I could with Soviet citizens. This was not easy to do. It was no pleasant experience to hear one's own country severely criticized and to be constantly out-debated in the bargain. I looked forward to the next chance meeting with a fellow Westerner so that I could get much-needed moral support and enjoy an evening's invective at the expense of Intourist and the "worker's paradise." But though I occasionally yielded to temptation, for the most part I kept true to my resolve and spent many hours in a completely Soviet environment. It was difficult, but interesting. I liked many of the people I met. Some of them apparently liked me. Though mistaken, they were obviously sincere. They wanted me to agree with them. The days went on, and strange things began to happen. I remember picking up a Soviet newspaper which featured an account of American activities in the Near East. "Oh, what are they doing now!" I asked myself, and stopped short; for I had thought in terms of "they," and it was my own country. Or I would become aware that I had been nodding to the points being made by my Soviet companion where before I had always taken issue. In short, when all around me saw the world in one way, I too found myself wanting to believe and belong.

And once I crossed the Soviet border on my way home, the process began to reverse itself. The more I talked with fellow Westerners, especially fellow Americans, the more I began to doubt the validity of my original impressions. "What would you expect them to say to an American?" my friends would ask. "How do you know that the person talking to you was not a trained agitator?" "Did you ever catch sight of them following you?" I never did. Perhaps I was naive. But, then, recently I reread a letter written to a friend during the last week of my stay. "I feel it is important," it begins, "to try to write to you in detail while I am still in it, for just as I could never have conceived of what I am now experiencing, so, I suspect, it will seem unreal and intangible once I am back in the West." The rest of the letter, and others I kept, contain the record of the experiences reported in this account.

In sum, I take my stand on the view that there *is* a mirror image in Soviet and American perceptions of each other and that this image represents serious distortions by *both* parties of realities on either side.

Bronfenbrenner's social-psychological analysis of Soviet-American interactions is postulated on the conviction that beliefs and attitudinal predispositions are central to understanding that interaction; implicitly, other factors impinging on the interaction process are "held constant" or ignored, such as the national circumstances the two countries found themselves in at the beginning of their rivalry and the strategic alignment systems operative in the world that influenced the way they acted toward one another. Moreover, the contribution that ideological incompatibilities made to the resultant tension is minimized in his interpretation. Nevertheless, the analysis is a lucid and perceptive account of one instance of interaction between states.

This article is essentially descriptive in emphasis, for its analysis is concerned primarily with a portrayal of the images the two societies held of each other. On this level, it is most difficult to assess the manner in which the descriptions of national images were constructed. A principal problem in the analysis is the observational procedure employed: We are not certain precisely whose images are being described, nor do we know the evaluative criteria that were employed in ascertaining the societies' beliefs. This is a problem inherent in all efforts to describe the attitudes of groups or collectivities such as nation-states, since, without rigorous sampling procedures and survey instruments, we have no way of judging whether the profile is representative of the opinions of the groups' members. Nevertheless, Bronfenbrenner's descriptions have considerable "face validity," in the sense that they possess a certain intuitive appeal. The descriptions must, however, be regarded as tentative in the absence of supporting evidence.

In another respect, Bronfenbrenner's diagnosis is explanatory, because his description of the images that the countries maintained toward each other is used to account for the subsequent behavior between them. Although he does not press the causal inferences very far, the author does explain interaction by identifying the attitudinal sources or causes of the hostility.

Explicitly explanatory analyses of international interactions are abundant in the scholarly literature. Perhaps the majority of these attempt to explain the cause of interstate antagonism and competition, although a variety of studies exist that attempt to explain why states interact the way they do in general. What follows is an example of a study that uses empirical data to test a set of theoretical propositions about competitive bargaining interactions. "The Calculus of Deterrence," by Bruce M. Russett, investigates the dynamics of one aspect of international interaction—deterrence, or the efforts of one actor to prevent another actor from doing something. One of the most prolific writers in the field of international relations, Russett has long been a persistent advocate of scientific techniques of investigation for international relations research. As you read his article, note particularly the methods of observation and analysis he employs to probe a phenomenon that is very difficult to research.

THE CALCULUS OF DETERRENCE

Bruce M. Russett

A COMPARATIVE STUDY OF DETERRENCE

A persistent problem for American political and military planners has been the question of how to defend "third areas." How can a major power make credible an intent to defend a smaller ally from attack by another major power? Simply making an explicit promise to defend an ally, whether that promise is embodied in a formal treaty or merely in a unilateral declaration, is not sufficient. There have been too many instances when "solemn oaths" were forgotten in the moment of crisis. On the other hand, more than once a major power has taken up arms to defend a nation with whom it had ties appreciably less binding than a formal commitment.

Some analysts like Herman Kahn maintain that the determining factor is the nature of the overall strategic balance. To make credible a promise to defend third areas the defender must have overall strategic superiority; that is, he must be able to strike the homeland of the attacker without sustaining unacceptable damage to himself in return (Kahn, 1960). This analysis implies, of course, a strategy which threatens to retaliate, even for a local attack, directly on the home territory of the major power antagonist. Advocates of a strategy of limited warfare retort that, in the absence of clear strategic superiority, the capacity to wage local war effectively may deter attack.

Other writers, notably Thomas C. Schelling, have suggested that the credibility of one's threat can be considerably enhanced by unilateral actions which would increase the defender's loss if he failed to keep his promise (Schelling, 1960). One of the best examples is Chiang Kai-shek's decision in 1958 to station nearly half his troops on Quemoy and Matsu. While the islands were of questionable intrinsic importance, the presence of so much of his army there made it virtually impossible for Chiang, or his American ally, to abandon the islands under fire.

All of these explanations tend to stress principally the military elements in what is a highly complex political situation. There are, however, numerous nonmilitary ways in which one can strengthen one's commitment to a particular area. A government can make it a matter of prestige with its electorate. A nation might even deliberately increase its economic dependence upon supplies from a certain area, the better to enhance the

Bruce M. Russett, "The Calculus of Deterrence," *Journal of Conflict Resolution* 7 (1963): 97-109. Copyright, 1963, by the University of Michigan. Reprinted by permission of the author and publisher.

This article is part of the research of the Yale Political Data Program. The author is grateful to Paul Y. Hammond for comments on an earlier draft.

Russett is a professor of political science at Yale University.

credibility of a promise to defend it. W. W. Kaufmann's classic piece identified the elements of credibility as a power's capabilities, the costs it could inflict in using those capabilities, and its intentions as perceived by the enemy. In evaluating the defender's intentions a prospective attacker will look at his past actions, his current pronouncements, and the state of his public opinion (Kaufmann, 1956, pp. 12-38).

Kaufmann's formulation is better than simpler ones that stress military factors almost exclusively, but it needs to be expanded and made more detailed. One must particularly examine the potential costs to the defending power if he does not honor his commitments. In addition, propositions about factors which determine the credibility of a given threat need to be tested systematically on a comparative basis. On a number of occasions, for example, an aggressor has ignored the threats of a major power "defender" to go to war to protect a small nation "pawn" even though the defender held both strategic superiority and the ability to fight a local war successfully. Hitler's annexation of Austria in 1938 is just this kind of case, and one where the aggressor was correct, moreover.

In this paper we shall examine all the cases during the last three decades where a major power "attacker" overtly threatened a pawn with military force, and where the defender either had given, prior to the crisis, some indication of an intent to protect the pawn or made a commitment in time to prevent the threatened attack.[1] A threat may be believed or disbelieved; it may be a bluff, or it may be sincere. Often the defender himself may not be sure of his reaction until the crisis actually occurs. We shall explore the question of what makes a threat credible by asking which threats in the past have been believed and which disregarded. Successful deterrence is defined as an instance when an attack on the pawn is prevented or repulsed without conflict between the attacking forces and regular combat units of the major power "defender." ("Regular combat units" are defined so as not to include the strictly limited participation of a few military advisers.) With this formulation we must ignore what are perhaps the most successful instances of all—where the attacker is dissuaded from making any overt threat whatever against the pawn. But these cases must be left aside both because they are too numerous to be treated in detail and because it would be too difficult to distinguish the elements in most cases. Who, for example, really was the "attacker"? Was he dissuaded because of any action by the defender, or simply by indifference? Such questions would lead to too much speculation at the expense of the careful analysis of each case in detail.

Deterrence fails when the attacker decides that the defender's threat is not likely to be fulfilled. In this sense it is equally a failure whether the defender really does intend to fight but is unable to communicate that intention to the attacker, or whether he is merely bluffing. Later we shall ask, from the viewpoint of the attacker, which threats ought to be taken seriously. At this stage we shall simply examine past cases of attempted deterrence to discover what elements are usually associated with a threat that is believed (or at least not disbelieved with enough confidence for the attacker to act on his disbelief) and therefore what steps a defender might take to make his threats more credible to his opponent. Table 1 lists the cases for consideration.[2]

These cases are not, of course, comparable in every respect. Particularly in the instances of successful deterrence the causes are complex and not easily ascertainable. Nevertheless, a systematic comparison, undertaken cautiously, can provide certain insights that would escape an emphasis on the historical uniqueness of each case.

Deterrence in Recent Decades

First, we may dismiss as erroneous some frequent contentions about the credibility of deterrence. It is often said that a major power will fight only to protect an "important" position, and not to defend some area of relatively insignificant size or population. As we shall see below, this is in a nearly tautological sense true—if, by "important," we include the enmeshment of the defender's prestige with the fate of the pawn, the symbolic importance the pawn may take on in the eyes of other allies, and particular strategic or political values attached to the pawn. But if one means important in terms of any objectively measurable factor like relative population or Gross National Product, it is not true.

As Table 2 shows, in all of our cases of successful deterrence—Iran, Turkey, Berlin, Egypt, Quemoy-Matsu, and Cuba—the pawn's population was well under 15 per cent, and his G.N.P. less than 5 per cent of that of the principal defender.[3] (Britain was not Iran's chief protector.) Yet in five of the eleven cases where the attacker was not dissuaded the territory in question represented over 20 per cent of the defender's population (Ethiopia, Czechoslovakia in the Sudeten crisis and again in 1939, Poland, and Rumania). Poland in 1939 constituted the largest prize of all, yet Hitler may not have been convinced that Britain and France would go to war to save it. Nor can one discover any special strategic or industrial importance of the pawn only in cases of success. Austria and both Czechoslovakian cases met these criteria but were nevertheless overrun, and the United States did not expect Communist China to fight for North Korea, despite its obvious strategic significance.

Clearly too, it is not enough simply for the defender to make a formal promise to protect the pawn. Only in one case of success was there what could be described as a clear and unambiguous commitment prior to the actual crisis (Berlin). In the others the commitment was either ambiguous (Iran, Cuba, Quemoy-Matsu) or not made until the crisis was well under way (Turkey, Egypt). The United States' principal precrisis commitment to Iran was the Big Three communique from Teheran in 1943 (written chiefly by the American delegation) guaranteeing Iranian "independence, sovereignty, and territorial integrity."[4] Britain was allied with Iran, but the Russians recognized that any effective resistance to their plans would have to come from the United States rather than from an exhausted Britain. In July 1960 Khrushchev warned that the Soviet Union would retaliate with missiles if the United States attacked Cuba, but this was later

TABLE 1

Seventeen Cases—1935-1961

Pawn	Year	Attacker(s)	Defender(s)
Success			
Iran	1946	Soviet Union	United States
			Great Britain—Secondary
Turkey	1947	Soviet Union	United States
Berlin	1948	Soviet Union	United States
			Great Britain } Secondary
			France
Egypt	1956	Great Britain	Soviet Union[a]
		France	
Quemoy-Matsu	1954-55	Communist China	United States
	1958		
Cuba	1961	United States	Soviet Union
		(support of rebels)	
Failure—Pawn Lost			
Ethiopia	1935	Italy	Great Britain
			France
Austria	1938	Germany	Great Britain
			France
			Italy
Czechoslovakia	1938	Germany	Great Britain
			France
Albania	1939	Italy	Great Britain
Czechoslovakia	1939	Germany	Great Britain
			France
Rumania	1940	Soviet Union	Great Britain
Guatemala	1954	United States	Soviet Union
		(support of Rebels)	
Hungary	1956	Soviet Union	United States
Failure—War Not Avoided			
Poland[b]	1939	Germany	Great Britain
			France
South Korea	1950	North Korea (supported	United States
		by China & Soviet Union)	
North Korea	1950	United States	Communist China

[a] Despite its efforts to restrain the attackers, the United States was not a "defender" in the Suez affair. It neither supplied arms to the Egyptians before the crisis nor gave any indication that it would employ military force against Britain and France. In fact, the United States government explicitly ruled out the use of military coercion. See **New York Times,** November 7, 1956.

[b] Possibly the Polish case is not really a failure at all, for Hitler may have expected Britain and France to fight but was nevertheless prepared to take the consequences. A. J. P. Taylor presents an extreme version of the argument that Hitler expected Poland and/or Britain and France to give in (Taylor, 1961).

TABLE 2

Size (Population and Gross National Product) of Pawn in Relation to Defender(s)

Pawn	Defender(s)	Pawn's Population as per cent of Defender's Population	Pawn's G.N.P. as per cent of Defender's G.N.P.
Success			
Iran	United States	12	a
	Great Britain	37	4
Turkey	United States	13	1.7
Berlin	United States	1.5	a
	Great Britain	4	3
	France	5	3
Egypt	Soviet Union	12	2
Quemoy-Matsu	United States	a	a
Cuba	Soviet Union	3	1.5
Failure—Pawn Lost			
Ethiopia	Great Britain	28	1.8
	France	31	2
Austria	Great Britain	14	7
	France	16	8
	Italy	16	17
Czechoslovakia (1938)	Great Britain	30	14
	France	34	16
Albania	Great Britain	2	a
Czechoslovakia (1939)	Great Britain	23	11
	France	26	12
Rumania	United Kingdom	33	11
Guatemala	Soviet Union	1.6	a
Hungary	United States	6	1.0
Failure—War Not Avoided			
Poland	Great Britain	73	25
	France	82	29
South Korean	United States	14	a
North Korea	Communist China	2	3

a Less than 1 per cent

Sources: Population—United Nations (United Nations, 1949, pp. 98-105; United Nations, 1962, pp. 126-37). G.N.P.—Norton Ginsburg (Ginsburg, 1962, p. 16). G.N.P. data are approximate and sometimes estimated.

qualified as being "merely symbolic" and the precise content of Soviet retaliation was left undefined. Neither Congress nor the President has ever stated the exact circumstances under which our formal guarantees of Taiwan would apply to the offshore islands.

Yet in at least six cases an attacker has chosen to ignore an explicit and publicly acknowledged commitment binding the defender to protect the pawn. Britain, France, and Italy were committed by treaty to Austria,

France by treaty to Czechoslovakia in 1938, France by treaty and Britain by executive agreement to Czechoslovakia in 1939, Britain by executive agreement to Rumania, Britain, and France by treaty with Poland, and China by public declaration to North Korea. In three others there was at least an ambiguous commitment on the "defender's" part that might have been more rigorously interpreted. By a treaty of 1906 Britain, France, and Italy pledged themselves to "cooperate in maintaining the integrity of Ethiopia," Britain and Italy agreed in 1938 to "preserve the status quo in the Mediterranean" (including Albania), and in the 1950's American officials made references to "liberating" the satellites that were tragically overrated in Hungary. Of the failures, in fact, only Guatemala and possibly South Korea lacked any verbal indication of their "protectors'" willingness to fight. (In these instances, the defenders showed their concern principally by sending arms to the pawns before the attack.) The analyst who limited his examination to the present cases would be forced to conclude that a small nation was as safe without an explicit guarantee as with one. At least such guarantees existed in fewer instances of success (one in six) than in cases of failure (six of eleven).

We must also examine the proposition that deterrence is not credible unless the defender possesses over-all strategic superiority; unless he can inflict far more damage on an aggressor than he would suffer in return. It is true that the successful deterrence of attack is frequently associated with strategic superiority, but the Soviet Union had, at best, strategic equality with the United States at the time of the Bay of Pigs affair. While Russia was clearly superior to Britain and France when it threatened to attack them with rockets in 1956, it just as clearly did not have a credible first strike force for use against their American ally.[5]

Furthermore, in at least five cases where the attacker was not dissuaded, it nevertheless appears that the defender definitely had the ability to win any major conflict that might have developed (in the cases of Ethiopia, Austria, Czechoslovakia in 1938, Albania, and South Korea) and in two others (Czechoslovakia in 1939 and Hungary) the defender had at least a marginal advantage. (*Post hoc* analysis of the relevant documents indicates this superiority was more often perceived by the attacker, who went ahead and took the chance it would not be used, than by the defender. Hitler consistently recognized his opponents' strength and discounted their will to use it.)

Even less is it necessary for the defender to be able to win a limited local war. Of all the cases of success, only in Egypt could the defender plausibly claim even the ability to fight to a draw on the local level. In the other instances the defender could not hope to achieve equality without a long, sustained effort, and local superiority appeared out of reach. Yet in at least two failures the defenders, perhaps individually and certainly in coalition, had local superiority (Ethiopia and Austria) and in four others (Czechoslovakia in 1938, Albania, and the Korean cases) the defenders seemed to have been more or less on a par with their prospective antagonists.[6]

Yet if these two kinds of capabilities—local and strategic—are analyzed together, it would seem that a defender may not be clearly inferior in both and yet hope to restrain an attacker. Although the Soviet Union could not dream of meeting the United States in a limited war in the Caribbean, at least in 1961 its strategic nuclear capabilities seemed roughly on a par with America's.[7] And although Russia was inferior to Britain-France-United States on the strategic level, Soviet chances of at least matching their efforts in a local war over Egypt seemed a little brighter. Success requires at least apparent equality on one level or the other—this is hardly surprising—but when we remember that even superiority on both levels has often been associated with failure we have something more significant. *Superiority*, on either level, is not a condition of success. *Equality* on at least one level is a *necessary*, but by no means *sufficient*, condition. The traditionally conceived purely military factors do not alone make threats credible.

Nor, as has sometimes been suggested, does the kind of political system in question seem very important, though it does make some difference. Often, it is said, a dictatorial power can threaten much more convincingly than a democracy because the dictatorship can control its own mass media and present an apparently united front. Democracies, on the other hand, cannot easily suppress dissenting voices declaring that the pawn is "not worth the bones of a single grenadier." This argument must not be overstated—four of our successful cases of deterrence involved a democracy defending against a dictatorship. Yet in all of these cases the democracy possessed strategic superiority, whereas the other two successes, by a dictatorship, were at best under conditions of strategic equality for the defender. And in all but two (North Korea and Guatemala) of the eleven failures the defender was a democracy. Thus a totalitarian power's control over its citizens' expression of opinion may give it some advantage, if not a decisive one—particularly under conditions when the defender's strategic position is relatively weak.

INTERDEPENDENCE AND CREDIBILITY

With some of these hypotheses discarded we may now examine another line of argument, the credibility of deterrence depends upon the economic, political, and military interdependence of pawn and defender. Where visible ties of commerce, past or present political integration, or military cooperation exist, an attacker will be much more likely to bow before the defender's threats—or if he does not bow, he will very probably find himself at war with the defender.

Military Cooperation

In every instance of success the defender supported the pawn with military assistance in the form of arms and advisers. In one of these cases, of course (Berlin) the defenders actually had troops stationed on the pawn's territory. The military link with Iran was somewhat tenuous, for Teheran received no shipments of American military equipment until after the 1946 crisis was past. Yet an American military mission was stationed in the country at the time, and 30,000 American troops had been on Iranian soil until the end of 1945 (Kirk, 1952, p. 150). America had given a tangible, though modest, indication of her interest in Iran. But in only five of the eleven failures were there significant shipments of arms to the pawn. France extended large military credits to Poland, and the British gave a small credit ($20 million) to Rumania. The Americans and the Chinese sent both arms and advisers to their Korean protégés. The Soviets sent small arms to Guatemala but no advisers, and they did not give any explicit indication of an intent to intervene in any American move against the Guatemalan government. A French military mission was stationed in Prague before and during the two Czechoslovakian crises, but no substantial amount of French equipment was sent (in part because of the high quality of the Czechoslovakian armament industry). In none of the other failures was there any tangible military interdependence. Some degree of military cooperation may not always be sufficient for successful deterrence, but it is virtually essential.

Political Interdependence

This is a helpful if not essential condition. Four of the instances of successful deterrence include some kind of current or recent political tie in addition to any current alliance. Western troops were stationed in Berlin and the three Western powers participated in the government of the city by international agreement. America and Nationalist China had been allies in a recent war. Turkey became allied with the Big Three toward the end of World War II. Iran had been occupied by British troops until early 1946 and American troops until the end of 1945. In the case of failures only four of eleven pawns had any significant former tie with a defender. Britain and Rumania were allies in World War I, as were the U.S.S.R. and Guatemala in World War II. Obviously, neither of these ties was at all close. The other two, however, were marked by rather close ties. United States forces occupied South Korea after World War II, and the R.O.K. government was an American protégé. The Communist Chinese had close party and ideological ties with the North Korean regime, and not too many decades previously Korea had been under Chinese sovereignty.

Economic Interdependence

We shall work with a crude but simple and objective measure of economic interdependence. In 1954 all countries of the world, other than the United States, imported a total of $65 billion of goods, of which 16 per cent came from the United States. South Korea, however, took 35 per cent of its total imports from the United States, a figure well above the world average. This will be our measure: does the pawn take a larger than average proportion of its imports from the defender or, vice versa, does the defender take a larger than average proportion of its imports from the pawn? To repeat, this is a crude measure. It does not tell, for example, whether the defender is dependent upon the pawn for a supply of a crucial raw material. But there are few areas of vital economic significance in this sense—almost every commodity can be obtained from more than one country, though not always at the same price—and attention to over-all commercial ties gives a broad measure of a country's general economic stake in another.[8] In none of the cases where this test does not show general economic inter-dependence is there evidence that the defender relied heavily on the pawn for a particular product.

In five of the six cases of successful deterrence either the pawn took an abnormally high porportion of its imports from the defender or vice versa. In the remaining case, the Iranian economy was closely tied to Britain if not to the United States, but in only three of the eleven failures was there interdependence between pawn and defender. A higher than average proportion of Austria's trade was with Italy, though not with France and Britain, the other two parties bound by treaty to preserve her integrity. Both Korean regimes also traded heavily with their defenders. Economic interdependence may be virtually essential to successful deterrence.

DIVINING INTENTIONS

Briefly we may also examine the question from the viewpoint of the at-tacker. If the defender's threat is not challenged, one may never know whether it truly expresses an intention to fight or whether it is merely a bluff. Perhaps the defender himself would not know until the circumstances actually arose. But we can examine the eleven cases where deterrence was not sufficiently credible to prevent attack. Previously we asked what dif-ferentiated the instances when the attacker pressed on from those in which he restrained his ambitions. Now, what distinguishes the cases where the defender actually went to war from those where he did not?[9]

"Size," as defined earlier, again is not crucial. Poland, for which Britain and France went to war, was a very large prize but neither North nor South Korea represented a significant proportion of its defender's popu-lation or G.N.P. Of the eight instances where the defender's bluff was suc-cessfully called, four of the pawns (Ethiopia, Czechoslovakia on both oc-casions, and Rumania) represented over 20 per cent of the defender's population and four (Austria, Czechoslovakia both times, and Rumania) over 5 per cent of its G.N.P. Proportionately "large" pawns were more often the subject of "bluffs" than of serious intentions. Nor is there nec-essarily a formal, explicit commitment in cases which result in war. There were such commitments over Poland and North Korea, but South Korea is an obvious exception. And there was such a commitment in the case of half the "bluffs" (Austria, Czechoslovakia twice, and Rumania), and a vague, ambiguous one in three other cases (Ethiopia, Albania, Hungary).

The state of the military balance does not seem to have much effect either. In at least four "bluffs" (Ethiopia, Austria, Czechoslovakia in 1938, and Albania) the defenders were clearly superior *over-all* and in two other

cases (Czechoslovakia in 1939 and Hungary) they were at least marginally
so. Yey despite their bad military position Britain and France fought for
Poland in 1939. And although the Chinese made some bold "paper tiger"
talk they really could have had few illusions about their position should the
United States counter their move into North Korea with its full conventional and nuclear might. In no instance where a defender fought did he
have the ability to win a quick and relatively costless *local* victory. But in
the two cases where the defender probably did have this ability (Ethiopia
and Austria) he did not employ it. Neither does the defender's political
system appear to matter much. The Chinese fought to defend North Korea,
but dictatorships did nothing to protect Austria and Guatemala.

Yet bonds of interdependence—economic, political, and military—do
turn out to be highly relevant. In every case where the defender went to
war he had previously sent military advisers and arms to the pawn. Only
four of the eight "bluffs" were marked by either of these activities, and
none by a significant level of both. The two Koreas both had important
prior political ties to their eventual defenders, but only two of the instances of "bluff" (Rumania and Guatemala) were marked by even very
weak ties of previous alliance. The two Korean states also were closely tied
economically to their defenders, but of all the seven instances of bluffs, only
Italy-Austria show a bond of similar strength. Again it is the nature of the
defender-pawn relationship, rather than the attributes of either party
separately, that seem most telling in the event.

We must be perfectly clear about the nature of these ties. Certainly
no one but the most inveterate Marxist would assert that the United States
entered the Korean War to protect its investments and economic interests.
The United States went to war to protect a state with which it had become closely identified. It was rather heavily involved economically in
Korea, and its prestige as a government was deeply involved. It had occupied the territory and restored order after the Japanese collapse; it had
installed and supported an at least quasi-democratic government; and it
had trained, organized, and equipped the army. Not to defend this country in the face of overt attack would have been highly deterimental to
American prestige and to the confidence governments elsewhere had in
American support. Even though it had made no promises to defend Korea
(and even had said it would not defend it in a general East-West war) the
American government could not disengage itself from the fate of the Korean
peninsula. Despite the lack of American promises, the American "presence"
virtually guaranteed American protection.

MAKING DETERRENCE CREDIBLE

It is now apparent why deterrence does not depend in any simple way
merely upon the public declaration of a "solemn oath," nor merely on the
physical means to fight a war, either limited or general. A defender's decision whether to pursue a "firm" policy that risks war will depend upon his
calculation of the value and probability of various outcomes. If he is to be

firm the prospective gains from a successful policy of firmness must be greater, when weighted by the probability of success and discounted by the cost and probability of war, than the losses from retreat.[10] The attacker in turn will determine whether to press his attack in large part on his estimate of the defender's calculation. If he thinks the chances that the defender will fight are substantial he will attack only if the prospective gains from doing so are great.[11]

The physical means of combat available to both sides are far from irrelevant, for upon them depend the positions of each side should war occur. A defender's commitment is unlikely to be believed if his military situation is markedly inferior to his enemy's. Yet even clear superiority provides no guarantee that his antagonist will be dissuaded if the defender appears to have relatively little to lose from "appeasement." At the time of the Austrian crisis Neville Chamberlain could tell himself not only that appeasement was likely to succeed, but that prospective losses even from its possible failure were not overwhelming. In particular, he failed to consider the effects appeasement would have on Britain's other promises to defend small nations. By autumn 1939, however, it was clear that further appeasement would only encourage Hitler to continue to disregard British threats to fight, as British inaction over Austria in fact had done.

Under these circumstances the effectiveness of the defender's threat is heavily dependent on the tangible and intangible bonds between him and the pawn. If other factors are equal, an attacker will regard a military response by the defender as more probable the greater the number of military, political, and economic ties between pawn and defender. No aggressor is likely to measure these bonds, as commercial ties, in just the way we have sketched them here, but he is most unlikely to be insensitive to their existence.

Strengthening these bonds is, in effect a strategy of raising the credibility of deterrence by increasing the loss one would suffer by not fulfilling a pledge. It illustrates in part why the American promise to defend Western Europe, with nuclear weapons if necessary, is so credible even in the absence of overwhelming American strategic superiority. Western Europe is certainly extremely important because of its large, skilled population and industrial capacity. Yet it is particularly important to the United States because of the high degree of political and military integration that has taken place in the North Atlantic Area. The United States, in losing Western Europe to the Communists, would lose population and industry, and the credibility of its pledges elsewhere. To put the case another way, America has vowed to defend both Japan and France from external attack, and there is much that is convincing about both promises. But the latter promise is somewhat more credible than the former, even were one to assume that in terms of industrial capacity, resources, strategic significance, etc., both countries were of equal importance. The real, if not wholly tangible, ties of the United States with France make it so.[12]

Interdependence, of course, provides no guarantee that the defender's threat will be believed. There have been a few cases where an attacker chose to ignore a threat even when relatively close interdependence existed. But if one really does want to protect an area it is very hard to make that intention credible *without* bonds between defender and pawn. If the United States wishes to shield a country it will be wise to "show," and even to increase, its stake in that country's independence. Because the strength of international ties is to some degree controllable, certain policy choices, not immediately relevant to this problem, in fact take on special urgency. Implementation of the Trade Expansion Act, allowing the American government to eliminate tariffs on much of United States trade with Western Europe, will have more than an economic significance. By increasing America's apparent, and actual, economic dependence on Europe it will make more credible America's promise to defend it from attack.

The particular indices of economic, military and political integration employed here are less important in themselves than as indicators of a broader kind of political and cultural integration, of what K. W. Deutsch refers to as mutual sympathy and loyalties, "we-feeling," trust, and mutual consideration (Deutsch, 1954, pp. 33-64). These bonds of mutual identification both encourage and are encouraged by bonds of communication and attention. Mutual attention in the mass media, exchanges of persons (migrants, tourists, students, etc.), and commercial activities all make a contribution. Mutual contact in some of these areas, such as exchange of persons, tends to promote contacts of other sorts, and often produces mutual sympathies and concern for each other's welfare.[13] This process does not work unerringly, but it does work frequently nevertheless. And these mutual sympathies often are essential for the growth of a high level of commercial exchange, especially between economically developed nations rather than nations in an essentially colonial relationship with each other.[14]

In addition to the loss of prestige and of tangible assets, there is yet another way in which a defender may lose if he fails to honor his pledge. New Yorkers would sacrifice their own self-esteem if they fail to defend Californians from external attack; some of the same feeling applies, in lesser degree, to New Yorkers' attitudes toward Britishers. Though broad and intangible, this kind of relationship is nonetheless very real, and knowledge of it sometimes restrains an attacker.

Communication and attention both produce and are produced by, in a mutually reinforcing process, political and cultural integration. The appendix to this paper demonstrates the degree to which economic, military, and political interdependence are correlated. All this raises the "chicken and egg" kind of question as to which comes first. In such a "feedback" situation there is no simple answer; sometimes trade follows the flag, sometimes the flag follows trade (Russett, 1963, ch. 4). Yet these are also to some extent independent, and the correlation is hardly perfect. From the data available one cannot identify any single factor as essential to deterrence. But as more are present the stronger mutual interdependence becomes, and the greater is the attacker's risk in pressing onward.

NOTES

[1]These definitions are employed purely in an analytical sense with no intention of conveying moral content. The British-French "attack" in 1956, for instance, was certainly provoked to a large extent by the Egyptians themselves.

[2]Note that we have excluded instances of protracted guerrilla warfare. While preventing and defeating guerrilla war is a major problem, the differences from the matters considered here require that it be treated separately. (See a forthcoming paper by Morton H. Halperin of Harvard University for a comparative examination of these cases.) The current Berlin crisis was not included because, at the time of writing, it was still unresolved. Also excluded are those cases of aggression in the 1930's and 1940's where no particular power had given a previous indication of a readiness to defend the pawn. By "previous indication" we mean either at least an ambiguous official statement suggesting the use of military force, or the provision of military assistance in the form of arms or advisers. The League of Nations Covenant is not considered such an indication because, barring further commitments by a particular nation, it is impossible to identify any one defender or group of defenders. Data on a number of factors are presented, for all of the cases, in the appendix.

[3]On the other hand one might argue that they were not of sufficient potential value to the attacker for him to run even a relatively slight risk that the defender might actually fight. A complete formulation involving these factors would have to include both the value of the pawn to the attacker and his estimate of the probability that the defender would fight. See below.

[4]See George Kirk on the Iranian case (Kirk, 1952, p. 473).

[5]In both of these instances we must recognize that the "attacker's" failure to persevere to defeat of the pawn was probably due less to Soviet threats than to pressures from the "attacker's" own allies and world opinion.

[6]On the military situation prevailing in various crises before World War II see Winston Churchill (1948, pp. 177, 270-1, 287, 336-7).

[7]American intelligence reports were, however, far from unanimous. By the end of 1961 it was clear to those with good information that the Soviets' strategic forces were distinctly inferior to America's.

[8]In the cases of Berlin and Quemoy-Matsu we must rely on trade figures for a larger unit (West Germany and Taiwan). West Germany conducted an above-average proportion of her trade with the United States and France in this period, but her trade with Britain was below average. Yet as Allied resolve in the Berlin crisis clearly depended upon American initiative it seems correct to include Berlin in the class of economically interdependent pawns.

[9]Remember that we have been dealing only with those cases in which deterrence was visibly in danger of failing, and not with instances where it was fully successful, i.e., where the attacker was dissuaded from ever making a serious explicit threat. As noted earlier the latter cases are extremely difficult to identify; nevertheless it seems likely that analysis would show similar results to those above. American protection of Western Europe is an excellent example. The political, economic, and military interdependence of Europe and the United States is great enough to make America's threat highly credible (though perhaps not as credible as we might sometimes wish).

[10]Formally, the defender will pursue a firm policy only if, in his calculation:

$$V_f \cdot s + V_w \cdot (1-s) > V_r$$

where

V_f = the value of successful firmness (deterrence without war)
V_w = the value (usually negative) of the failure of firmness (war)
V_r = the value (usually negative) of retreat
s = the probability that firmness will be successful.

Daniel Ellsberg presents a related formulation (Ellsberg, 1960).

[11]Precisely, he will press the attack only if:

$$V_a \cdot s + V_w \cdot (1-s) > V_o$$

where

V_a = the value of a successful attack (no war)
V_w = the value (usually negative) of an attack which is countered (war)
V_o = the value of doing nothing in this instance (no attack, no war)
s = the probability of a successful attack.

[12]This point is further illustrated by the 1962 Cuban crisis. The American government took great pains to indicate that it was reacting to the threat of Soviet missiles on the island, and only demanded their removal, not the overthrow of the Castro regime. To have directly threatened the existence of a Communist government in which the Soviets had such a heavy military and economic investment would have carried a much greater risk of Soviet military retaliation.

[13]The theoretical and empirical literature on this point is voluminous and cannot be discussed in more detail here. I have presented elsewhere a general theoretical examination of these problems and their application to Anglo-American relations (Russett, 1963).

[14]Few markets are perfectly analogous to the model of perfect competition, as the products of two sellers are seldom identical, at least in the mind of the buyer. Customs, habits, traditions, and "myths" about the goods or the seller differentiate two seemingly identical products. A seller who speaks the language and understands the mores of his customers has a great advantage over one who does not. Past habits can affect current prices through credit terms. Goods coming across a previously established trade route can be shipped more cheaply than those across one which has not yet developed much traffic.

REFERENCES

Churchill, Winston S. *The Second World War*, I, *The Gathering Storm*. Boston: Houghton, 1948.

Deutsch, Karl W. *Political Community at the International Level*. Garden City, N.Y.: Doubleday, 1954.

Ellsberg, Daniel. *The Crude Analysis of Strategic Choice*, RAND Monograph P-2183. Santa Monica, Calif.: RAND Corporation, 1960.

Ginsburg, Norton. *Atlas of Economic Development*. Chicago: University of Chicago Press, 1962.

Kahn, Herman. *On Thermonuclear War*. Princeton, N.J.: Princeton University Press, 1960.

Kaufmann, W. W. (ed.). *Military Policy and National Security*. Princeton, N.J.: Princeton University Press, 1956.

Kirk, George. *The Middle East in the War: Royal Institute of International Affairs Survey of International Affairs, 1939-46*. New York: Oxford University Press, 1952.

Russett, Bruce M. *Community and Contention: Britain and America in the Twentieth Century*. Cambridge, Mass.: Mass. Institute of Technology Press, 1963.

Schelling, Thomas C. *The Strategy of Conflict*. Cambridge, Mass.: Harvard University Press, 1960.

Taylor, A. J. P. *The Origins of the Second World War*. New York: Atheneum, 1962.

United Nations. *Demographic Yearbook, 1948*. New York: United Nations, 1949.

———. *Demographic Yearbook, 1961*, New York: United Nations, 1962.

APPENDIX:
Presence or Absence of Various Factors Alleged to Make
Deterrent Threats Credible

Column groups: **Attacker Holds Back** (Iran, Turkey, Berlin, Egypt, Quemoy-Matsu, Cuba) — **Attacker Presses On**: *Defender Does Not Fight* (Ethiopia, Austria, Czechoslovakia (1938), Albania, Czechoslovakia (1939), Rumania, Guatemala, Hungary) and *Defender Fights* (Poland, South Korea, North Korea).

	Iran	Turkey	Berlin	Egypt	Quemoy-Matsu	Cuba	Ethiopia	Austria	Czechoslovakia (1938)	Albania	Czechoslovakia (1939)	Rumania	Guatemala	Hungary	Poland	South Korea	North Korea
Pawn 20% + of defender's population	✻						x	x			x	x			x		
Pawn 5% + of defender's G.N.P.								x	x		x	x			x		
Formal commitment prior to crisis	?		x		?	?	?	x	x		?	x	x	?	x	x	
Defender has strategic superiority	x	x	x	x			x	x	x	x	?			?	x		
Defender has local superiority								x	x	?	?					?	?
Defender is dictatorship					x	x	✻					x					x
Pawn-defender military cooperation	x	x	x	x	x	x		x			x	x	x		x	x	x
Pawn-defender political interdependence	x	x	x		x							x	x		x	x	
Pawn-defender economic interdependence ✻	x	x	x	x	x		✻								x	x	

Key: x Factor present
    ? Ambiguous or doubtful
    ✻ Factor present for one defender

Deterrence is essentially a bargaining maneuver in which one state attempts to influence another state to refrain from doing something that the first state does not want done. However, identification of the various techniques by which one state might deter another and assessment of the efficacy and utility of those techniques have not been easy intellectual tasks. They require the formulation of generalizations about deterrence that are valid across time and place. This is precisely what Russett has attempted to do in his comparative cross-national study of deterrence.

Note how Russett draws upon existing literature for theoretical hypotheses about deterrence as a bargaining strategy. He thus uses others' speculations and theorizing as a source of explanations that may be put to empirical tests. His task, then, is to subject theory to data to see whether they are confirmed or discomfirmed by the evidence.

Data are generated by precise and systematic procedures of observation. The author has selected his cases or instances of deterrence by clearly specified criteria. One may object to the criteria, but at least the reader has a basis for knowing the reasons why the cases were selected for study.

Note also how the various hypotheses are tested. Russett has first defined the concepts contained in the propositions under investigation, so that what he means by "successful" or "unsuccessful" deterrence is explicit. This process of definition has enabled the author to make then an estimate about the validity of the various propositions under consideration. The result is a tentative but penetrating analysis that generates many provocative insights into deterrence as an international bargaining process.

The next reading, like the one before it, is explanatory in emphasis. It, too, assess the causes for observed interaction processes. But unlike the Russett cross-national comparative investigation of the determinants of a general type of behavior—deterrence—the explanations provided in the following study are of conflict interactions occurring between a discrete set of actors in a particular confrontation. Written by Edward E. Azar, this case study attempts to delineate some of the crucial factors that promote and diminish conflict between antagonistic states. In reading this selection, take special note of the rigorous manner in which the author defines his concepts and specifies his observational base in terms of identifiable overt conduct. That data base is from an extensive event/ interaction data collection (COPDAB, or Conflict and Peace Data Bank). which is one of many data sets emerging from the events data research movement. Azar has been a pioneer in the generation and analysis of event/interaction data for the quantitative study of international relations.

CONFLICT ESCALATION AND CONFLICT REDUCTION IN AN INTERNATIONAL CRISIS: SUEZ, 1956

Edward E. Azar*

INTRODUCTION

Conflict research has already advanced some very useful conceptual and empirical discoveries concerning the structure and process of international conflict escalation. Some of the more basic findings suggest that when two parties involve themselves in a conflict situation, they tend to escalate the intensity, scope, and frequency of their negative signals; they tend to

---

* My thanks go to the Department of Political Science, the Institute for Research in Social Science, and the University Research Council at the University of North Carolina at Chapel Hill for their support—and to Thomas Goins, David Pansius, Louise Richey, Thomas Sloan, and Robert Taylor for their assistance. I am indebted to Joseph Ben-Dak, Barry Blechman, Davis Bobrow, Nazli Choucri, Paul Conn, Robert North, and J. David Singer for their criticisms and helpful comments. I am especially grateful to Clinton Fink for his invaluable guidance which helped me write this paper.

Edward E. Azar, "Conflict Escalation and Conflict Reducation in an International Crisis: Suez, 1956," *The Journal of Conflict Resolution,* XVI, 2 (June 1972), pp. 183–201. Reprinted by permission of the author and publisher.

Azar is a professor in the Department of Political Science at the University of North Carolina.

make more visible or even possibly compound their areas of incompatibility; they tend to raise the intensity of their mutual images; and they tend to engage in or increase the rate of a potentially destructive arms race (Boulding, 1961; North, 1963; Richardson, 1960; Singer, 1962; Smoker, 1966; Wright, 1965).

Conflict reduction on the other hand is less well understood. However there is enough empirical and theoretical work on which further research may be based. For example we know that motivating an opponent to clarify his signals extremely well may produce favorable responses, reduce the chances of further negative signals, and probably induce conflict reduction (Quester, 1970). There is some evidence that the pressure of national and international opinion on decision-makers can induce a lowering of hostile activities (Randle, 1970; Rothstein, 1970). Carroll's (1968) work on how wars end, Timasheff's (1965) work on the transition from war to peace and from revolution to order, Osgood's (1962) work on GRIT, and the variety of gaming research on conditions for producing higher proportions of cooperative responses provide us with useful concepts, ideas, and findings about the movement from high levels of conflict to reduction of hostilities. O'Connor's (1969) study of modern war suggests that conflict reduction resides in the parties' ability to contain their hostilities through a willful effort to combat the pathological and other forces which maintain a hostile situation.

The present study aims to contribute to the understanding of conflict reduction in international crises. It focuses on the level and type of interaction manifested by the signals exchange between conflicting parties and the role that these signals play in generating or deterring future hostilities. Some general assumptions and definitions are introduced, and descriptive hypotheses concerning escalation and de-escalation in international crises are presented. These hypotheses are then tested using events data from the Suez Crisis of 1956. Finally a suggested set of correlates and determinants of conflict reduction are posited and discussed.

INTER-NATION INTERACTION: ASSUMPTIONS AND DEFINITIONS

International actors tend to express their policies toward one another in the form of verbal and/or physical *signals*. An international signal is an inter-nation *event* which has the following characteristics: On a specific *date* a specific *actor* directs an activity toward a specific *target* regarding an *issue* of mutual concern. The date is the day on which the signal is reported by a reputable and publicly available source; actors and targets are nations, organizations, or movements which have attained international or regional significance; activities are verbal or physical actions, reactions, and interactions; and issue-areas include the items about which actors and targets interact or signal one another (Azar, 1970). International signals are units of overt behavior which international actors receive, interpret, and act upon. They vary in frequency and content intensity and are scaled either implicitly or explicitly by an international actor in order to better assess his own behavior as well as that of his target.

The frequency and level of friendliness or hostility of inter-nation signals are partly dependent on the frequency and intensity of previously exchanged signals, since some have the capability of generating others. The entire sequence of antecedent and consequent signals therefore establishes a pattern which can be studied longitudinally. This is not to argue that one inter-nation signal strictly causes another but rather that certain signals tend to flow or occur simultaneously and that some nonzero level of interdependence exists between international signals. We do suggest however that the process of event-generation depends on the interaction situation itself as well as on the decisions made by the parties to the conflict and that a nation's decisions are affected not only by its responses to stimuli provided by the other nation, but also by the signals which it or its own subsystems previously generated.

Over a period of time any two nations establish between them an interaction range which they perceive as "normal." This *normal relations range* (NRR) is an interaction range (on a scale from very friendly to very hostile) which tends to incorporate most of the signals exchanged between that pair and is bound by two critical thresholds—an *upper and a lower threshold*. The upper critical threshold is that level of hostility above which signals exhibited by either member of the interacting dyad are regarded as unacceptable to the other. Interaction above the present upper critical threshold (or present upper tolerable limit) for more than a very short time implies that a crisis situation has set in. The lower critical threshold on the other hand is that level of friendliness beyond which signals between the members imply that some integrative shift in their relations—the inverse of a crisis—has occurred.

Changes in the level of a dyad's NRR may occur (albeit slowly) due to changes in each actors' domestic and international situation, attributes, or behavior. Although it would be useful to study the conditions under which these shifts occur, and the time it takes to bring them about, for the present we simplify our task by assuming that a dyad's NRR does not change significantly during a relatively short period of time, such as six months to one year.

Conflict escalation is the movement of a dyad to an interaction space above the upper critical threshold of its present NRR. Conflict reduction is the movement of that dyad to an interaction space below its immediate upper critical threshold. This space can be within its previous NRR or somewhere below it. Although it is very important to focus on how a dyad moves toward or even below its lower critical threshold (i.e., toward the more friendly or cooperative end of the scale), we do not explore that possibility here. This paper is concerned only with those factors which allow a pair of nations in a crisis to shift their interactions back below the upper critical threshold.

THE LITERATURE ON CORRELATES AND DETERMINANTS OF ESCALATION AND DE-ESCALATION

Motivation

Nations like other social organizations tend to define for themselves a preferred state-of-affairs which includes those situations they wish to attain as well as ones they wish to avoid (Miller *et al.*, 1960). These desired states-of-affairs or preferences are established by a nation's examination of its strategic situation vis-à-vis its international targets and can involve the following: (a) an inventory and rank-ordering of preferences; (b) an evaluation of the costs and chances of achieving or approximating such preferences; (c) an assessment of the type and level of behavior necessary to achieve or approximate these preferences; and (d) a modification or reranking of preferences (preference modulation). It may be difficult for an observer to discern these steps, because decision-makers do not usually make such a process public and because these are done incrementally. Also depending on a nation's capabilities and domestic and international difficulties, it is conceivable that some nations might follow an *ad hoc* approach in defining their strategic preferences.

A conflict situation between a pair of nations tends to arise from their pursuance of directly incompatible preferences, where the success of one would inflict a cost on the other (Schelling, 1960). Thus in their attempt to achieve their preferences nation-states tend to define the saliency of the issues and the costs they are willing to incur in order to achieve them. As their preference incompatibility increases, it is likely that these nations will intensify the volume and threat content of their signals in a manner which they feel will allow them to achieve or approximate their desired state-of-affairs (Pruitt, 1965).

Wright (1965) has argued that changes in the level of hostilities between nations are influenced by the saliency of the issues over which conflicts arise, and that rather than occurring by accident war is generally used as an instrument of policy. As hostile interactions escalate, parties tend to place higher values on certain issues and tend to marshal their domestic and international resources for the purpose of achieving the goals or preferences they associate with their salient issues. He found that conflicting nations tend to begin their hostile interactions by applying pressure short of military force to resolve their perceived inconsistencies. If however they fail to achieve their goals, they tend to intervene militarily or go to war to dictate a solution.

It is true however that if two nations find that their costs have been too high when compared with their gains or that there is no possible means of achieving their objectives, they are likely to (a) lower their aspiration level and/or (b) reorder their preferences. These choices are made not on the basis of a nation's own situation but on the basis of the information it has about its target's preference schedule, costs, and past and anticipated behavior. Thus if interacting nations perceive that their preferences or priorities have been achieved, it is probable that they will formulate new preferences and raise their level of expectations (see Timasheff, 1965, pp. 91–98).

Frequency and Intensity of Inter-Nation Hostile Signals

Symmetrical and asymmetrical signaling during conflict escalation and reduction. In a conflict situation interactions between a pair of nations tend to contain or imply some level of violence or hostility. Although some inter-nation signals may express a degree of cooperation, when two nations are locked into an escalatory spiral they tend to exhibit "selective perception," thus becoming more sensitive to the relatively hostile signals of their opponent than to the relatively cooperative ones. And the greater the sensitivity of a nation to threatening signals in some area, the more likely it is that that nation will perceive a signal in that area and will assess the signal as hostile. This may account for the inconsistency of a nation that perceives two equally hostile signals directed from two sources as significantly different in their hostility content. It is probable however that this would not hold true at the extremes of a continuum of hostile behavior. A very cooperative action would most likely be viewed correctly in most instances, and similarly a highly hostile action would probably be viewed as highly hostile. Although ambiguous signals may be exchanged between two conflicting nations, such ambiguity tends to disappear when two nations begin to interact outside the critical thresholds of their normal relations range (NRR).

In his conflict studies North (1967) has shown that when inter-nation hostilities reach crisis proportions (i.e., high levels of violent behavior), a tit-for-that phenomenon develops—thus producing an increase in the frequency and relative distribution of interactions. These studies show that as actors increase the exchange of hostile *verbal messages* toward one another, they are likely to exchange more hostile *physical messages* as well. Thus in terms of our model as nations begin to increase the rate of their verbal hostile signals, they are likely to move toward the upper critical threshold of their NRR. This escalatory process depends upon a nation's own strategic preferences and cost tolerance as well as its assessment of its opponent's signals toward that nation (Milburn, 1971; O'Connor, 1969; Timasheff, 1965).

Wright has described these inter-nation escalatory moves and countermoves as "mechanical" conflict behavior or a tit-for-tat pattern. Thus as a nation becomes threatened due to a sharp increase in the hostile signals received from its opponent, then that nation is likely to respond with similar acts. In other words nations that enter into a conflict situation are likely to escalate their hostile interactions symmetrically, and this symmetry manifests itself in terms of the frequency and level of hostility.

Does this symmetry in hostile interactions manifest itself during conflict reduction as well as it does during conflict escalation? There is limited evidence to suggest that inter-nation interactions during conflict reduction do not follow the tit-for-tat pattern (Azar, 1970, 1971a). On the other hand we feel that more knowledge about this phenomenon is necessary. For example does the asymmetrical pattern of signaling during conflict reduction hold for nations with a relatively hostile NRR as well as for those with a relatively friendly NRR? If yes, why? How do we explain this phenomenon in order to understand how conflict may be reduced? Although we will not be able to answer these questions with the 1956 Suez data alone, we hope to explore some explanatory hypotheses toward the end of this paper for the purpose of defining some worthwhile areas of investigation for students of conflict reduction.

The first descriptive hypothesis which emerges from the above discussion is that when two or more nations perceive themselves as parties to a conflict situation and when these parties begin exchanging hostile signals such that both nations begin to move toward or beyond the upper critical threshold of their NRR, *nations will exhibit a symmetrical signaling pattern during the escalatory phase of the conflict and a slightly asymmetrical pattern during the de-escalatory phase.*

The temporal distance between hostile signals in a conflict situation. McClelland (1961) has shown that as international actors escalate their hostile interactions to the point of crisis where they begin to exchange violent verbal and physical threats, the simple volume of their interactions increases substantially in comparison to their precrisis relations. From his study of East-West interactions Corson (1969) has found that since 1945 periods of high tension and threat tended to be characterized by an increase in the volume of conflict events.

Conversely Milburn (1971) has found a significant positive correlation between a nation's ability to seek a crisis settlement and that nation's capacity to delay hostile response to its target nation. Both McClelland and Corson have argued that noncrisis periods tended to be characterized by a reduction in the simple volume of interactions as compared to the crisis periods.

These studies suggest therefore that during escalation and de-escalation there is a high degree of association between volume and intensity of hostile signals. They imply that as the level of signaled hostility increases, the time interval between signals decreases (i.e., their frequency per unit of time increases), and that as the level of signaled hostility decreases, the time interval between signals increases. Thus as the conflict escalation spiral begins to develop, the length of time (temporal distance) intervening between hostile signals drops significantly, and as conflict reduction sets in, the temporal distance between hostile signal rises sharply.

In terms of our model, we posit another descriptive hypothesis, namely *as nations begin to move up toward (or above) the upper critical threshold of their NRR, the temporal distance between hostile signals decreases.* Conversely *as nations begin to move their interactions back toward (or below) the upper critical threshold of their NRR, the temporal distance between hostile signals increases.*

Shifts from escalation to reduction of signaled hostility between nation-states. Although conflicting nations can maintain hostile signaling for long periods (as in lengthy wars), we have enough evidence that there are forces which more frequently motivate them to move their interactions below the upper critical threshold of their NRR or even to begin to cooperate after having experienced a brief period of intense hostility. Some of these forces or conditions are (a) frustration or attainment of preferred situations or responses; (b) sharp increases in actual or perceived costs; or (c) significant changes in the domestic or international conditions (Carroll, 1969; Hermann, 1971; Milburn, 1971; O'Connor, 1969; and Timasheff, 1965). These do not exhaust all the possibilities and they may differ from one conflict situation to another. Although we will not formally test these explanatory hypotheses, we will *explore* them in order to get behind the signal-exchange data that we use to test the first two descriptive hypotheses.

METHOD

For the purpose of testing the above hypotheses we used 835 signals exchanged between Egypt and its opponents (Britain, France, Israel) from July 26, 1956 (the day Nasser nationalized the Suez Canal Company), through January 11, 1957 (about the time when all occupying forces had either withdrawn or were about to withdraw from Egyptian territory). These signal events were gathered from eleven publicly available and reputable sources which comprise part of the set of sources we employ at the Conflict and Peace Data Bank (COPDAB) at the University of North Carolina at Chapel Hill (see Azar, 1971b).

The Hostility-Friendliness Scale

At COPDAB we assume that events are measurable in terms of some scale and that every event contains some degree of "violence," "friendship," "hostility," etc. ranging from very low to very high. The intensity of the

TABLE 1

13 POINT SCALE OF MANIFEST INTER-NATION HOSTILITY–FRIENDLINESS*

Region II:
    13. Nation A engages in an all-out war against Nation B.
    12. Nations A and B engage in limited war activities.
    11. Nation A initiates subversion in Nation B.
    10. Nation A encounters domestic politicomilitary violence.
     9. Nation A increases its military capabilities.
     8. Nation A makes a protest directed against Nation B.
     7. Nation A experiences limited internal political difficulties.

Region I:
     6. Nations A and B communicate regarding issues of mutual concern.
     5. Nation A receives support for its internal and/or external policies.
     4. Nations A and B establish a friendship agreement among themselves.
     3. Nation A extends economic aid to Nation B.
     2. Nations A and B establish a regional organization among themselves.
     1. Nations A and B merge to form a nation-state.

*Region II comprises points 7 to 13 and describes the high violence or more hostile region of the scale. Region I comprises points 1 to 6 of the scale and describes the low violence or more friendly region.

violence contained in each of COPDAB's 100,000 events has been established by using a 13-point scale which ranges from very friendly (point 1 on the scale) to very hostile (point 13).

In Table 1 we reproduce the thirteen marker-points of our scale, which was devised by conducting a battery of ranking tests and through the use of the paired comparison technique as described by Torgerson (1958). The reliability and validity of both the coding and scaling procedures were evaluated and estimated through a series of several experimental investigations described in Azar (1970).

Establishing the Normal Relations Range

There are a number of ways to estimate the NRR of a pair of nations. The problem stems from the lack of universally acceptable criteria as to what nations will and will not tolerate or expect from one another. International allies for example and nations with a common cultural base tend to interact cooperatively and therefore establish for themselves an NRR toward the more cooperative side of the scale. On the other hand nations which have had incompatible preferences and a history of hostile relations tend to establish an NRR toward the more hostile end of the scale. Thus signals which would do very little to damage the relations between nations with a normally hostile NRR would probably precipitate a crisis for the normally cooperative nation-states.

We maintain that there are three ways for estimating the threshold of an NRR for any pair of nations:

(1) *Empirically*—by content, analyzing statements of key decision-makers as they express acceptable or tolerable limits within which their target nations can behave toward them without a need for a reassessment of the existing relations between them;

(2) *Historically*—by inventorying points preceding the present inter-nation crisis to determine the kind of event-mix which motivates each member of the dyad to engage in more conflictual or more friendly acts; and

(3) *Statistically*—by establishing reasonable normal distribution curves and continuous updating procedures.

In this paper we opted for the statistical approach and used different time parameters for computing the NRR than were used to test the hypotheses. We computed the relative distribution of international signals for each of the scale values for the months May–September 1956, and on the basis of these distributions we established the NRR for each dyad by employing an arbitrary criterion—the scale values which comprise the middle 85 per cent of all the signals exchanged between any pair of nations plus two scale points, one on each side of this range. A total of 320 events entered into these NRR computations, including 240 of the 835 events used for hypothesis testing.

We used data from these five months for the following reasons:

(1) From February–April 1956, Egypt and Israel were engaged in a very hostile interaction situation over the *fedayeen* and other outstanding problems, but they had moved back to their pre-February "normal" level beginning in May of that year. Thus in order not to bias the level of their NRR, we decided to begin in May and continue through September or one month before large scale military activity had set in over Suez. We felt that the period from May through September 1956 tended to portray more accurately that dyad's normal pattern of interactions.

(2) During these five months British-Egyptian relations included a variety of events ranging from British promises to give Egypt aid to build the Aswan Dam to the leveling of charges and countercharges over the nationalization of the Suez Canal Company. French-Egyptian relations vacillated between holding meetings to normalize relations and discuss outstanding issues to the leveling of charges and countercharges over Egyptian support to the Algerian Liberation Movement.

(3) By computing the relative distribution of events at various levels of hostility during noncrisis periods, one can (a) reduce the chances of contaminating the NRR computation with data from the crisis period, and (b) allow it to detect a crisis by the shifts of the distribution towards a higher percentage of events at the higher levels of hostility.

Testing the Hypotheses

The 835 events for the period July 26, 1956, to January 11, 1957, were coded, scaled, and grouped into subsets such as "Egypt's signals toward Israel," "Israel's signals toward Egypt," etc. In order to test the first hypothesis, concerning the symmetry and asymmetry of signaled hostilities, we decided to separate inter-nation hostile signals from non-hostile signals by using the scale value of each signal. Signals with values 7 to 13 were labeled "hostile" and grouped in 10-day intervals. We then computed a percentage score for each interval for each dyad based on that dyad's total number of signals exchanged during the entire 170-day period. Furthermore we decided to graph these results, visually inspect these time-series graphs, and address ourselves to the data. We felt that to compute correlations between hostile signals of A toward B and hostile signals of B toward A would be a correct statistical procedure but somewhat unsatisfactory for these events data. We were very sure that a high degree of correlation existed because of the nature of the time-series events data.

We grouped these data into 10-day intervals only as a matter of convenience. We wanted a reasonable spread of the data over time so we could detect shifts in the hostile signaling of our actors, and we found that 10-day intervals produced fewer empty cells than one-week intervals did and that they produced a longer spread ($n = 17$) than two-week intervals ($n = 12$). For the purposes of making inferences no interval width is necessarily superior to any other.

For testing the second hypothesis concerning the relationship between level of hostility and temporal distance between hostile events, we examined the frequencies of events at each scale value for three distinct periods: (a) the "precrisis" period from July 26, 1956, through October 29–30, 1956—the three-month period which preceded the actual military intervention of Israel, Britain, and France; (b) the "acute crisis" period from October 29–30, 1956, through November 7, 1956—the approximately one-week period of military intervention, ending when the British, French and to a large extent the Israelis accepted the U.N. ceasefire resolution; and (c) the period from November 8, 1956, through January 11, 1957 —the period when conflict reduction was achieved.

There may be those who would find it either more convenient or even more appropriate to establish a different set of time parameters for the Suez precrisis or crisis periods. However the above parameters appear very useful and satisfactory, given our notion of the normal relations range. As the following discussion will show, after October 29 Israeli-Egyptian hostile interactions had moved above the upper critical threshold of their NRR (i.e., above point 10 of the scale) and had maintained themselves in that region until the first part of November (roughly November 7 or 8, 1956). British-Egyptian and French-Egyptian hostile relations moved above their upper critical threshold (above 9) on October 31, 1956, and continued in that region until the end of the first week of November. While it is true that some subsequent interactions, such as Egyptian signals toward Britain and France, moved above the upper critical threshold, these were only sporadic signals and did not elicit hostile reactions from either Britain or France.

Finally for exploring hypotheses concerning the determinants of conflict reduction, we examined the events in relation to other evidence concerning the preferences, perceptions, and changing environments of the foreign policy decision-makers in these four countries.

RESULTS

Table 2 presents the distribution of events exchanged between Egypt and its three opponents from May through September 1956. As these results indicate, over 90 per cent of the Egyptian-British and Egyptian-French interactions during that period ranged between scale values 6 and 8 and 86 per cent of the Egyptian-Israel interactions ranged between 6 and 9. Therefore both the British-Egyptian and French-Egyptian NRRs were between 5 and 9 on the 13-point scale, and the Israeli-Egyptian NRR was from 5 to 10. Thus when French and British interactions with Egypt moved above 9 and when Israeli-Egyptian interactions moved above 10, these countries had shifted into a crisis situation. On the other hand when the Egyptian-British and French-Egyptian interactions moved to below 9 and when the Israeli-Egyptian interactions moved below 10, then for that time period conflict reduction had set in.

The first hypothesis states that hostile interaction during escalation will exhibit a symmetrical or tit-for-tat pattern, but that during deescalation

EDWARD E. AZAR

TABLE 2

PERCENT HOSTILE SIGNALS AT EACH SCALE VALUE FOR THE PERIOD MAY–SEPTEMBER 1956*

Scale value	Egypt toward and from Britain (n = 146)	Egypt toward and from France (n = 69)	Egypt toward and from Israel (n = 105)
13	0	0	0
12	0	0	0
11	0	0	8
10	0	0	2
9	2	0	8
8	53	48	48
7	0	0	5
6	40	43	25
5	3	1	0
4	2	7	4
3	0	0	0
2	0	0	0
1	0	0	0

*Percentage figures are rounded off.

it will exhibit a slightly asymmetrical pattern. The relevant data are shown in Table 3, which contains a summary of the distribution of the hostile scores for each 10-day interval for each dyad. These data are represented graphically in Figures 1–3.

The Suez conflict appears to be a very good case for the symmetrical exchange of hostile signals hypotheses. Our data show that from July 26 through November 7, 1956 (i.e., the escalation period), Egyptian-

TABLE 3

HOSTILE SIGNALS OF NATION DYADS PER 10-DAY INTERVALS AS A PERCENT OF TOTAL SIGNALS OF DYADS FROM JULY 26, 1956, THROUGH JANUARY 11, 1957*

Time periods	Britain toward Egypt	Egypt toward Britain	France toward Egypt	Egypt toward France	Israel toward Egypt	Egypt toward Israel
July 26, 1956–August 4	7.69	5.07	10.40	4.06	1.12	3.66
August 5–August 14	4.73	3.55	1.16	0.81	1.12	0.00
August 15–August 24	0.00	2.03	0.00	3.25	2.80	4.88
August 25–Sept. 3	2.95	4.06	0.00	1.62	3.52	6.10
Sept. 4–Sept. 13	3.55	4.06	5.81	1.62	1.68	2.44
Sept. 14–Sept. 23	0.59	2.03	0.00	2.91	1.12	2.44
Sept. 24–Oct. 3	0.00	0.51	0.00	0.00	0.00	1.22
Oct. 4–Oct. 13	1.18	1.52	0.00	0.81	1.12	1.22
Oct. 14–Oct. 23	0.00	1.02	0.00	0.81	3.93	1.22
Oct. 24–Nov. 2	8.28	6.09	11.62	10.50	17.97	18.30
Nov. 3–Nov. 12	14.79	10.66	16.27	12.19	12.35	3.66
Nov. 13–Nov. 22	4.73	5.58	2.32	8.13	8.98	8.54
Nov. 23–Dec. 2	4.73	3.05	3.48	9.06	5.05	7.32
Dec. 3–Dec. 12	5.33	3.05	1.16	1.62	1.68	0.00
Dec. 13–Dec. 22	2.96	3.05	2.32	4.87	2.24	4.88
Dec. 23, 1956–Jan. 1, 1957	0.59	1.52	0.00	0.00	3.52	2.44
Jan. 2–Jan. 11	0.59	2.53	0.00	0.00	0.00	1.22
Total percent hostile signals	62.70	59.38	52.20	57.30	68.20	69.54
Total signals for dyad	169	197	86	123	178	82

*Percent of hostile signals = total hostile signals for the dyad per 10-day interval divided by total signals for the dyad in 170 days multiplied by 100.

British, Egyptian-French, and Egyptian-Israeli behavior tended to exhibit a tit-fot-tat pattern. The data show that after a series of verbal threats, accusations, and counteraccusations, and at times small border incidents. Israeli-Egyptian interactions moved above the upper critical threshold of their NRR on October 29, 1956. This was followed by British-Egyptian and French-Egyptian interactions on October 31, 1956. Thus by the end of October the four nations were in a crisis situation with plans to increase the scope and intensity of their hostile signals. The data show that up to November 7, 1956, all three dyads behaved similarly, giving hostile responses for hostile stimuli.

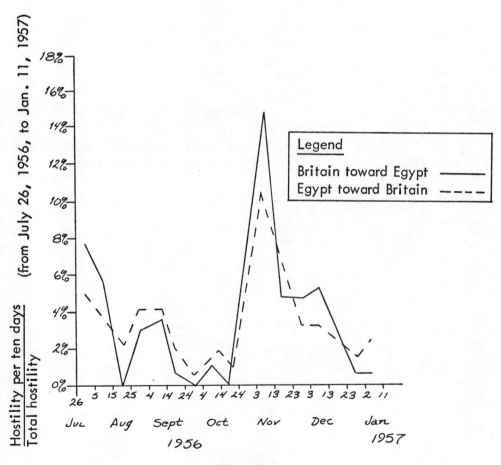

FIGURE 1

Hostile signals per 10-day period between Britain and Egypt as a percentage of their total signals from July 26, 1956, through January 11, 1957

After November 8, 1956 (the approximate date of the parties' acceptance of the U.N. ceasefire resolution), British-Egyptian signals maintained the same pattern exhibited during escalation, but the French-Egyptian and Israeli-Egyptian interactions exhibited a slightly dissimilar stimulus-response pattern. For example during the first days of the conflict Egypt reduced its physical hostile signals towards Israel by withdrawing its forces from Sinai in the face of the better trained and tougher Israeli armed forces, but Egypt continued its verbal attack against Israel and encouraged some unsuccessful *fedayeen* activities against Israel from the surrounding Arab areas of Jordan, Syria, and Lebanon. Also Egypt continued its defensive actions against Britain and France, who by the first week of November had destroyed one major portion of

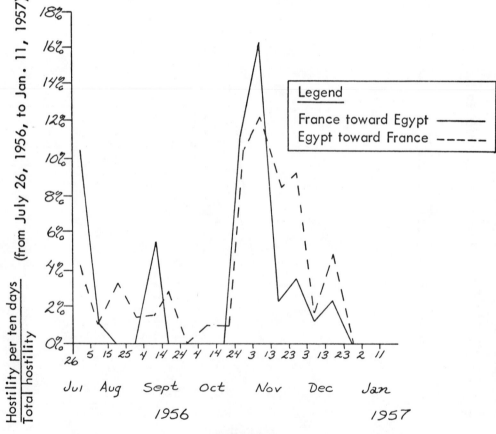

FIGURE 2
Hostile signals per 10-day period between France and Egypt as a percentage of their total signals from July 26, 1956, through January 11, 1957

Egypt's small air force and occupied strategic positions around the Suez canal area. After November 7 both Britain and France stopped their military strikes against Egypt and announced plans to withdraw their armed forces from the Suez area. France was not as receptive to the idea of withdrawal before very clear conditions regarding navigation rights and compensations to Canal Company shareholders were publicly accepted by Nasser. Furthermore both Israel and France had other goals beyond the Suez question to which they wanted Nasser to agree before bringing the hostilities to a full end. France for example wanted Nasser to stop both political and military aid to the Algerians. Israel wanted Egypt to stop encouraging the *fedayeen* raids against Israel, to allow Israeli shipping through Suez and Aqaba, and to stop its anti-Israeli

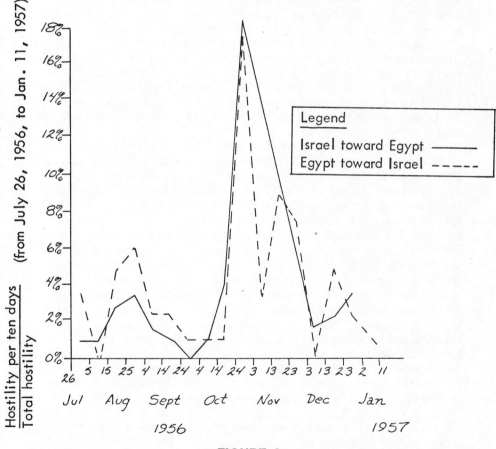

FIGURE 3
Hostile signals per 10-day period between Israel and Egypt as a percentage of their total signals from July 26, 1956, through January 11, 1957

196 EDWARD E. AZAR

activities in the Middle East and around the world. Obviously some of these demands were met for the moment and others were denied and even compounded. Thus Israeli hostile interactions with Egypt continued for a few days after British and French hostilities had stopped. In fact Israeli armed forces were the last forces to withdraw from Egyptian territory.

We observed from the data that the pattern of hostile signaling was clearly symmetrical during the escalation period (July 26–November 7), but not during the conflict reduction period. We found that after Egyptian hostile signals toward Israel had dropped below the upper critical threshold of their NRR, Israel continued its hostile actions against Egypt for more than three weeks. We also found that after France dropped its hostile actions against Egypt, the latter did not lower its anti-French hostilities in response to French signals. Instead Egypt continued a fairly high level of anti-French signaling. In both of these cases there was a lag between offers of conflict reduction and responses to these offers.

The second hypothesis suggests that when nations are in a crisis situation, they will make many more hostile acts per unit of time, and conversely when they begin to reduce the hostile content of their signals, they tend to increase the time intervals between hostile signals. In very general terms this hypothesis says that a relationship exists between the hostile *content* of signals and the *density* of these signals per unit of time.

The data in Table 4 provide a partial test of this hypothesis. The number of events in Period C (crisis) divided by the length of that period (one week) is clearly much higher than the same ratios for Periods P (precrisis) and R (reduction). The mean level of hostility is also higher in Period C. A careful inspection of the data reveals this hypothesis would have to be qualified for conflict reduction periods.

The data show that as these nations cross the upper critical threshold of their NRR and establish a state of acute crisis between them, they begin to behave somewhat differently than the hypothesis suggests. For example, Britain and Egypt seem to have behaved quite similarly in terms of reducing the temporal distances between their hostile events during the intense crisis period and increasing them during conflict reduction. France and Egypt however behaved differently toward one another. As France began to reduce the temporal distance between its signals, Egypt began to increase the distance except toward the latter part of November 1956. On the other hand, from mid-September through the end of October 1956 as Israeli hostile signals increased and the temporal distances between them decreased, Egyptian hostile signals seem to have been reduced and the temporal distances between the Egyptian signals increased. During the conflict reduction period Egyptian-Israeli relations exhibited a pattern very similar to that of the period between July 26, 1956, and September 15, 1956. In other words hostile charges and countercharges were used as a bargaining tactic and a lag of two to five days tended to characterize the distance between an Israeli hostile stimulus and Egyptian hostile response. The following discussion is an exploration of the reasons for the differentiated behavior of these four nations.

TABLE 4

TOTAL DYADIC SIGNALS AT EACH SCALE VALUE FROM JULY 26, 1956–JANUARY 11, 1957[a]

Scale value	Britain toward Egypt			Egypt toward Britain			France toward Egypt			Egypt toward France			Israel toward Egypt			Egypt toward Israel		
	P[b]	C	R	P	C	R	P	C	R	P	C	R	P	C	R	P	C	R
13	—	12	—	—	8	1	—	10	1	—	—	—	—	8	—	—	2	—
12	—	5	—	—	2	7	—	—	1	—	5	—	9	27	3	—	3	—
11	—	—	3	—	—	1	—	—	—	—	4	4	1	—	1	8	5	—
10	—	—	—	—	—	—	—	—	—	—	—	—	—	—	—	—	1	—
9	4	13	1	48	15	22	20	5	9	21	15	23	18	2	1	—	—	—
8	34	—	33	—	—	—	—	—	—	—	—	—	3	12	36	12	6	20
7	—	—	—	48	6	21	13	1	13	27	1	12	3	10	25	6	3	10
6	18	—	34	—	2	3	—	—	1	—	—	—	—	—	6	—	—	—
5	—	2	4	3	2	—	3	1	7	—	4	—	—	—	11	1	4	1
4	—	—	5	—	—	—	—	—	—	3	4	1	—	—	—	—	—	—
3	—	—	—	—	—	—	—	—	—	—	—	—	—	—	—	—	—	—
2	—	—	—	—	—	—	—	—	—	—	—	—	—	—	—	—	—	—
1	—	—	—	—	—	—	—	—	—	—	—	—	—	—	—	—	—	—
Total events	56	32	81	99	33	65	37	19	30	52	31	40	34	61	83	27	24	31

[a] n = 835 events.
[b] P = precrisis period (July 26, 1956–Oct. 29-30, 1956); C = conflict escalation during the acute crisis period (Oct. 29-30, 1956–Nov. 7, 1956); and R = conflict reduction period (Nov. 8, 1956–Jan. 11, 1957).

Why did the four participants in the Suez crisis reduce their hostilities? We have suggested earlier that nations who are involved in a crisis situation will probably reduce their hostilities and move to their precrisis NRR if they achieve or frustrate their goals, if they incur heavy costs, or if they feel pressured by changes in the domestic and international condition. The 1956 Suez crisis appears to be a useful case for exploring these possibilities.

An investigation of a number of relevant sources has yielded the following rank-ordering of major Israeli strategic preferences (see Azar, 1970):

(1) Protection of the territorial integrity and sovereignty of the Israeli nation-state, specifically protection of Israeli citizens against *fedayeen* attacks;

(2) Need to strengthen Israel's military capability and particularly her air force;

(3) Need to end Egyptian economic boycott of Israel—specifically Egypt's closing of the Gulf of Aqaba to hamper Israeli shipping;

(4) Avoidance of military confrontation with Israeli neighbors and in particular to make Egypt renounce her objective of reducing Israel to impotence by force; and

(5) Reduction of Nasser's increasing prestige in the region and the world, which would tend to reduce the level of threat against Israel, whether from Egypt or the other Arab states.

Although British and French strategy may have included more preferences than the list below, we feel that the following were the major strategic preferences relevant to the Suez crisis of 1956:

(1) A demand that Nasser rescind his orders nationalizing the Suez Canal Company;

(2) A campaign to reduce Nasser's growing prestige in the Middle East;

(3) France furthermore wanted Nasser to stop aid to the Algerians and stop transfer of Russian arms from Egyptian territory to the Algerian nationalists; and

(4) In more general terms both European powers wanted to maintain the influence they had enjoyed in the Middle East before Nasser came to power and they felt that undermining Nasser's government and continuing to control Suez would accomplish these over-all objectives.

In the case of Israel, Britain, and France the anticipated costs did not seem to deter them from going to war with Egypt. According to Dayan (1965, pp. 12–13) even as far back as 1955 Israel adopted the principle of going to war to remove Egypt's blockage of Aqaba. As the *fedayeen* attacks increased and as more threats began to accumulate, the anticipated costs were perceived as tolerable and necessary.

The international situation seemed encouraging to Israel, France, and Britain: (a) The U.S.S.R. would probably be deterred by the U.S.; (b) although not supportive of the tripartite attack against Egypt, the U.S. would not come out against the attack just a few days before the American presidential elections; and (c) the countries of the region were weak enough that a quick and successful military operation might achieve the above objectives with minimal regional and international costs such as alliance rifts, international negative reactions, etc.

In addition Israel saw the opportunity in a much larger context. This episode would allow Israel to stop the *fedayeen* attacks by liquidating their bases and by inducing or forcing Egyptians to stop their support of the *fedayeen* or to use Gaza as a base for their future operations. Diplomatically Israel would warn the West about the new Egyptian arms sources, namely the Soviet bloc countries. Israel would stress the potential threat of a Soviet-dominated Middle East. Furthermore Israel would emphasize that a strong Israel in the region would be an insurance policy against Soviet domination of this vital region. Thus Israel would induce the West and primarily the U.S. to supply her with more arms.

With these perceptions, preferences, and strategies, the Israelis, British, and French formed an *ad hoc* alliance designed to pool the resources of these nations in their military attack on Egypt. On October 29, 1956, the Israelis moved into Sinai. This step "was designed according to plans worked out in advance, to give an 'excuse' to the British and French to intervene in order to 'protect' the Suez Canal" (Safran, 1969, p. 53). On the following day the British and French gave their ultimatum to both Israel and Egypt to withdraw from the Suez area and announced that their troops would land in the Suez zone to "secure" navigation through the Canal. The Egyptians rejected the ultimatum as tantamount to surrender of sovereignty, and on October 31, 1956, the British and French began their operations against Egypt. From November 1 until November 6 (at the peak of the crisis) Egyptian targets were hit by the three powers and Egypt's air force effectiveness was reduced to nil.

The United States assumed a leading role in opposing the tripartite attack on Egypt. The U.S.S.R. supported the U.S. and the U.N. efforts and began sending threatening notes to Britain, France, and Israel. By November 6–7, 1956, the British and French agreed to a ceasefire immediately and to a speedy withdrawal when a U.N. Emergency Force was available to take over their positions in the Suez zone. On November 8 Israel officially agreed to withdraw from the territory it had occupied, but in fact did not leave until early 1957.

Thus by November 6–7, 1956, Britain and France had changed their preferences—demanding that Egypt rescind her laws of nationalization of the Suez Canal. They began to argue that Egypt should accept international supervision of the Canal rather than run it alone. Egypt however objected to this plan. Finally France and Britain further altered their objectives and accepted control of the Suez by Egypt if the latter would repatriate the British and French shareholders of the nationalized Suez Canal Company. This last preference was very close to Egypt's position.

Most Israeli preferences until the end of the first week of November remained roughly the same. However, Israel preferred that Egypt allow

Israel the use of the Suez Canal and that international supervision of the Canal would be sufficient despite nationalization. The Israelis felt that the implications of Egypt's policy with respect to their use of the Suez and Aqaba were tantamount to cutting off Israel from the rest of the Asian and African world. The reversal of such a policy however implied an indirect recognition of Israel and a possible step to an improvement of future Israeli-Egyptian relations.

Thus the Israelis began to bargain with the Egyptians over the conditons and timetable of their withdrawal from Sinai. The heavy American pressure on the Israelis to withdraw from Sinai, and oddly enough the heavy British pressure on Israel to withdraw immediately from Sinai after Britain had accepted and implemented its withdral plans, forced the Israelis to drop some of their demands and hope for Western protection of their vital interests. Although on November 9 the Israeli leadership began a campain suggesting that they had won their main objectives, the Egyptian-Israel interactions between November 9 and January 11, 1957, indicate that the Israelis were not happy about terminating the Sinai campaign without securing firm Egyptian commitments about acceptable future Arab-Israeli relations. Of the four nations Egypt incurred the largest portion of the objective costs during the Suez conflict. About 3,000 Egyptians were killed in comparison to 300 Israelis, and a very small number of British soldiers were wounded during this operation. During the first two weeks of November 1956 Israeli objective costs remained fairly low. However there were other subjective costs which Israel had incurred, namely the sharp differences between Israeli and U.S. policies would have cost Israel a reduction in U.S. economic and military aid. On the whole Israel was more successful in achieving her strategic preferences than were the British or the French: (1) Israel weakened Egypt's military capability (90 Egyptian planes were either downed or damaged, 1,000 vehicles and 10,000 tires along with other material were confiscated by the Israelis); (2) Israel demonstrated that her military forces were qualitatively superior to those of the Arab states, resulting in a psychic payoff to Israeli military forces; and (3) the victory of controlling Gaza, Sinai, and Aqaba had a psychological effect on the masses in terms of increased support for the regime and the state. Thus by November 10 the expected and real gains outweighed the subjective and objective costs for the Israelis.

After mid-November Israel's anticipated costs began to actualize. France and Britain had withdrawn from Egypt; the U.S. threatened sanctions; the maritime nations did not come to the aid of Israel to promote her use of the waterways; and the Suez increasingly became an Egyptian-owned waterway. Moreover international pressure intensified to compel Israel to withdraw from the occupied territory.

Furthermore Israel had not produced the desired response from Egypt to change its preferences or significantly alter its strategies. Thus for Israel the objective and subjective costs after mid-November were increasing compared to the real gain. International public opinion was branding them as occupiers and expansionists. Israeli leaders began to modulate their preferences and stopped demanding Egyptian guarantees of security and free navigation rights before withdrawing; instead they settled for partial assurances from the U.S. and the U.N. that these measures would be satisfied. After November 10–15 Israeli-Egyptian conflict reduction began and by late November they had returned to within their NRR of pre-October 29, 1956. Although after December 1956 there were some border incidents and a continuation of charges and counter-charges, these were not of the same magnitude (i.e., they did not move their interactions to above the NRR).

We have found that the symmetry of hostile interactions hypothesis holds well during escalation but not during de-escalation. We found also that the temporal distance between hostile signals hypothesis holds only for British-Egyptian relations but not for the other dyads. These led us to develop an exploratory hypothesis which posits that as costs (objectively and subjectively) increase, as preferences are modulated or reranked, and as public opinion in favor of de-escalation increases, nation-states who are in the midst of a crisis are likely to move toward the temporary reduction of hostile interactions by moving back to within their precrisis normal relations range.

In order to explain the discrepancies in the temporal distance and symmetry of hostile signals hypotheses in the Suez case, we suggest the following tentative explanation. The Suez crisis of 1956 was *more or less* a British-Egyptian affair with France and Israel acting as important direct participants and the U.S. and U.S.S.R. providing the indirect and psychological influence. We suggest that the 1956 crisis was precipitated at that particular time by the British-Egyptian quarrel over a number of strategic issues in the Middle East including Nasser's nationalization of the Suez Canal. This does not necessarily contradict the position that Israel had been contemplating a limited war with Egypt. It merely suggests that Egypt had focused its responses mainly against Britain because the rest of the Middle East had to be eliminated as a first step to reducing French and other Western powers' influence in the region. Furthermore Nasser had described Israel as a Western agent and had argued that an attack on British interest and influence would constitute the first step to strangling Israel and its other Western supporters.

Verbal and physical interactions between Britain and Egypt during the 1956 Suez crisis support the above interpretation. Furthermore they lend themselves to the view that official Egyptian policy directed all of its diplomatic, economic, and military resources against Britain for the above reasons and also because: (a) Britain was a colonial power in the Middle East and therefore an attack on Britain would harness world public opinion in support of Egypt; and (b) when British influence weakened in the Middle East, Egyptian influence over the oil-rich and other strategically located Arab states would tend to increase.

Since Egypt appears to have seen Britain as the central opponent in the conflict, Egyptian verbal and physical activities tended to be primarily directed against Britain. Thus the lack of symmetry of hostile signaling and the discrepancies in event distribution between Egypt, Israel, and France can be attributed to Egypt's skewed distribution of attention among the three belligerents. Egypt saw it as profitable to concentrate on attacking Britain as colonial, as hostile, and as a conflict instigator, and it appears that Egypt's strategy had succeeded for that particular crisis situation.

CONCLUSIONS

We are convinced that more cases must be investigated before the relationships posited above can be firmly established. We feel that we have identified some useful directions for our future research on conflict reduction. We maintain that conceiving of crisis as the movement of dyadic interactions above the upper critical threshold (or the point beyond which national leaders feel that they are justified in using all kinds of actions to deter an opponent who has exhibited intolerable behavior) is realistic and helpful; it provides us with the notion of relativity in crisis analysis. Thus the kind of interactions which might be construed as having reached crisis proportions for one dyad would probably be seen as normal relations for another dyad.

This line of reasoning allows us to be realistic about the interactive role of events and it provides us with a first step for events analysis and may allow us to move out of the purely descriptive situation in which we find ourselves into a reasonable level of causal analysis. In this connection conflict reduction analysis appears to be a justifiable strategy of research for those who wish to undertake conflict resolution analysis between nation-states.

From a policy point of view conflict reduction is an interim step between highly conflictual and fairly cooperative behavior and it may be achieved in a gradual manner by manipulating the temporal distances between events (e.g., the number of days intervening between any two hostile events) and by the containment of these interactions within a reasonable limit of hostility, namely the normal relations range of any two nations.

REFERENCES

Ackoff, R., et al. A Model Study of Escalation and De-escalation of Conflict. Philadelphia: University of Pennsylvania, 1967.

Azar, E. "The Quantification of Events for the Analysis of Conflict Reduction." Paper presented at the Seventh North American Research Conference of the Peace Research Society (International), November 11–12, 1969.

————. "The Analysis of International Events," Peace Research Reviews, 1970, 4 (1, Nov.), 1-113.

————. "Conflict and Peace Data Bank: A Codebook." Studies of Conflict and Peace, The University of North Carolina, Chapel Hill, 1971b.

Boulding, K. Conflict and Defense: A General Theory. New York: Harper and Row, 1961.

Carroll, B. "How Wars End: An Analysis of Some Current Hypotheses," Journal of Peace Research, 1969 (4), 295-321.

Dayan, M. Diary of the Sinai Campaign. London: Weidenfeld and Nicholson, 1966.

Fink, C. "Some Conceptual Difficulties in the Theory of Social Conflict," Journal of Conflict Resolution, 1968, 12 (4, Dec.), 412-60.

Hermann, C. "Alternative Theories of International Crisis Behavior." Paper presented at the Conference on Political Theory and Social Education, Michigan State University, February 5–6, 1971.

McClelland, C. "The Acute International Crisis," *World Politics*, 1961, *41*, 182-204.

Milburn, T. "The Management of Crises." In C. Hermann (ed.), *Contemporary Research on International Crises*. New York: Free Press, 1971.

Miller, G., et al. *Plans and the Structure of Behavior*. New York: Holt, Rinehart, and Winston, 1960.

Newcombe, A. "Initiatives and Responses in Foreign Policy." *Peace Research Reviews*, 1969, *3* (3), 1-122.

North, R. C. "Perception and Action in the 1914 Crisis," *Journal of International Affairs*, 1967, *21* (1), 16-39.

———. "The Behavior of Nation-States: Problems of Conflict and Integration." In M. Kaplan (ed.), *New Approaches to International Relations*. New York: St. Martin's Press, 1968.

———, and C. Osgood. "From Individual to Nation." Unpublished paper, Stanford University, 1963.

O'Connor, R. G. "Victory in Modern War," *Journal of Peace Research*, 1969 (4), 367-84.

Osgood, C. *An Alternative to War or Surrender*. Urbana: University of Illinois Press, 1962.

Pruitt, D. "Definition of the Situation as Determinant of International Action." In H. Kelman (ed.), *International Behavior*. New York: Holt, Rinehart, and Winston, 1965.

Quester, G. "Wars Prolonged by Misunderstood Signals," *Annals*, 1970 (Nov.), 30-39.

Randle, R. "The Domestic Origins of Peace." *Annals*, 1970 (Nov.), 76-85.

Raser, J. "Deterrence Research: Past Progress and Future Needs," *Journal of Peace Research*, 1966 (4), 297-327.

Richardson, L. F. *Arms and Insecurity: A Mathematical Study of the Causes and Origins of War*. Chicago: Quadrangle Books, 1960.

Rothstein, R. "Domestic Politics and Peacemaking: Recognizing Incompatible Imperatives," *Annals*, 1970 (Nov.), 62-75.

Safran, N. *From War to War: The Arab-Israeli Confrontation, 1948–1967*. New York: Western Publishing, 1969.

Schelling, T. *The Strategy of Conflict*. Cambridge, Mass.: Harvard University Press, 1960.

Singer, J. D. *Deterrence, Arms Control, and Disarmament: Toward A Synthesis in National Security Policy*. Columbus: Ohio State University Press, 1962.

———. "Soviet and American Attitudes: A Content Analysis of Elite Articulations." Report of Project Michelson, U.S. Naval Ordinance Test Station, China Lake, California, January 1964.

———. "Escalation and Control in International Conflict: A Simple Feedback Model," *General Systems*, 1970, *15*.

Smoker, P. "Integration and Escalation: A Study of the Three World Arms Races." Northwestern University, Sept. 1966.

Timasheff, N. *War and Revolution*. New York: Sheed and Ward, 1965.

Wright, Q. "The Escalation of International Conflict," *Journal of Conflict Resolution*, 1965, *9* (4, Dec.), 434-49.

Azar's study of a particular case of conflict escalation and conflict reduction was designed to derive nomothetic generalizations about the characteristics of conflict management that may be applicable to other situations or types of interstate interactions. That is, his goal was to investigate intensely a particular instance of conflict cycles in order to generate hypotheses about the process in general. The reader should note the care the author exercises in emphasizing that the findings emergent from his analysis are merely suggestive of the kinds of processes that may be operative in other contexts and among other actors. He thus takes cognizance of the fact that a single case study can never prove a hypothesis, but it can be used to obtain propositions and insights about social processes that can then be tested with many cases in order to ascertain the validity of the hypothesis.

Although Azar's study and the preceding one by Russett are both systematic and explanatory, they may nevertheless be differentiated and compared. Russett uses quantitative techniques to deal with a small number of cases. In contrast Azar uses quantitative techniques to trace the patterns of interaction of a few actors over time; hence, many instances of behavior are quantitatively analyzed rather than a small set of actions. Thus, unlike the Azar study, which has many complimentary examples in the literature, the Russett study is one of a few using specific cases to generate hyotheses about interactions. Other examples include Peter Wallensteen (166), who studied the use of economic sanctions to modify national behavior, and Coplin and J. Martin Rochester (35), who have studied the ways in which international organizations effect conflict interactions among states. Both the Russett and Azar contributions, however, provided us with empirically informed hypotheses about, respectively, deterrence and conflict behavior between interacting pairs of states. Because both indicate the causes, or antecedents, of the phenomenon they have investigated, they suffice as examples of explanatory analysis.

A final feature of the Azar and Russett selections should be noted. This is that both studies, while explanatory in emphasis, provide us with information that has prescriptive implications for the policy-maker. For instance, Azar's development and use of the Normal Relations Range (NRR) suggests how that instrument might be employed to monitor interactions among states in order to anticipate when relations may erupt into hostility; moreover, his finding that conflict reduction may be facilitated by the suspension, or postponement, of action toward the target serves to prescribe an appropriate way of behaving in future interstate interactions. On the other hand, Russett's findings about the determinants of effective deterrence serve to inform the policy-maker of the conditions under which certain types of behavior will be most efficacious in deterring behavior. Hence, explanatory studies are frequently able to tell us not only why states interact the way they do, but also how they can act most effectively, given specified goal preferences. What this illustrates is that empirically grounded explanatory hypotheses contain prescriptive implications for how states should act.

Our next selection addresses the analysis of international interactions from yet another perspective. Like Angell, Herbert C. Kelman focuses his attention on the determinants and effects of intersocietal contact among people; that is, he examines the effects that transnational participatory experiences have on the participants' images about the members of other societies with whom they come into contact. Yet, rather than merely

*monitoring changes in the level of transnational interaction, Kelman in-
terpets what such fluctuations mean for the nature of international society.
His study is thus evaluative and his conclusions, derived from his assessment regarding the conditions that facilitate or inhibit favorable attitude
change, are explicitly prescriptive. They allow him to propose specific
action in light of the information reviewed in his survey.*

INTERNATIONAL INTERCHANGES:
SOME CONTRIBUTIONS FROM THEORIES
OF ATTITUDE CHANGE*

Herbert C. Kelman

Proponents of international educational, cultural, and scientific interchanges usually assume that such activities have the potential for increasing
international understanding and improving mutual attitudes. Insofar as
this assumption is correct—and the evidence, though not entirely consistent,
does lend it support—theories of attitude change can contribute to our
understanding of the nature of the attitudinal effects that international
interchanges may produce and the conditions that enhance the effectivness
of such interchanges.

Whatever the attitudinal effects of international interchanges may be,
do they have any relevance for the course of international politics and
for creating the conditions for a peaceful world order? Even if such
activities invariably produced more favorable attitudes in the participants,
is it reasonable to suppose that favorable attitudes developed through
personal contact can overcome the realities of a conflict of interests? If
conflicts between nations are based primarily on incompatible goals rather
than on lack of understanding, can increased understanding contribute
greatly to their resolution? I shall address myself to these questions before

---

* This paper was prepared for the panel on "International Educational, Cultural, and Scientific Interchanges: What Theory Do We Have?" chaired by
Michael J. Flack and held at the meetings of the International Studies Association
in Saint Louis, March 22, 1974. The paper draws on material from four earlier
publications (Kelman, 1962; Kelman, 1965; Kelman, 1967; and Kelman & Ezekiel,
1970).

Herbert C. Kelman, "International Interchanges: Some Contributions from
Theories of Attitude Change," *Studies in Comparative International Development*
(forthcoming). Reprinted by permission of the author and publisher.

Kelman is professor of social psychology at Harvard University.

turning to an examination of the nature of attitude changes that international contacts may produce and of the conditions conducive to attitude change in a favorable direction.

POLITICAL RELEVANCE OF INTERNATIONAL INTERCHANGES

One can distinguish four types of effects of international interchanges that may, in turn, have an impact on the relations between two nations and the ways in which conflicts between them are resolved: (1) development of a network of relationships cutting across national boundaries; (2) reduction in the level of tension between the two nations; (3) increased commitment to an internationalist ideology; and (4) increased openness in attitudes toward the other nation, especially among key individuals in each nation.

1. The most important source of the political relevance of international exchange and cooperation, in my opinion, is its contribution to the development of human networks that cut across national boundaries. Participation in such activities, if they are successful, is likely to lead to the establishment of ongoing relationships around common professional concerns among individuals representing different nationalities. These relationships have functional significance for the individuals in being directly relevant to their own professional interests and to the effective performance of their professional roles. Thus, individuals and groups from different countries become committed to international cooperation not as an abstract value, but as a concrete vehicle for carrying out personally important activities and pursuing their immediate and long-range goals. They become involved in a network of interdepedent individuals and groups without reference to national differences, and are likely to develop a sense of loyalty to it. What is crucial here is that this loyalty cuts across national lines; it need not be antagonistic to or competitive with national loyalty, but is simply independent of it (cf. Guetzkow, 1955; Kelman, 1968).

Coser (1956) points out that modern pluralistic societies are themselves "sewn together" by the existence of multiple group affiliations of individuals, which "make for a multiplicity of conflicts crisscrossing society" (p. 79). Thus, for example, individuals who are members of antagonistic groups in the economic sphere may, at the same time, be members of the same religious group and thus stand together in a conflict with other religious groups. Because the lines of conflict between these multiple groups do not converge, deep cleavages along a single axis are prevented. In similar fashion, the development of *networks based on professional and other interests that cut across national boundaries* can contribute to the stability and integration of the international system. It would do so not by eliminating conflicts, but by counteracting tendencies toward complete polarization—toward subordinating all relationships to a single basic conflict along national lines.

Insofar as groupings that cut across national lines are important to individuals in the enactment of their various roles—in other words, insofar as individuals have become tied into a pattern of genuine interdependency —they will resist a definition of the international system along strictly national lines, in which national affiliations supersede and subsume all other affiliations. Moreover, they will have something at stake in maintaining the integrity of the international system, since its breakdown would also mean the breakdown of the cross-national networks in which they are involved. As more and more cross-cutting ties develop through international exchange and cooperation, such vested interest in a pluralistic and stable international system is likely to increase and ever stronger barriers to the breakdown of the system are likely to arise.

2. If two nations that are in conflict with each other are, at the same time, involved in exchanges and cooperative ventures, the level of tension that marks their over-all relationship is likely to be reduced. They are more likely to engage in at least some interactions that are free of hostility and mutual threat, and that provide opportunities for communication and for the discovery of common values and interests. Needless to say, these more positive interactions will not cause the basic conflict between the two nations to vanish and will not persuade them to abandon the pursuit of incompatible goals. Such contacts can, however, contribute to the creation of an *atmosphere in which these basic conflicts can be negotiated more effectively and political settlements can be achieved.*

A history of conflict between two nations makes it extremely difficult to negotiate political agreements, even though such agreements would clearly benefit both sides, because of the cumulative erosion of mutual trust. Positive interactions between the two nations in areas outside of those on which their conflict centers, by reducing the level of tension, may help to build up some degree of mutual trust and thus at least make it somewhat likely that serious negotiations on the issues in conflict will get under way. Moreover, the establishment of cooperative relationships in some domains may help to counteract tendencies toward complete polarization of the conflicting nations and may thus make it easier to find ways of "fractionating" the conflicts between them. Fisher (1964) has argued very persuasively that fractionating conflict—"dividing up the issues and considering them separately in small units" (p. 109), rather than treating each as part of a total ideological confrontation—may reduce the risk of war and at the same time facilitate achievement of specific national goals.

3. International interchanges—provided they are intrinsically useful and satisfying—are likely to increase world-mindedness and commitment to an internationalist ideology among the participants. Wide adoption of this type of value framework would seem to be necessary to provide the ideological underpinnings to a peaceful world order. In the short run, peaceful settlement of conflicts is more likely where there is an acceptance of the legitimacy of supranational organizations and a willingness to surrender some degree of national sovereignty to them. In the long run, the stability and effectiveness of such supranational organizations will depend on the acceptance—as fundamental values governing the relations between

nations—of the concepts of international (in contrast to strictly national) security, nonviolence in the settlement of conflicts, and responsibilty for human welfare on a world-wide basis. As the rate of international exchange and cooperation increases, it seems reasonable to suppose that ideological changes in these directions will become more widespread.

Such changes in the belief systems of individuals, in and of themselves, are not likely to produce major changes at the institutional level. New institutional arrangements develop only when their functional significance becomes widely apparent. Thus, for example, it can be argued that the major impetus for the development of the European Economic Community came, not from an ideological commitment to the idea of a united Europe, but from the recognition that economic operations can be made more efficient and profitable if they can be planned and coordinated with reference to a wider geographical area. Nevertheless, it is probably true that the existence of supporting beliefs within the societies—such as (in the case of EEC) the belief in the idea of a united Europe, along with the postwar disenchantment with traditional nationalism—facilitates the establishment of new institutional arrangements by providing an ideological framework ready to incorporate them. In the same sense, then, international exchange and cooperation may contribute to the development and strengthening of international political institutions by *increasing the ideological readiness for them among inflential segments of the participating nations*, even though the major force toward the development of such institutions is likely to come from functional requirements rather than from an abstract commitment to an internationalist ideology.

4. Participants in international interchanges do not universally and necessarily come away from these experiences with wholly favorable attitudes toward the other nation or nations involved. Yet the indications are that such experiences can and usually do produce some very important attitude changes—provided the experiences themselves are personally and professionally satisfying to the participants. Moreover, participants in such activities are likely to develop personal ties to the other country and to certain individuals within it, and thus a sense of personal involvement in its fate. Such increased understanding and involvement, though not likely to overcome real conflicts of interests that exist between the nations, can be expected to create a greater openness in individuals' attitudes toward the other nation. A continuing pattern of cooperation and exchange between two nations, involving many individuals who are in leading positions within their own societies, should then *create a greater predispostion within each nation to trust the other nation, to perceive it as nonthreatening, and to be responsive to it* (Pruitt, 1965). If conflicts arise between nations whose citizens have been having close and friendly contacts, there should be less of a tendency in each nation to perceive threatening intent in the other and to formulate the issue in black-and-white terms, and a greater readiness to communicate with one another and to seek accommodation.

NATURE OF ATTITUDE CHANGES PRODUCED
BY INTERNATIONAL INTERCHANGES

The kinds of attitude changes that can be expected to result from participation in international exchanges and other cooperative activities are well
illustrated by a study of the attitudes of a group of broadcasting specialists
from sixteen different countries who spent four months in the United
States (Kelman and Ezekiel, 1970). During this period they participated
in various professional and academic seminars, they visited broadcasting
facilities, and they traveled through various parts of the country. A variety
of procedures were used to evaluate the effectiveness of this program.
One of these consisted in a detailed questionnaire, completed by the
participants shortly before they arrived in the United States and again
about nine months to a year after they had returned home. In order to be
confident that changes from the before- to the after-questionnaires can
indeed be ascribed to participation in the exchange program, we also
questioned a control group of nonparticipants from the same countries
as the participants, with comparable status and experience, who filled out
the two questionnaires at the same times as the participants, but who did
not come to the United States during the period in between.

From past studies, we knew that there is no particular reason to expect
an increase in over-all favorableness toward the United States as a result
of such a visit, even under the best of circumstances. Those who start out
with negative attitudes may find confirming evidence for them; those who
start out with positive attitudes may have little room for change in the
favorable direction; and those who start out with neutral attitudes may
find things they like balanced by things they dislike. Thus, marked changes
on the dimension of favorablesness do not represent a realistic goal of
international exchange programs—nor is the uncritical accepance of all
features of the host country even a desirable goal. I would argue that the
most important outcomes of such programs are changes in the cognitive
structure—for example, in the complexity and differentiation—of images
of the host country. Changes on these cognitive dimensions are more
meaningful in the long run than global increases in favorableness, which
are often based on incomplete understanding and are likely to be quite
ephemeral. Cognitive changes suggest the development of a fuller, richer,
more detailed image of the other society and a greater understanding of
that society on its own terms.

Thus our major interest was in assessing changes in cognitive structure—in particular, changes in the complextity and differentiation of our
respondents' images of America and of American broadcasting. To this
end, we developed an over-all index of "differentiation," based on responses to a series of questions. Participants in the program registered
an increase on this index, whereas controls actually registered a slight
decrease. The difference between the two groups was statistically significant
and suggests very strongly that the participants did indeed develop more
complex and differentiated images of America and American broadcasting
as a result of their experiences. This finding is particularly noteworthy in

view of the fact that our respondents were quite sophisticated and relatively knoweldgeable about America and American broadcasting to begin with.

Questionnaire responses also revealed a change on the evaluative dimension: Compared to the controls, participants became more favorable in their general images of America and Americans as a result of their experience. These evaluative changes, however, are not as marked as those on the dimension of differentiation. The pattern of change in attitudes toward American broadcasting is also interesting. Participants, when compared to controls, actually became less favorable in their attitudes toward American television. On the other hand, they were more likely to conclude —after their visit—that American experience in broadcasting can potentially contribute to the development of broadcasting in their own countries. In short, having observed American television in some detail, they tended to like it less, but at the same time they were more aware of valuable lessons that they could learn from it.

The findings that I have just summarized underline the limitations in using favorableness toward the host country and its institutions as a criterion for evaluating international interchanges. These limitations can be seen more clearly in Table 1, which juxtaposes changes from the before- to the after-questionnaires on the four dimensions discussed above. To make the dimensions comparable, the table simply presents the percentage of participants and the percentage of controls who have shown changes on each dimension. We see, first of all, that there is a very large difference between participants and controls on the cognitive dimension: Participants showed a much greater increase in the differentiation of their images of America and American broadcasting. Changes on the evaluative dimensions are considerably smaller and inconsistent in direction. Thus, participants, as compared to controls, did become more favorable in their general attitude toward America, but they actually became less favorable (whereas the controls showed no net change) in their general attitude toward American TV. Finally, it is clear that favorableness toward American broadcasting itself is not a unitary dimension: Though participants became less favorable toward American TV in general, they became more favorable in their view of the potential contributions that American experiences could make to broadcasting in their own countries.

This pattern of results suggests quite clearly some of the subtleties that must be kept in mind as one assesses the impact of an international exchange experience on participants' attitudes toward the host society. Specifically, our conclusions are likely to be misleading (1) if we assess change solely on the evaluative dimension, rather than assigning an important place in the analysis to the cognitive dimensions of attitudes; (2) if we treat the host society as a unitary object, rather than taking into account the likelihood that different patterns and institutions of the society may be evaluated quite differently; and (3) if we treat the evaluation of the society or even of a specific pattern or institution within it as a unitary dimension, rather than exploring the possibility that it may be evaluated favorably along one dimension and unfavorably along another.

FACTORS FACILITATING AND INHIBITING
FAVORABLE CHANGE

International interchanges clearly have the potential for producing, among each set of participants, an openness to the other country, a readiness to accept it on its own terms, and an appreciation for at least some of its features. To what extent this potential is actualized depends on the conditions surrounding the experience—on the presence of various facilitative factors and the absence of various inhibitory ones.

Exchange of Persons

Let us examine first the situation in which nationals of country A come to country B for a period of months or years as students, trainees, scholars, or temporary employees. Such sojourns have often led to the development of favorable attitudes as well as personal ties and feelings of identification with the host country.

Studies of exchange students and other social-psychological investigations provide a number of hints about the variables determining the probability that favorable attitudes will develop. An important variable, for example, is the opportunity the visitor has for genuine contact with nationals of the host country and for involvement in various aspects of its life. Another important and obvious factor is what happens in the course of the contact—what treatment the visitor receives at the hands of the host. Early studies on race relations, such as those by Allport and Kramer (1946), suggest that favorable changes (on the part of the host as well as the visitor) are most likely to take place if the contact is at an equal status. Finally, the more positive and rewarding the visitor's general experience has been, for whatever reason, the more likely he is to become positive toward the country and its people.

It is not enough, however, to consider variables that would facilitate change. It is also necessary to pay deliberate attention to the various barriers to favorable change. These barriers derive in part from the preconceptions and motivations of the visitors. A visitor who starts out with hostile attitudes toward the host country may confirm them by being selective in his perception and by avoiding or reinterpreting information that does not fit his preconceptions. Also, he is likely to minimize communication or handle his interactions in such a way that they will tend to confirm his unfavorable attitudes and expectations.

There are various circumstances under which a visitor will be especially motivated to avoid favorable information about the host country and to seek out negative features. A visitor who is sensitive about his national status, for example, and feels that his country is being downgraded may defend himself against these feelings by rejecting the host country and accentuating its weaknesses. This seemed to be a strong factor in the reaction of Indian students in America interviewed by Lambert and Bressler (1956). Sometimes a visitor may resist positive information in line with the demands of a reference group back home to whom he expects to report on his experiences—and who will be expecting an unfavorable report (Zimmerman and Bauer, 1956). Or a visitor who is not well established in his home situation and is tempted by opportunities in the host country may derogate that country as a way of coming to grips with his own ambivalence (Bailyn and Kelman, 1962).

Even in the absence of motivation toward negative attitudes, barriers to favorable change may derive from the individual's experiences in the host country. If his over-all experience in the host country is for some reason frustrating or unsatisfying, perhaps because of his work situation or his living arrangements or social isolation, he will be less likely to be open to the favorable information about the host country to which he is also exposed. Or particular negative experiences may interfere with the visitor's ability to see the positive features of the host country, even though these are isolated experiences and the visitor has in general been treated with kindness and friendliness. This would be particularly true if unfortunate experiences occurred early in the stay and thus affected the visitor's whole strategy of interaction from the beginning. It would also be true if an experience touched on a particularly sensitive area—for example, if the visitor were confronted with an act of discrimination because of his color.

Even some of the deliberate attempts of the hosts to provide the visitor with positive experiences may have unintended boomerang effects because of the needs, the sensitivities, and the cultural background of the visitor. If his privacy is scrupulously respected, he may feel there is a lack of interest in him. If, on the other hand, an exaggerated interest in him is evinced, he may also be resentful: He may feel that he is being treated as a curiosity and that people are eager to hear about the quaint customs of his primitive country. As the Lambert and Bressler (1956) study suggests, people who are sensitive about their national status relative to the host country will be particularly resentful of any implication that they are being patronized.

To make exchange programs fruitful, it is clear that ways must be found of providing the visitor with rewarding experiences and positive contacts, while at the same time taking account of the various barriers to change that may arise even under favorable conditions. The experiences must be such that the visitor's own motivations to overcome these barriers are mobilized and that he senses the host's interest in him without feeling patronized and exploited. The real challenge is to provide the visitor with attractive and engaging opportunities that do not interfere with his freedom to make independent choices and to organize his life and activties in line with his own needs. Two types of opportunities seem especially well designed to do this: (1) opportunities for genuine involvement in an ongoing enterprise and (2) opportunities for interpersonal involvement with people in the host country.

1. In the professional or educational setting to which the visitor is attached, it is important that he become a full-fledged participant, in-

tegrally related to some aspect of its ongoing activities. Such involvement increases the likelihood that the experience will be rewarding, maximizes the opportunities for meaningful contacts with nationals of the host country —whether as individuals or as colleagues or as people with whom the visitor shares common interests and goals—and facilitates the formation of substantial and lasting ties via an important joint activity. Insofar as possible, he should be treated not as a visitor, who is in a special category and requires special attention, but as a regular member of the organization —albeit a temporary one—whose participation in its ongoing activities is desired, needed, and even expected. Ignoring him and according him special treatment are both ways of classifying him as an outsider and thus losing out on the dynamic potential that is contained in an integral relationship to the host institution.

2. The formation of a personal relationship to nationals of the host country is often a very important part of the visitor's experience, providing rewarding interactions while he is there and often leading to the establishment of lasting ties. Such relationships, of course, cannot be planned, but it is possible to provide opportunities for person-to-person contact, for example, by inviting the visitor to meet a local family and to participate in some aspect of community life. As already suggested, however, hospitality programs of this sort are likely to backfire if they are patronizing, ritualistic, or impersonal. The visitor needs to sense a personal interest in him and needs to see that the host is enjoying the relationship and getting something out of it. He must be regarded as an individual—equal to his hosts, valuable in his own right—who at the moment happens to be living in a foreign country, which partly determines his current interests and needs but certainly does not circumscribe them. Thus he should not be constantly confronted with the request to speak about his own country or to express his opinions about the host country. In short, he should be treated as a person, not as a specimen. His special status can and should be a criterion for initiating the interaction, but it should not be the sum and substance of that interaction.

In sum, I am proposing that *the exchange experience is most likely to produce favorable attitudes if it provides new information about the host country in the context of a positive interaction with some of its people.* The visitor is engaged in some meaningful activity with nationals of the host country; he is working on a joint problem in which both are involved; he is participating in the give-and-take of a warm, personal, and individualized relationship. He is not merely presented with some objective evidence that these are nice people, but he knows them from his own experience. The very fact that he has worked and lived with people in the host country—and found these experienecs rewarding—mobilizes his own motivations to see the country in a favorable light.

Though I have focused on the visitor, similar considerations enter into the effects of the exchange program on the attitudes of the host toward the visitor and his country. He too is most likely to show favorable attitude change if he has the opportunity for genuine involvement with the visitors as colleagues and as individuals.

Foreign Aid Projects

Special considerations arise in international interchanges that take place in the context of foreign aid projects. I shall address myself specifically to the situation in which personnel from country A are sent into country B (typically a less developed country) to administer an aid program, or to provide training or direct assistance to the local population.

Aid programs of this type provide opportunities for nationals of the two countries to work together on a joint problem, to accomplish things together, to get to know each other in the process. In this respect, foreign aid programs have the same potential for producing attitude change as any kind of program that provides for contact, especially around a common problem. Here, as in exchange programs, the probability that favorable attitudes will develop depends on the amount of genuine contact that takes place, on the extent to which the contact is at an equal status, on the way the representative of the other country conducts himself in the course of the contact, and on the opportunities for establishing a give-and-take relationship.

A special potential for favorable attitude change is inherent in the very existence of an aid program in that there is a tendency for people to like those who benefit them (as well as those whom they have benefited). At the same time, the experience of receiving help engenders great ambivalences. Thus the *way* in which help is given in a foreign aid project is all important in determining whether the resulting attitudes in the recipient country will be more favorable or less so.

The usual barriers to change that derive from the aid recipients' preconceptions about the donor country function in this situation as much as in other types of international interchange. In addition, however, there are strong forces conducive to hostility toward the donor country inherent in the very nature of the aid situation. The fact that nationals from the donor counry have come to his country to give aid is concrete evidence, from the recipient's point of view, of his own inferior status. The situation has obvious implications of an unfavorable comparison, damaging to the recipient's self-esteem and conducive to the generation of hostility. Such hostility is most naturally directed at the one who, by giving, underlines the recipient's inferiority. Under these circumstances, the recipient will be motivated to deny the donor's "kindness," to interpret his aid as being based on ulterior motives, to be particularly attentive to any weaknesses and flaws in the program, and so on. The strength of these tendencies will depend, of course, on the extent to which the particular character of the aid program is such as to elicit inferiority feelings in the recipient. But we cannot minimize the possibility that such forces will arise—and even the possibility that the greater the actual "kindness" of the donor, the greater the hostility that is generated. This paradox is inherent in foreign aid projects, despite their potential for favorable attitude change.

The way in which the foreign aid personnel conduct themselves in the country in which they are stationed has a great bearing, of course, on the attitudes that develop. The favorable effect of a generous and useful aid project may be completely wiped out because of unfavorable impressions created by those who administer the project. The behavior of the personnel takes on particular significance, however, in view of the special sensitivities engendered by the aid situation. The national of the recipient country is likely to be particularly attentive to and resentful of anything that reminds him of his inferior status. There are many ways—direct and indirect, obvious and subtle—in which the aid personnel can communicate such reminders through their own behavior: by living at a standard that is clearly higher than that of the local population, particularly if they are ostentatious about it; showing a patronizing attitude toward the local population, comporting themselves as benefactors, or acting like an occupation force; and by failing to learn the local language, showing a lack of respect for the local institutions, ignoring the local customs, and "sticking together" in isolation from the rest of the community—in short, by behaving in a way that implies that the recipient country is not worthy of their attention. Given the forces toward rejecting the donor country that are inherent in the aid situation, it is understandable that this type of behavior on the part of the aid personnel will create barriers to the development of favorable attitudes and may even .result in increased hostility.

The real challenge in this field is to find ways of giving aid that will *enhance* the recipient's status in the process. Recipients of an aid program that has this character are not likely to dismiss it as manipulative and based on ulterior motives. They are far more likely to interpret it as a genuine act of friendship, and to develop increasingly favorable attitudes toward the donor. In the light of this, if the full potential of foreign aid programs for favorable attitude change is to be realized, it seems crucial, in my view, that status-enhancing features be built into (1) the project itself and (2) extraproject relationships.

1. In selecting a focus for the aid program, it is important to look for a project that is fairly directly related to people's immediate needs—that represents a way of dealing with a problem they face all the time and recognize; a project that can be executed fairly simply and that is likely to have fairly immediate results; and a project of such a nature that it can soon be taken over by the recipients, given their skills and facilities. In carrying out this project, the donors should make every effort to use the recipients' special knowledge, experience, and skills and, at the same time, should be training local people so that as soon as possible they will be able to handle the whole project by themselves.

A project selected and carried out in this way demonstrates to the recipient that he is held in high esteem and actually serves to raise his status in a visible way—now he can do something that he could not do before, and he can continue to do it without further help; he has become more skilled and less dependent in the process. Contrast this to a large-scale, highly specialized project which leaves the recipient physically better off but does not make *him* "better" as a person in any way. Such large-scale projects can be very useful from the point of view of attitude change at a later stage, when the local population has become more aware of their execution. The initial projects, however, should be so selected that they make a visible difference in the individual recipient's immediate life and provide the opportunity for status-enhancing interactions. Under these circumstances, the recipient will be open to favorable information about the donor—and, of course, such information will be forthcoming to the extent that the donor communicates a genuine interest in the recipient and regards him as a full equal.

2. While the donor-recipient relationships in the project itself are essential in determining the effectiveness of the program, the extraproject relationships between donor and recipient are also of great importance. The selection, training, and preparation of the people sent abroad are, of course, major determinants of the kinds of relationships that become possible. Aid personnel should be prepared to live simply, to live as equals of their counterparts in the local population and in direct contact with them—a requirement that has been built into the Peace Corps program. They should learn the language and customs of the country and develop some appreciation for what the country has to offer. That is, they should not only "know" the customs, so as to avoid offending the local population, but have a genuine interest in the local culture. Under these conditions, relationships based on a mutual give-and-take are likely to develop spontaneously and communication at an equal status becomes possible. The local population is likely to regard the aid personnel as people like themselves, as people who respect them and are interested in them—rather than people who consider themselves superior and are interested only in exploiting the local population for their own advantage. In short, the ingredients will be present for a relationship that will enhance the status and the self-esteem of the recipients.

It is of special importance to this relationship that the recipients have the opportunity to *give* something to the donors, to reciprocate for the help that they are receiving. This may be, for example, by feeding the aid personnel, by entertaining them in their homes, by inviting them to their festivals and celebrations, by introducing them to various aspects of their own culture. These acts of giving will, of course, be meaningful only if the aid personnel have communicated a genuine interest in *taking* what is being offered—if they have given some indication that they would regard an invitation as a special treat, that they are really interested in learning about the local culture, and so on. And it is not enough merely to pretend that such an interest exists. This desideratum underlines the importance of one aspect of the selection and preparation of aid personnel that is often neglected. In addition to arousing the aid personnel's desire to help the receiving country, it is also necessary to arouse their real interest in what the country has to offer them.

Foreign aid projects have great potential for producing favorable attitudes not only among the recipients toward the country but also among the aid personnel toward the recipient country. Strong forces in the direction of such attitudes are generated by the fact that the aid personnel are stationed in that country and that they are dedicated to helping it. There are also barriers to change, however. Change is less likely, for example, if interactions with the local population are at an unequal status; and attitudes may even increase in hostility if the population is unreceptive and seemingly "ungrateful." In general, an aid program characterized by the features I have been discussing is likely to be most effective in changing the donor's attitudes toward the recipient as well as the recipient's attitude toward the donor.

Conclusion

The general assumption in the foregoing discussion has been that *providing new information* about another country and people in the course of international interchanges is a necessary but by no means sufficient condition for favorable attitude change. It is also essential that this information be provided in the context of a *positive interaction* between the nationals of the countries involved. Given such a context, participants have both a greater opportunity and a stronger motivation to see the other country in a favorable light. The other's qualities are more likely to be visible in a concrete, immediate way, and at the same time each participant is more likely to expose himself to communication and contact and thus to open himself to the impact of the new information.

What is more, strong forces toward the restructuring of perceptions of the other country derive from the fact that one has participated in a friendly interaction with nationals of that country and that he himself has *engaged in friendly behavior toward them*. The participant's own friendly behavior toward nationals of the other country becomes an element that enters into his definition of that country and ultimately into his evaluation of it. It is often true that we define an object in terms of the way in which we have behaved toward it: our own action becomes, in a sense, a salient characteristic of the object. This, in turn, creates a readiness to evaluate the object in a way that takes this new characteristic into account (Kelman, 1974). Thus, if the situation in which the nationals of two countries interact is so structured that the one finds himself taking friendly actions toward the other—or actions that imply friendliness—then he is likely to define the other as someone to whom he has been friendly (someone with whom he has agreed, someone with whom he has cooperated, someone with whom he has broken bread), and to be ready to change his attitude toward him accordingly. When, in this context of friendly action, he is exposed to new information that calls for a restructuring of his attitude toward the other nation, he will be considerably more receptive to it.

Engaging in friendly behavior toward nationals of another country thus creates a powerful potential for attitude change. The behavior itself, however, is not enough. It merely provides the motivation and openness for examining and accepting favorable information. It is *the joint occurrence of friendly behavior toward the other and genuinely new information about him* that makes favorable attitude change possible.

REFERENCES

Allport, G. W.; and Kramer, B. M. "Some Roots of Prejudice," *Journal of Psychology*, 1946, 22: 9-39.

Bailyn, L.; and Kelman, H. C. "The Effects of a Year's Experience in America on the Self-Image of Scandinavians," *Journal of Social Issues*, 1962, *18* (1): 30-40.

Coser, L. A. *The Functions of Social Conflict*. New York: Free Press, 1956.

Fisher, R. "Fractionating Conflict." In R. Fisher (ed.), *International Conflict and Behavioral Science*. New York: Basic Books, 1964, pp. 91-109.

Guetzkow, H. *Multiple Loyalties*, Princeton, N.J.: Princeton University Press, 1955.

Kelman, H. C. "Changing Attitudes Through International Activities," *Journal of Social Issues*, 1962, *18* (1): 68-87.

———. "Social-Psychological Approaches to the Study of International Relations: The Question of Relevance." In H. C. Kelman (ed.), *International Behavior: A Social-Psychological Analysis*. New York: Holt, 1965, pp. 556-607.

———. "International Cooperation and Attitude Change." In F. L. Ruch, *Psychology and Life*. 7th ed. Chicago: Scott, Foresman, 1967, pp. 677-84.

———. "Education for the Concept of a Global Society, *Social Education*, 1968, *32*, 661-66.

———. "Attitudes Are Alive and Well and Gainfully Employed in the Sphere of Action," *American Psychologist*, 1974, *29*, 310-24.

Kelman, H. C.; and Ezekiel, R. S. *Cross-National Encounters: The Personal Impact of an Exchange Program for Broadcasters*. San Francisco: Jossey-Bass, 1970.

Lambert, R.; and Bressler, M. *Indian Students on an American Campus*. Minneapolis: University of Minnesota Press, 1956.

Pruitt, D. G. "Definition of the Situation as a Determinant of International Action." In H. G. Kelman (ed.), *International Behavior: A Social-Psychological Analysis*. New York: Holt, 1965, pp. 393-432.

Zimmerman, C.; and Bauer, R. A. "The Influence of an Audience on What Is Remembered," *Public Opinion Quarterly*, 1956, *20*: 238-48.

Substantively, the foregoing study addresses itself to an important aspect of international interactions: What international educational, cultural, and scientific interchanges have potential for promoting mutually favorable attitudes in participating nations. It distinguishes four types of attitudinal effects of interchanges that may have an impact on the political relations between participating nations; it then proceeds to examine the nature of attitude changes that international contacts may produce. The contention that emerges from this treatment is that the most important changes are on cognitive, rather than evaluative, dimensions. Contact through international interchanges affects how we think about the world more than it does our liking or disliking of the people with whom we come into contact. This is relevant policy, for the argument prescribes a way of behaving by suggesting that international interchanges can help to create the conditions for peaceful conflict resolution. It further suggests that it would be unrealistic to expect such changes in attitude to assure peace between two nations that have conflicting interests.

Kelman concludes his interpretation of the circumstances that encourage or inhibit favorable attitude changes by proposing that favorable change is facilitated only when genuinely new information about the country and people is provided in the context of a positive interaction between nationals of the participating countries. Finally, some implications of this proposition for the organization of personnel-exchange programs and foreign-aid projects are assessed.

Methodologically, two features of Kelman's prescriptive study are worth noting. First, we may note that his analytic mode resembles a style frequently found in the traditional literature: A review of previous theoretical studies is conducted to arrive at an interpretation through logical deduction. What is atypical about his analytic style is that, while it is judgmental, it is based on a review of research that is empirical and verifiable rather than impressionistic. That is, while Kelman's conclusions are based on literature citations, the literature that is cited contains findings that have been substantiated with evidence and testing. Their validity and reliability are therefore higher than are those of studies based on intuition and conjecture. Consequently, while the author's conclusions are not built from empirical inquiry with supporting data, they are derived from the empirical studies of previous scholarship. Kelman's synthesis of this knowledge, therefore, deserves a higher regard than do synthetic studies that refer to impressionistic accounts.

Secondly Kelman's study is noteworthy because of the similarity it shares with Angell's previous selection dealing with transnational participation. Angell's inductive account of the growth of transnational contact across national borders was informative descriptively, but in many respects it raised more questions than it answered. For instance, in describing the growth rates of transnational participation, Angell's account left us hanging with regard to what those rates mean, ultimately, for the future of international relations; in particular, what is the relationship between this growth of actual contact and the attitudes that the parties to the contact are likely to develop? Here is where a study of Kelman's type can make a real contribution. By putting empirical findings in perspective with the theoretical literature, Kelman has offered an interpretation of those findings; his assessment tells us what increased contact among societies may mean. Thus, through theory empiricism can be rendered more comprehensible. Moreover, Kelman's analysis demonstrates how empirically informed findings can be converted into policy prescriptions.

Finally, we will look at yet another style in which prescriptive analysis of international interactions may be conducted. The article that follows was written by a political scientist, J. David Singer, and a diplomatic historian, Melvin Small. Together they have produced a large number of scholarly investigations into the sources of international war and are principal investigators of the massive Correlates of War Project, a series of quantitative studies of characteristics of the international system since 1815. The present effort is designed to demonstrate the contribution social science can make to our understanding of foreign-policy interactions. To this end, the "state of the world" messages devised by the Nixon

Administration are examined for the ideas they contain about the conditions that promote war and peace, and these ideas are expressed as predictive propositions that can ultimately be used for foreign policy-making purposes. The ideas implicit in the state of the world message are thus frequently prescriptive, stated in a normative format: "If you want to achieve x, *engage in behavior* y." *These prescriptive statements, as Singer and Small demonstrate, may be tested with empirical evidence to estimate their plausibility and to ascertain the extent to which they are valid. Their study is therefore designed to show how rigorous social science methodology can be applied to international policy prescriptions for refinement as well as for rejection of false assumptions.*

WAR IN HISTORY AND IN THE STATE
OF THE WORLD MESSAGE

J. David Singer and Melvin Small

Among the several "movements" of the past decade, one of the more interesting and durable is the social indicators movement. In an effort to cope with the increasing complexities of social planning, as well as with the increasing militance of the socially disadvantaged, practitioners and academics have sought to develop more effective tools for the planning, executing, and evaluating of social policy. Central to that enterprise has been the effort to convert many of the vague notions associated with "quality of life" into more precise and operational language. As a result, we now have quantitative indicators which are designed to tap or reflect not only such tangible conditions as "full employment" or "national product, but more elusive conditions such as the job satisfaction, health care, educational achievement, and environmental quality of a given population.[1]

As these illustrations make clear, the historical origins are found largely in the area of economic activity, with such measurement occurring in the "softer" sectors only in the more recent period. While it is likely —for reasons which will become clear as this paper unfolds—that some

J. David Singer and Melvin Small, "Foreign Policy Indicators: Predictors of War in History and in the State of the World Message," *Policy Sciences,* 5 (1974). Reprinted by permission of the authors and publisher.

Singer is a professor of international relations at the University of Michigan, and Melvin Small is a professor of history at Wayne State University.

of us may have gone overboard in our enthusiasm for these more contemporary indicators, they have already begun to demonstrate their utility.[2] In the foreign policy sector, on the other hand, the utility of indicators has been largely ignored. Outside of the thoughtful exhortations of Bobrow, one finds little explicit attention to the kinds of indicators that might be developed, or to the ways in which they might improve the efficacy and/or humaneness of national foreign policies.[3] In the paper at hand, we hope to focus attention on some of the possible applications of foreign policy indicators and to illustrate the potential that may already lie close at hand.

INDICATORS AND THEIR FOREIGN POLICY APPLICATIONS

In this opening section, before turning to our specific assignment, we cover a number of preliminary points. First, we attempt to define what we mean by indicators, how they are devised and evaluated, and how they may be differentiated. We then go on to summarize their possible roles in the policy process. Following these preliminaries, we will turn to a more specific application of certain indicators that we have devised in the context of a rather different enterprise.

Indicators as Proxies

When we speak of indicators in the context of social phenomena, it is useful to distinguish between two different usages of the term. The first and most familiar usage is in the sense of a proxy, surrogate, symptom, representation, measure, or index. That is, many of the concepts that we use in describing social phenomena do not have easily observed empirical referents. Rather, we make an inferential leap of greater or lesser magnitude from some trace or proxy, which we *do* observe, back to the unobserved phenomenon. The condition or event in which we are interested may be unobserved because it has occurred in the past and is gone from sight, or is spread over too broad a space, or has too many component elements, or is sufficiently intangible to lie beyond the human senses. To illustrate, we may infer the severity of a war from the battle death estimates that are compiled afterward, or the industrial capability of a nation from its steel production, or the material quality of life from infant mortality rates, or the ego strength of an individual from his responses to certain projective tests, or the efficacy of a therapeutic treatment from the patients' average stay in hospital.

In other words, we try to "operationalize" the more elusive concept or variable by devising a procedure through which its presence, strength, or rate of change might be indirectly measured or inferred. If the same operation or procedure, applied to the same phenomenon, gives the same "reading" regardless of who conducts it or when, we say that the index or indicator is a *reliable* one. But devising reliable indicators is only part of the struggle to "observe" the unobserved. More difficult and ambiguous is the *validity* of an indicator: the extent to which it really does tap or reflect the phenomenon we claim to be getting at and measuring. Whereas reliability is easily demonstrated by repeated observational tests, validity always remains partially a matter of judgment. There are, however, some ways in which we can go beyond mere assertion as to the validity of an indicator. One is the extent to which an alternative indicator of the allegedly identical phenomenon gives us a set of readings which are highly correlated with those produced by the original indicator. For example, caloric intake might correlate highly (but negatively) with infant mortality, suggesting that both might be valid indicators of material quality of life; or the energy consumption of a nation might correlate highly with its steel production, strengthening our confidence in the validity of both as indicators of industrial capability.

A second strategy is to ascertain whether the readings on our indicator conform to what one's model or "theory" would predict. If, for example, our model predicts that the "diplomatic interdependence" of pairs of nations should decrease as their trade decreases, and the number of nations with whom they both have diplomatic relations does indeed decrease following a decline in their trade, we have some grounds for believing that the number of nations with whom they both have relations is a valid indicator of diplomatic interdependence. But when all is said and done, the most important test is that of "face validity": Are those with expertise persuaded that the indicator really taps the unobserved phenomenon? And that usually rests, in turn, on the extent to which we believe that: (a) changes in the unobserved phenomenon of interest lead to, or cause, commensurate changes in the value of the indicator; (b) changes in the value of the proxy or trace that serves as the indicator will lead to, or cause, commensurate changes in the actual event or condition of interest; or (c) the values of the variable and its alleged indicator at least rise and fall together, despite the absence of any causal link. In the last case, it may merely be that some third factor exercises an equally strong impact on both the variable and its indicator.

Indicators as Predictors

Shifting now from the use of indicators as proxies for, or traces of, some less readily observed phenomenon, there is a second and more complex role for social indicators. This is the predictive or early warning role, and while the reasoning behind it and the difficulties encountered are rather similar, the focus is somewhat different. Thus, even though a proxy indicator might, in principle, be one whose value or magnitude we observe *prior to* the inferred value or magnitude of the unobserved variable or phenomenon, this is rarely the case. More frequently, the indicator's value rises and falls simultaneously with, or subsequent to, changes in the value or magnitude of the variable itself. But in both cases, we postulate a high covariation or correlation between the two.

More important than temporal sequence, however, is the fact that a predictive indicator is assumed to co-vary *with another indicator* rather than with an unobserved concept or variable. On the one hand, this means that it is much easier to demonstrate the covariation or correlation between the predictor and the outcome. But on the other hand, it means that we have to deal with the problems of reliability and validity at *both* ends of the chain. This set of relationships may be illustrated by way of the following simple diagram:

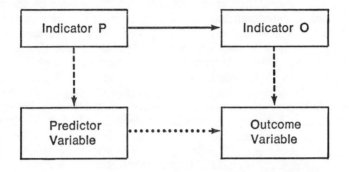

The broken vertical lines leading down from the indicators to the variables emphasize that the latter will often lie below some threshold of direct observability, and their presence or strength will thus have to be inferred from the presence and strength of the indicators which we devise to represent them. The solid line between indicators P and O reminds us that it is a simple matter to observe the correlation or covariation between our predictive and outcome indicators.

But the very simplicity of ascertaining the correlation between indicators can often mislead us into thinking that we have, by that operation, ascertained the predictive and perhaps even the causal connection between our unobserved variables. If we are merely inferring a *predictive* relationship between the variables, the only threat to that inference lies in the validity and the reliability of our two indicators. But if we want to infer, from a strong correlation between indicators P and O, that changes in the predictor variable *cause* changes in the outcome variable, all sorts of difficulties arise. Since, however, our concern here is *not* with explanation and causality, but only with the more manageable problem of early warning and prediction, we can sidestep these philosophical issues for the nonce. Suffice it to say, then, that the weak dotted line conveys the tenuousness of any causal link between the two variables, as well as the extent to which the predictive link between them depends on the quality of their respective indicators.

The Policy Uses of Indicators

Bearing in mind these two meanings of indicator, as well as the dangers of overinterpretation, let us next mention some of the ways in which each type of indicator might be used for policy purposes. They may, of course, be useful not only in (a) the formulation of policy but also in (b) the monitoring of its execution, and (c) the evaluation of its success.

In the formulation stage, we may use both the proxy and the predictor. The *former* is used to tell us something of the state of the world at the moment and the direction and rate of change in the conditions and events of interest. The *latter* may help us to predict which outcomes are most likely to arise out of certain conditions, and thus which of these conditions should be perpetuated (or modified) in order to arrive at (or avoid) some future outcome. In the monitoring stage, we rely primarily on proxy indicators, hoping that they can tell us whether or not the assigned or agreed actions have been executed, and how close certain of the transition conditions are to those which we predicted and thought of as necessary to a successful outcome. And in the evaluation stage, we again turn to proxy indicators to measure the success of the policy, by observing the discrepancy between the ultimate outcome and that which we had predicted and preferred. Moreover, such objective evaluation can be utilized for self-correcting feedback purposes and provide the basis for change in our predictive models. That is, if the outcome is not as predicted, we know that the appropiate predictor conditions were not those the model led us to believe, and that other preconditions will have to be established.

For predictive indicators to be of much use, however, they must not only satisfy the measurement criteria of reliability and validity. Whereas the historian or political scientist is often satisfied with the construction of an indicator that merely meets these two criteria—on the assumpton that it will in due course be scientifically useful—the policy-maker must demand more. He or she must be satisfied that it is also a *dependable* predictor. Either through his own experience or on the basis of highly credible academic research, he must be persuaded that, in a reasonably large number of cases, the indicator turns out to be a solid predictor. Now, some will ask *how* solid a job of prediction the indicator or index must do before it becomes useful in the policy process. Some officials will insist on 100 per cent performance and will shy away from any indicator unless there is a demonstrated correlation of 1.0 between it and the hoped for, or feared, outcome. The purist would, for example, refuse to take seriously a prediction that increased military pressure by A leads to increased diplomatic resistance from B unless that association has *always* occurred.

This seems overly conservative in two ways. First, it ignores the hard fact that foreign offices are always playing the odds, and, no matter how unconscious the operation may be, the estimation of probabilities goes into almost all predictions. Second, this very tendency to think probabilistically reflects an important reality of the political world: Very few events or conditions *are* certain. It is not only the state of our knowledge about diplomatic behavior and the changing state of the global system; it is also that *some* degree of randomness will always inhere in these phenomena. Thus, we urge that, at this early stage in the development of solid knowledge about international politics, we set more modest and realistic standards. We are not prepared to state what the performance level of an indicator should be in order to take it seriously, but we would point out that—if track records *were* kept—most of us would be pleased to do better than two out of three on nonroutine predictions.[4]

INDICATORS IN THE STATE OF THE WORLD MESSAGE

So much, then, for the usefulness of foreign policy indicators in the abstract. Let us shift now to a more specific real world context, in which we find some promising signs of an increased role of such indicators. Reference is to the "state of the world" message inaugurated by President Nixon and his special assistant for national security affairs, Henry Kissinger.

The first of these was presented to the Congress—and the wider world at home and abroad—at the beginning of Nixon's second year in the White House (February 18, 1970). Entitled *U.S. Foreign Policy for the 1970's: A New Strategy for Peace,* it represented both a report on the Administration's first year of foreign policy stewardship and a statement of predictions and preferences regarding the near and middle future. Linked in style and timing to the traditional State of the Union message, it was quickly dubbed—with official encouragement—the "state of the world" message. The second and third ones (February 25, 1971, and February 9, 1972) were similar in form and orientation to the first and, like their predecessor, carried the peace theme in the subtitle.

While there is always some tendency to dismiss such reports as self-serving propaganda and political smokescreen, these state of the world messages obviously have other purposes as well.[5] In addition to assuring the Congress, the media, and the domestic public of the Administration's competence, patriotism, far-sightedness, and commitment to peace, the document also meets two other important needs. One is that of communicating a range of signals to other governments, friendly and otherwise, and to some of the world's intergovernmental organizations, in a fairly general and noncommittal fashion. The other is to provide guidance and legitimation to U.S. officials in Washington and in the field.

Finally, although the authors may not have so intended, the state of the world message provides in one place the sort of general overview of world politics which policy analysts may explore for a variety of purposes. One might, by techniques ranging from those of biblical exegesis to quantitative content analysis, search for all sorts of patterns, trends, deviations, inconsistencies, subtle clues, blunt warnings, articulated and unarticulated premises, and so forth.[6] Our purpose is more limited, and our technique quite simple.

Given the persistence of the "peace" theme in all three messages to date, we sought to tap the Administration's collective views as to which particular events and conditions make for peace, conflict, and war in the modern global system and its subsystems. More specifically—and even allowing for the possibility of intentionally misleading statements or deliberately vague interagency compromise phrases—the document offers an excellent opportunity to identify the sorts of indicators used by this

Administration, implicitly or explicitly, to predict to, or away from, war. Once these indicators have been "teased out" of the document, we might then be able to convert them into more operational language and then ascertain the extent to which they *have* been dependable predictive indicators in the past. That is, given the tendency of the U.S. and other foreign policy establishments to base their forecasts on "lessons of the past" and what "history tells," it is not inappropriate to ask how closely those "lessons" conform to the systematically observed regularities.

In so doing, however, we cannot overemphasize the tentative nature of this comparison. First, despite a conscientious effort to avoid it, we may have misinterpreted the phraseology of these reports and attributed a position to the Administration which is not justified. This danger is more real when dealing with pre-operational statements, and as foreign-policy-makers begin to speak in more precise terms, via the use of indicators, the possibility of misinterpretation will, of course, decline. Second, we are looking here at only a small part of the historical evidence: that which has been generated by a single project. When the work of such scholars as North and Rosecrance and their colleagues is brought to bear, a more adequate test of these historical predictions (or post-dictions) will be possible.[7] And, third, given the tentative nature of the results emerging from the Correlates of War project and the others mentioned, it would be premature to claim that we have really pinned down the historical correlations to which we refer.

What we have attempted here, then, is a two-step operation involving these reports. First, we have selected from them a number of predictive statements which embody—if only implicitly—the idea of early warning indicators in the area of war and peace. These are statements which predict that certain preconditions will increase the probability of war for the international system, its regions, or certain specific nations. Second, we have translated these statements into more operational language, using the indicators which had been devised earlier for the Correlates of War project. Rather than spell out the reasoning and procedures behind each of these indicators here, we will cite the book or article in which that information can be found.[8] And, third, we have asked how regularly the predictor indicators and the war outcomes have been associated in the manner postulated by the Administration. Thus, in each of the following sections, we will offer the predictive statement as it appears in one of the three state of the world reports, summarize how we convert the predictor variable into an operational indicator, and examine the extent to which it *has* been correlated with war over the century and a half from the Congress of Vienna through 1956.[9]

Acceptance of War Leads to More War

Let us turn now to the first of the predictors we have selected for discussion from the state of the world messages. One of the more widely accepted propositions in the folklore of international politics is that war begets war, on the premise that (a) the victorious initiator of war will seek to repeat his success; (b) another will be encouraged by the example; or (c) the defeated party will, alone or with others, move as soon as feasible to settle old scores. In any event, we find in the 1972 report (p. 148) the proposition that "the resort to military solutions, if accepted, would only tempt other nations in delicately poised regions of tension to try the same."

The predictive indicator, like most of those used in diplomacy, can be interpreted (and thus operationalized) in several ways. Beginning with the loosest, we can interpret "resort to military solutions" as war in general. Historically, *does* war lead to war? During the 150 years from 1816 through 1956, 93 serious international wars began (wars with 1,000 or more battle deaths). How often were such wars followed by another within the same or the subsequent year? [10] It turns out that 53 (57%) of the 93 wars were so followed by another war. But what does this tell us about war contagion? For instance, how likely is it that those 53 wars could have been followed by war by sheer chance alone?

TABLE 1a
Frequency with Which War Years Are Followed by War Years, 1816–1965

		War Year?		
		Yes	No	
War	Yes	41	39	80
Follows?	No	29	41	70
		70	80	150

$$\chi^2 = 1.45$$
$$\phi = .09$$

To test this null hypothesis (that it *was* mere chance), we use the *year* as our unit of analysis, and ask whether years during which international war began were more likely to be followed by another war beginning in the same or the subsequent year than those years in which *no* war began. It turns out that the 93 wars in our study began in 70 different years. Of those 70 war years, 51 saw the onset of one war, 16 saw two wars begin, 2 years saw three wars, and one year was cursed with the onset of four. Of the 51 single war years, 22 were followed by at least one war in the subsequent year. Those 22, plus the 19 multiple-war years, make a total of 41 years in which war that began in one year was followed by at least one more beginning in the same or the subsequent year.

Expressing these figures in the contingency table (Table 1a), we find that we cannot reject the null hypothesis. That is, 41 war years and 39 nonwar years were followed closely by war, and this is a negligible difference. Looking at it another way, 29 of the war years and 41 of the nonwar ones were followed by nonwar years. Again, while this latter difference is greater than the first, and is also in the predicted direction, the two sets of differences could have occurred by chance alone, as reflected in the chi-square (χ^2) value of 1.45 and the very weak phi (ϕ) coefficient of .09.[11]

		TABLE 1b 19th Century					TABLE 1c 20th Century		
		War Year?					War Year?		
		Yes	No				Yes	No	
War	Yes	31	21	52	War	Yes	10	18	28
Follows?	No	14	18	32	Follows?	No	15	23	38
		45	39	84			25	41	66

$$\chi^2 = 2.00 \qquad\qquad\qquad \chi^2 = 0.10$$
$$\phi = .15 \qquad\qquad\qquad\quad \phi = .04$$

Given the possibility of important differences between the 19th and 20th centuries, however, it behooves us to examine them separately. In the 19th, the differences are in the direction predicted by the war-leads-to-war proposition. But in the 20th, we find that while 10 war years were followed by more war, 15 were not, suggesting that war is more likely to begin in a "fresh" setting, rather than on the heels of another. In neither case, however, are the differences sufficiently clear to reject the hypothesis that the configurations could have occurred by chance alone.

A slightly more restricted interpretation of the war-leads-to-more-war prediction is to divide the international system into its major geographical regions and see whether the contagion proposition stands. Given the fact that each region will have fewer wars over the full time span than will the system as a whole, we are not surprised to find even less evidence for the contagion hypothesis in this case. Over-all, only 40 per cent of the wars in any given region occurred within the same or following years of one another. So far, then, to treat the occurrence of military hostilities as an indication that others will soon follow is to be unduly pessimistic.

The alert reader may, however, object to our equating of the specific resort to military solutions with war in general. Perhaps the proposition refers to individual nation entries into war, and given the fact that some wars (20 of the 50 interstate wars, or 40%) involved more than two parties, it is worth recomputing our contagion indicators.[12] On that basis, we find that the prediction is again not very solidly based. That is, if we look at all 189 nation-entries into war for the entire period, only 87 of them (46%) occurred within the year or two of a prior war's onset.

But this may *still* be too general an interpretation of the Administration's proposition. Perhaps the phrase "if accepted" may well be essential to an understanding of the authors' meaning that the victim of armed attack was not promptly and vigorously joined by others who came to its defense. Thus, we now ask how frequently we find such cases followed by susequent resort to force. Since the question here is whether different kinds of wars are more or less likely to be followed by war, we return to the *war* rather than the *year* as the unit of analysis.

Restricting ourselves to the 50 interstate wars which mark the 1816–1965 period (thus excluding the colonial and imperial wars, which rarely engaged third parties), we find that 13 were marked by such intervention on the side of those who were attacked, while 37 were not. Since 6 of the 13 former cases (46%) were soon followed by another war and 15 of the 37 latter were (43%), it would appear to make little difference whether "resort to military solutions" was accepted by the rest of the system or not. That is, wars in which the victim is left to fight alone are not significantly more likely to be followed by more war than those in which the victim of armed attack *is* joined by others.

TABLE 2

		Victim Aided?		
		Yes	No	
War	Yes	6	15	21
Follows?	No	7	22	29
		13	37	50

$$\chi^2 = .12$$
$$\phi = .05$$

Alternatively, "accepted" could be interpreted to mean that the initiators were "permitted" to emerge victorious, and that under *those* conditions, war might beget more war. Here, we again find the evidence mixed. Thus, of the 50 interstate wars in our population of cases, the initiators won 34 of them. In 12 of those 34 cases (35%), renewed interstate warfare broke out in the near future. Conversely, on those 16 occasions in which the initiator did *not* win, the number followed by war was 9 (56%). While this is a higher proportional figure, it is not quite enough to justify the counter conclusion that peace is best preserved by permitting the initiator to win.

TABLE 3a

		Initiator Wins?		
		Yes	No	
War	Yes	12	9	21
Follows?	No	22	7	29
		34	16	50

$$\chi^2 = 1.96$$
$$\phi = .20$$

In this context, we might again ask whether the historical evidence is more solid in one or the other of our two centuries. In the 19th, which saw 27 of the 50 interstate wars, 19 were won by the initiator. But only 6 of those 19, or 32%, were followed by war, while 6 of the 8, or 75%, which were *lost* by the initiator, were so followed. In this case, we *can* reject the null hypothesis that war outcome makes no difference; rather, the pattern is in the opposite direction (Cramer's ϕ of .40). In other words, for the 19th century, wars which the initiator *lost* were more likely to be quickly followed by another, initiated by either the same or another state.

TABLE 3b						TABLE 3c					
19th Century						20th Century					
		Initiator Wins?						Initiator Wins?			
		Yes	No					Yes	No		
War	Yes	6	6	12		War	Yes	7	2	9	
Follows?	No	13	2	15		Follows?	No	8	6	14	
		19	8	27				15	8	23	
	$\chi^2 = 4.30$						$\chi^2 = 1.03$				
	$\phi = .40$						$\phi = .21$				

What about the 20th century? Here we find that 7 of the 15 (47%) wars won by the initiator in this century were soon followed by war, while only 2 of the 8 (25%) in which the initiator lost were so followed —making for a pattern just the reverse of the 19th century experience. However, in this century, the relationship, while supporting the Administration's prediction, is not strong enough (Cramer's ϕ of .21) to allow ready acceptance of the hypothesis that the initiator's winning is more likely to lead to another war.

So far, we have found little support for the notion that wars in which the victim nations are defended by other nations are less likely to be followed by another war than wars in which the victim is not defended. The same holds for the notion that defeating the initiator will inhibit the prompt beginning of other wars. But there is one further question which we may ask at this point. Among those specific cases (13) in which the victim nation *is* defended by others, are the wars won by the initiator more likely to be followed by war? The answer might be surprising to some. In those 13 cases, the initiator was defeated 9 times. However, 5 of the 9 were followed by another interstate war beginning in the same or the subsequent year, while only one of the 4 (or 25%) in which the initiator won—in spite of the fact that others came to the defense of the victim—was followed by war. While we cannot reject the null hypothesis that there is no difference in this case (primarily because of the small N), the relationship is moderate (Cramer's ϕ of .28). There is, therefore, some tentative evidence that "punishing" (by defeating) war initiators does not prevent other wars from quickly erupting, and that coming to the defense of an attacked nation and defeating the "aggressor" not only does *not* deter future aggression, but, on the contrary, may even lead to further war. Thus, the "acceptance" of war, by itself, is not a particularly dependable early warning indicator of future war.

Weakness Leads to War

A close corollary of the proposition that the global community's acquiescence in the initiation of war will lead to more war is that which tells us that relative weakness leads to war. This may be interpreted as both a national level and a more general, system level, prediction, with weaker nations being more vulnerable and therefore more likely to have to fight in self defense, and with weakness on the part of the "peace loving" (or "status quo"?) nations serving as a temptation to the stronger. This type of predictive statement finds repeated expression in all three of the Administration's reports on the state of the world. It appears in particularly crisp language on page 4 of the first of these: "Peace requires strength. So long as there are those who would threaten our vital interests and those of our allies with military force, we must be strong. American weakness could tempt would-be aggressors to make dangerous miscalculations." And the theme is echoed in 1972: "American weakness would make no contribution to peace. On the contrary, it would undermine prospects for peace."

In discussing the relationship, past or predicted, between war-proneness and national power or strength, we quickly come face to face with the familiar question, "What is power?" . . . First, there is the difference between power base or power potential, on the one hand, and military preparedness or other indices of force in being, on the other. Second, the bases of power have changed across time. Third, a nation's capacity to exercise influence may range considerably across space. The indicator we employ here is a very general one, and that limitation should be kept in mind as the discussion unfolds.[13]

We use a straightforward measure in which we combine six factors: steel production, energy consumption, urban population, the square root of total population, armed forces size, and military expenditure. For more thorough analyses, we use several different combinations and weightings of these six, but here we will merely compute each nation's share of each element's distribution in the system, and then compute its mean percentage share. Thus, if a nation has 8% of the system's armed forces, steel production, and urban population, and 12% of its military expenditures, energy consumption, and total population (5), its composite score would be 10%. In the analysis at hand, restricted to the major powers only for the 150-year period, the rankings and scores turn out to be remarkably close to those that a diplomatic historian might expect; in other words, the face validity of the indicators—as a reflection of *general* power potential—appears to be quite high. (For a more restricted test, and perhaps one more appropriate to the Administration's argument, we might use the military dimensions only, or better yet, an indicator which reflects the fraction of over-all capabilities which has been allocated to military preparedness.)

Using this composite indicator, *does* it turn out that major powers are more likely to get into war, or to be attacked, when they are (a) nearer the bottom of the capability scale or (b) experiencing a decline in relative power? In the table below, we present a rough summary of where each major power stood vis-à-vis the others in that subset on the eve of most of its wars, as well as the direction in which its capabilities tended to be moving at that time, in regard to the subsystem average score.

TABLE 4
Capabilities of Major Powers Predicting
to Their Entry into Interstate Wars

	Capability Above the Average		Capability Below the Average	
	Not Falling	Falling	Not Falling	Falling
United States	0	5	1	0
England	1	2	0	3
France	4	3	1	4
Germany/Prussia	2	0	3	1
Austria-Hungary	0	0	1	4
Italy/Sardina	0	0	5	4
USSR/Russia	5	3	0	1
China	1	0	2	3
Japan	0	0	5	1
Totals	13	13	18	21

First, if we add all four columns for all the war experienced by system members when they (and their successor states) were major powers, we find a total of 65 nation–war experiences. Of these, 26 occurred when the specific power had a capability score *above* the average of all powers, while 39 occurred when they were *below* the mean. To the extent that we have a valid indicator of strength and that the average score constitutes a reasonable cutting point between the weaker and the stronger, the Administration's prediction finds historical support. Next, we ask whether that pattern is reinforced by the association between the nations' war experiences and the rise, stability, or decline in their capability scores. Here we find a modest difference: 34 occur when the major power's score is falling, and 31 when it is either rising or holding steady. As to the combined "effect" of both scores, the 13–13 and 18–21 figures reinforce the impression that present strength is moderately important and that direction of change is of minor consequence. On the other hand, the U.S. experience is unique in that 5 of its 6 wars began while it was in the upper half, but on the decline.

TABLE 5
Relative Strength of Initiators in Major Power Wars

	Initiator Stronger	Initiator Weaker
Initiator Rising	Seven Weeks WW II	Ital. Unif. Russo-Jap. (04) WW I Russo-Jap. (39) Korean
Initiator Falling	Crimean Franco-Pruss.	

It is, of course, one thing to ask whether the nations' strength vis-à-vis all the other major powers helps us predict to their general war proneness, and quite another to ask whether relative strength predicts to war in a more specific context. Thus, we now inquire as to the relative capabilities of the major powers vis-à-vis those others who *initiate* war against them over these 150 years. Here our question is whether the initiator and its allies are stronger or weaker than their victims in those 9 wars in which there was one or more major power on each side.[14] As Table 5 shows, these 9 wars do not quite fall into the pattern predicted by the Administration. That is, the nations which were actually attacked were appreciably *stronger* than the initiators in 5 of these 9 wars, and in 2 of the others (Franco-Prussian and World War II's opening round), both sides were virtually equal in capabilities. In the Crimean War, France and England enjoyed a marked superiority, but it is not altogether clear that we should label them as initiators. On the other hand, in the Seven Weeks War of 1865, the victim (Austria-Hungary) *was* appreciably weaker than the initiating powers, but only because Prussia and Sardinia had joined forces for the occasion.

As to the possible effects of *changes* in capability, a corollary of the state of the world proposition finds stronger support. That is, if we look at direction and magnitude of change (averaged if more than one power was involved on either side), we find that the initiator's direction of change was more favorable than the defender's in 7 of the 9 cases. In 5 of those 7, the defender's score showed an *absolute* decline during the half decade prior to the war, and the initiator's showed an absolute decline only once. Further support for the weakness-leads-to-war argument is that we find *no* cases in which the initiators were both weaker *and* experiencing a disadvantageous trend. Or to put it another way, our limited historical experiment tends to confirm the belief that major power wars are often initiated by nations which are relatively inferior, but gaining vs-à-vis the leaders. This may not be precisely the way in which the Administration formulated its proposition, but it is sufficiently close to cause alarm. That is, there is little hope for keeping the peace unless one power or bloc is not only stronger, but increasing in capability vis-à-vis the potential initiator.

Alliances Help to Deter War

As intimated in the previous sections, the likelihood of war and the nature of its outcome will depend not only upon the relative strength of the would-be initiator and its victim. The capabilities of allies can often be conclusive. But it is usually too late to begin forming alliances once war has begun, or even on its eve; as a matter of fact, of the 177 formal alliances established during the 150 years under study, only 8 were consummated during, or within the three months preceding, hostilities. This tendency, by itself, suggests that practitioners have generally shared the Administration's view that "we must build an alliance strong enough to deter those who might threaten war" (1970, p. 27).

TABLE 6
Correlations Between Alliance Aggregation and Onset of War

Predictors	No. of Wars	Nation Months	Battle Deaths
Total period:			
% of nations in any alliance	.00	.27	.26
% of nations in defense pacts	−.01	.05	−.01
% of majors in any alliance	.01	.20	.20
% of majors in defense pacts	.00	.11	.09
19th century:			
% of nations in any alliance	.03	−.09	−.24
% of nations in defense pacts	.00	.10	−.23
% of majors in any alliance	−.21	−.18	−.34
% of majors in defense pacts	−.16	−.28	−.45
20th century:			
% of nations in any alliance	.00	.23	.21
% of nations in defense pacts	−.02	.05	.04
%of majors in any alliance	.34	.31	.28
% of majors in defense pacts	.19	.12	.04

Such an inquiry requires three different foci. First, is the international system less war-prone when alliance levels are high? Second, are the nations which join into most of the alliances also the ones which experience the least war? Third, does high alliance involvement on the eve of war make a nation less likely to be drawn into that war?

Before examining the historical correlations between alliance levels and war, we should summarize the operations and reasoning behind our indicators. Despite the relative ease of identifying all formal alliances (at least after the archives are opened) and differentiating among their types, ours represents the first published effort to convert that diplomatic information into machine-readable, quantitative indicators. First, we only include written treaties of alliance between and among sovereign states. Second, we differentiate among (a) defense pacts, in which the signatories contract to *fight alongside* one another if either is "attacked"; (b) neutrality or nonaggression pacts, in which the obligation is to *not fight against* the other; and (c) ententes, which oblige the signatories to *consult* in the event, or imminent likelihood of, hostilities. Third, we exclude (a) highly asymmetric alliances and treaties of guaraneee; (b) collective security arrangements such as the League and the U.N., in which the potential attacker may well be one of the signatories; and (c) general declarations of nonviolent behavior, such as the Kellogg-Briand Pact or the Geneva Conventions.

With all alliances, members, and dates recorded, we then combine the information in order to measure, for each year, what percentage of the *system's* members are in one or more alliances of each type; these are our alliance aggregation indicators. For each *nation*, we ascertain the number of alliance commitments of each type it has with different classes of nations each year, in order to get its alliance commitment index.

Turning now to the question at the systemic level of analysis, we ask whether the amount of war which began in every three-year period since 1816 was indeed lower when the alliance aggregation indicators were high. For the entire period, the pattern is not particularly strong, but what pattern there is does not point in the direction predicted in the state of the world report. And as the correlation matrix shows, the higher the alliance aggregation level, the higher the amount of war in the next three years for the current century.[15]

For the 19th century, on the other hand, Mssrs. Nixon, Kissinger, *et al.,* do appreciably better in their predictions (or, more literally, post-dictions). First, almost all of the signs are in the postulated direction, with war magnitudes down when alliance levels are up. Further, several of the correlation coefficients are high enough to have been unlikely to occur by chance alone. Finally, defense pacts among majors seem to exercise a particularly strong downward effect on war as reflected in battle-connected fatalities. But as the state of the world report reminds us, "perceptions framed in the 19th century are hardly relevant to the new era we are now entering" (1970, p. 136).[16]

Shifting now to the individual nations, we concentrate on the major powers alone and again find a very mixed pattern. As the correlation

TABLE 7
Correlations Between Major Power Alliance
Involvement and War Experience

Predictors	No. of Wars	Months of War	Battle Deaths
All alliances	.60	−.39	.13
Defense pacts	.42	−.45	.07
Neutrality pacts	.25	−.07	−.47
Ententes	.67	.01	.049
Alliances with majors	.00	−.26	−.49
Defense with majors	−.03	−.37	−.28
Neutrality with majors	.11	−.23	−.58
Ententes with majors	.00	.08	−.66

matrix indicates, the high alliance joiners have a consistent tendency to get into more wars, but for those war experiences to be shorter, on the average, and slightly less bloody than those of the low joiners. Of more than passing interest is the tendency of those majors which limit themselves to neutrality pacts with all other nations to sustain fewer battle deaths than those which join ententes. On the other hand, entering defense and neutrality pacts with other majors seems to have virtually no correlation with the frequency of war entry, but clearly helps to keep their war months and battle deaths low. One possible inference to draw (subject to the reservation in the following paragraphs) is that, if major powers do choose to go into alliances, they should do so only with other majors and, above all, avoid ententes with minor powers.

As implied earlier in this section, these coefficients tell us nothing of the temporal sequence; a nation *could* have most of its alliance involvement in one historical epoch and its wars in another. Thus, a more realistic test for the proposition that alliances deter war is to examine the extent to which high alliance involvement is followed by low war experience for the nations, and vice versa.

What we examine here is the frequency with which major power membership in one or more alliances in a given year is followed by entry into interstate war during that same year or within the two following years. As the contingency table shows, there is virtually no discernible pattern. Of the 648 major power alliance membership years, 116 (18%) are followed by war entry, while 532 (82%) are not. While this looks as if alliance membership reduces war experience, we next note that of the 239 nation-years not marked by alliance membership, 44 are nevertheless followed by entry into war and 195 are not. These percentages are also 18% and 82% respectively, identical to those for years in which these

TABLE 8

		In Alliance?		
		Yes	No	
Enters	Yes	116	44	160
War?	No	532	195	727
		648	239	887

$$\chi^2 = .03$$
$$\phi = 0.0$$

nations *were* in alliances. The similarity of these ratios is confirmed when we compute the χ^2 and ϕ coefficients, each of which is negligible. In other words, membership in alliances seems to have had little effect on the historical likelihood of major powers getting into war or remaining at peace.[17]

System Polarization Leads to War

As nations forge alliance bonds and establish other diplomatic, commercial, or cultural links with one another, the over-all system configuration can take on a variety of patterns. To the extent that they link up in a diffused fashion, the system will look rather multicentric or multipolar, but as the system's members are drawn into one of two opposing blocs, the pattern becomes increasingly bicentric or bipolar. Most students of international politics and some practitioners expect such polarization to lead to heightened probabilities of war, largely on the ground that the normal cross-cutting diplomatic ties and interaction opportunities are replaced by rigid divisions into friend or foe. The authors of the state of the world message are no exception, and in the 1972 version (p. 16), they have the President speaking of the improved chances for peace among the major powers, concluding that this "has been rendered possible by the end of the bipolar rigidity which characterized the postwar world."

In the Correlates of War project, this link between system structure and war has been a central—if frustrating—preoccupation. The frustration arises from the great difficulty of devising a valid indicator of how polarized (or more precisely, how bicentric) the system is at any point in time. One such indicator is based on the fraction of normal pairwise bonds (those the system would have had in the absence of any alliances) which were lost in a given year via the concentration of its members into opposing blocs. More specifically, and restricting our index construction to the major power subset only, we first computed the maximum number of dyads that *could* be formed, using the standard formula of $N(N - 1) \div 2$. Next, we eliminated all normal pairwise bonds which were lost via (a) alliance partners, between whom competition is less likely; (b) members of opposing alliances, between whom cooperation is less likely; and (c) alliance members and the target nation against whom they were aligned, since cooperation between them is also less likely.[18] By dividing the number of normal bonds (with their mix of cooperation and conflict) that would have obtained *in the absence of alliances* into the number of normal bonds lost via the three routes noted above, we get one possible indicator of polarization.[19]

Employing the A and B versions of this indicator, what sort of

TABLE 9
Correlations Between Polarization and War in Interstate System (I)

	Predictors	No. of Wars	Nation Months	Battle Deaths
Total	Polar. A	−.03	.08	.15
Period	Polar. B	.01	.13	.19
19th	Polar. A	−.21	−.32	−.33
cent.	Polar. B	−.12	−.23	−.28
20th	Polar. A	.27	.15	.19
cent.	Polar. B	.26	.28	.31

historical association do we find between polarization and war? As the correlation matrix shows, the impact of polarization for the entire period is a negligible one. More interesting is the perfectly consistent difference in signs between the two centuries. The polarization of the system in each three-year period predicts negatively to all of our indicators of systemic war in the next three years for the 19th century. And in the current century, as polarization rises, so does war. But we should emphasize that, despite the clear pattern, the correlation coefficients are quite weak, with all but three of them likely to have occurred by chance alone.

Let us now shift to a more complex, and more promising, indicator of system polarization, developed by one of our associates in the project. Here, we apply the "smallest space analysis" technique to each year's nation-by-nation alliance matrix, with the polarization index based on the extent to which the resulting clusters of nations group around and along the dominant axis which emerges. The closer the pattern is to a small number of tightly clustered groupings, the more polarized the system.[20]

Using this more complex indicator, do we find that the Administration's view of the polarity-war association is borne out by history? We computed the bivariate correlations using the indicator summarized above, and then went on to recompute them, using an indicator which reflected military manpower as well as the alliance bonds between all pairs of nations. And as the correlation matrix shows, we used—because it gives the clearest differentiation in the later analyses—cutting points other than the intercentury break. Three generalizations are suggested by the correlation coefficients. First, the pattern is pretty much the same for all three time periods. Second, few of the coefficients are statistically significant. And, third, while the two *war* indicators give virtually identical results, the alternative *polarization* indicators point in opposite directions. That is, if the polarization index merely reflects the way in which the clusters of nations fall (i.e., unweighted), we find a consistently positive association with the onset of war. But when we reduce the "noise" generated by the less powerful (or militarily prepared) nations, and weight the configurations by armed force size, the association is negative. Even though armed force size is a very crude indicator of either prepardeness or military capability, it does produce an index of greater face validity.

TABLE 10
Correlations Between Polarization and War
in Interstate System (II)

Predictors		Nation Months	Battle Deaths
Total	Unwtd. Polar.	.13	.11
Period	Wtd. Polar.	−.33	−.41
1815–1919	Unwtd. Polar.	.11	.13
	Wtd. Polar.	−.15	−.28
1850–1964	Unwtd. Polar.	.17	.23
	Wtd. Polar.	−.39	−.46

Faced with these very mixed results within and between the two sets of analyses, Wallace then went on to test for a possibly more complex historical relationship between system polarization and war. Following (and operationalizing) the Rosecrance hypothesis that the system will be more war-prone when it is either very high *or* very low on polarization, he tested a curvilinear model.[21] The results are summarized in the matrix below, with the multiple R^2 reflecting the amount of variance around the mean accounted for by the weighted polarization indicators. Contrary to all of our prior findings, we now find a clear and consistent pattern, except for the 1815–1919 period.[22] Thus, despite the tentative nature of our indicators, there remains a strong suggestion that the Administration is on reasonably solid historical ground in predicting that high polarization levels make for a more war-prone system. By and large, when the system has been *either* very diffuse or highly polarized, interstate war has increased. Needless to say, while there is discernible movement away from the post–World War II polarization pattern, we are a very long way from the equally dangerous extreme of virtually *no* alliance pattern.

TABLE 11
Multiple R^2 Values for Weighted
Polarization vs. Interstate War

	Nation Months	Battle Deaths
Total Period	.61	.77
1815–1944	.70	.78
1815–1919	.15	.16
1850–1964	.60	.77

International Organization Contributes to Peace

Despite some important differences, formal alliances and international governmental organizations (IGOs) are both formal institutions set up by governments in order to make, *inter alia*, a less warlike international system. Regardless of whether their membership patterns create a more or less polarized system, and despite the positive emphasis of IGOs and the negative emphasis of alliances, it is generally understood that both can help reduce the incidence of war. One recent finding in support of this notion is that both the number and size of IGOs show a sharp increase on the heels of war, suggesting that statesmen tend to turn to them while still in their "never again" frame of mind.[23] And despite some private criticism and erratic sustenance, the U.S. has tended to endorse such organizations as the League and the U.N. Thus, in the 1970 state of the world message, the Nixon Administration termed the achievements of the U.N. as "impressive." In support of that evaluation, the document notes that "the U.N. provides a forum for crisis diplomacy and a means for multilateral assistance. It has encouraged arms control and helped nations reach agreements extending the frontiers of international law. And it offers a framework for private discussions between world leaders, free of the inflated expectations of summit meetings" (p. 104).

This implied prediction that the system and its members will experience less war as IGOs grow and flourish may be scrutinized in two ways. One is to see whether changes in the amount of such organizations has led to any rise or fall in the incidence of war. The other is to see whether the amount of shared membership predicts to the frequency with which specific nations get into war with each other. Turning to the first analysis, at the systemic level, we measure the amount of such organization in the system by counting the number of IGOs, and the number of nation memberships therein, every half-decade since the Congress of Vienna. These give us our first two indicators, and our third is generated by weighting each nation membership by its diplomatic importance score.[24] And since our hypothesis might be more effectively tested by examining *rates* of growth (or decline), we add a fourth indicator: percentage change in weighted memberships during the half-decade.

As the top half of Table 12 makes clear, the amount of intergovernmental organization in the system in each half-decade has no discernible impact on the incidence of war in the following half-decade. Our rank order correlation coefficients show that if we rank all the 30 periods on each of the IGO and onset of war indicators, the pattern will be very close to a random one. And if we examine the product moment correlations, the only generalization we might draw is that the amount of IGO in the system may make war slightly less freqeunt, but somewhat more lengthy and bloody.[25]

TABLE 12
Correlations Between Amount of IGO and War

Predictors	Number of Wars	Nation Months	Battle Deaths
Rank order			
Number of IGOs	.01	.07	.10
Simple memb.	.00	.06	.09
Wtd.	−.02	.06	.08
% Chg. in memb.	−.05	.07	.06
Product moment			
Number of IGOs	−.06	.26	.22
Simpl memb.	−.08	.23	.20
Wtd. memb.	−.07	.27	.23
% Chg. in wtd. memb.	−.19	−.04	.03

These patterns must be treated in a very skeptical fashion, not only because they range from nearly invisible to very weak, but also because any system level analysis is insensitive to the identity of the nations; it may well be that those which account for most of the IGO membership are not the ones which account for most of the war. Second, there has been a dramatic upward trend in the number and size of IGOs since 1816, and since wars have become slightly less frequent and somewhat longer and bloodier, the statistical results are far from surprising.

Shifting from systemic level predictions to those at the *dyadic* level, does the existence of intergovernmental organization bonds help us anticipate whether or not the specific pairs of nations will be more or less war prone than those with few or no such bonds? In partial support of the Administration's prediction, it does turn out that those nations whose shared IGO memberships decline during a given half-decade tend to become involved in war more frequently than those whose bonds remain constant or actually increase. Furthermore, those pairs of nations whose shared memberships drop to half or fewer of their original level (controlling for the upward historical trend) are virtually certain to go to war against one another.[26]

Despite this latter—and not surprising—finding, the general impact of intergovernmental organization on war, by itself, is a negligible one. Perhaps a better early warning indicator regarding IGO and war is that implied in the same section as the opening quotation: "But we have had to recognize that the U.N. cannot by itself solve fundamental international disputes, especially among the superpowers. . . . We cannot expect it to be a more telling force for peace than its members make it" (p. 105).

CONCLUSION

In our effort to illustrate ways in which contingent predictions ("if _____, then _____") in foreign policy might be improved via the use of operational indicators, we have merely scratched the surface. First of all, we have selected such predictions from only one set of documents reflecting a single nation and single government. Second, we have only selected those which could be examined in the light of a small part of a single research project. Third, all of the contingent predictions are of a simple bivariate nature, with a single predictor variable; and while many practitioners and researchers tend to think in essentially bivariate terms, a moment's pause reminds us that few outcomes in international politics are likely to be "determined" by a single factor. Furthermore, we have addressed ourselves primarily to the prediction problem in policy-making and have ignored many critical issues ranging from the decisional setting through effective implementation. Nor have we wrestled with the differentiation between variables which might have a great deal of predictive or explanatory power and those which—while not theorectially powerful—may offer opportunities for conscious and timely human intervention.

On the other hand, this modest exercise should convey an idea of the possibility that we may indeed "learn from history." If we can frame our policy prediction statements in more precise language, we are already partway to the construction of reliable and valid indicators. If we can begin to approach history in a systematic and rigorous fashion, rather than merely ransack it for arguments and analogies that are convenient at the moment, we can begin to accumulate a fair amount of existential and correlational knowledge. If we can assimilate that knowledge through a multi-theoretical taxonomy, we can begin to develop modest islands of explanatory knowledge. If that knowledge can be integrated into alternative theories, these can be put to further historical test. And, from the more successful and accurate theories, additional predictions can be made. This sequential scenario is, of course, very close to what any serious policy analyst would seek. As the President's staff noted early in the first state of the world message, "Our actions must be the products of thorough analysis, forward planning, and deliberate decision. . . . We must know the facts: intelligent discussions . . . and wise decisions require the most reliable information available. . . . We must know the alternatives: we must know what our real options are, and not simply what compromise has found bureaucratic acceptance" (pp. 17–18).[27]

Having sounded this moderately sanguine note, however, it now behooves us to back off and face up to some of the more critical issues that confront the applied scientist. First, there is the question of whether social scientists should be concerned with the policy implications of their research. Should we actively emphasize those implications, ignore them, or intentionally conceal them, to take the three dominant views? Further, should we make available to some governments and not to others? To some political parties and not others? To some agencies or bureaus and not others? In the short run, of course, these remain fairly academic questions, given (a) the paucity of even our correlational and predictive (not to mention explanatory) knowledge and (b) the skepticism of foreign office types the world over.

But as (and if) the proposed trend continues and our knowledge base becomes more solid, these can emerge as increasingly salient questions. To respond in an indirect fashion, we have no illusions that all the disasters that befall mankind are a consequence of ignorance or incompetence; nor do we urge that if we merely understood more fully the consequences of our actions, life would be less nasty, brutish, or short. Similarly, we do not suggest that there is little difference between the "good guys" and the "bad guys" in classifying nations, regimes, agencies, or individuals. But we would nevertheless argue that an applied social science is an essential concomitant of any related efforts to move toward a world of peace, prosperity, and justice.

Further, the same extension and diffusion of knowledge which can make policy-makers become more sophisticated and insightful regarding the issues which confront them can also serve to distenthrall the general citizen.[28] Whether cheerleader, nay-sayer, or victim of governmental decisions, the man in the street can become a more critical and knowledgeable participant in the governmental process. And, in doing so, he or she will increasingly blunt one of the major weapons of demagogues, bigots, warmongers, or imperialists: the combined ignorance which permits the leader, as well as the led, to believe the most ill-founded and vicious propaganda.

This consideration leads us, with some reluctance, to the unattractive issue of pseudo-science or scientism. Not only the general citizen and the politician, but the specialists in foreign and defense ministries—especially the latter—are always in danger of being taken in by research that *looks* like science. To some extent, the universities, but more often the think tanks and industrial research firms, are well populated with "number jugglers" whose reports have a decidedly scientific aura to them. The background factors that make for shoddy work are all too familiar: (a) Today's strategic analyst or Middle East specialist was yesterday's expert on traffic safety or water pollution; (b) a large fraction of the organization's business comes from a mission-oriented client, such as the U.S. Air Force; (c) time pressures often guarantee a quick and dirty job on contract research.[29]

But most often the source is simple ignorance at the client's end as well as at the researcher's end. This need not be surprising, given the durability of the three-culture problem in today's world. Sir Charles Snow reminds us of the gulf between the scientific culture and the humanistic culture, but he neglects to emphasize that those of the former class are no less ignorant of the social sciences than those of the latter; engineers, physicists, and systems analysts often have even more erroneous notions about social systems (and how to study them) than poets, lawyers, or businessmen.

Thus, we conclude with an emphasis on not only the familiar need for more research, but the less familiar one of the need for a very different kind of "education for world affairs." In the primary and secondary schools, in colleges and graduate schools, and, perhaps more critically, in the public and private discussion of public policy questions, it is essential that we move out of the Neanderthal era. Superstition was of little use in understanding the weather or predicting whether a tunnel would withstand a given water pressure, and medieval notions of human physiology were of little help in diagnosing and curing disease. Why should we hope that such primitivism will suffice in the solution of foreign policy problems? Until we move beyond them, human beings will have to live—and all too often, die—with the consequences of decisions made and executed by the kinds of half-educated foreign ministers and simple-minded defense ministers who have loomed all too large recently on the American foreign policy horizon.

NOTES

1. For some examples and discussions, see U.N. Department of Economic and Social Affairs, *Report on the World Social Situation,* (New York: United Nations, 1957–); Raymond A. Bauer (ed.), *Social Indicators* (Cambridge: MIT Press, 1966); Eleanor Sheldon and Wilbert E. Moore (eds.), *Indicators of Social Change* (New York: Russell Sage Foundation, 1968); Commission on the Social Sciences National Sciences Board, *Knowledge into Action: Improving the Nation's Use of the Social Sciences* (Washington, D.C.: National Science Foundation, 1969); U.S. Department of Health, Education, and Welfare, *Toward a Social Report* (U.S. Government Printing Office, Washington, D.C., 1969); Otis Dudley Duncan, *Toward Social Reporting: Next Steps* (New York: Russell Sage Foundation, 1970); Amitai Etzioni, "Indicators of the Capacities for Societal Guidance," *The Annals of the American Academy of Political and Social Science,* 388 (March 1970); and Fred R. Harris (ed.), *Social Science and National Policy* (Chicago: Aldine-Atherton, 1970). One of the earliest efforts to tap a particularly remote social condition is in Norman Bradburn and David Caplovitz, *Reports on Happiness* (Chicago: Aldine, 1965). And for one attempt to apply social indicators to the quality of life in the global system, see J. David Singer, "Individual Values, National Interests, and Political Development in the International System," in Horowtiz (ed.), *Studies in Comparative International Development* (Beverly Hills, Calif.: Sage, 1971).

2. A recurrent theme in the criticism is that expressed by Irving Kristol in "In Search of the Missing Social Indicators," *Fortune* (August 1, 1969): "These statistics are organized primarily for management purposes. . . . We can account for public money spent [for example] on mental health, but we haven't the faintest idea whether our mental health is getting better or worse. More than that, we don't even have as yet the conceptual apparatus that would enable us to say what we *mean* by mental health, much less permit us to measure it by a series of index numbers."

Other criticisms—especially of many economic indicators—are their failure to reflect inequalities in distribution, the assumption that advertising or military expenditures are social "goods," and their inability to tap the more general concepts of welfare. In response to the latter criticism, one economist retorted: "Producing a summary measure of social welfare is a job for a philosopher-king, and there is no room for a philosopher-king in the federal government." Arthur Okun, "Should GNP Measure Social Welfare?" *Brookings Bulletin* 8/3 (1971): 4–7.

3. See Davis Bobrow and Judah Schwartz (eds.), *Computers and the Policy Making Community* (Englewood Cliffs, N.J.: Prentice-Hall, 1968): Davis Bobrow, "International Indicators," American Political Science Association (September 1969); and Davis Bobrow, "Political and Social Forecasting," National Bureau of Standards, Gaithersburg, Maryland (March 1970).

4. In one of the few efforts to estimate such performance, Jensen found that U.S. State and Defense Department respondents scored 67% and 63% respectively on 25 predictions made in 1965 re diplomatic events which did or did not occur in the next half-decade; see Lloyd Jensen, "Predicting International Events," Philadelphia: Temple University (February 1972).

Among the discussions of international event prediction, and tentative efforts to devise predictive indicators, are: Stuart Carter Dodd, "A Barometer of Perceived International Security," *Public Opinion Quarterly* 9/2 (Summer 1945): 194–200; Gaston Bouthoul, "Les Barometres Polémologiques," *Etudes Polémologiques* 1 (1971): 1–26; Rudolph Rummel, "Forecasting International Relations: A Proposed Investigation of Three-Mode Factor Analysis," *Technological Forecasting* 1 (1969): 197–216; Arthur Vogel, "Toward a Foreign Policy Reporting System," *World Affairs* 133/2 (September 1970); Uolevi Arosalo, "East-West Trade as a Potential Indicator of International Tension," *Instant Research on Peace and Violence* 3 (Tampere, Finland, 1971): 120–25; Norman Z. Alcock, "The Prediction of War," Ontario: Canadian Peace Research Institute, 1972; Alan G. Newcombe, Nora S. Newcombe, and Gary D. Landrus, "The Development of an Inter-Nation Tensiometer," *International Interactions* 1/1 (1974): 3–18.

5. James Reston, in *New York Times* (February 19, 1970), likened the first one to a maxicoat in that "it is long, it covers a lot of territory, and it conceals the most interesting parts." Other media reactions included that of David Lawrence in *U.S. News and World Report* (February 28, 1972, p. 92), who saw the third report "as one of the most weighty, most serious, and best argued statements of American foreign policy to be made since the end of the Second World War." The Palm Beach *Post-Times* (February 12, 1972), on the other hand, described the same one as "an election year exercise in political propaganda," full of "chest-beating superlatives" set in "gloss and glitter."

6. For a systematic, if somewhat superficial, effort to tap the superpowers' operational codes during the late 1950s via the State Department *Bulletin, Pravda,* etc., see J. David Singer, "Soviet and American Foreign Policy Attitudes: Content Analysis of Elite Articulations," *Conflict Resolution* 8/4 (December 1964): 424–85.

7. See, as illustrative, Robert North and Nazli Choucri, *Nations in Conflict: National Growth and International Conflict* (San Francisco: W. H. Freeman,

1975), and Richard Rosecrance, *Action and Reaction in World Politics* (Boston: Little, Brown, 1963).

Some would say post-diction or retro-diction, but it seems reasonable to speak of pre-diction, even in the past, as long as we have not yet observed and recorded the unfolding of events or the extent to which the predictor and outcome variables did indeed co-vary.

8. For the rationale, procedures, and data on the incidence of war at the systemic, regional, pairwise, and national levels, see J. David Singer and Melvin Small, *The Wages of War, 1816–1965: A Statistical Handbook* (New York: Wiley, 1972). As these dates imply, those wars that had not ended—or even begun— by December 31, 1965, are not included: the several Indochina Wars, the Six Day War in the Mideast, the Football War, and those in Yemen, Aden, and Angola.

   A useful summary of the over-all project will be found in J. David Singer, "The Correlates of War Project: Interim Report and Rationale," *World Politics* 24/2 (January 1972): 243–70.

9. We must differentiate here between the generalizations which can be drawn from a study of comparable cases out of the past and the sort of dynamic models which can be generated and tested from an examination of the processes which link these cases together as they unfold across time. As Bobrow reminds us in "International Indicators," p. 5, without adequate models "we have no more than descriptive trend plots which lack explanatory power and ignore interaction effects."

10. Throughout this section, we use this time span of 1–2 years as a reasonable measure of "following soon," etc., since a longer period would obliterate all distinctions between interwar intervals. That is, with 93 international wars over the century and a half, we get an average of almost 2 wars every 3 years, meaning that almost all three-year periods would see war following war. And with 50 interstate wars, or an average of one every three years, we get an even more conservative test of the proposition.

11. Of the many coefficients in use for the statistical interpretation of 2×2 contingency tables, we use chi-square (χ^2) as the conventional index of deviation from randomness, and Cramer's phi (ϕ), which serves as a supplemental index in order to estimate the strength of association. Whereas the latter has the virtue of ranging from 0 to 1.0, χ^2 values have varying upper limits; furthermore, one must then go to a probability table to ascertain how likely it was for the computed value to occur by chance alone, given the number of cells in the matrix.

12. Interstate wars are differentiated from extra-systemic ones in that the former (N-50) have at least one sovereign state member of the system on each side, whereas the latter (N-43) see system members fighting against colonies and other less-than-sovereign national entities which do not qualify for system membership.

13. The data acquisition procedures, sources, theoretical arguments, and resulting scores will be found in J. David Singer and Melvin Small, *The Strength of Nations: Comparative Capabilities Since Waterloo* (forthcoming).

14. We must emphasize that we are only identifying the nations which took the first act of war and initiated military hostilities. This is *not* always (as in the Franco-Prussian War) the side whose behavior made the war most likely. To ascertain that with any confidence requires a very detailed and reproducible coding of the events leading up to the war, and we are now engaged in that enterprise; see Russell Leng and J. David Singer, "Toward a Multi-Theoretical Typology of International Behavior" (forthcoming). We included as participants only the major powers, and then only if they had troops in combat from the onset of hostilities or within three months thereof.

15. In the following statistical analyses, we have intentionally avoided any strong emphasis on or preoccupation with statistical significance levels. Our reasons

are four: (a) Our intention here is to illustrate an approach, not to emphasize our findings; (b) bivariate findings are, by themselves, not sufficiently important to merit detailed interpretation; (c) the use of significance tests in analyzing populations, rather than samples, remains a matter of spirited debate; and (d) such debate here would distract us from more interesting questions. To illustrate, see Denton E. Morrison and Ramon E. Henkel (eds.), *The Significance Test Controversy* (Chicago: Aldine, 1970).

16. This may, however, be too hasty a conclusion·on the authors' part. The report alludes frequently to the dramatic changes in the international system at different points in time, but some of these may be more apparent than real. Without valid and reliable proxy indicators which measure the state of the system across time, we have no way of telling how much change occurred, in which system attributes, and when.

17. These results are in partial contrast to those which emerged from a study of *all* system members; see J. David Singer and Melvin Small, "National Alliance Commitments and War Involvement, 1818–1945," *Peace Research Society Papers* 5 (1966): 109–40.

18. For the reasoning behind this "loss of interaction opportunity" indicator, see Karl Deutsch and J. David Singer, "Multipolar Power Systems and International Stability," *World Politics* 16/3 (April 1964): 390–406. For the specific computations and statistical analyses, see J. David Singer and Melvin Small, "Alliance Aggregation and the Onset of War, 1815–1945," in Singer (ed.), *Quantitative International Politics: Insights and Evidence,* (New York: Free Press, 1968) 247–86.

19. One of the difficulties of devising a valid index of polarity is evident in the correlation matrix below, where we use two alternative indices. The first (A) is based on our identification of which nations were the "targets" of each major power alliance. But in quite a few alliance patterns, diplomatic historians show little consensus as to which nations—if any—the alliances were directed against. In those cases, we recomputed the bipolarity indicator (B), using alternative target nations or none at all.

20. For the rational, detailed procedures, and the results summarized here, see Michael Wallace, "Alliance Polarization and War in the International System, 1815–1964: A Measurement Procedure and Some Preliminary Findings," Montreal: Canadian Political Science Association, June 1972.

21. See Richard Rosecrance, "Bipolarity, Multipolarity, and the Future," *Journal of Conflict Resolution* 10/3 (1966): 317–27. Our equation is:

$$Y = a - b_1\chi + b_2\chi^2 - b_3\chi^3 + b_4\chi^4 + e$$

where,

a = intercept term
b = regression weights
χ = weighted polarization
e = residual term or unexplained variance,

and where,

$$b_1 \geq b_2 \geq b_3 \geq b_4$$

22. This is partially due to the fact that the equation "fits" the interwar and immediate post–WW II period very well, bringing up the R^2 values for all sets of observations which include that period, while it fits the immediate pre–WW I period very poorly, bringing the 1815–1919 values down.

23. Those data, as well as the index construction and analyses, are presented in the following papers: Michael Wallace and J. David Singer, "Inter-Governmental Organization in the Global System, 1816–1964: A Quantitative Description," *International Organization* 24/2 (Spring 1970): 239–87; and J. David Singer and Michael Wallace, "Inter-Governmental Organization and the Preservation of Peace, 1816–1965: Some Bivariate Relationships," *International Organization* 24/3 (Summer 1970): 520–47.

24. Our indicator of a nation's diplomatic importance is the number of diplomatic missions in its capital during each half-decade. Originally, we weighted these to reflect the differences among ambassadors, ministers, and chargés d'affaires but found that virtually the same rankings are produced without such weighting. See J. David Singer and Melvin Small, "The Composition and Status Ordering of the International System, 1815–1940," *World Politics* 18/2 (January 1966): 236–82; and Melvin Small and J. David Singer, "The Diplomatic Importance of States, 1816–1970: An Extension and Refinement of the Indicator," *World Politics* 25/4 (July 1973): 577–99.

25. The combined or indirect impact may, however, be more substantial. One of our recent studies found that when IGO levels showed a relative decline, arms spending tended to increase throughout the interstate system, and that in turn predicted to increases in war. See Michael Wallace, "Status, Formal Organiza- tion, and Arms Levels as Factors Leading to the Onset of War, 1820–1964," in Bruce M. Russett (ed.), *Peace, War, and Numbers* (Beverly Hills, Calif.: Sage, 1972), pp. 49–69. The negative correlation between IGO levels and military ex- penditure also give some indirect support to the proposition that the U.N. "has encouraged arms control."

26. For the indicators and analyses, see Kjell Skjelsbaek, "Shared Memberships in Intergovernmental Organizations and Dyadic War, 1865–1964," in Edwin Fedder (ed.), *The United Nations: Problems and Prospects* (Saint Louis, Mo.: Center for International Studies, 1971), pp. 31–62.

27. In the first issue of the *Journal of Conflict Resolution* (1957, p. 94), Quincy Wright proposed the establishment of a "world intelligence center" among whose missions would be the measurement of "the changing atmosphere of world opinion [and] the changing condition of world politics." Such a use of foreign policy indicators, whose scores would be published on a weekly or monthly basis by an independent global institute, could appreciably enhance the accuracy and credibility of the facts and help clarify the range of alternatives to which the Administration alludes.

28. As to the problems of communicating social science results to the policy-maker, see Philip Burgess, "International Relations Theory: Prospect, 1970–1995," American Political Science Association, Los Angeles, Calif., 1970, pp. 9–14, and Charles Hermann, "The Knowledge Gap: The Exchange of Information Between the Academic and Foreign Policy Communities," American Political Science Association, Chicago, 1971.

29. A more affirmative view of these institutions is in Roger Levien, "Independent Public Policy Analysis Organizations: A Major Social Invention," Rand Corpo- ration, Santa Monica, Calif., November 1969.

The preceding article shows the role that social science indicator sys- tems can play in the formulation and evaluation of public policy. Indicators, the authors argue, serve as operational (usually quantitative) manifesta- tions, representations, or "proxies" of a given state of affairs and permit us to measure the extent to which certain conditions are present or absent in the global system. In this proxy form, they permit us to monitor a system, measure changes in it, and thereby prescriptively evaluate the execution or outcome of a policy process. They also allow us to ascertain observed historical correlations among factors bearing on international relations; and, while these correlations fail to inform us about causal connections, they do provide us with one basis for prediction in future policy cases.

Several prescriptions about how the United States might effectively act to create the kind of world it would like are contained in the state of the world message. Singer and Small seek to test these hypotheses by using an indicator system to ascertain the extent to which each of the postulated associations has actually obtained in the international system during the past one hundred fifty years. What their empirical study tells us is that there is some marked inconsistency between their findings and what the administration's view of history "tells us." Although their findings must be regarded as tentative at best until further replicative research can confirm them, the study clearly suggests ways in which indicators might improve our capacity to learn from history. In the process, prescriptive analysis can be improved by enabling us to differentiate empirically informed prescriptions from advocated behavior based on folklore. If nothing else, this study should serve to illustrate that policy prescriptions with respect to international relations can be supported on more than mere opinion, subjective belief, and assertion.

4

The Analysis of the International System

When we look at international relations from the perspective of a *social system*, we examine the totality of events and processes that we have described in a piecemeal fashion throughout the preceding two chapters. If this were a textbook on American politics, we would have introduced the idea of a social system much earlier, because in American politics certain institutions like the Presidency, Congress, and the Supreme Court permeate all political activities to such a degree that it would be futile to describe American politics without describing the American political system first. In withholding the discussion on the international system until the last part of the book, we have assumed that a great deal about international relations can be understood by looking at the actors and their interactions without first discussing the nature of the international system.

At some point, however, it is necessary to apply the general concept of a system as it is now employed throughout the social sciences. As we might expect, the international political system differs radically in a number of crucial areas from most domestic political systems; nevertheless, the general concept of political system can be applicable to certain aspects of international relations that we have not yet discussed. Before continuing to examine certain features of the past, present, and possible future international system, we will briefly describe what we mean by the term international system.

The international *political* system may be viewed as a set of semi-autonomous—in law and in fact—political units organized on a territorial basis. Called nations or states, these political units that now encompass the earth act independently and collectively toward each other in a large number of issue areas. The state is a particular kind of political organization that claims control over a specific piece of territory and interacts with other states in a number of ways—one of which is to maintain its own territorial integrity or control. The international political system is a system of states each of which claims control within its boundaries and acts to maintain that control. Whether a particular state seeks to expand its control over the territory of another state is not relevant to the definition of the system, although it appears that for many years a significant number of states have endeavored to do just that. While the definition does not assume that states necessarily compete with other states, it also does not assume that the states will respect the territorial integrity of others—only that they will claim the right to control and protect their own territory.

Our description of the international political system sounds almost as if we are describing a nonsystem, because it focuses on the actors in the system rather than on the laws and institutions that shape the behavior of the actors. We emphasize the state because the international political system is a *decentralized* political system. In Chapter 3, we noted that the legal, social, and economic settings for international interactions were decentralized and fragmented, and that the states acting independently still made many of the crucial decisions affecting international law and the world economy. Similarly, political conditions among states are determined by what the states acting both individually and collectively decide to do. Although central institutions like the United Nations or the World Court do exist, their authority is limited by the will of the states.

While the central authority in the international political system is weak and the activties of the states determine the major conditions within the system, it is still valuable to look at international relations through the concept of the international system. Certain patterns of activities that have occurred regularly for hundreds of years indicate that, when threats to the system as a set of semi-autonomous, territorially organized political units arise, the states collectively act to meet that threat. We will discuss these activities in the subsequent readings. Other factors also make it valuable to consider the totality of events among nations as a social system. In addition to the growth of a number of international institutions such as the United Nations, penetration of states into affairs makes the concept of the international system useful. This type of penetration may in the long run change the entire structure of the international political system by making the state less viable as a form of political organization, or it may produce more elaborate international institutions. No matter what the implications, however, these factors—as we shall see in this chapter—make international relations more than just the anarchic activities of a number of competing states.

In the remaining material, then, we will attempt to assemble the analytic pieces we have developed in the preceding chapters within the framework of the discussion of the international system. Building on our study of the foreign policy–making process and the behavior of inter- governmental organizations as well as on our presentation of the nature of interactions among states, we will discuss the international system from several perspectives. First, we will look at the manner in which various structural characteristics of the historical international system, such as its evolving alignment configuration and its legal order, have served to in- fluence the behavior of nations. Second, we will investigate some of the mechanisms states have devised to maintain the international system against serious threats to it as a way of organizing the world politically. Finally, we will examine some proposals for transforming the present system, particularly those proposals concerning the way states will be dealing with each other in the future and to the role that the state, as a form of political organization, will be playing in future international relations.

Analytically, our discussion of the international system will be in terms of the descriptive, explanatory, and prescriptive tasks of inquiry we have delineated throughout the book. Consequently, we will explore how scholars have constructed descriptions of past and current patterns of social interaction among states, investigate how analysts have attempted to account for and explain transformations in the structure of the international system observed to have occurred over time, and examine prescriptive studies that address the problem of directing change in the behavior of nations in the global system. This discussion will all be couched in the terms of general systems theory. General systems theory is primarily a framework that views social phenomena as a complex of elements in dynamic interaction, wherein units are seen as responding to other units as well as to their external environments and subcomponents. In international affairs, the international system consists of the dominant patterns of relations between basic units (i.e., nation-states) as they are affected by environmental factors, such as the distribution of the world's resources, and subsystemic factors, such as the internal makeup of the units comprising the system. Analytically, we use the concept of the system to order facts as an aid to interpretation. When one analyzes international relations in terms of the interactions between units and subsystems, attention is drawn to the interdependence of units and their interrelationships. Thus, the international *system* can be diagnosed as a set of global properties structuring the behavior of states in interaction. Let us look briefly at some of the varieties of research that analyze international relations in these terms.

At the risk of oversimplifying the voluminous literature dealing with the international system, it may be suggested that most of it is concerned essentially with one of two types of questions. About half of it examines how the international system maintains itself; that is, it looks at *systemic maintenance* as a central problem and inquires into the conditions that promote international stability and equilibrium and the circumstances that transform systems into new patterns of relationship. The other half focuses on forecasting and analyzing trends in the international system, with the goal of projecting the nature of future international relations. This focus seeks to anticipate future world conditions from a global perspective. This dichotomy of system maintenance and systemic prognostication may be used to classify existing literature in terms of a number of other distinctions. We will treat each body of literature separately in order to facilitate discussion.

1. Literature relevant to the maintenance of the international political system can be divided into a number of categories. First, historical writers trace the evolution of patterns of interactions among states and assess the significance of the patterns for international stability. Second, theoretical

scholars have written expositions about the maintenance of the international system, many of which are prescriptive. Third, some writers have offered explanations about system maintenance and transformation through sets of explicitly developed concepts and relationships. Finally, some attempt to assess the significance and implications of contemporary trends for stability and equilibrium in the international system.

Much of the literature deals with the history of international systems. We will discuss only those works that strive for a theoretical framework. In addition to the work of Raymond Aron (6 and 7), at least four interesting efforts assess the history of the international political system in an explicit theoretical framework. A good starting point is Edward Vose Gulick's (55) discussion of the "balance of power framework" and his application of that framework to the politics of the post-Napoleonic period. Osgood and Robert Tucker (112) attempt to trace technological, military, political, moral, and ethical trends to analyze the maintenance of the international political system. John H. Herz (66) observes the impact of technological conditions on the system. Finally, Richard N. Rosecrance (128) traces the history of the international political system through nine "international systems," corresponding to the rise and fall of various states and coalitions as well as to general conditions. These works, together with more conventional historical works, including Charles Petrie (114), Taylor (160), and Garrett Mattingly (95) will provide an excellent overview of the history of the international political system.

A large number of works deal theoretically with how the international system may be maintained; some of these have identified the main theories or ideas about how the international system *should* be maintained. Surveys are provided by Frederick H. Gareau (51) and Paul Seabury (144). Ernst B. Haas (56 and 57) has examined the various uses of the term "balance of power," concluding that it has served as an analytic concept for scholars as well as an ideological rationale for policy by decision-makers.

In addition, the student is advised to read Edward H. Carr (25) for a classic discussion of the ideas of system maintenance during the interwar period. Kenneth Waltz (167) surveys the entire history of Western thought on the question of "causes" of war, while Inis Claude (29 and 30) has evaluated a number of major conceptions relating to what he calls the "management of power," including the balance of power and collective security.

A number of essays construct explanations or conceptual models of the international political system and its maintenance. Martin Wight's short essay (170) has provided the essential framework for a number of writers on the idea of the balance-of-power system. Morton A. Kaplan (77) presents six models of the international system, two of which correspond to historical periods. Because his analysis is regarded as a classic study of international relations from the perspective of systems theory, we have included an early version in the selected readings. Another study investigating the same problem is Liska's (93) application of the concept of equilibrium developed by some economists to the international political system. Finally, George Modelski (105) has developed models that contrast international political systems based on agrarian states with those based on industrial states.

Finally, attempts to generalize about conditions in the international system and their probable future impact can be found in the literature. Liska (93) is one of a number of writers who have discussed the role of alliances in the maintenance of the international system. Lewis F. Richardson (123) is one who has explored implications of arms races for system maintenance.

Contemporary conditions that create the threat of large-scale warfare, and the viability of various attempts to meet those conditions, are examined from a number of angles. William T. R. Fox (48), Herz (66), Aron (6), and Osgood and Tucker (112) discuss the underlying conditions of threats to the present international political system. Nuclear proliferation is discussed in Brody (22) and Rosecrance (128). The area of disarmament and arms control is studied in Singer (149) and David Edwards (43); and Claude (29), David Wainhouse, *et al.* (165), and Lincoln F. Bloomfield (16) examine the role of international organizations in crisis situations.

2. A second set of questions in the analysis of international systems relates to the probable evolution of global characteristics in the future. Here the analyst is interested primarily in describing and explaining trends in the international system. Because policy-makers must predict the consequences of the decisions they make, there has been a traditional concern with estimating the efficacy and outcome of alternative courses of action. International relations, like every field in which men are deeply involved, is thus heavily populated by scholars attempting to predict the future. From the intuitively based and often policy-prescriptive writings of scholars such as Carr (25) and John Wear Burton (24) as well as statesmen such as George W. Ball (10) to the projections of existing trends from a firm empirical foundation, as in Russett (137), most writers have at some time set out to write about trends—past, present, and future. Also, systematic projections of possible new futures or relevant utopias have been made by writers such as Greenville Clark and Louis B. Sohn (28), Bloomfield (16), and Richard A. Falk and Richard J. Barnet (44). These are joined by fictional efforts to describe new hells as imagined by George Orwell (110).

For a view of technological conditions in the near future, see Kahn and Anthony J. Wiener's (76) social, economic, and political dimensions for the year 2000. War and peace are contemplated by a number of writers in a volume entitled *Preventing World War III* (177), and another group (162) discusses other international aspects of the future. But these works only begin to suggest the multitude of published efforts being made to forecast the nature of the future world. A number of extensive research projects into the future are also currently under way, whose findings have not yet been released. Bertrand de Jouvannel's *Futuribles* project in France represents an ambitious example.

In the field of international politics, much speculation into the future international system is found in the political integration literature, particularly in the area of regional integration. In an excellent volume about the integration of political communities at various levels, Jacob and James V. Toscano (72) indicate that the term "integration" means many things to many scholars, particularly in international integration. In addition to the arguments concerning the functionalist approach, as in David Mitrany (104), Haas (58), and James P. Sewell (145), one can identify a number of other approaches. One major approach is found in the work of Deutsch and other scholars using Deutsch's general framework. Examples are Russett (139), Deutsch, *et al.* (38), Merritt (101), and Hayward R. Aker, Jr., and Donald Puchala (3). This approach is clearly related to Deutsch's earlier work on nation building. Haas's work represents an approach that shifts somewhat from integration as a process of political unification (59) to integration as the development of different systems of political organization (58). Another approach using the general viewpoint of the sociology of organization concentrates on the development of political unions among states. A final approach treats integration as a theory or ideology. Mitrany (104), for example, argues for certain types of integration, while Claude (30) has examined the theoretical assumptions many writers make. For a general view of the literature concerning regional as well as global integration, the student is advised to read (in addition to those already cited) Ronald J. Yalem (178) as well as collections of essays found in such anthologies as *International Political Communities* (38). Also, journals like *International Organization* and the *Journal of Common Market Studies* contain a great deal on integration.

A number of studies trace the relationship of various types of integrative relationships (trade, mail flow, and so forth) to bargaining behavior. Richardson (121, 122, and 123) and Paul Smoker (153 and 154) investigate patterns of trade and the outbreak of conflict. Russett (136 and 137) examines the effect of social and economic interactions on foreign-policy strategies. In addition, Chadwick F. Alger (1) observes the role of intergovernmental organizations on bargaining behavior among states, and Ole R. Holsti and Robert C. North (68) view the relationship of economic trends such as gold flow to political activity in events leading up to World War I. Singer and Small (151 and 152) have examined patterns of alliance behavior and the outbreak of war.

While hardly exhaustive, the above survey should serve to suggest the breadth, scope, and variety of research at the international system level of analysis. Nearly every dimension of interstate relations is amenable to analysis in systemic terms, and consequently the body of literature dealing with global characteristics and their transformation is extensive. While the product of this effort has been to produce much knowledge in several "islands of theory" (as, for example, in the process of political integration), many areas of inquiry remain undeveloped and noncumulative; moreover, little progress has yet been made in connecting these islands together to construct a general theory of behavior in the international system. Nevertheless, the remarkable success that has been achieved in the last twenty years of research indicates that such a general theory may some day be emergent.

As the preceding review has indicated, research at the level of the international system has been fragmented between descriptive, explanatory, and prescriptive analyses. Let us now sample some of this investigative effort in order to understand better the nature of the global system and to appreciate better the costs and benefits of conducting research in the descriptive, explanatory, and prescriptive modes.

SELECTED READINGS

Because a system is considered to consist, at a minimum, of a set of interrelated units and their interrelationships, analysis of international systems begins with a description of the nations and the behavior that tie them together. An attempt to describe international relations as a whole begins with the assumption that the behavior in the system is governed by repetition, regularity, and order. The descriptive study of international systems, therefore, is a form of macroanalysis, in that it seeks to discover and generalize about the characteristic patterns of relationships occurring within a particular span of history. In the reading selection that follows, written by Morton A. Kaplan, the author attempts to devise various models or descriptions of the way the international community either has organized itself or may in the future organize itself for interaction and the maintenance of the global community itself. With this essay, Kaplan, a prolific contributor to the field of international politics and foreign policy, presaged much of the work that followed on the nature of the global system. Since it is a classic study and goes far in demonstrating how a subject as complex as the international system might be studied, it deserves our serious attention. In reading the article, note in particular Kaplan's specification of the assumptions he is making about reality and the methodological points he emphasizes in rationalizing his investigative procedure.

MODELS OF INTERNATIONAL SYSTEMS

Morton A. Kaplan

I

A number of theoretical considerations underlie this essay. One is that some pattern of repeatable or characteristic behavior does occur within the international system. Another is that this behavior falls into a pattern because the elements of the pattern are internally consistent and because they satisfy needs that are both international and national in scope. A third is that international patterns of behavior are related, in ways that can be specified, to the characteristics of the entities participating in international politics and to the role functions they perform there. A fourth is that international behavior can also be related to other factors such as military and economic capability, communication and information, technological change, demographic change, and additional factors well recognized by political scientists.

Just as it is posible to build alternative models of political systems, e.g., democratic or totalitarian, and of family systems, e.g., nuclear families, extended families or monogramous or polygamous families, so it is possible to build different models of international systems. The models can be given an empirical interpretation and the specific propositions of the models can be tested. In the last part of this paper, some specific tests will be suggested.

The aspiration to state testable propositions in the field of international politics is useful provided some degree of caution is observed concerning the kinds of propositions one proposes to test. For instance, can a theory of international politics yield a prediction of a specific event like the Hungarian revolution of October 1956? The answer probably must be negative. Yet why make such a demand of theory?

Two basic limitations upon prediction in the physical sciences are relevant to this problem. In the first place, the mathematics of complicated interaction problems has not been worked out. For instance, the physical scientist can make accurate predictions with respect to the two-body problem, rough guesses with respect to the three-body problem, and only very incomplete guesses concerning larger numbers of bodies. The scientist cannot predict the path of a single molecule of gas in a tank of gas.

Morton A. Kaplan, "Balance of Power, Bipolarity and Other Models of International Systems," *The American Political Science Review*, 51, 3 (1957). (Abridged.) Copyright 1957 by the American Political Science Association. Reprinted by permission of the author and the APSA.

Kaplan is a professor of political science and chairman of the Committee on International Relations at the University of Chicago.

In the second place, the predictions of the physical scientist are predictions concerning an isolated system. He does not predict that so much gas will be in the tank, that the temperature or pressure of the tank will not be changed by someone, or even that the tank will remain in the experimental room. He predicts what the characteristic behavior of the mass of gas molecules will be if stated conditions of temperature, pressure, etc., hold.

The engineer deals with systems in which many free variables enter. If he acts wisely—for instance, in designing aircraft—he works within certain constraints imposed by the laws of physics. But many aspects of exact design stem from experiments in wind tunnels or practical applications of past experiences rather than directly from the laws of physical science.

The theory of international politics normally cannot be expected to predict individual actions because the interaction problem is too complex and because there are too many free variables. It can be expected, however, to predict characteristic or modal behavior within a particular kind of international system. Moreover, the theory should be able to predict the conditions under which the system will remain stable, the conditions under which it will be transformed, and the kinds of transformations that may be expected to take place.

II

Six alternative models of international systems will be presented in this paper. These models do not exhaust the possibilities for international organization but they represent positions along a scale of political organization, with the unit veto system exhibiting the smallest degree of political integration and the hierarchical system the greatest. The six international systems are the "balance of power" system, the loose bipolar system, the tight bipolar system, the universal system, the hierarchical system, and the unit veto system.

In their present stage of development the models are tentative and may be less complex than the real phenomena to which they refer. Yet, if they have some degree of adequacy, they may permit a more meaningful organization of existing knowledge and more productive organization of future research.

Only two of the models—the "balance of power" system and the loose bipolar system—have historical counterparts. Greater attention will be given to these in this paper. The other four are projections based upon requirements of internal consistency and of relationships to other political and economic factors. They function both to illustrate possible transformations of the loose bipolar system and as possible predictions of the theory when the transformations are explicitly linked to the conditions that will bring them into being.

The first system to be examined is the "balance of power" international system. Quotation marks are placed around the term to indicate its metaphoric quality.

The "balance of power" international system is an international social system which does not have as a component a political subsystem. The actors within the system are exclusively national actors, such as France, Germany, Italy, etc. Five national actors—as a minimum— must fall within the classification "essential national actor"[1] to enable the system to work.

The "balance of power" international system is characterized by the operation of the following essential rules, which correspond to the elements of the characteristic behavior of the system: (1) increase capabilities but negotiate rather than fight; (2) fight rather than fail to increase capabilities; (3) stop fighting rather than eliminate an essential actor; (4) oppose any coalition or single actor which tends to assume a position of predominance within the system; (5) constrain actors who subscribe to supranational organizational principles; and (6) permit defeated or constrained essential national actors to re-enter the system as acceptable role partners, or act to bring some previously inessential actor within the essential actor classification. Treat all essential actors as acceptable role partners.

The first two rules of the "balance of power" international system reflect the fact that no political subsystem exists within the international social system. Therefore, essential national actors must rely upon themselves or upon their allies for protection. However, if they are weak, their allies may desert them. Therefore, an essential national actor must ultimately be capable of protecting its own national values.

The third essential rule illustrates the fact that expansion beyond certain limits would be inconsistent with nationality. It is not necessary to raise the question whether capabilities place limits on appetites or whether more basic national values are inconsistent with unlimited national expansion.

The fourth and fifth rules give recognition to the fact that a predominant coalition or national actor would constitute a threat to the interests of other national actors. Moreover, if a coalition were to become predominant, then the largest member of that coalition might also become predominant over the lesser members of its own coalition. For this reason members of a successful coalition may be alienated, although they may also be able to bargain for more from the threatened national actors.

The sixth rule states that membership in the system is dependent only upon behavior which corresponds with the essential rules or norms of the "balance of power" system. If the number of essential actors is reduced, the "balance of power" international system will become unstable. Therefore, maintaining the number of essential national actors above a critical lower bound is a necessary condition for the stability of the system. This is best done by returning to full membership in the system defeated actors or reformed deviant actors.

Although any particular action or alignment may be the product of "accidents," i.e., of the set of specific conditions producing the action or alignment, including such elements as chance meetings or personality factors, a high correlation between the pattern of national behavior and the essential rules of the international system would represent a confirmation of the predictions of the theory.

Just as any particular molecule of gas in a gas tank may travel in any direction, depending upon accidental bumpings with other molecules, particular actions of national actors may depend upon chance or random conjunctions. Yet, just as the general pattern of behavior of the gas may represent its adjustment to pressure and temperature conditions within the tank, the set of actions of national actors may correspond to the essential rules of the system when the other variables take the appropriate specific values.

Thus, by shifting the focus of analysis from the particular event to the type of event, the seemingly accidental events become part of a meaningful pattern. In this way, the historical loses its quality of uniqueness and is translated into the universal language of science.

The number of essential rules cannot be reduced. The failure of any rule to operate will result in the failure of at least one other rule. Moreover, at this level of abstraction, there does not seem to be any other rule that is interrelated with the specified set in this fashion.

Any essential rule of the system is in equilibrium [2] with the remaining rules of the set. This does not imply that particular rules can appear only in a particular international system. The first two rules, for instance, also apply to bloc leaders in the bipolar systems. However, they are necessary to each of the systems and, in their absence, other rules of the two systems will be transformed.

The rules of the system are interdependent. For instance, the failure to restore or to replace defeated essential national actors eventually will interfere with the formation of coalitions capable of constraining deviant national actors or potential predominant coalitions.

The equilibrium of the set of rules is not a continuous equilibrium but one that results from discrete actions over periods of time. Therefore, the possibility of some change operating to transform the system becomes great if sufficient time is allowed.

It is relatively easy to find historical examples illustrating the operation of these rules. The European states would have accepted Napoleon had he been willing to play according to the rules of the game.[3]

The restoration of the Bourbons permitted the application of rule three. Had such a restoration not been possible, the international system would immediately have become unstable. Readmission of France to the international system after restoration fulfilled rule six.

The European concert, so ably described by Mowat, illustrates rule one. The *entente cordiale* illustrates rule four and the history of the eighteenth and nineteenth centuries rule two. Perhaps the best example of rule three, however, can be found in the diplomacy of Bismarck at Sadowa, although his motivation was more complex than the rule alone would indicate.

It is not the purpose of this essay to multiply historical illustrations. The reader can make his own survey to determine whether international behavior tended to correspond to these rules during the eighteenth and nineteenth centuries.

Apart from the equilibrium within the set of essential rules, there are two other kinds of equilibrium characteristic of the international system: the equilibrium between the set of essential rules and the other variables of the international system and the equilibrium between the international system and its environment or setting.

If the actors do not manifest the behavior indicated by the rules, the kind and number of actors will change. If the kind or number of actors changes, the behavior called for in the rules cannot be maintained.

In addition, the essential rules of the "balance of power" international system may remain in equilibrium for a number of values of the other variables of the system. Some changes in capabilities and information for instance may be compatible with the rules of the system, while others may not.

Indeed, if the value of one variable changes—for instance the capabilities of a given coalition—the system may not maintain itself unless the information of some of the actors changes correspondingly. Otherwise a necessary "counter-balancing" shift in alignment may not take place. Some shifts in the pattern of alliance may be compatible with the rules of the system and others may not.

If the rules of the "balance of power" international system are consistent with the actions of the national actors in the eighteenth and nineteenth centuries, the system may well have appeared to be an absolute system to observers and the "balance of power" a rule of universal applicability. But since the described system is not consistent with the present bipolar international system, it is clear that the system operated only under fixed conditions. To account for the change from one system to the other, it is necessary to isolate the critical conditions for the maintenance of the "balance of power" system.

The changes in conditions that may make the "balance of power" international system unstable are: the existence of an essential national actor who does not play according to the rules of the game, such as one whose essential rules are oriented toward the establishment of some form of supranational political organization; failures of information which prevent a national actor from taking the required measures to protect its own international position; capability changes which become cumulative and which thus increase an initial disparity between the capabilties of essential national actors; conflicts between the prescriptions of different rules under some conditions; difficulties arising from the logistics of the "balancing" process, the small number of essential actors, or an inflexibility of the "balancing" mechanism.

An important condition for stability concerns the number of essential national actors. If there are only three, and if they are relatively equal in capability, the probability that two would combine to eliminate the third is relatively great. It is possible that the third actor may not be eliminated and that, after defeat, it would participate in a new coalition with the weaker of the victorious powers. But clearly the probability of such an outcome—necessary to the stability of the system—rises if the number of essential actors is greater than three. Mistakes or failures in information can be tolerated more easily if the number of actors is greater. Therefore, only some numerical lower bound will give sufficient flexibility to the "balance of power" system to permit the required shifts in alliance as conditions change.

Coalitions with many members may regard loosely attached members with equanimity. The role of the nonmember of the coalition also will be tolerated. When there are a large number of loosely attached actors or nonmembers of an alliance, any change of alliance or addition to an alliance can be "counter-balanced" by the use of an appropriate reward or the cognition of danger to the national interest of some actor. There are many national actors to whom these bids may be made.

When, however, there are very few loosely attached or nonmember actors, a change in or an addition to an alignment introduces considerable tension into the international system. Under these circumstances, it becomes difficult to make the necessary compensatory adjustments.

For the same reasons, coalition members will have more tolerance for the role of "balancer," i.e., the actor who implements rule four, if the international system has a large number of members and the alignments are fluid. Under these conditions, the "balancer" does not constitute a lethal threat to the coalition against which it "balances."

If, however, there are only a few essential actors, the very act of "balancing" may create a permanent "unbalance." In these circumstances the tolerance of the system for the "balancing" role will be slight and the "balance of power" system will become unstable.

Instability may result although the various national actors have no intention of overthrowing the "balance of power" system. The wars against Poland corresponded to the rule directing the various national actors to increase their capabilities. Since Poland was not an essential national actor, it did not violate the norms of the system to eliminate Poland as an actor. The Polish spoils were divided among the victorious essential national actors. Nevertheless, even this cooperation among the essential national actors had an "unbalancing" effect. Since the acquisitions of the victorious actors could not be equal—unless some exact method were found for weighting geographic, strategic, demographic, industrial, material factors, etc., and determining accurately how the values of these factors would be projected into the future—a differential factor making the system unstable could not easily be avoided.

Even the endeavor to defeat Napoleon and to restrict France to her historic limits had some effects of this kind. This effort, although conforming to rules four, five, and six, also aggrandized Russia and Prussia, and hence upset the internal equilibrium among the German actors. This episode may have triggered the process which later led to Prussian hegemony within Germany and to German hegemony within Europe. Thus, a dynamic process was set off for which shifts within alignments or coalitions were not able to compensate.

The logistical or environmental possibilities for "balancing" may be decisive in determining whether the "balancing" role within the "balance of power" international system will be filled effectively. For example, even had it so desired, the Soviet Union could not have "balanced" Nazi pressure against Czechoslovakia without territorial access to the zone of potential conflict. In addition, the intervening actors—Poland and Rumania—and possibly also Great Britain and France, regarded Soviet intervention as a threat to their national interests. Therefore, they refused to cooperate.

It is possible that a major factor accounting for British success in the "balancing" role in the nineteenth century lay in the fact that Great Britain was predominantly a naval power and had no territorial ambitions on the European continent. These facts increased the tolerance of other national actors for Britain's "balancing" role. As a preponderant maritime power, Great Britain could interfere with the shipping of other powers and could also transport its small armed forces to the zone of conflict. It could afford to maintain only a small army, because it was able to use its naval capabilities to dispel invading forces. Even so, Palmerston discovered occasions on which it was difficult to play the "balancing" role either because it was difficult to make effective use of Britain's limited manpower or because other powers displayed little tolerance for the role.

The "balance of power" system in its ideal form is a system in which any combination of actors within alliances is possible so long as no alliance gains a marked preponderance in capabilities. The system tends to be maintained by the fact that, even should any nation desire to become predominant itself, it must, to protect its own interests, act to prevent any other nation from accomplishing such an objective. Like Adam Smith's "unseen hand" of competition, the international system is policed informally by self-interest, without the necessity of a political subsystem.

The rise of powerful deviant actors, inadequate counter-measures by nondeviant actors,[4] new international ideologies, and the growth of supranational organizations like the Communist bloc, with its internationally organized political parties, sounded the death knell for the "balance of power" international system.

In its place, after an initial period of instability, the loose bipolar system appeared. This differs in many important respects from the "balance of power" system. Supranational actors participate within the international system. These supranational actors may be bloc actors like NATO or the Communist bloc or universal actors like the United Nations. Nearly all national actors belong to the universal actor organization and many—including most of the essential national actors—belong to one or the other of the bipolar blocs. Some national actors, however, may be nonmembers of bloc organizations.

In distinction to the "balance of power" international system, in which the rules applied uniformly to all national actors, the essential rules of the loose bipolar system distinguish, for instance, between the role functions of actors who are members of blocs and those who are not.

In the "balance of power" system, the role of the "balancer" was an integrating role because it prevented any alliance from becoming predominant. In the ideal form of the system, any national actor is qualified to fill that role. In the loose bipolar system, however, the integrating role is a mediatory role. The actor filling it does not join one side or the other, but mediates between the contending sides. Therefore, only non–bloc members or universal actor organizations can fill the integrative role in the loose bipolar system.

The functioning of the loose bipolar system depends upon the organizational characteristics of the supranational blocs.[5] If the two blocs are not hierarchically organized, the loose bipolar sytem tends to resemble the "balance of power" system, except that the shifting of alignments takes place around two fixed points. Such shifting is limited by the functional integration of facilities, since a shift may require the destruction of facilities and the reduction of the capabilities of the shifting national actor. Shifting in alignment tends also to be limited by geographic and other logistic considerations. Nevertheless, the bloc actors constitute relatively loose organizations and the international system itself develops a considerable flexibility.

If one bloc has some hierarchical organizational features and the other is not hierarchically organized, a number of consequences can be expected. The hierarchical or mixed hierarchical bloc will retain its membership, since functional integration will be so great that it would be difficult for satellite members to withdraw or to form viable national entities if they did.[6] The relative permanence of membership in the bloc constitutes a threat to nonmembers. Therefore, such a bloc is unlikely to attract new members except as a consequence of military absorption or political conquest by a native political party which already had associate membership in the bloc through the medium of an international party organization. The irreversible characateristics of membership in such a bloc constitute a threat to all other national actors, whether associated in a bloc or not.

The nonhierarchical bloc has a looser hold over its members but is more likely to enter into cooperative pacts of one kind or another with non–bloc members. The pressure emanating from the hierarchically organized bloc, however, is likely to force the nonhierarchically organized bloc to integrate its bloc activities more closely and to extend them to other functional areas, or alternatively to weaken and undermine the bloc.

If both blocs subscribe to hierarchical integrating rules, their memberships become rigid and only uncommitted states can, by choosing an alignment, change the existing lineup. Any action of this sort, however, would tend to reduce the flexibility of the international system by eliminating nations not included in blocs. Non–bloc member actors therefore would be more likely to support one or the other of the blocs on specific issues rather than to support either in general. If both blocs are hierarchically organized, their goals are similar—hierarchical world organization—and incompatible, since only one can succeed in leading such a world system.

With only two major groupings in the bipolar system, any rapid change in military capabilities tends to make this system unstable. For this reason, possession of a larger stockpile of atomic and thermonuclear weapons by both major blocs is a factor for stability within the system.

The rules of the loose bipolar system follow:

1. All blocs subscribing to hierarchical or mixed hierarchical integrating principles are to eliminate the rival bloc.
2. All blocs subscribing to hierarchical or mixed hierarchical integrating principles are to negotiate rather than to fight, to fight minor wars rather than major wars, and to fight major wars—under given risk and cost factors—rather than to fail to eliminate the rival bloc.
3. All bloc actors are to increase their capabilities relative to those of the opposing bloc.
4. All bloc actors subscribing to nonhierarchical organizational principles are to negotiate rather than to fight, to increase capabilities, to fight minor wars rather than to fail to increase capabilities, but to refrain from initiating major wars for this purpose.
5. All bloc actors are to engage in major war rather than to permit the rival bloc to attain a position of preponderant strength.
6. All bloc members are to subordinate objectives of universal actors to the objectives of their bloc but to subordinate the objectives of the rival bloc to those of the universal actor.
7. All non–bloc member national actors are to coodinate their national objectives with those of the universal actor and to subordinate the objectives of bloc actors to those of the universal actor.
8. Bloc actors are to attempt to extend the membership of their bloc but to tolerate the nonmember position of a given national actor if the alternative is to force that national actor to join the rival bloc or to support its objectives.
9. Non–bloc member national actors are to act to reduce the danger of war between the bloc actors.
10. Non-bloc members are to refuse to support the policies of one bloc actor as against the other except in their capacities as members of a universal actor.
11. Universal actors are to reduce the incompatibility between the blocs.
12. Universal actors are to mobilize non–bloc member national actors against cases of gross deviation, e.g., resort to force by a bloc actor. This rule, unless counterbalanced by the other rules, would enable the universal actor to become the prototype of a universal international system.

Unlike the "balance of power" international system, there is a high degree of role differentiation in the loose bipolar system. If any of the roles is pursued to the exclusion of others, the system will be transformed. If one bloc actor eliminates another, the system may be transformed into a hierarchical system. If the universal actor performs its function too well, the system may be transformed into a universal international system. Other variations are possible.

The tight bipolar international system represents a modification of the loose bipolar system in which non–bloc member actors and universal actors either disappear entirely or cease to be significant. Unless both blocs are hierarchically organized, however, the system will tend toward instability.

There is no integrative or mediatory role in the tight bipolar system. Therefore there will tend to be a high degree of dysfunctional tension in the system. For this reason, the tight bipolar system will not be a highly stable or well integrated system.

The universal international system might develop as a consequence of the functioning of a universal actor organization in a loose bipolar system. The universal system, as distinguished from those international systems previously discussed, would have a political system as a subsystem of the international social system. However, it is possible that this political system would be of the confederated type, i.e., that it would operate on territorial governments rather than directly on human individuals.

The universal international system would be an integrated and solidary system. Although informal political groupings might take place within the system, conflicts of interest would be settled according to the political rules of the system. Moreover, a body of political officials and administrators would exist whose primary loyalty would be to the international system itself rather than to any territorial subsystem of the international system.

Whether the universal international system is a stable system or not depends upon the extent to which it has direct access to resources and facilities and upon the ratio between its capabilities and the capabilities of the national actors who are members of the system.

The hierarchical international system may be democratic or authoritarian in form. If it evolves from a universal international system—perhaps because the satisfactions arising from the successful operation of such a universal international system lead to a desire for an even more integrated and solidary international system—it is likely to be a democratic system. If, on the other hand, the hierarchical system is imposed upon unwilling national actors by a victorious or powerful bloc, then the international system is likely to be authoritarian.

The hierarchical system is a political system. Within it, functional lines of organization are stronger than geographical lines. This highly integrated characteristic of the hierarchical international system makes for great stability. Functional cross-cutting makes it most difficult to organize successfully against the international system or to withdraw from it. Even if the constitution of the system were to permit such withdrawal, the integration of facilities over time would raise the costs of withdrawal too high.

The unit veto international system is one in which all actors possess such great capabilities that an aggressor—even if it succeeded eventually in destroying an actor—could be destroyed in return. Within this system, each actor relies upon itself exclusively for its own protection, rather than upon alliances.

The unit veto system is maintained by mutual threat. Therefore the dysfunctional tension within it is likely to be quite high. For this reason, actors may succumb to threats, i.e., they may lose nerve, or they may launch an aggressive venture simply because they cannot stand the tension. As a consequence, the unit veto international system is not likely to have a high degree of stability.

III

History will still remain the laboratory for research, since controlled experiments, for the most part, are out of the question in the field of international politics. Yet the normal modes of historical investigation are not adequate for the confirmation of a theory of international politics.

The mere statement of the alternative models of international systems necessitates the collection of information relevant to their validation, in particular, of information dealing with the patterns of national interactions. It is significant that the simple task of counting various kinds of interactions has never been seriously attempted in the literature, and that this information is essential to the description of the international system.

Some consequences of the theory which can be empirically tested are fairly obvious. For instance, the rules of the "balance of power" system specify a great fluidity in the formation of alliances and groupings with respect to particular issues. The analysis of national interactions during the "balance of power" period should test this consequence and should also permit a more detailed specification of the characteristics of the "balance of power" system.

If the theory is correct, there should be a difference between the "balance of power" and bipolar systems with respect to the frequences of certain groupings. For instance, in the "balance of power" system, groupings will depend primarily upon the interests of nations in particular situations. Therefore, they will tend to break up as soon as the interests are satisfied or forestalled. New groupings should continue to depend upon particular interests. Therefore, there should be great variety in the groupings.

In the loose bipolar system, on the other hand, groupings will depend upon long range rather than particular interests. Therefore, some alignments will have an extremely high probability and others an extremely low probability. The study of interaction patterns in the two systems should serve both to test these propositions and to permit a closer comparison of the characteristics of the two systems.

To be more specific, the "balance of power" system postulates that any alignment is as probable as any other alignment prior to a consideration of the specific interests which divide nations. Moreover, any particular alignment should not *a priori* predispose the same nations to align themselves with each other at the next opportunity. Was there, therefore, any period of the "balance of power" system during which the fluctuations in alignments did not shift as the theory predicts? If there were, some other factors must be located to account for the pattern of preferences.

It is also possible that the system of alignments became more rigid over time, i.e., that any one alignment increased the probability that that alignment would recur in the future. If so, an element of instability would be found within the system. Of course, the frequency of interactions is not identical with the predisposition to interact. Other variables complicate the picture. Nevertheless, if it is true historically that the frequency of interactions changed in some systematic manner, this in itself would have great importance.

If some important patterns of behavior are discovered, an effort should then be made to discover whether they are linked to internal system characteristics, e.g., increasing probability of repeating previous patterns of alignment, or whether they are linked to external factors, e.g., technological change, or to some combination of the two.

Still additional consequences may be derived from the rules of the various international systems. Although the problems involved in testing these propositions may prove difficult, the problems nevertheless arise in the area of empirical theory and are brought to attention by abstract theoretical considerations.

NOTES

[1] The term "essential actor" refers to "major power" as distinguished from "minor power.'

[2] This kind of equilibrium is not mechanical like the equilibrium of a seesaw, which re-establishes itself mechanically after a disturbance. Instead, it is a "steady state" or homeostatic equilibrium which maintains the stability of selected variables as the consequence of changes in other variables. For instance, the body maintains the temperature of blood in a "steady state" by perspiring in hot weather and by flushing the skin in cold weather. The international system is not simply stable but in Ashby's sense is ultrastable. That is, it acts electively toward states of its internal variables and rejects those which lead to unstable states. See W. Ross Ashby, *Design for a Brain* (New York: John Wiley & Sons, 1952), p. 99, for a precise statement of the concept of ultrastability.

[3] It is nevertheless true that, since Napoleon threatened the principle of dynastic legitimacy, the system would have been strained. The principle of legitimacy, for quite some time, reduced the suspicions which are natural to a "balance of power" system.

[4] Britain and France violated rules one, two, four, five, and six in the 1930's.

[5] Extensional definitions would identify NATO as relatively nonhierarchical and the Communist bloc as mixed hierarchical. If the Communist bloc were to be so integrated that national boundaries and organizational forms were eliminated, it would become fully hierarchical.

[6] In this connection, it is noteworthy that the Yugoslavs were able to resist the drastic Soviet demands for economic integration. Tito's withdrawal would have been much more difficult—and perhaps impossible—had this not been the case.

The purpose of Kaplan's analysis is to describe various models of the ways in which national members of the global community may regularize, or pattern, their relationships with one another. In using the term "model," Kaplan seeks to stress to the reader the fact that he is constructing explicitly simplified versions of reality. A model of a social process, like a model of anything, facilitates our understanding of our subject of inquiry by systematically distorting the subject so as to exaggerate certain features and minimize the importance of others. Although a model is a simplified distortion, it aids understanding by permitting us to see salient attributes more readily.

The models of the international system Kaplan provides are based on his interpretation of the distinguishing characteristics of two actual historical systems as well as on his image of a number of hypothetical international systems. The study is thus more sociological and typological than dynamic; that is, it aims more at classifying types of international systems than it does at explaining how one type of system maintains itself or transforms itself so as to be superseded by another type of system. The study does not tell us why history consists of a potential succession of international systems that are distinctive, and which replace preceding ones. Hence, the longitudinal aspect of time and the dynamics of system change are largely ignored. Instead, only descriptions of alternate structures of international systems are offered.

In some respects, the analytic mode of this study is best seen as heuristic theory. The descriptions of variant models of international systems are constructed in a nonrigorous fashion; they are based on impressions from unorganized information. As such, they are deductive and logical rather than inductive and empirical. Because we do not know precisely what is being looked at—the set of variables, or the empirical foundation for many of the assumptions (for example, national actors are rational and the national interest consists exclusively of the survival motive)—we have little basis for ascertaining whether Kaplan's mental constructs make empirical sense. The cogency and veracity of descriptive models constructed in this manner are thus difficult to assess. This should not, however, be considered a major deficiency when we recall that the author himself acknowledges that few, if any, existing international systems conform with the models of hypothetical systems that are offered. Because his descriptive models are designed for the heuristic purpose of stimulating thinking about the nature of the international system, the utility of the treatment must be evaluated in terms of the number and kinds of hypotheses that can be derived and tested.

In other respects, Kaplan's study might be considered explanatory and prescriptive. While as theoretical frameworks the models are designed to facilitate descriptive comparison with the actual behavior of nations in historical periods, they are explanatory, in the sense that they postulate causes for the maintenance of each system. By indicating the conditions that serve to preserve each type of system within permissible limits of variation, Kaplan thus provides an explanation of system maintenance. Moreover, the models are prescriptive, in the sense that the propositions that may be derived contain implications for the types of policies states may pursue to alter the characteristic behavior of a prevailing system. In addition, the models are all used for the normative purpose of evaluating each model's potential contribution for achieving system stability. In a sense, then, they provide prescriptions for the kind of system that should be created in order to enhance the prospects for interstate peace. Thus, we see that a descriptive model of the nature of the international system may serve explanatory and prescriptive functions, as well.

Our second reading selection in this chapter was written by one of the editors of this volume, William D. Coplin. The author turns his attention in this investigation to another salient attribute of the international system: the international legal culture of the global system. The international legal order is a global property that some analysts have been prone to dismiss as irrelevant and immaterial to the actual conduct of states. Yet, if one acknowledges that how states think about the international system is important and sometimes causative of how they act in it, then it becomes apparent that those images are structured and communicated primarily as premissible. Coplin's article seeks to describe the functions that international law may be examined for clues to the attitudes states hold about the nature of international society and the kinds of behavior they regard as permissible. Coplin's article seeks to describe the functions that international legal rules perform in the global system as well as how those rules have evolved over time since the advent of the state system.

INTERNATIONAL LAW AND ASSUMPTIONS ABOUT THE STATE SYSTEM

William D. Coplin

Most writers on international relations and international law will examine the relationship between international law and politics in terms of the assumption that law either should or does function only as a coercive restraint on political action. Textbook writers on general international

William D. Coplin, "International Law and Assumptions About the State System," *World Politics*, 17 (July 1965): 615-34. (Abridged.) Footnotes have been renumbered to appear in consecutive order. Reprinted by permission of the author and publisher.

Coplin is director of the International Relations Program at Syracuse University.

politics like Morgenthau [1] . . . make the common assumption that international law should be examined as a system of coercive norms controlling the actions of states. . . . The assumption that international law is or should be a coercive restraint on state action structures almost every analysis, no matter what the school of thought or the degree of optimism or pessimism about the effectiveness of the international legal system.[2] With an intellectual framework that measures international law primarily in terms of constraint on political action, there is little wonder that skepticism about international law continues to increase while creative work on the level of theory seems to be diminishing.[3]

Therefore, it is desirable to approach the relationship between international law and politics at a different functional level, not because international law does not function at the level of coercive restraint, but because it also functions at another level. In order to illustrate a second functional level in the relationship between international law and politics, it is necessary to examine the operation of domestic law. In a domestic society, the legal system as a series of interrelated normative statements does more than direct or control the actions of its members through explicit rules backed by a promise of coercion. Systems of law also act on a more generic and pervasive level by serving as authoritative (i.e., accepted as such by the community) modes of communicating or reflecting the ideals and purposes of the societies. The legal system functions on the level of the individual's perceptions and attitudes by presenting to him an image of the social system—an image which has both factual and normative aspects and which contributes to social order by building a consensus on procedural as well as on substantive matters. In this sense, law in the domestic situation is a primary tool in the "socialization" [4] of the individual.

International law functions in a similar manner: namely, as an institutional device for communicating to the policy-makers of various states a consensus on the nature of the international system. The purpose of this article is to approach the relationship between international law and politics not as a system of direct restraints on state action, but rather as a system of quasi-authoritative communications to the policy-makers concerning the reasons for state actions and the requisites for international order. It is a "quasi-authoritative" device because the norms of international law represent only an imperfect consensus of the community of states, a consensus which rarely commands complete acceptance but which usually expresses generally held ideas. Given the decentralized nature of law-creation and law-application in the international community, there is no official voice of the states as a collectivity. However, international law taken as a body of generally related norms is the closest thing to such a voice. Therefore, in spite of the degree of uncertainty about the authority of international law, it may still be meaningful to examine international law as a means for expressing the commonly held assumptions about the state system.

The approach advocated in this article has its intellectual antecedents in the sociological school, since it seeks to study international law in relation to international politics. Furthermore, it is similar to that of the sociological school in its assumption that there is or should be a significant degree of symmetry between international law and politics on the level of intellectual constructs—that is, in the way in which international law has expressed and even shaped ideas about relations between states. It is hoped that this approach will contribute to a greater awareness of the interdependence of international law and conceptions of international politics.

Before analyzing the way in which international law has in the past reflected and continues today to reflect common attitudes about the nature of the state system, let us discuss briefly the three basic assumptions which have generally structured those attitudes.[5] First, it has been assumed that the state is an absolute institutional value and that its security is the one immutable imperative for state action. If there has been one thing of which policy-makers could always be certain, it is that their actions must be designed to preserve their state. Second, it has been assumed that international politics is a struggle for power, and that all states seek to increase their power. Although the forms of power have altered during the evolution of the state system, it has been generally thought that states are motivated by a drive for power, no matter what the stakes. The third basic assumption permeating ideas about the international system has to do with maintaining a minimal system of order among the states. This assumption, symbolized generally by the maxim "Preserve the balance of power," affirms the necessity of forming coalitions to counter any threat to hegemony and of moderating actions in order to avoid an excess of violence that could disrupt the system.

It is necessary at this point to note that an unavoidable tension has existed between the aim of maintaining the state and maximizing power, on the one hand, and of preserving the international system, on the other. The logical extension of either aim would threaten the other, since complete freedom of action by the state would not allow for the limitation imposed by requirements to maintain the system, and a strict regularization of state action inherent in the idea of the system would curtail the state's drive for power. However, the tension has remained constant, with neither norm precluding the other except when a given state was in immediate danger of destruction. At those times, the interests of the system have been subordinated to the drive for state survival, but with no apparent long-range effect on the acceptance by policy-makers of either set of interests, despite their possible incompatibility. The prescriptions that states should be moderate, flexible, and vigilant [6] have been a manifestation of the operation of the system. Together, the three basic assumptions about the state system have constituted the conceptual basis from which the policy-makers have planned the actions of their state.

I. CLASSICAL INTERNATIONAL LAW AND THE IMAGE OF THE STATE SYSTEM

Almost every legal aspect of international relations from 1648 to 1914 reinforced and expressed the assumptions of the state system. State practices in regard to treaties, boundaries, neutrality, the occupation of new lands, freedom of the seas, and diplomacy, as well as classical legal doctrines, provide ample illustration of the extent to which the basic assumptions of the state were mirrored in international law.

The essential role of treaties in international law reflected the three assumptions of the state system. First, treaty practices helped to define the nature of statehood. Emanating from the free and unfettered will of states, treaties were the expression of their sovereign prerogatives. Statehood itself was defined in part as the ability to make treaties, and that ability presupposed the equality and independence usually associated with the idea of the state. . . .

Treaty law also contributed to the evolution of the classical assumption regarding the maintenance of the international system. Both explicitly and implicitly, treaties affirmed the necessity of an international system. . . . Also, many treaties reaffirmed earlier treaty agreements, contributing to the idea that the international system was a continuing, cooperative unity.[7] Therefore, treaties usually reminded the policy-maker that the maintenance of the international system was a legitimate and necessary objective of state policy.

Finally, treaties affirmed the necessity and, in part, the legality of the drive for power. The constant juggling of territory, alliances, and other aspects of capability was a frequent and rightful subject of treaty law. Treaties implicitly confirmed that power was the dynamic force in relations between states by defining the legal criteria of power and, more important, by providing an institutional means, subscribed to by most of the members of the system, which legalized certain political transactions, such as territorial acquisition and dynastic exchange. . . .

A final category of international law which reinforced the assumptions about the state system was the law of diplomacy. The legal rationalization behind the rights and duties of diplomats (i.e., since diplomats represent sovereign states, they owe no allegiance to the receiving state) emphasized the inviolability of the state which was an essential aspect of the classical assumptions.[8] At the same time, the very fact that even semi-hostile states could exchange and maintain ambassadors emphasized that all states were part of a common international system.[9] Finally, the classical functions of a diplomat—to make sure that conditions are not changing to the disadvantage of his state and, if they are, to suggest and even implement policies to rectify the situation—exemplified the rule of constant vigilance necessary in a group of states struggling for power. Therefore, in their own way, the laws of diplomacy expressed all three of the assumptions of the state system.

The assumptions of the state system were reinforced not only by the legal practices of states but also by the major international legal theories of the classical period. Three general schools of thought developed: the naturalists, the eclectics or Grotians, and the positivists. In each school, there was a major emphasis on both the state and the state system as essential institutional values. . . .

Therefore, there was a consensus among the classical theorists of international law that international politics had two structural elements: the state, with its rights of freedom and self-preservation; and the system, with its partial effectiveness in maintaining a minimal international order. That the theorists never solved the conflict between the idea of the un-fettered sovereign state, on the one hand, and a regulating system of law, on the other, is indicative of a conflict within the assumptions of the state system,[10] but a conflict which neither prevented international lawyers from writing about an international legal order nor kept policy-makers from pursuing each state's objectives without destroying the state system.

Although the norms of classical international law sometimes went unheeded, the body of theory and state practice which constituted "inter-national law as an institution" nonetheless expressed in a quasi-authoritative manner the three assumptions about international politics. It legalized the existence of states and helped to define the actions necessary for the preservation of each state and of the system as a whole. It reinforced the idea that vigilance, moderation, and flexibility are necessary for the pro-tection of a system of competing states. And finally, international law established a legalized system of political payoffs by providing a means to register gains and losses without creating a static system. In fact, this last aspect was essential to the classical state system. With international law defining certain relationships (territorial expansion, empire building, etc.) as legitimate areas for political competition, other areas seemed, at least generally in the classical period, to be removed from the center of the political struggle. By legitimizing the struggle as a form of political competi-tion rather than as universal conflict, international law sanctioned a form of international system that was more than just an anarchic drive for survival.

II. CONTEMPORARY INTERNATIONAL LAW AND THE ASSUMPTIONS OF THE STATE SYSTEM

As a quasi-authoritative system of communicating the assumptions of the state system to policy-makers, contemporary international law no longer presents a clear idea of the nature of international politics. . . . Inter-national law today is in a state of arrested ambiguity—in a condition of unstable equilibrium between the old and the new. As a result, it no longer contributes as it once did to a consensus on the nature of the state system. . . .

The Challenge to the State and the System

The current legal concept of the state is a perfect example of the arrested ambiguity of contemporary international law and of the threat that this condition represents to the assumptions of the state system. On the one hand, most of traditional forms used to express the idea of statehood are still employed. Treaty-makers and statesmen still write about "respect for territorial integrity," the "right of domestic jurisdiction," and the "sovereign will of the high contracting parties." . . . On the other hand, certain contemporary developments contrast sharply with the traditional territory-oriented conceptions of international law.[11] With the growth of international entities possessing supranational powers (e.g., ECSC), the legal idea of self-contained units based on territorial control lacks the clear basis in fact that it once enjoyed. . . .

Other developments in contemporary international law represent, theoretically at least, a challenge to the assumption that the state and its freedom of action are an absolute necessity for the state system. Most noticeable has been the attempt to develop an international organization which would preserve a minimal degree of order. . . .

Like the League [of Nations], the United Nations was to replace the state as the paramount institutional value by establishing a constitutional concert of powers. However, it has succeeded only in underscoring the existing tension between the drive to maintain the state and the goal of maintaining the system. In the Charter itself, the tension between the state and the system remains unresolved.[12] Nor does the actual operation of the United Nations provide a very optimistic basis for the hope that tension will be lessened in the future. . . .

A more serious challenge . . . is the changing relation of the individual to the international legal order. In the classical system, international law clearly relegated the individual to the position of an object of the law. Not the individual, but the state had the rights and duties of the international legal order. . . .[13] The idea that the individual rather than the state is the unit of responsibility in the formulation of policy has a long intellectual tradition; [14] however, it is only recently that norms associated with that idea have become a part of international law.

Although the role of the individual in international law is small and the chances for its rapid development in the near future are slight, it represents a more vital challenge to traditional international law and to the assumptions of the state system than either international or regional organizations. Since the principle of collective responsibility (of the state) rather than individual responsibility has traditionally served as the infrastructure of the rights and duties of states,[15] the development of a place for the individual in the international legal system that would make him personally responsible would completely revolutionize international law. At the same time, by making the individual a higher point of policy reference than the state, the development of the role of the individual represents a challenge to the assumption once reflected in classical international law that the preservation and maximization of state power is an absolute guideline for policy-makers. The evolving place of the individual in the contemporary international legal system, then, is contrary to the traditional tendency of international law to reaffirm the absolute value of the state. . . .

III. INTERNATIONAL LAW AND THE REALITY OF CONTEMPORARY INTERNATIONAL POLITICS

Contemporary international legal practice, then, is developing along lines which represent a threat not only to traditional concepts of international law but also to the assumptions of the state system. . . . Actually, of course, the traditional conceptions of international law and the classical assumptions about international politics are not extinct.[16] Rather, there is in both international law and politics a perplexing mixture of past ideas and current developments. The only thing one can be sure of is that behind the traditional legal and political symbols which exist today in a somewhat mutated form, a subtle transformation of some kind is taking place.

It is not possible to evaluate the line of future development of the assumptions about the state system or the international legal expression of those assumptions from the work of contemporary theorists of international law. The most apparent new expressions are those that propose increased formalizations of world legal and political processes.[17] On the other hand, much international legal theory today seems to be dedicated to an affirmation of the traditional assumptions of international politics. Political analysts like Hans Morgenthau,[18] E. H. Carr,[19] and George F. Kennan,[20] and legal theorists like Julius Stone,[21] P. E. Corbett,[22] and Charles De Visscher,[23] are predisposed to "bring international law back to reality."

This trend toward being "realistic" occupies the mainstream of current international legal theory. . . .[24]

The desire of contemporary theorists to be "realistic" has been crucial to the relationship between contemporary international law and the assumptions of the state system. . . . When they talk about adjusting international law to the realities of power, they usually have in mind the traditional reality of international politics. . . . Much contemporary international legal theory, then, has not contributed to the development of a new consensus on the nature of international politics but instead has reinforced many of the traditional ideas.

In order to understand more fully the relation of international law to world politics, it is necessary to do more than examine law merely as a direct constraint or political action. . . . In the contemporary period, where the international legal system is relatively decentralized, and international politics is subject to rapid and profound development, it is necessary to avoid a conceptual framework of international law which breeds undue pessimism because it demands too much. If international law does not contribute directly and effectively to world order by forcing states to be peaceful, it does prepare the conceptual ground on which that order could be built by shaping attitudes about the nature and promise of international political reality.

NOTES

[1] Hans J. Morgenthau, *Politics Among Nations* (New York, 1961), 275-311. The entire evaluation of the "main problems" of international law is focused on the question of what rules are violated and what rules are not.

[2] There are a few writers who have tried to approach international law from a different vantage point. For a survey of some of the other approaches to international law and politics, see Michael Barkun, "International Norms: An Interdisci-

plinary Approach," *Background* (August 1964): 121-29. The survey shows that few "new" approaches to international law have developed beyond the preliminary stages, save perhaps for the writings of F. S. C. Northrup. Northrup's works (e.g., *Philosophical Anthropology and Practical Politics* [New York, 1960], 326-30) are particularly significant in their attempt to relate psychological, philosophical, and cultural approaches to the study of law in general, although he has not usually been concerned with the overall relationship of international law to international political action. Not mentioned in Barkun's survey but important in the discussion of international law and politics is Stanley Hoffmann, "International Systems and International Law," in Klaus Knorr and Sidney Verba, eds., *The International System* (Princeton, 1961), 205-38. However, Hoffmann's essay is closer in approach to the work by Kaplan and Katzenbach than to the approach developed in this article. Finally, it is also necessary to point to an article by Edward McWhinney, "Soviet and Western International Law and the Cold War in a Nuclear Era of Bipolarity: Inter-Bloc Law in a Nuclear Age," *Canadian Yearbook of International Law*, I (1963), 40-81. Professor McWhinney discusses the relationship between American and Russian structures of action, on the one hand, and their interpretations on international law, on the other. While McWhinney's approach is basically similar to the one proposed in this article in its attempt to relate international law to politics on a conceptual level, his article is focused on a different set of problems, the role of national attitudes in the contemporary era on ideas of international law. Nevertheless, it is a significant contribution to the task of analyzing more clearly the relationship between international law and politics.

[3] See Richard A. Falk, "The Adequacy of Contemporary International Law: Gaps in Legal Thinking," *Virginia Law Review*, 50 (March 1964): 231-65, for a valuable but highly critical analysis of contemporary legal theory.

[4] See Gabriel A. Almond and James S. Coleman, eds., *The Politics of the Developing Areas* (Princeton, 1960), 26-31, for an explanation of the concept of socialization.

[5] The following discussion of the assumptions of the state system is brief, since students of international politics generally agree that the three assumptions listed have structured most of the actions of states. This agreement is most complete concerning the nature of the "classical" state system. The author is also of the opinion that these assumptions continue to operate today in a somewhat mutated form. (See his unpublished manuscript "The Image of Power Politics A Cognitive Approach to the Study of International Politics," chaps. 2, 4, 8.) Note also the agreement on the nature of classical ideas about international politics in the following: Ernst B. Haas, "The Balance of Power as a Guide to Policy-Making," *Journal of Politics*, 15 (August 1953): 370-97; Morton A. Kaplan, *System and Process in International Politics* (New York, 1957), 22-36; and Edward Vose Gulick, *Europe's Classical Balance of Power* (Ithaca, N.Y., 1955).

[6] See Gulick, 34; and for a discussion of principles of moderation, flexibility, and vigilance, *ibid.*, 11-16.

[7] For a treaty which expressed the necessity of keeping prior obligations, see *Treaty of Aix-la-Chapelle, 1748,* in Browning, ed., *English History Documents*, Vol. X (New York, 1963).

[8] For the relationship of the assumption of statehood and the functioning of diplomatic immunities, see a discussion of the theoretical underpinnings of diplomatic immunities in Ernest L. Kelsey, "Some Aspects of the Vienna Conference on Diplomatic Intercourse and Immunities," *American Journal of International Law*, 88 (January 1962): 92-94.

[9] Morgenthau, 547.

[10] See Georg F. von Martens, *The Law of Nations: Being the Science of National Law, Convenants, Power & Founded upon the Treaties and Custom of Modern Nations in Europe*, trans. by William Cobbett (4th ed., London, 1829), 123-34, for the intellectual and legal problems growing out of the assumption that states may

legally maximize power but that they also have a responsibility "to oppose by alliances and even by force of arms" a series of aggrandizements which threaten the community.

¹¹ For a survey of current challenges to traditional international law, see Wolfgang Friedmann, "The Changing Dimensions of International Law," *Columbia Law Review*, 62 (November 1962): 1147-65. Also, see Richard A. Falk, *The Role of the Domestic Courts in the International Legal Order* (Syracuse, 1964), 14-19, for a discussion of the fact that while there is a growing "functional obsolescence" of the state system, the assumptions of the state system continue to operate for psychological and political reasons.

¹² Compare Articles 25-51, or paragraphs 2-7 in Article 2, for the contrast between system-oriented and state-oriented norms.

¹³ See P. E. Corbett, *Law and Society in the Relations of States* (New York, 1951), 53-56, for a discussion of the place of the individual in classical international law.

¹⁴ According to Guido de Ruggiero, *The History of European Liberalism* (Boston, 1959), 363-70, the liberal conception of the state has always assumed that the individual was the absolute value, though this idea has not always been operative.

¹⁵ For an excellent discussion of the role of collective responsibility in international law, see Hans Kelsen, *Principles of International Law* (New York, 1959), 9-13, 114-48.

¹⁶ As in the past, international lawyers are still concerned with definitions and applications of concepts of territorial integrity, self-defense, and domestic jurisdiction, and policy-makers are still motivated by the traditional ideas of state security and power. However, the traditional political and legal symbols have been "stretched" to apply to current conditions.

¹⁷ E.g., Arthur Larson, *When Nations Disagree* (Baton Rouge, La., 1961); or Grenville Clark and Louis B. Sohn, *World Peace Through World Law* (Cambridge, Mass., 1960). These theorists and others who fall under this classification are "radical" in the sense that what they suggest is antithetical to the assumptions of the state system as traditionally developed. These writers are not necessarily utopian in their radicalism. This is especially true since adherence today to the traditional assumptions might itself be considered a form of (reactionary) radicalism. However, the radical scholars, in the sense used here, are very scarce, especially among American students of international law. Today there is a very thin line separating the few radical scholars from the more radical polemicists of world government.

¹⁸ Morgenthau writes (277): "To recognize that international law exists is, however, not tantamount to asserting that . . . it is effective in regulating and restraining the struggle for power on the international scene."

¹⁹ E. H. Carr, in *The Twenty Years' Crisis, 1919-1939* (London, 1958), 170, writes: "We are exhorted to establish 'the rule of Law' . . . and the assumption is made that, by so doing, we shall transfer our differences from the turbulent political atmosphere of self-interest to the purer, serener air of impartial justice." His subsequent analysis is designed to disprove this assumption.

²⁰ George F. Kennan, *Realities of American Foreign Policy* (Princeton, 1954), 16.

²¹ Julius Stone, *Legal Control of International Conflict* (New York, 1954), introduction.

²² Corbett, 68-79, 291-92.

²³ De Visscher writes [*Theory and Reality in Public International Law* (Princeton, 1957), (xiv)]: "International law cannot gather strength by isolating itself from the political realities with which international relations are everywhere impregnated. It can only do so by taking full account of the place that these realities occupy and measuring the obstacle which they present."

²⁴ The programs of the 1963 and 1964 annual meetings of the American Society of International Law exemplify the way in which the concern for reality (as power)

has come to dominate international legal theory. In the 1963 program, the relationship between international law and the use of force was not discussed by international legal theorists but by two well-known writers on the role of conflict in international politics. The 1964 program manifested the same tendency. It centered on the question of compliance with transnational law, a topic treated in a socio-political framework by most panelists. This point is not to be taken as a criticism of the two programs, both of which were excellent and very relevant, but as proof of the assertion that the mainstream of contemporary theory of international law is significantly oriented to the role of power.

The preceding study is exemplary of qualitative historical description. The author has sought to describe changes in the structure of the international legal culture as they have evolved through long periods of time. The descriptions are made from an impressionist comparison of the writings of international legal scholars. While it is possible, in principle (e.g., Kegley, 79), to base such descriptions on information derived from more systematic observational procedures, such as content analysis, such research operations are tremendously costly and difficult to conduct in a reliable manner. Changes in the legal rules of the global system have hitherto never been scientifically measured and monitored. Thus, we should regard the descriptive account provided here as suggestive and tentative rather than definitive. The article is designed to generalize, in a macroanalytic manner, about fluctuations in legal norms and beliefs and to suggest conceptually a number of hypotheses regarding the nexus that obtains between systemic beliefs about behavior, on the one hand, and subsequent actual behavioral patterns, on the other. The descriptions and hypotheses that emerge from this exploratory analytic exercise are all amenable to testing and verification.

In another sense, Coplin's study is explanatory. It attempts to account for the reasons that systemic prescriptions regarding appropriate national behavior have undergone changes and to indicate, by implication, the philosophical and cultural sources of national conduct. The observed discrepancy between the way states act and the way international legal norms say they should act is explained by Coplin as resulting from the fact that international law does not operate as a political constraint system, as domestic legal systems do. Thus, by reorienting our thinking about the functions that international legal norms perform in the global system, Coplin has offered an explanation of the role that international law plays in the system.

Coplin's essay on international law concentrates on a basic international mechanism for maintaining the international system and preserving its salient structural characteristics. By tradition, statesmen and analysts alike have tended to interpret (for sometimes dubious reasons) international law as a global attribute that serves to enhance the prospects for stability. Some have seen legal rules as a conflict-resolution device that facilitates and encourages international peace, while others—observing that international law restricts and limits the policy options of states— have regarded international legal norms as a technique for preserving the status quo. *Still others—noting the justifications for violence inherent in much of Western international law—have interpreted international law as promotive of the continuation of the war system. Regardless, however, of how one interprets the consequences and effects of international law, all interpreters share in common the assumption that international law is somehow related to the incidence and magnitude of international war and the probability of its occurrence. All observers thus see international law as a global attribute bearing on the maintenance of the international system.*

Another central component of the international system that states-men and scholars alike have traditionally viewed as relevant to the maintenance of the international system is the number and type of inter-national organizations extant. Although there is a rich folklore about the role of intergovernmental organizations in the system, there is little in the way of hard information about the functions that these institutions perform or the contribution that they make to the maintenance of system stability. This is unfortunate because intergovernmental organizations are an important element in the international environment. Because their membership, purposes, and scope of activity transcend national boundaries, we may assume that they constitute a segment of the international system that affects the relations of those states that make up the system. They not only provide an institutional setting for nation-states to interact in but are international actors themselves. And yet their influence on international political relations and the probability of war is difficult to observe systematically.

In the following article, J. David Singer and Michael Wallace under-take a systematic and scientific investigation of the implications of intergovernmental organizations for the preservation of peace. They thus address a series of empirical questions that have not yet been confronted with data. In reading this study, the reader is advised to take special notice of the precise observational rules and rigorous analytic procedures employed.

INTERGOVERNMENTAL ORGANIZATION AND THE PRESERVATION OF PEACE, 1816–1964: SOME BIVARIATE RELATIONSHIPS

J. David Singer and Michael Wallace

In the three centuries or so since the modern international system began to take on its present shape, its component members have come together in a wide variety of organizations, for a wide variety of purposes. Those who act on behalf of the nations have turned to international organizations to oversee peace settlements, to strengthen their collective defense capacity, to mediate conflicts between themselves, to discourage interference from the outside, to harmonize their trade relations, to supervise international waterways, to accelerate the production of food, to codify diplomatic practice, and to formalize legal proceedings. Some organizations are established primarily for the neutral purpose of making coexistence possible, others for the more affirmative purposes of positive cooperation. Some have been directed toward the modification of the system, others toward the preservation of its status quo.

Whether the orientation is positive, neutral, or even negative, the preservation of peace is generally one of the prime considerations of the organization's architects. As Inis L. Claude has so well put it:

> In the realm of international organization, the essential criterion of legitimacy is relevance to the prevention of war; almost any multilateral program can be justified with, and hardly any can be justified without, the claim that it promises to promote conditions conducive to international peace.[1]

There are, admittedly, some occasions on which nations organize for rather less benign purposes. But even when the organization appears aggressive on its surface, those who created it often seek only to deter a potential enemy, to intimidate an adversary into capitulation without war, to postpone a struggle that might otherwise be imminent, or, at worst, to so organize that a potentially long and bloody stalemate might be replaced with a quick and relatively inexpensive victory. Furthermore, most of these

J. David Singer and Michael Wallace, "Intergovernmental Organization and the Preservation of Peace, 1916–1964: Some Bivariate Relationships," *International Organization*, 24, 3 (Summer 1970): 520-47. (Abridged.) Footnotes have been re-numbered to appear in consecutive order. Reprinted by permission of the author and publisher.

Wallace is an assistant professor political science at the University of British Columbia.

military oriented activities are carried on via temporary arrangements, and rarely do they lead to the creation of international organizations as traditionally defined. That is, seldom do they see the establishment of a permanent headquarters, a multinational secretariat, and regularized budgetary provisions.

Beyond this, of course, are the concerns of those who study international organizations, publicize their activities, or seek to strengthen and multiply the organizational bonds between the nations. Outside of that small and dwindling group which looks to international organization as merely another vehicle for the perpetuation of its own short-run national interests, most of us assume or hope that such institutions somehow do contribute to international peace. More particularly, we assume that they have contributed, however modestly, to some reduction in the incidence of war in the past and, more importantly, are likely to do so in the future.[2]

The purpose of this article is to search out the preliminary evidence for these interpretations of the past and predictions of the future. Specifically, our intent is to ascertain the extent to which international organization in some of its several manifestations has, during the past century and a half, correlated with the rise and fall in the incidence of war.

Before turning to the evidence, however, two points need to be emphasized. First, we believe that any search for generalization in world politics must be based on a fairly long historical period, and we therefore view with skepticism any proposition based on the observation—no matter how systematic and operational—of events and conditions within a brief and limited time (or space) frame. At the same time, we fully appreciate that the longer the period under examination, the greater the possibility that the separate decades will differ markedly from one another in terms of the environment within which our phenomena occur. But the amount of such change must be treated as an empirical question, not as a matter of assertion. The position taken here is that, despite the dramatic changes in certain attributes of the international system since the Napoleonic wars, they do not invalidate the search for recurrent patterns during that admittedly tumultuous epoch. We will return to this problem in our conclusion.

A second, and closely related, point is that an analysis which is based on only two sets of variables must, of necessity, be incomplete. That is, because other factors may be intervening to affect the outcome, there is always the chance that any correlation which is found between international organization and fluctuations in the incidence of war might well be a spurious one. But, since we do not know with any certainty *which* additional variables are likely to be most potent in accounting for any such correlation and since in any event we cannot gather the data for all possible variables at once, we must begin somewhere. In so doing, we have no illusion that we are discovering the causal connections—or absence thereof—between international organization and war; we have only an appreciation that anytime we can ascertain the statistical relationship between two sets of variables over time, we are enlarging the base upon which a fuller understanding must ultimately rest.

THE INCIDENCE OF WAR IN THE INTERSTATE SYSTEM

In order to examine the relationship between international organization and war over the past 150 years, the initial step is to ascertain precisely how much war the interstate system has experienced in the past, and it is to that mission which this section is assigned. That task must await, however, completion of a preliminary operation: defining our empirical domain.

The Interstate System and Its Composition

No empirical observations can be intelligently appraised unless we know which cases, events, or conditions were *in*cluded and which were *ex*cluded from the observations. We are as justifiably skeptical of the relevance of a set of cases which are too distant in time or space or too few in number as we are of those which result from a conscious "ransacking" of history in pursuit of just those cases which support our argument. In other words, we must either define our universe or draw a representative sample therefrom before any data-based generalizations can be made. For the purposes at hand, we should insist on a universe which is fairly long in terms of the life of the international system and broad in terms of the political units and regions which are embraced. On both the temporal and the spatial dimensions, however, there is always the chance that overly large sectors may contain highly diverse subsectors, such that important empirical differences are concealed within the overall rubric.[3] Hence, the generality of any findings in a study such as this can—and ultimately should—be assessed by subdividing the system at hand into its regional and functional subsystems and dividing the time span into several more limited periods. This we will do in a subsequent analysis.

Following the practice adopted in a larger project which is designed to ascertain which variables show a consistent correlation with international war, let us set the temporal limits between January 1816, with the close of the Napoleonic wars, and December 1964, the most recent year for which comprehensive data on our several variables [are] now available. Within that time framework, we have identified and delineated those national political units which qualified for inclusion in the interstate system, a universe ranging from 23 nations in 1816 to 122 in 1964.[4]

While the precise coding criteria and data-making procedures are presented elsewhere, a brief summary is in order here. We defined as members of the interstate system all national political entities which, at a given time, had—in the judgment of the historical scholars—the standard attributes of independence and statehood.[5] For those entities whose statehood was ambiguous, diplomatic recognition from the United Kingdom and France up to 1920, and membership in the League of Nations or the United Nations since then, served as the final criterion; a population minimum of one half million was also required, unless the nation was a member of either organization. The shifting population of the system, as generated by these procedures, is shown in Table 1.

TABLE I: NATION MEMBERS OF THE INTERSTATE SYSTEM, 1816–1964

Western Hemisphere			
United States	1816	Hesse Grand Ducal	1816–1867
Canada	1920	Mecklenburg-Schwerin	1843–1867
Cuba	1902	Poland	1919–1939
Haiti	1859		1945
Dominican Republic	1887	Austria-Hungary	1816–1918
Jamaica	1962	Austria	1919–1938
Trinidad-Tobago	1962		1955
Mexico	1831	Hungary	1919
Guatemala	1849	Czechoslovakia	1918–1939
Honduras	1899		1945
Salvador	1875	Sardinia	1816–1859
Nicaragua	1900	Italy	1860
Costa Rica	1920	Papal States	1816–1860
Panama	1920	Two Sicilies	1816–1861
Colombia	1831	Modena	1842–1860
Venezuela	1841	Malta	1964
Ecuador	1854	Parma	1851–1860
Peru	1838	Tuscany	1816–1860
Brazil	1826	Albania	1914–1939
Bolivia	1848		1944
Paraguay	1896	Serbia	1878–1918
Chile	1839	Yugoslavia	1919–1941
Argentina	1841		1944
Uruguay	1882	Greece	1828–1941
			1945
Europe		Cyprus	1960
		Bulgaria	1908
England	1816	Romania	1878
Ireland	1922	Russia	1816
Holland	1816–1940	Estonia	1918–1940
	1945	Latvia	1918–1940
Belgium	1830–1940	Lithuania	1918–1940
	1945	Finland	1919
Luxemburg	1920–1940	Sweden	1816
	1944	Norway	1905–1940
France	1816–1942		1945
	1944	Denmark	1816–1940
Switzerland	1816		1945
Spain	1816	Iceland	1944
Portugal	1816		
Hanover	1838–1866	*Africa*	
Bavaria	1816–1870	Gambia	1965
Prussia	1816–1870	Mali	1960
Germany	1871–1945	Senegal	1960
Germany West	1955	Dahomey	1960
Germany East	1954	Mauritania	1960
Baden	1816–1870	Niger	1960
Saxony	1816–1867	Ivory Coast	1960
Württemberg	1816–1870	Guinea	1958
Hesse Electoral	1816–1866	Liberia	1920

TABLE 1—Continued

Sierra Leone	1961	United Arab Republic (Egypt)	1937
Ghana	1957	Syria	1946–1958
Togo	1960		1961
Cameroon	1960	Lebanon	1946
Nigeria	1960	Jordan	1946
Gabon	1960	Israel	1948
Central African Republic	1960	Saudi Arabia	1927
Chad	1960	Yemen	1926
Congo (Brazzaville)	1960	Kuwait	1961
Congo (Kinshasa)	1960		
Upper Volta	1960	*Asia-Oceana*	
Uganda	1962	Afghanistan	1920
Kenya	1963	China	1860
Tanzania	1961	Mongolia (Outer)	1921
(Tanganyika-Zanzibar)		Taiwan	1949
Zanzibar	1963–1964	Korea	1888–1905
Burundi	1962	Korea North	1948
Rwanda	1962	Korea South	1949
Somali	1960	Japan	1860–1945
Ethiopia	1898–1936		1952
	1941	India	1947
Zambia	1964	Pakistan	1947
Malawi	1964	Burma	1948
South Africa	1920	Ceylon	1948
Malagasy (Madagascar)	1960	Nepal	1920
		Thailand (Siam)	1887
Middle East		Cambodia	1953
Morocco	1847–1911	Laos	1954
	1956	Vietnam North	1954
Algeria	1962	Vietnam South	1954
Tunisia	1956	Malaysia (Malaya)	1957
Libya	1952	Singapore	1965
Sudan	1956	Philippines	1946
Iran (Persia)	1855	Indonesia	1949
Turkey	1816	Australia	1920
Iraq	1932	New Zealand	1920

We can now turn to the specification of our dependent variable—that factor against which our various measures of international organization will be correlated. In order to ascertain the frequency and other measures of the incidence of war, some brief verbal definitions must first be developed. Following Quincy Wright's *Study of War* categorization but using somewhat more operational criteria, we postulate four types of war: interstate, imperial, colonial, and civil. Only the first of these will concern us here, but the general distinctions are worth noting.[6]

As its name clearly implies, an *interstate* war is one in which at least one of the participating entities on each side was a qualified nation member of the interstate system. An *imperial* war is defined as one in which only one side included a state member of the system, and the major adversary was a relatively independent national entity which did not, however, qualify for system membership. A *colonial* war is one in which again only one side included a member of the system, but the major adversary, rather than being independent, had been, either before or after the war, a protectorate or dependency of the system member against whom it was fighting. A *civil* war is one in which the system member's armed forces were involved in sustained combat against domestic rebellious forces, whether the latter enjoyed insurgency status or not. If a system member intervened militarily on the side of the rebels and its forces sustained 1,000 or more battle deaths, the war became an internationalized civil war and would therefore be included under the interstate war rubric. And, for *any* of these three types of war to be included in the overall study, it had to lead to a minimum of 1,000 battle-connected deaths among the military personnel of the system members participating.

Once we had separated wars from all other instances of armed conflict and had classified them as above, the next step was to measure not only the frequency but also the magnitude and severity of the interstate wars. In *The Wages of War* (1972), we spell out in considerable detail the procedures by which wars were classified and quantified, along with a number of analyses of the resulting data; thus, as in defining the population of the system, only a brief summary of the coding procedures and criteria is needed here.[7] Very simply, every war is scaled in terms of its *magnitude,* measured in nation-months, and *severity,* measured in battle-connected fatalities among system member participants. We also devised three indicators of each war's *intensity*—measured as the ratio between battle deaths and, respectively, nation-months, armed forces size, and total population of the participating nations.

If space were available, we would then show a table listing each of the 50 interstate wars and its duration, magnitude, and severity, along with the dates during which each participant was involved and its battle-connected deaths. In that raw form, the data would be of limited use, however. For the purposes of a time series analysis, we need to calculate the amount of war which began and ended during each of the half-decade periods, so that the fluctuating frequency, magnitude, and severity measures could be correlated with those for international organization during the period covered in the study. When we come to those analyses, the data will be aggregated and presented in the appropriate format.

THE AMOUNT OF INTERGOVERNMENTAL ORGANIZATION IN THE SYSTEM

Having summarized the procedures by which we defined our empirical domains and having measured the incidence of war within these domains, we can now proceed to a discussion of our *in*dependent variables. So far, we have used "international organization" in its most general sense; it is now time to define its several meanings and to outline the operational procedures by which it may be measured. This will be a somewhat lengthier process, not only because it is probably intrinsically more difficult to develop measures of international organization which are both reliable and valid, but also because little prior work of an operational nature has gone into the enterprise.[8] And if we are to make any well-founded statements regarding the efficacy of international organization in the prevention of war, a minimum requirement is that we ascertain fluctuations in the amount of war and in the amount of international organization over the years and then ascertain the extent to which they rise and fall together. Of course, even if we discover a strong positive or negative *correlation* between the two sets of variables, we cannot automatically assume a strong *causal* relationship between them. We will return to the interpretation of our correlations later, but the immediate task at hand is to propose, justify, and describe certain measures of international organization.

The Number of Intergovernmental Organizations

The most obvious and undifferentiated indicator of the extent to which international organization has been instituted among the members of the system is a gross reflection of magnitude: How many organizations are there in existence each year and how many nations do they embrace? Such gross measures can be refined, first, by differentiating between the various types of organizations that are found and, second, by differentiating between the classes of nations which belong to them. Among the differentiations we can make between international organizations, the most widely accepted one is between those which are intergovernmental (hereafter called IGO's) and those which are nongovernmental (NGO's). Thus, one procedure would be to use as one index the total number of IGO's and NGO's in existence in the total system year by year and then go on to a more refined index which counts the number in each group separately. There are, however, several good reasons for not doing so and for restricting our analysis to IGO's only. First of all, despite the large amount of research in the field, no scholar has yet seen fit to find out how many organizations existed each year, which ones they were, and which nations belonged to each. Such a delineation of the population, for IGO's or for NGO's, for the very recent past or for the more distant past, has not (to our knowledge) been undertaken as of the present. The nearest attempt to produce such information has been the pioneering, but incomplete, work of the Union of International Associations and the League of Nations.[9] Given the cost and complexity of gathering [these] data, only one set should be generated at a time, and we decided to use IGO's only in this particular study.

In addition to the obvious difference in the reliability and completeness of the information available, a relevant theoretical factor strongly suggests the superiority of IGO's for our purposes here. Even while recognizing the overlap in functions between the two types and the occasional ambiguity in differentiating between them, those embracing national governments offer a more valid measure of the amount of organization devoted directly to the reduction of international war. That is, membership in an IGO represents the decision of a government, and it is governments that ultimately make decisions for war or for peace. Moreover, most IGO's deal with activities that come closer to matters of war and peace than do most NGO's, even though, once more, we must admit the presence of an appreciable overlap. In sum, then, we use IGO's here because they offer an index which seems to be least costly, most reliable, and most valid.

Now, some will agree with this distinction but insist that we have not gone far enough. They might contend that we still fail to discriminate between the most and least "important" (or relevant or powerful) or that we might do well to distinguish between those which are "really" intended to contribute to peace and those which are little more than a façade for preserving the distribution of power or wealth in the system. We think such comments are well taken in principle but that they pose two serious problems. First, such discriminations would require a detailed investigation into the origins or history of each IGO if we are to avoid a purely idiosyncratic classification. Better, in our judgment, to begin with a somewhat more gross set of categories than to create capricious subcategories which reflect little more than one's personal (and not reproducible) biases. Second, and more important, a cardinal rule of research strategy is to avoid refinement of one's data until certain brush-clearing analyses have been completed. Thus, as we or others follow up this first primitive—but essential—investigation, it will become increasingly appropriate to seek a finer breakdown, but for the moment we are persuaded that it would be unwarranted.

Nation Membership in Intergovernmental Organization

Having made and justified this rather gross distinction between the international organizations themselves, we do, however, go on to refine our measures in terms of certain attributes of their memberships. Quite clearly, the importance of an IGO at any point in time cannot ignore the difference between one which is composed of a few small nations and one which includes many nations, including the most powerful. Our measure, then, must reflect both (1) the sheer size of each organization in terms of member nations and (2) the diplomatic importance of those nations. This refinement is achieved by adding to our first measure (mere number of IGO's in the system) two additional ones. The second reflects total size of international governmental organization and is measured by the *number of nation memberships* in all IGO's year by year. The third reflects not only the simple number of nation memberships but goes a step further and weights each such membership by the "diplomatic importance" score of the nation in question.

Since these procedures, like those for defining the composition of the system and for identifying and measuring war, are quite complex and detailed, we will only summarize them here.[10] First of all, for an international organization to qualify as an IGO under our criteria, it must be composed of at least two qualified nation members of the interstate system, must have a permanent secretariat, headquarters, and a regular budget, and must hold at least one general conference per decade. Second, the organization must have been established by a formal agreement, convention, or treaty between national governments. Third, the organization must not be the subsidiary of any other IGO, must not be serviced by the same secretariat as another, must not be an *association* of separate IGO's and must not have been replaced by another which successfully claims de facto jurisdiction over the same functions and/or regions. As to the IGO's *size,* only full participating members, as opposed to those with associate status, are counted; but a system member's colony or dependency can serve to provide the basis for an indirect membership if that metropolitan nation is *not* a member.

Once we have ascertained the number of IGO's in the system for each year and have identified the number of nations belonging to each, we turn to the third step in measuring the "amount of IGO." As indicated above, this involves a search for the number of diplomatic missions in each nation's capital. Computed twice per decade for all system members, this figure reflects in an approximate fashion the diplomatic importance which all the other system members attribute to the host nation.[11] This score is then "normalized" by dividing it by the total number of nations in the system for that year. Thus, by ascertaining what percentage of the system's nations posted diplomatic missions (at the rank of chargé d'affaires or above) to each other, we had an index which was comparable across time regardless of how large the system was.

To recapitulate, we began with the number of qualifying IGO's in the system each year, then counted the total number of nation memberships in these organizations, and, finally, weighted each membership by the normalized diplomatic importance score of the relevant member. The resulting figures are called "amount of intergovernmental organization" (or amount of IGO) and the results—collapsed into five-year periods— are shown in Tables 2 and 5, in the context of our several analyses.

CORRELATIONS BETWEEN INTERGOVERNMENTAL ORGANIZATION AND WAR

Having summarized the rationale behind our basic indicators plus the procedures by which they were operationalized, we may now turn to the major concern of the article. This is, of course, the extent to which interstate war and intergovernmental organization have been statistically associated over the past century and a half. At the risk of some redundancy, let us reiterate that no *causal* association is claimed or implied in the data analyses or interpretations which follow and that each set of bivariate correlations will require cautious and conservative interpretation. Our inquiry will be addressed to two main questions: First, what sort of evidence is there that statesmen believe that (or behave as if) intergovernmental organization is an important means of reducing war? Second, is there any evidence that such beliefs, if they exist, are historically justified?

Belief in the Efficacy of Intergovernmental Organization

There are, of course, several strategies by which we might get at the extent and intensity of elite (or public) belief in the efficacy of IGO as a means for the reduction of interstate war. One strategy would be to content analyze their private and their public statements, as recorded in memoirs, intragovernmental memoranda, diplomatic correspondence, speeches, press conferences, party platforms, and the like. For those of our own era, the interview might provide a useful if ancillary approach. Another approach, while less direct, might be more valid, and that is to examine the actual behavior of governments and their decisionmakers; this, of course, reflects the premise that verbalizations may conceal more than they reveal, while actual policy decisions often provide the most accurate indicator of the really *operative* beliefs. Within this second strategy, one of the more revealing indicators might well be the extent to which governments attempt to strengthen or increase the role and amount of such international institutions in the wake of each war experience. That is, even while recognizing that few statesmen believe that IGO's *by themselves* can guarantee the preservation of peace in the system, we would be quite justified in inferring that a discernible increase in the commitment to intergovernmental organization in the various postwar periods of the past 150 years reflects the conviction that their role is of considerable importance. What sort of evidence do we find in support of such an inference?

In Table 2 we have assembled our data showing three different measures of the amount of war which *ended* during each half decade since 1816, along with two measures of the amount of IGO *established* and three measures of the amount of IGO that *existed* during each half decade.

The first thing we notice is the dramatic spurt in the creation of new IGO's and weighted nation memberships during the periods following World War II (i.e., 1945–1949, as well as later), World War I (i.e., 1920–1924 and 1925–1929), the Russo-Japanese War (i.e., 1905–1909), and to a lesser extent after the Russo-Turkish, Pacific, and Central American wars (i.e., 1885–1889 and 1890–1894). These figures would suggest that quite a few statesmen *did,* when the costs and tragedies of war were still fresh in their memories, seek to avoid further slaughter via the establishment of new or additional intergovernmental organizations.

Rather than select out the more dramatic indications of this tendency, however, let us take the entire period under investigation and see whether the relationship between the termination of war and the creation of new IGO has indeed been a regular and recurrent phenomenon. We do this by examining the statistical association between the amount of war which ended in each half decade and several indicators of the increase (or occasional decrease) in the amount of intergovernmental organization

found in the wake of such wars. The former is the number of nation-months and battle deaths resulting from all interstate wars; for IGO, we actually measure the net change figures, reflecting both the establishment of new organizations and the loss of previously existing ones, in terms of their number and their total nation memberships. And as Table 3 indicates, we explore the effect of differing time spreads to see whether these lead to any changes in the pattern.

It will also be noted that we run these correlations in two ways, using both a rank-order (Kendall's Tau) and product-moment (Pearson's r) statistic. This is because of the questionable propriety of using a product-moment correlation on interval-type data when [these] data do not approximate a normal distribution, and neither the war nor the IGO data satisfy that condition. Moreover, the product-moment (or parametric) type of analysis is considered inappropriate for data whose values are not independent of one another from one observation to the next. This is a modest problem as far as the war data [are] concerned but a serious one vis-à-vis the IGO figures, since they show so strong a secular trend pattern. On the other hand, rank-order correlations are sensitive only to the fact that one period is higher or lower than another on a given measure and do not reflect *how much* higher or lower it is. Thus, in order to satisfy the need for a conservative measure as well as one which responds to the wide range of war and IGO scores over time, we utilize and report both sets of analyses in Tables 3, 4, and 6.

A second statistical matter is that of significance levels in our correlation coefficients. All those which are significant at the .05 level or better are italicized, and those which satisfy the .01 threshold are in bold face. We realize that one school of thought holds that significance levels are appropriate only when dealing with a sample and should not be used when the data represent . . . a full population. Our response is threefold. First, even in a population, one may speak of the probability of a given correlation appearing by chance alone, and the .05 and .01 indicate that these correlation coefficients had only a 5 percent or 1 percent probability of occurring by sheer chance. Second, there must be some threshold above which a coefficient is strong enough to be theoretically interesting, and these are the conventional thresholds in social science. To put it another way, if a correlation coefficient is very unlikely to occur by chance alone and also accounts for about 52 percent of the variance around the means in the results (as does the .72 correlation between nation-months of war ending and number of new nation memberships in IGO in the subsequent decade) it is worth noticing. Third, in a certain sense, we *are* working with a sample rather than a complete population. That is, even though we have all the IGO and war cases for the period at hand, these results only reflect the configurations revealed by our particular measures and observational procedures; hence, they may be thought of as a sample of the patterns that could have been generated by a wide variety of measures. In addition, some might contend that we also have a sample here in the sense that there were many other historical configurations and associations which *could* have occurred but

TABLE 3: CORRELATIONS BETWEEN AMOUNT OF WAR ENDING IN EACH PERIOD AND INCREASES IN AMOUNT OF IGO

	Changes during Following Period			Changes during Two Following Periods			Changes during Same and Following Periods		
	Number of IGO's	Simple Memberships	Weighted Memberships	Number of IGO's	Simple Memberships	Weighted Memberships	Number of IGO's	Simple Memberships	Weighted Memberships
Rank-Order:									
Nation-Months	.20	.21	.10	.42	.39	.37	.22	.22	.20
Battle Deaths	.20	.22	.11	.42	.41	.37	.23	.26	.23
Product-Moment:									
Nation-Months	.53	.40	.02	.65	.72	.56	.64	.51	.18
Battle Deaths	.47	.34	—.06	.54	.55	.31	.59	.46	.18

did not. Perhaps more important, we believe that our findings generalize to the post-1964 international system (if not the pre-1816 one) and thus represent only a time-bound sample of that larger, but not yet observed, population.

Turning, then, to the rank-order and product-moment correlations in Table 3, we look first at the extent to which the amount of war ending in one period correlates with the net change in IGO during the following five-year period. The differential effect of the two statistics is readily apparent. That is, the extent to which the periods which merely *rank* high on war termination are the ones followed by periods which also rank high in increased intergovernmental organization appears to be rather slight, ranging from .10 to .22. But if we shift from the rank-order to the more sensitive product-moment measure of association, we find that all six coefficients are considerably higher now, ranging up to .53.

Some might urge, however, that we have examined too brief a time spread and that the effect of war on the growth in IGO might not be evident unless we allow more time for that alleged effect to be felt. Thus, let us now consider the relationship between war termination and the net increase in IGO during the *two* half decades following that termination. These results suggest that there may well be something to the argument that postwar IGO takes as long as a decade to establish, since these correlation coefficients are consistently higher than those produced by the shorter time spread. Again, the type of statistic used can make an appreciable difference, with the six rank-order coefficients ranging from .37 to .42 and the product-moment ones reaching to .72. On the other hand, all but one of the twelve had less than a 5 percent probability of occurring by sheer chance.

Despite the increase in correlation values when we utilize the longer postwar time spread, there is need to consider a counter argument. A glance at the data in Table 2 shows that the half decade periods are so defined that several major wars end in the *early* part of such periods; examples are the Crimean (1856), Franco-Mexican (1887), Russo-Japanese (1905), and the world wars (1918 and 1945). If the IGO data were available on a more discriminating time scale and we were permitted to use briefer observation periods (of perhaps two years' duration) we might find that a larger fraction of the war termination data would fall in a period *preceding* that in which new IGO was established. One possible way of ascertaining the effect of our aggregation procedures is to measure the dependent variable during the decade which *includes* the end of the wars; thus, the relationship measured is that between the amount of war which ended during the 1870–1874 period (for example) and the net change in IGO during both the 1870–1874 and 1875–1879 periods. Using this set of observations, we find that the expected increase in association is not justified; both sets of correlation coefficients decline. While the decline is modest for the product-moment scores, it is quite sharp for the rank-order ones.

Worth noting in several of these correlations, regardless of the time period used for measuring the dependent variable, is that the mere *number* of IGO's correlates with war in a somewhat higher fashion than do the nation membership scores. This should occasion no surprise. Even though there seems to be this clear upsurge in the creation of new organizations after wars, there is probably a temporary *decrease* in the number of nations which are available to join them. This is, of course, due to the fact that wars often lead to the disappearence, or temporary occupation, of the defeated states, plus the fact that it often takes several years for other defeated states to re-establish their legitimacy as members of the comity of nations.

Another regularity is the already noted tendency of the product-moment correlations to be consistently higher than those which merely reflect the ranking of the periods. This is largely a consequence of the pattern which we found in the early visual inspection of Table 2. That is, the really dramatic increases in IGO seem to follow on the heels of the most severe and drawn-out wars, and while those magnitudes have little effect on rank-order correlations, they do show clearly when the more sensitive product-moment statistics are used.

In sum, Tables 2 and 3 show that whether we use visual inspection, rank-order correlation, or product-moment correlation, and regardless of which measures we use, it turns out that most of the new intergovernmental organization in the world has been established in the decade following the most warlike periods, while little such growth occurred in the decades following the relatively peaceful periods.

The above patterns suggest, in turn, a final way of examining the possible impact of war on IGO. We might focus, not on a measure which reflects the *new* organization created after wars, but on the amount still in existence. That is, if we recognize that many organizations fall into a serious state of disrepair and lose many members just before, and during, many wars, the fact that they are often resurrected and refurbished after the war years would be another indication of their perceived value. But since such revitalization often takes less time than the creation of new IGO's let us look only at the single period immediately following each five-year measure of the amount of war ended. As Table 4 reveals, there is indeed a moderately high set of associations between the amount of war which terminated in each period and the amount of IGO still existing in the following half decade. From these twelve correlations—all but one of which had less than a 5 percent probability of occurring by chance alone—it is reasonable to infer that statesmen have frequently acted as if they believed that the creation or continuation of such institutions might offer one way of reducing war in the future.

Of course, that *is* only an inference, and it falls far short of constituting proof of such beliefs. These patterns in the growth and re-establishment of IGO could well be accounted for by other phenomena. One such might be the need to institutionalize the large reconstruction efforts that are usually necessary after major warfare. Another might be the fact that the normal growth in the system's interdependence had led to the perceived need for more IGO's, and since their creation in wartime is difficult, the postwar surges and resurrections could have been largely

TABLE 4: CORRELATIONS BETWEEN AMOUNT OF WAR ENDING IN EACH
PERIOD AND AMOUNT OF IGO EXISTING IN NEXT PERIOD

	Number of IGO's	Simple Memberships	Weighted Memberships
Rank-Order: Nation-Months	.30	.31	.30
Battle Deaths	.33	.34	.33
Product-Moment: Nation-Months	.50	.46	.37
Battle Deaths	.41	.38	.30

a result of accumulated pressures. Not to be overlooked, too, is the possible effect of the secular trends noted earlier, since wars have tended to become somewhat more severe (if not more frequent) over time, while the amount of IGO has risen exponentially. Despite these possibilities, however, we are persuaded that the peacekeeping motive was a fairly critical one, never too far from the minds of those who had only recently experienced the tribulations of war. The next, and more important question, is this: To what extent have we been justified in looking to IGO as a possible vehicle for the reduction or prevention of war?

Does IGO Reduce the Incidence of War?

In order to ascertain whether or not the existence of intergovernmental organization has had a discernible effect on the frequency, magnitude, and severity of interstate war during the century and a half since the Napoleonic wars, our data need . . . to be rearranged and then reanalyzed. That is, our IGO data must be converted from periodic readings of the amount *created* to readings of the amount which *existed* during each of 30 periods. And our war data must be converted from readings of the amount of war which *ended* during each half decade to readings of the amount which *began* during each period. And instead of placing the war data first and then examining the extent to which [they] predict . . . to changes in IGO, we must now put the IGO data first and see whether [their] fluctuations predict to fluctuations in the amount of war during the subsequent period. In Table 5, we present a number of IGO and interstate war measures in the form which permits such an analysis.

TABLE 5: EXISTING IGO AND CHANGES VERSUS ONSET OF WAR, 1816–1964

Period	Number of IGO's	Simple Nation Memberships	Weighted Nation Memberships (Normalized)	Percentage Change Weighted Memberships	Number of Wars Begun	Nation-Months Begun	Battle Dead from Wars Begun (000's)
1816–1819	1	6	2.3	—	0	0	0
1820–1824	1	6	1.9	17.2	1	14.0	1.0
1825–1829	1	6	2.0	9.3	2	35.0	133.0
1830–1834	1	6	1.8	12.5	0	0	0
1835–1839	2	18	6.3	251.9	0	0	0
1840–1844	2	18	5.9	−6.5	0	0	0
1845–1849	2	18	6.0	2.6	4	75.0	34.0
1850–1854	2	18	5.8	3.1	2	128.5	265.3
1855–1859	3	24	8.7	49.3	3	26.0	35.0
1860–1864	3	21	7.9	−9.8	5	135.0	27.5
1865–1869	6	54	20.9	165.5	2	31.5	37.0
1870–1874	7	65	28.9	38.5	1	27.5	188.0
1875–1879	9	106	51.4	77.6	2	188.5	299.0
1880–1884	11	136	62.4	21.5	1	24.0	12.0
1885–1889	17	203	107.6	72.4	1	1.0	1.0
1890–1894	21	267	131.6	22.3	1	16.0	15.0
1895–1899	23	299	157.7	19.9	2	14.0	12.0
1900–1904	30	412	205.1	30.0	1	39.0	130.0
1905–1909	43	639	321.4	56.7	3	30.0	12.0
1910–1914	49	753	394.8	22.8	4	656.5	8,663.0
1915–1919	51	826	435.5	28.9	1	83.0	50.0
1920–1924	72	1336	454.6	4.4	0	0	0
1925–1929	83	1528	634.6	39.6	1	170.0	130.0
1930–1934	89	1639	743.4	17.2	1	33.0	60.0
1935–1939	86	1697	810.7	10.3	5	1,017.0	16,129.0
1940–1944	82	1560	760.8	−6.2	0	0	0
1945–1949	120	2284	1032.3	35.7	1	19.0	8.0
1950–1954	142	2684	1041.5	.9	1	516.5	2,000.0
1955–1959	167	3338	1340.3	28.7	2	4.0	35.0
1960–1964	192	4436	2008.2	49.8	2	5.0	17.0

Visual inspection of the several IGO and war measures in this set of data leads to a less distinct impression than one gets from Table 2; no clear pattern seems to emerge. That impression turns out to be quite well founded, as the three upper rows in each set of correlations shown in Table 6 indicate. Thus, the strongest product-moment association—that between the number of weighted nation memberships in all IGO's for each half decade and the number of nation-months of interstate war which began in the following half decade—is a low .27.

While all eighteen of these correlations are quite low, they are not without interest. The fact that those predicting to magnitude and severity (but not frequency) are positive would suggest that there is indeed a weak but discernible historical association between the amount of IGO in the system and the amount of war which follows. But a second, and closer, look at Table 5 tells us why. Note, first of all, the almost unbroken upward trend in the number and size of IGO's over the 150 years. Note, also, that even though there is no discernible trend (up or down) in the *number* of interstate wars over time, there is a slight increase in their magnitude (i.e. nation-months) and an even stronger increase in their severity, as measured in battle-connected fatalities. And, as might well be expected, when any two sets of variables show a secular trend in the same direction over time, there is bound to be *some* positive correlation between them.

When the data analyst is confronted with this sort of problem and wants to make certain that his statistical results are not misleading, he has several choices. The most obvious and widely used solution is to partially de-trend the data by using a different version of the same basic variables. Thus, rather than use (as our independent variable) the sheer *amount* of IGO existing in each period, we can use the *percentage change* between that period's score and that of the prior period, as found in Table 5. This differs from our previous measure of net change in that the percentage change from one period to the next gives us a normalized index. That is, a change from 100 to 110 will be no different than one from 10 to 11, thus permitting comparisons across a long span of time, while eliminating the effects of the general upward trend.

What results emerge when we use (lower set of rows in Table 6) as our independent variable, not the amount of *existing* IGO, but the percentage *change* between the period under consideration and that which preceded it? The already weak product-moment associations for magnitude and severity decline even further, and the rank-order correlations show almost no change. Even though there is also an upward trend in the net increase of IGO, this strengthens the impression that the weak positive correlation between IGO and war *is* primarily an artifact of the secular trends and that there is basically no association between these two sets of phenomena. . . .

Interpreting the Findings

Two major regularities have turned up in this preliminary investigation into the relationship between international governmental organization and interstate war since the Congress of Vienna. First, we found a consistently positive correlation between the termination of war and the establishment of new organization: At the close of highly warlike periods, the creation of new IGO is high, and at the close of peaceful ones, that creation is low. Second, we found almost no discernible correlation between the amount of such organization existing in any period and the amount of war which began in the following period: The amount of IGO has almost no effect on the amount of war which the system experiences. . . .

Why is it that international governmental organization has, to date,

TABLE 6: CORRELATIONS BETWEEN AMOUNT OF IGO IN EACH PERIOD AND
AMOUNT OF WAR BEGINNING IN NEXT PERIOD

	Number of Wars Begun	Nation-Months Begun	Battle Deaths Begun
Rank-Order:			
Number of IGO's	.01	.07	.10
Simple Memberships	.00	.06	.09
Weighted Memberships	—.02	.06	.08
Percentage Change in Weighted Memberships	—.05	.07	.06
Product-Moment:			
Number of IGO's	—.06	.26	.22
Simple Memberships	—.08	.23	.20
Weighted Memberships	—.07	.27	.23
Percentage Change in Weighted Memberships	—.19	—.04	.03

exercised no effective impact on the incidence of interstate war? Granting that things might have been worse *without* such organization, it still behooves us to ask why they were not better. Three general interpretations come to mind, and each may be worth a brief discussion.

First, there is the "threshold" argument, which goes somewhat as follows: The evidence adduced in the earlier portions of the article is not persuasive because, as large in space and time as the domain may be, its time span is much too limited. As world history goes, it is little more than a brief interlude. And more time, perhaps much more time, is needed before the slow and painful growth of international organization can approach that critical threshold above which it can effectively mediate and control conflict between nations. The argument, in sum, is that nineteenth- and twentieth-century international organization is still too weak to preserve peace but that given more time, it will indeed eliminate war from the global scene.

We find this argument not at all persuasive. The facts on which it is based seem to be incontrovertible, but it overlooks one important consideration. As has been pointed out before,[12] even though international organizations are becoming more numerous and larger in membership and resources over time, they are invariably based not only on territorial national states as their major component but on the continuing and virtually untrammelled sovereignty of these states. One might even argue that, whether national states are becoming more powerful or not, international governmental organization is doing little to diminish and quite a bit to perpetuate that power.[13] Thus, if the present pattern and basis are continued, there is little reason for believing that they—or more particularly, their secretariats—will acquire sufficient power to exercise any effective control over the behavior and interaction of their member states.

A second possible explanation of these discouraging results is that of the functionalists.[14] Put in rather general terms, one version contends that we have been moving perhaps too quickly and directly in the establishment—if not proliferation—of political and security organizations and much too slowly in establishing organizations with a social and economic orientation. Rather than seek to control the nations directly through security-oriented organization, the functionalist would emphasize the establishment of specialized organizations designed to encourage and facilitate interstate cooperation in the less sensitive sectors of national life. As these collaborative activities expand to the satisfaction of the member governments and those who influence them, the tendency toward more cooperation and toward stronger organizations would increase, spilling over inevitably into the political and security sectors. Thus, the functionalist might go on, it is not so much that we have not had sufficient time, but that we have failed to use that time effectively. If we begin now to accelerate the growth in number, size, and function of these more specialized organizations, in due course we will have not only nations which are more cooperative but political and security organizations which will be powerful enough to help reduce the incidence of war.

We find this argument slightly more persuasive than the threshold argument, but not much. Its strength lies, in our judgment, in its awareness that behavior, attitude, and structure are highly interdependent and that any movement toward a more peaceful world must be accompanied by profound changes in all three sets of variables. Likewise, it recognizes the extent to which high cooperation *within* politically aligned blocs (or unions) tends to sharpen and exacerbate the conflicts *between* such blocs and unions.

But this argument still rests essentially on the belief that territorial states can "learn cooperation," thus overlooking the way in which the incentives of domestic politics and the constraints of international politics will continue, in combinaton, to keep cooperative behavior down to rather minimal and strategically "acceptable" levels. Moreover, by any measure one cares to use, it is quite evident that more nations have participated in more "functional" organizations, governmental or nongovernmental, than in security-oriented ones. Finally, there is the assumption—in our judgment quite naïve—that organizations devoted to such purposes become highly technical, problem-oriented, administrative agencies and therefore quite removed from the "dysfunctional" political concerns and pressures of foreign ministries, defense ministries, political parties, pressure groups, and other political realities. It may well be possible to remove certain activities and decisions from the conflict-ridden "political" sectors of the world, but this will happen not by defining them as technical and therefore nonpolitical but by having so much knowledge that policy matters become, more and more, questions of applied science and, less and less, matters of rhetoric and logrolling.

A third basic interpretation is that of the world federalists. They would contend that it is not the lack of time, nor the tendency to focus on the wrong problems, but rather the fact that these IGO's have never received sufficient power that has been responsible for the ineffective impact of international organization. They have grown in number, membership, staff, and budget, but—the federalist would claim—they have grown little if at all in their authority over the member states. Thus, if certain political and security functions had been transferred from the territorial states to the IGO's and if the organs of these IGO's could have taken decisions which were binding on the members, they might have been considerably more effective in avoiding or reducing war. The logic of this argument strikes us as unassailable, but we will never know whether things *might* have been different.[15]

Other possible explanations for the poor performance of international organization might readily be imagined, but none that accept the basic premises of the traditional approaches strike us as satisfactory. From the theoretical position taken here, *no* international organization (governmental or otherwise) solution is likely to prove satisfactory. To the contrary, our view is that war is basically inherent in the continued coexistence of the nation-state and the international system as we know it. Why should this be?

If we consider national political elites as decisionmakers who must operate in two different sets of environments more or less simultaneously, the reasoning becomes more clear. Looking first at the environment provided by the international system, incompatibilities of interests between nations seem inevitable. There are many scarcities, and nations must compete for them: markets, supplies, routes, bases, votes, prestige, and so forth. In competing for these scarcities, the normative rule clearly is the well-known doctrine of "self-help," and despite some occasional advances in international law, the only contraint consistently applied to the exercise of that norm is the disastrous doctrine of "auto-limitation." What other interpretation can one make, faced with the continued belief in, and behavior consonant with, the principle of national sovereignty? This reinforcing combination of belief and behavior creates, of course, the most critical scarcity of all: security.

In the normal course of things, the standard procedures and institutions of bilateral and multilateral diplomacy will, all too often, flounder on the rocks of domestic politics. Whether we look at states which are highly democratic or highly autocratic, once they become involved in a foreign conflict there are certain widely recognized temptations facing the domestic "outs." The "ins" of whatever political complexion almost always engage in some consistent policies of preparing their nation for conflict: They encourage *some* xenophobia, allocate *some* human and industrial resources to preparedness, and generally engage in certain minimal amounts of deterrence vis-à-vis one or more other nations. Depending on the extent and duration of the preparedness program, the "hard-liners" have *some* sort of power base in the society and some sort of public receptivity to which they can appeal.

If the party or faction in power moves in a conciliatory direction during such a foreign conflict, the domestic opposition will find it difficult to resist the temptations thus created. That is, the opposition is quite likely to appeal for a stronger and firmer policy against the enemy of the moment and can always count on some support from those who stand to gain—psychologically, financially, or politically—from a more bellicose policy. And if the governing party does indeed take a hard line early in the conflict, it further strengthens the position of other hard-liners in or out of power, thus making it difficult and costly to engage in serious negotiations later. And, of course, each additional allocation of resources to one nation's preparedness not only reduces the domestic range of options but, by creating less security for the adversary, gives an impetus of the same sort to *its* domestic alignments. In sum, we see nothing in any of the international organization approaches which is likely to break into this highly structured and self-aggravating international system and lead to a more pluralistic, multiunit, self-correcting state of affairs in world politics.[16]

CONCLUSION

Despite the rather undifferentiated nature of our measures of intergovernmental organization and some of the inferential leaps which are required, the evidence seems, for the moment, relatively unambiguous. First, these findings suggest that policymakers show a distinct tendency to turn to IGO's as one possible means of reducing the incidence of war or (at least) demonstrating their commitment to its reduction. Second, the correlations show that any confidence in its efficacy is ill founded indeed. We must reiterate, however, that these simple bivariate analyses are only a first-phase, brush-clearing operation. Having detected these very general patterns in the relationship between IGO and war, it is now necessary to get on to more detailed sorts of investigations. While we have indicated, along the way, some possible directions which such investigations might take, it would be presumptuous to lay out an extended research strategy here.

Suffice it to say, even though *insights* into the roots of war may come in a single revealing flash, *knowledge* will come primarily in a series of modest data-based increments. We trust that this inquiry and the data which it has generated will provide the basis for a rapid upsurge in the rate at which those increments of knowledge will appear. If war, as Clemenceau noted, is too important to be left to those who merely hope for victory (i.e., the generals), peace is too important to be left to those who merely hope for *it*.

NOTES

[1] See Inis L. Claude, "Economic Development Aid and International Political Stability," in Robert W. Cox (ed.), *Politics of International Organization* (New York, 1970).

[2] Some will object to the implication here that peace is more or less equivalent to the absence of war and will insist that peace is something more than that; granted, but certainly the absence of war is necessary to the presence of peace.

[3] A suggestive discussion of this so-called ecological fallacy is in W. S. Robinson, "Ecological Correlations and the Behavior of Individuals," *American Sociological Review,* June 1950 (Vol. 15, No. 3), pp. 351-57. We would emphasize, however, that there are certain inferences from groups to their components and vice versa which are quite legitimate and do not run afoul of this fallacy; for a detailed discussion and partial rebuttal, see J. David Singer, "Man and World Politics: The Psycho-Cultural Interface," *Journal of Social Issues,* July 1968 (Vol. 25, No. 3), pp. 127-56.

[4] A summary of the project (following largely from the work of Wright and Richardson) is found in J. David Singer, "Modern International War: From Conjecture to Explanation," in A. Lepawsky (ed.), *The Search for World Order: Studies by Students and Colleagues of Quincy Wright* (New York: Appleton-Century, 1971); see also Quincy Wright, *The Study of War* (2 vols; Chicago: University of Chicago Press, 1942), and Lewis F. Richardson, *Statistics of Deadly Quarrels* (Pittsburgh, Pa., Boxwood Press, 1960).

[5] For the basic criteria and the empirical results of our coding rules, see J. David Singer and Melvin Small, "The Composition and Status Ordering of the International System: 1815–1940," *World Politics,* January 1966 (Vol. 18, No. 2), pp. 236-82; and Bruce M. Russett, J. David Singer, and Melvin Small, "National Political Units in the Twentieth Century: A Standardized List," *American Political Science Review,* September 1968 (Vol. 62, No. 3), pp. 932-51.

[6] We are by no means suggesting that wars other than interstate ones are of no interest or importance or that intergovernmental organization has no relevance for imperial, colonial, and civil wars. To the contrary, we are persuaded that there is indeed a close connection between all types of mass violence in world politics and that in our own age the distinctions between these four types of war will become increasingly blurred. But no intelligent analysis of the relationship between international organization and *all* forms of war can be made without the inclusion of several additional variables and a finer breakdown of intergovernmental organizations into more discriminating categories. We hope, in due course, to attend to such a follow-up study.

[7] While we believe very strongly in the need to spell out, in precise detail, the procedures by which one's data [are] acquired or generated, along with the line of reasoning which persuades one that the resulting numbers are indeed valid indicators of the concept at hand, space limitations preclude doing this for each of the variables used in this article. Therefore, the reader is referred in each case to the basic study in which the data [are] presented for the first time. In the case of our war data, see J. David Singer and Melvin Small, *The Wages of War, 1816–1965: A Statistical Handbook* (New York: John Wiley & Sons, 1972). [These] data [are] also available in raw form from the International Relations Archive of the Inter-University Consortium for Political Research, University of Michigan.

[8] Among those efforts, none of which is quite satisfactory for the purposes intended here, are Robert C. Angell, "An Analysis of Trends in International Organizations," Peace Research Society (International) *Papers,* 1965 (Vol. 3), pp. 185-95; Paul Smoker, "Nation-State Escalation and International Integration," *Journal of Peace Research,* 1967 (Vol. 4), pp. 61-75; and Raymond Tanter, "Theories of International Political Development," in M. Hass (ed.), *Behavioral International Relations* (Scranton, Pa.: Chandler Publishing Co., 1972).

[9] See *Yearbook of International Organizations* (Brussels: Union of International Associations); also *The 1,978 International Organizations Founded Since the Congress of Vienna* (Brussels: Union of International Associations, 1957).

[10] For the procedures and the basic data in detail, see Michael Wallace and J. David Singer, "Intergovernmental Organization in the Global System, 1815–1964: A Quantitative Description," *International Organization,* Spring 1970 (Vol. 29, No. 2), pp. 239-87.

[11] The rationale and detailed procedures are described fully in J. David Singer and Melvin Small, *World Politics* (Vol. 18, No. 2), pp. 236-82. Originally, we based the attributed diplomatic importance score on the *ranks* of the missions as well as their sheer number, but the status ordering produced by the simpler index correlated well above .90 with the more complex one for four sample years.

[12] See Maurice Bourquin, *L'Etat souverain et l'organisation internationale* (Etudes nationales sur l'organisation internationale) (New York: Manhattan Publishing Co., for the Carnegie Endowment for International Peace, 1959).

[13] In a recent paper, we are reminded that the economic development program of the U.N. system is directed toward making national sovereignty meaningful, not reducing it to meaninglessness. It is aimed at assisting states in achieving genuine and effective statehood, not at promoting their merger into larger groupings. See Inis Claude. Even though, in practice, there have been discernible violations of the principles of sovereignty, it is difficult to quarrel with Claude's interpretation of the original motivations.

[14] The classic formulation remains David Mitrany, *A Working Peace System* (Chicago: Quadrangle Books, 1966), and the most thorough, if basically sympathetic, critique is Ernst B. Haas, *Beyond the Nation-State: Functionalism and International Organization* (Stanford, Calif.: Stanford University Press, 1964).

[15] For a provocative and detailed exposition and application of the world federalist view, see Grenville Clark and Louis B. Sohn, *World Peace Through World Law* (Cambridge, Mass.: Harvard University Press, 1958).

[16] This is a considerable simplification of the postulated model; for a fuller discussion, involving the role of schools, labor groups, mass media, etc., see J. David Singer, "The Political Matrix of International Conflict," in Elton McNeil (ed.), *The Nature of Human Conflict* (Englewood Cliffs, N.J.: Prentice-Hall, 1965), and J. David Singer, "Escalation and Control in International Conflict: A Simple Feedback Model," in *General Systems: Yearbook of the Society for General Systems Research,* Vol. 15 (Ann Arbor: Society for General Systems Research, 1970). It should be noted that this is by no means a conspiratorial model: Everyone merely does what "comes naturally"!

———

This article is a paragon of scientific research. It defines a theoretically interesting problem in a meaningful manner by reviewing previous speculation about the consequences of intergovernmental organizations for the maintenance of international peace; it accumulates a body of evidence from a long historical period by precisely defined operational rules; it probes the empirical data by statistical procedures to ascertain whether the observed correlational relationships between IGO's and war are occurring by chance; and it interprets the generalizations that emerge from the analysis in order to assess their theoretical significance. The study thus employs scientific methodology to build verifiable knowledge about a phenomenon that has hitherto been treated only in terms of intuition and impression.

The research mode is explicitly explanatory. Although the authors begin with a longitudinal description of the temporal fluctuations of their major variables, they then intercorrelate these variables to measure the extent to which they are associated and co-vary. Correlational analysis allows us to determine the extent to which two or more factors are related and tend to occur together. A correlational statement thereby defines the extent to which independent and dependent conditions go together. While the correlations fail to tell us the degree to which one variable causes another, they facilitate the construction of explanations by informing us of the manner in which one factor (e.g., the number of IGO's) contributes to, and is related to, the other (e.g., the preservation of peace). The first factor is said to explain or account for the second in the sense that variations in the latter are associated with variations in the former. While correlation can never establish causation, correlational knowledge permits one to make causal inferences and can enable one to determine the absence of causal relatationships. Thus, when Singer and Wallace find (1) that the termination of war is associated with the establishment of new intergovernmental organizations, and (2) that the number of IGO's has almost no significant effect on the amount of war that the system experiences, these findings may be used to postulate causal regularities. The inductively derived propositions tell us that highly warlike periods tend to precipitate the creation of new international institutions, but that the number of intergovernmental organizations in the system fail to diminish the probability of new wars. The correlations explain the effects, therefore, of one set of conditions in terms of the other. Note, however, that the authors take care to warn of the dangers intrinsic in reading too much into such bivariate relationships. Because the findings explain one set of conditions in terms of another set of conditions, the "explanations" are necessarily single factor theories and consequently deficient. We do not live in a bivariate world where social phenomena are caused by single factors. The authors therefore encourage the peace science community to employ the findings that they uncover in their correlational analysis in more sophisticated, multivariate research in order more precisely to unravel the chain of causation that exists in the real world. Their study is thus exploratory rather than definitive. It provides us with the basic building blocks of causal, or explanatory, theory.

The two preceding selections have dealt with two distinct mechanisms for maintaining the international system and enhancing the prospects for system peace and stability. The first examined the potential contribution that international law can make to that goal by providing rules for orderly national conduct and interstate competition, and the second assessed the contribution that internatonal, or intergovernmental, organizations can make to the preservation of peace. A third mechanism, or system-wide process, for the maintenance of international security may also be identified: the amalgamation of previously independent nations into a larger political entity through a process of political integration. The idea behind this approach is that competition and violence between states are partly caused by the existence of territorially defined sovereign states, and that the removal of these national boundaries would reduce intersocial competition. Integration and functionalist theory assumes that conflict reduction will commence when parties develop loyalties to one another and create institutions and symbols that will serve to perpetuate and increase the affiliations of people toward the integrated political unit. Thus, by co-operatively working on common functional problems, nations can integrate themselves into a new unit.

The following article, by Karl W. Deutsch, attempts to explore some of the antecedent and precipitant conditions that facilitate the growth and integration of political communities. Deutsch has been a prolific writer in integration studies and has contributed widely to the international relations literature in general. In reading his analysis of factors that serve to exert integrative influences, note in particular his style of presentation and the manner in which he formulates his hypotheses.

THE GROWTH OF NATIONS: SOME RECURRENT PATTERNS OF POLITICAL AND SOCIAL INTEGRATION

Karl W. Deutsch

At many places and times, tribes have merged to form peoples; and peoples have grown into nations. Some nations founded empires; and empires have broken up again into fragments whose populations later attempted again to form larger units. In certain respects, this sequence appears to describe a general process found in much of history. This process shows a number of patterns which seem to recur, and which to a limited extent seem to be comparable among different regions, periods, and cultures.

Karl W. Deutsch, "The Growth of Nations: Some Recurrent Patterns of Political and Social Integration," *World Politics*, 5, 2 (1953): 168-95. (Abridged.) Footnotes have been renumbered to appear in consecutive order. Reprinted by permission of the author and publisher.

Deutsch is professor of government at Harvard University.

Such recurrent patterns of integration, like other relative uniformities in history, raise the problem of the comparability or uniqueness of historical events. Yet the search for such relative uniformities in politics and history is essential to the pursuit of knowledge in these fields. No historical or political analysis can be written without the use of general concepts in which some notions of uniformity are necessarily implied.[1] Indeed, such recurrent patterns offer a background of similarities against which differences can stand out, and against which investigators can evaluate the specific and perhaps unique aspects of each particular case of national or supra-national integration.

At the same time, the study of the growth of nations may reveal cumulative change. It may suggest that the present period is unique in respect to both the extent of nationalism and the potentialities for supra-national organization. To the student of contemporary politics, it may further suggest specific problems of research and policy in the on-going process of social and political integration on the national as well as the international level.

Before discussing the recurrent problems of national integration, it may be well to note the use of a few terms. For the purposes of our discussion, a distinction is made between a *society*, which is defined as a group of persons who have learned to work together, and a *community*, which is defined as a group of persons who are able to communicate information to each other effectively over a wide range of topics.[2] A similar distinction is adopted between a *country*, which denotes a geographic area of greater economic interdependence and thus a multiple market for goods and services, and a *people*, which is a group of persons with complementary communications habits. A *nation* is then a people which has gained control over some institutions of social coercion, leading eventually to a full-fledged *nation-state;* and *nationalism* is the preference for the competitive interest of this nation and its members over those of all outsiders in a world of social mobility and economic competition, dominated by the values of wealth, power, and prestige, so that the goals of personal security and group identification appear bound up with the group's attainment of these values.[3]

While peoples are found at almost any period in history, nationalism and nations have occurred during only a few periods. A nation is the result of the transformation of a people, or of several ethnic elements, in the process of social mobilization. Thus far, however, the processes of social mobilization and communication have at no time included all mankind. The "universal states" listed by A. J. Toynbee as stages in the distintegration of particular civilizations [4] were superficial short-cuts, rather than solutions to the problem of the unity of mankind.

Periods of "universal states" have left behind them, however, a number of widespread languages, such as Latin, Greek, or Arabic; and a measure of cultural assimilation among certain social groups such as the nobility, town population, or the clergy of some "universal church." [5] The results have somewhat resembled a *layer-cake pattern,* with a high degree of cultural assimilation and participation in extended social com-

munication among the top layers of society; a lesser degree on the intermediate levels; and little or no assimilation or participation among the
mass of the population at the bottom.[6]

In several parts of the world, the cycle—from local isolation to
"universal" empire and back to a new age of localism [7]—has been traversed
more than once. Yet the cycle has usually shown a net gain, in the sense
that there has been a gain in man's technological and scientific command
over nature,[8] and that some of the most important cultural, intellectual,
moral, and spiritual traditions of the earlier civilization have tended to
survive that civilization in which they arose, and continue, often as a
"universal church" or religion, to influence the development of new peoples
and new regions. . . .[9]

The processes of partial social mobilization and of nation-building
have been recurrent phenomena in history, at least in certain general
characteristics. What uniformities can we find in this growth of nations
in the past? And in what ways is our own age different in respect to the
growth of nations from any age that has gone before?

SOME POSSIBLE SPECIFIC UNIFORMITIES

Uniformities which have been found in the growth of nations include
the following:

1. The shift from subsistence agriculture to *exchange economies.*
2. The social mobilization of rural populations in *core areas* of denser
settlement and more intensive exchange.
3. The growth of *towns,* and the growth of social mobility within
them and between town and country.
4. The growth of *basic communication grids,* linking important rivers,
towns, and trade routes in a flow of transport, travel, and migration.
5. The differential accumulation and *concentration of capital* and
skills, and sometimes of social institutions, and their *"lift-pump" effect* on
other areas and populations, with the successive entry of different social
strata into the nationalistic phase.
6. The rise of the concept of *"interest"* for both individuals and
groups in unequal but fluid situations, and the growth of *individual self-
awareness* and awareness of one's predispositions to join a particular group
united by language and communications habits.
7. The awakening of *ethnic awareness* and the acceptance of *national
symbols,* intentional or unintentional.
8. The merging of ethnic awareness with attempts at *political compulsion,* and in some cases the attempt to transform one's own people
into a privileged class to which members of other peoples are subordinated.

Some of these similarities may be discussed briefly.

The Shift to Exchange Economies

The shift from subsistence agriculture to an exchange economy seems to have characterized all cases of wide national integration which I have been able to find. Where the exchange economy came to embrace the bulk of the population and to bring many of them into direct contact with each other in the interchange of a wider variety of goods and services, there we find a tendency to "national" or at least regional, linguistic, and cultural "awakening," provided only that sufficiently large numbers of individuals enter the exchange economy and its more intensive communication *faster* than they can be assimilated to another "alien" language or culture.

Where these shifts take place, the ethnic and in part the linguistic situation becomes, as it were, loosened or softened, and capable of settling again into new and different molds. The awakening of the Slavic population of the Balkans, and the rise of regions of greater intensity of trade and exchange around which the revived Serbian and Bulgarian languages and nationalities were constituted, may perhaps serve as illustrations.[10]

Further Social Mobilization and Integration in Core Areas

The shift to an economy and culture based on wider interchange takes place at different times and different rates of speed in different regions. The result is often the existence of more "advanced" regions side by side with more "underdeveloped" ones. The former are then often in a position to function as centers of cultural and economic attraction for some of the populations of the latter, and thus to become nuclei of further integration. The "when" is thus often as important and sometimes more important than the "where," and the processes of social mobilization and partial integration are truly historical in the sense that each step depends to a significant extent on the outcome of the step that went before.

Political geographers have sought to identify *core areas* around which larger states were organized successfully in the course of history. Characteristic features of such core areas are unusual fertility of soil, permitting a dense agricultural population and providing a food surplus to maintain additional numbers in non-agricultural pursuits; geographic features facilitating military defense of the area; and a nodal position at an intersection of major transportation routes. Classic examples of such core areas are the Ile de France and the Paris basin, or the location of London.[11]

It should be noted that the density that makes a core area is one of traffic and communication rather than mere numbers of passive villagers densely settled on the soil. Thus the dense population of the Nile valley seems to have been less effective as a wider center of integration than the sparse population of the Arab territories beyond Mecca and Medina, who more than compensated for their smaller numbers by their proportionately far greater mobility, activity, and traffic.

The theory of core areas, however, cannot account for the persistence of some states and the failure of others. What counts for more may well be what happens within each core area, and perhaps particularly what happens in its towns.

The Growth of Towns, Mobility, and Ties Between Town and Country

There is no developed nation, it appears, without towns which have or have had a period of considerable growth, of mobility within the towns, and of increasing ties of social mobility, communication, and multiple economic exchange between town and country.

There have been towns, of course, where one or more of these conditions did not exist, and to that extent national development has been incomplete, absent, halted, or retarded. On the other hand, to the extent that there was such growing mobility and communication within towns and between town and country, national development was accelerated.

The Growth of Basic Communication Grids

Most nations do not seem to have grown from single centers. Many nations have had several capitals and have shifted their central regions several times in the course of their history. Even the classical example of growth around one center, France, has long had two capital cities, Paris and Orleans; and some significant phases of the unification of the French language took place at the Champagne fairs and along the trade routes leading through that region—not to mention the role of the North-South routes and connections in helping the North to consolidate its victory over separatist and Albigensian elements in the Midi during the religious wars of the thirteenth century.[12]

The same notion of a basic grid seems to be applicable to the unification of China, Russia, Switzerland, Canada, and the United States.[13] It would be interesting to investigate the relationship of such a grid to the incomplete unification and more recent separation of the areas that now comprise India and Pakistan.

The Differential Concentration of Capital, Skills, and Social Institutions

A major factor in national differences and national pride today are the differences in the general standard of living. To some extent such differences tend to cut across the differences between social classes; there is a social, moral, or traditional component in what is considered "bare subsistence" in a given community, or in what counts as "luxury" in another; and a significant part of what is considered the poor population in a relatively wealthy community may be appreciably better off in terms of physical goods and services than even many of the relatively well-off members of a poor or economically backward people. This difference between the generally prevailing standards of wealth, comfort, and opportunity among different regions or peoples has sometimes been called the *Kulturgefälle* ("the drop in the level of culture") by German writers who have employed this concept to bolster claims to German supremacy or exclusiveness vis-à-vis the populations of Eastern Europe and the Balkans.

Behind the differences in the standards of living lie differences in levels of productivity and in the supply of factors of production, that is, in the material means to pursue any one of a wide range of conceivable ends regardless of the difference in importance assigned to some of these ends relative to others in some particular culture. These differences in productivity may involve geographic factors such as soils, water supplies, forests, mineral deposits, and the absence of obstacles to transportation. All such geographic factors, however, depend on specific technologies to give them significance. Every concentration of natural resources requires, therefore, a concentration of productive skills and knowledge if men are even to know how to use them; and resources as well as skills require a concentration of invested *capital* if they are to be used in fact.

It should be clear that, as technology progresses, the relative importance of the man-made factors of production, such as capital and skills, has tended to increase relative to the importance of the few natural facilities which once were the only ones that more primitive technologies could exploit. There is reason to believe that present-day differences in living standards are due far less to differences in natural factors of production, and far more to differences in the supply of skilled labor, schools, housing, and machinery.

Particular peoples and nations may then tend to crystallize, as it were, around particular concentrations of capital and technology, or of particular social institutions which offer individuals greater opportunities for the pursuit of the goods or factors which they have learned to desire.

The effects of differential standards of living and of productivity operated long before the Industrial Revolution, but they were increased by its coming. Where large economic or industrial developments have taken place, they have had a "lift-pump" effect on the underlying populations. They have induced migrations of populations to the regions of settlement, employment, and opportunity, and put these newcomers into intensive economic and political contact with the locally predominant peoples, and with each other. This physical, political, and economic contact had one of two cultural and linguistic consequences: either it led to national assimilation, or, if national assimilation to the dominant group could not keep pace with the growing need for some wider group membership for the newcomer, then the "lift-pump" effect would tend to lead eventually to a new growth of nationalism among the newly mobilized populations. Eventually, it might result in the assimilation of some previously separate groups, not to the still-dominant minority, but to the "awakening" bulk of the population.

Both national assimilation and national resurgence thus respond in a "lift-pump" situation to the power of the "pump." The intensity and appeal of nationalism in a world of sharply differentiated income and living standards perhaps may tend to be *inversely proportional to the barriers to mobility between regions and classes,* and *directly proportional to*

*the barriers against cultural assimilation, and to the extent of the economic
and prestige differences between classes, cultures, and regions.*

Seen in this light, the rise of nationalism and the growth of nations
have some semi-automatic features, even though they have other features
which are by no means automatic. As the distribution of scarce rewards
is made unequal by economic or historic processes; as men learn to desire
the same kinds of rewards; as they fail to be assimilated to the language
and culture of the dominant group; and as they succeed in becoming assimilated with other men who possess cultural and language habits more
compatible with their own—as all these processes go on, situations conducive to nationalism are created without anyone's deliberate intention.

The Concept of Self-Interest and
the Experience of Self-Awareness

The concept of a nation is bound up with that of a national interest.
Already the non-national or proto-national institutions of the city-state
and the princely state imply the notion of group interests and interests
of state, and all these notions of national, state, or city interests imply in
turn the interests of individuals. But this concept of individuals with
interests has itself gained its present importance only gradually in the
course of certain developments of history.[14] Even today different regions
and civilizations ascribe to it different degrees of significance, and it may
lose again in the future much of its present importance.

At bottom the notion of interest perhaps implies a situation in which
men are pitted against each other in a competitive situation in which some
of them can improve or even maintain their positions only at the expense
of others. The word "interest" denotes, then, the ensemble of an individual's chances for improving or maintaining his position against all
competitors, and thus, indirectly, the amount and effectiveness of disposi-
tion of his resources applicable to the competitive situation in which he
finds himself. Such competitive situations may be relatively vague and unpredictable, or they may be formalized and hence in part predictable to
a more or less high degree. The more predictable they are, the more easily
can they be recognized as competitive by the participants.

As men leave the relative security of villages and folk cultures for
the mobility and uncertainty of travel, towns, and markets, and for the
competition of wealth-getting, politics, and warfare, they may find greater
opportunities and rewards for aggressiveness and self-assertion; and at the
same time they may come to feel more poignantly the loneliness, the loss
of security, and the loss of context and meaning in their lives which the
transition to the new ways of life entails.

Nationalism is one peculiar response to this double challenge of
opportunity and insecurity, of loneliness and power. Men discover sooner
or later that they can advance their interests in the competitive game of
politics and economics by forming coalitions, and that they stand to gain

the firmer these coalitions can be made, provided only that they have been made with individuals and groups who have to offer in this game the largest amount of assets and the least amount of liabilities. To form the firmest possible connections with the most promising group of competitors would seem to be sound long-run strategy. With which group such firm connections can be formed is by no means arbitrary: in politics and economics such coalitions will depend to a significant degree on social communication and on the culture patterns, personality structures, and communications habits of the participants. Their chances of success will thus depend to some degree on the links that make a people, the ties of nationality.

Organization along ethnic or national lines is by no means the only type of alignment which may be tried in the competitive game. Yet of all these probable patterns of organization, ethnic or national alignments often combine the greatest strength and resilience with the greatest adaptability to a competitive world. So long as competitive institutions continue to prevail, nationalism can mobilize more people and organize them more firmly than can many competing types of organization. The potential rewards of nationalism then grow in proportion to the potential resources of wealth and power to which members of a particular people have, or can gain, access on preferred terms.

To develop thus the economic, intellectual, and military resources of a territory and a population, *and to knit them together in an ever tighter network of communication and complementarity based on the ever broader and more thorough participation of the masses of the populace*—all this is sound power politics; and those who carry out such policies tend to be rewarded by the long-run outcome of this contest.

What may fit the necessities of the competitive game may also fit some inner needs of its participants. Ages of social mobilization, of rapid changes in the traditional social contexts, tend to be ages of increasing self-doubt and self-awareness for the individuals who live in them. The questions "Who am I?" "Whom do I resemble?" "In whom can I trust?" are asked with a new urgency, and need more than a traditional answer.

As a man seeks answers to these questions he must try to take stock of himself, of his memories, his preferences, and his habits, of the specific images and indeed of the specific words in which they were conveyed and in which they are now stored in his mind. As old cultural or religious patterns, beliefs, and ceremonies become questionable, self-searching must lead back to the childhood memories and the mother tongue, in terms of which so many experiences have been acquired, and out of which, in a sense, the individual's character and personality have been built up. When men seek for themselves, they thus may come to find their nationality; and when they seek the community of their fellows, they may discover once again the connection between ethnic nationality and the capacity for fellowship. Instances of this process can be found even in antiquity: it is well known that Socrates enjoined upon his pupils the imperative, "Know thyself," and that Socrates' pupil, Plato, proposed that all Greeks should henceforth cease to plunder or enslave their fellow Greeks, but should rather do these things to the barbarians.[15]

Our hypothesis finds some confirmation in a well-known pattern in the history of nationalism and the biographies of nationalist leaders. Many emotionally, culturally, and politically sensitive individuals react to a sojourn abroad, i.e., away from their native region or culture, with a far stronger assertion of nationalism and of allegiance to their own language, culture, and people. This precipitating crisis in the lives of many nationalists has been dubbed the *Fremdheitserlebnis* ("the experience of strangeness"), and it has been described repeatedly in the literature of nationalism.[16]

From Group Awareness to the Nation-State

Individual awareness of one's language and people may appear to be a matter of personal psychology, even though there are social situations which make such awareness more probable. Group awareness, on the other hand, seems clearly a matter of social institutions. Some secondary symbols are attached to some aspects of group life and are repeated and disseminated over and over again by an organization or institution, often for a purpose that has nothing to do with nationality, or which might even be opposed to it. After a time, the institution may change or disappear, the organized repetition of the symbols may cease—but if there were enough of a primary reality capable of being symbolized, *and if there had been going on that basic process of social mobilization* which has been described earlier, then the results of the dissemination of those symbols may well prove irreversible.

Given these underlying conditions, symbols and institutions of group awareness may be produced quite unintentionally. A process of social mobilization may even transform the function of existing symbols or institutions so as to turn them into agencies of group awareness, regardless of their original purposes.

Once the process of group consciousness has started, however, there appear also the deliberate pioneers and leaders of national awakening. There appear grammarians who reduce the popular speech to writing; purifiers of language; collectors of folk epics, tales, and songs; the first poets and writers in the revised vernacular; and the antiquarians and historians who discover ancient documents and literary treasures—some genuine, some forged, but all of them tokens of national greatness.

Side by side with the awakeners of national pride and fashioners of symbols appear the first organizers. There arise the first social circles and literary societies where the formerly despised native language is read or spoken. There follow the first benevolent societies, fraternal orders, credit cooperatives, and all the devices of mutual credit, support, or insurance, which now begin to collect the financial resources of the awakening nationality. There appear the organizers of the first schools, singing societies, athletic organizations, agricultural colleges, which herald the array of all the organizations for cultural, physical, and technological improvement which characterize every full-fledged modern nation.

Together with all this activity we find the gradual acceptance, or the deliberate proposal, of national symbols, of national colors, flags, animals, and flowers, of anthems, marches, and patriotic songs, from the "Rule Britannia" and the "Marseillaise" of the eighteenth century to the *"Nkosi sikelel i Africa"*—"God Save Africa"—of today's nationalist South African Negroes.[17] How all these symbols, maps, anthems, flags, and flag-salutes are then taught and impressed upon the populations and their children by informal group pressure and the media of mass communication as well as by all the coercive powers of the state and its system of compulsory public education—this is a story that has been told often and well by students of these late stages of the nation-building process.[18]

What does this process accomplish, and what does it aim at? When a nation has been built up, and when it has been reinforced finally by the full compulsive power of the state, then four things have been accomplished.

1. A relatively large community of human beings has been brought into existence who can communicate effectively with each other, and who have command over sufficient economic resources to maintain themselves and to transmit this ability for mutual communication to their children as well. In other words, there has been brought into being a large, comprehensive, and very stable human network of communication, capable of maintaining, reproducing, and further developing its channels.

2. There has been both an effective accumulation of economic resources and a sufficient social mobilization of manpower to permit the social division of labor necessary for this process and to permit its continuation.

3. There has been a social accumulation and integration of memories and symbols and of individual and social facilities for their preservation, transmission, and recombination, corresponding to the level of mobilization and integration of material and human resources, or even pointing beyond it.

4. There has been at least some development of the capacity to redirect, re-allocate, or form a new combination of economic, social, and human resources as well as of symbols and items of knowledge, habit, or thought—that is to say, of the capacity to learn. Some of the social *learning capacity* is developed invisibly in the minds of individuals; some of it can be observed in the habits and patterns of culture prevailing among them; some of it finally is embodied in tangible facilities and specific institutions. Together, all these constitute the community's capacity to produce and accept new knowledge or new goals, and to take the corresponding action.

On all four counts, it should be evident, the nation represents a more effective organization than the supra-national but largely passive layer-cake society or the feudal or tribal localisms that preceded it.

On all these counts, there may be considerable contrasts between different nations. The social models accepted for imitation, the established institutions, the economic practices, and the methods of compulsion within each nation are all intimately connected with the cultural traditions and leading social classes currently prevailing there. Whether a leading class of businessmen or farmers or wage earners will prove more hospitable to accumulation of resources and to efficient dynamic innovation in their use may depend not merely on the general outlook to be found prevailing in each particular stratum, but also—and perhaps sometimes crucially— on the particular cultural goals and traditions which have become accepted by that particular class in that particular nation.[19] Yet, the impression remains that even the worst-led nation represents, relative to its numbers of population, a greater amount of social communication facilities, of economic resources, and of social learning capacity than any pattern of ethnic or social organization preceding it.

Where does this process aim? The nation has been valued as a means of social advancement. In a world of extreme differences between living standards, men have tended to use the nation as an instrument to improve their own standards relative to those of their neighbors. The intrinsic bias of this process has been, where the opportunity offered itself, to produce in the temporarily most successful nation a sociological pattern reminiscent of a *mushroom cloud*. The stem of this social mushroom was formed by the "national solidarity" between the poorest and the lower-middle strata of the nation; the poorest strata, both rural and urban, however, tended to be somewhat less in relative numbers, and offered their members greater chances for "vertical mobility" than was the case in other less "successful" nations. The middle and upper strata, on the other hand, tended to form the crown of the mushroom; they tended to be somewhat larger in number than the corresponding group in other nations, with a greater propensity to spread out horizontally into new positions of privilege or control over new territories, populations, or capital resources, and correspondingly with at least somewhat greater opportunities to accept in their midst newcomers from the less favored strata of their own nation.

It is perhaps this sociological explosion into a mushroom cloud that has been at the heart of the transitory popularity of empire-building. Nationalism typically has led to attempts at empire or at least at establishing privileges over other peoples. The essence of this empire-building has been perhaps the attempt at ruling without sharing, just as the essence of nationalism has been the attempt at improving the position of one's "own" group without any sharing with "outsiders." To the extent that this process was successful it could only tend ultimately to transform the whole nation into a privileged class, a *Herrenvolk* lording it over servant peoples, as the Nazis dreamed of it, or a small, select population monopolizing vast natural resources or accumulations of technological equipment regardless of the fate of the rest of mankind. In reality, this state has probably never been achieved; and where it was even partially approximated, the results in the long-run were anything but lasting. Invariably, thus far, the same nation-building process which had permitted one nation to get temporarily on top of its neighbors subsequently raised up other nations to weaken or destroy it.

From this it might seem at first glance that the whole process of the rise and decline of nations has been cyclical, with only the names of the actors changing in an endlessly repeated drama. Closer scrutiny may show that this is not the case, and that some tentative inferences may be drawn from the events and processes surveyed.

THE UNIQUENESS OF THE PRESENT PERIOD

Our survey offers no support for the belief of many nationalists that nations are the natural and universal form of social organization for mankind. But neither does it confirm entirely the opposite view held by many thoughtful and distinguished observers—the view that nations are exclusively the product of the modern period and of Western civilization.[20] Perhaps the impression that remains might be summed up by saying that the West has gone much farther on a road which all the world's great civilzations have traveled to some extent.

NOTES

1. The alternative views that all history is random, or that all important historical events are unique, involve grave philosophic difficulties. Historians who criticize the search for certain historical uniformities by their colleagues use in effect other uniformities which they prefer. Similar considerations apply to much of the debate about uniformities in other fields of social science. All knowledge involves the matching of patterns, and thus requires at least some similarities between some aspects of the events or processes studied. It thus requires some degree of relative uniformity among the processes to be investigated, in order to enable each science to proceed beyond the relatively simple and the relatively uniform to the recognition and study of those situations which are relatively complex and unique. Simplicity and uniformity, in this view, are not sweeping metaphysical assumptions about all aspects of all processes. They are properties of those aspects of processe which were first selected for investigation, or first investigated with success. With the growth of each science, this concern with the simple and the uniform reveals itself as a steppingstone to the study of more difficult matters. Cf. H. T. Pledge, *Science Since 1500*, New York, 1947, which supersedes, in this respect, the view of E. A. Burtt, *The Metaphysical Foundations of Modern Physical Science*, London, 1932, and J. H. Randall, Jr., *The Making of the Modern Mind*, 2d ed., Boston, 1940, pp. 227-29.
2. Cf. K. W. Deutsch, *Nationalism and Social Communication*, Cambridge, Mass., and New York, 1953.
3. *Ibid.;* and "Nationalism and the Social Scientists," in L. Bryson, *et al.*, eds., *Foundations of World Organization: A Political and Cultural Appraisal*, New York, 1952, pp. 9-20, 447-68. On recent studies in this field, cf. K. W. Deutsch, *An Interdisciplinary Bibliography on Nationalism, 1935–1951*, Boston, 1953.
4. *A Study of History*, London, 1939, IV, pp. 2-3.
5. For examples of such limited assimilation during and after the expanding phase of certain civilizations or universal states, see *ibid.*, Vols. I-VI, *passim*, and the appendix on "Lingue Franche" in Vol. V, pp. 483-526. Cf. also A. C. Woolner, *Languages in History and Politics*, London, 1938; and H. A. Innis,

Empire and Communication, Oxford, 1950, and *The Bias of Communications,* Toronto, 1952. On particular languages, see Woolner, *op. cit.,* pp. 109-48, 156-67; H. A. R. Gibb, *The Arabs,* Oxford, 1940; George Antonius, *The Arab Awakening,* Philadelphia, 1939, p. 16; P. K. Hitti, *History of Syria Including Lebanon and Palestine,* New York, 1951, pp. 483-89.

6. Cf. Royal Institute of International Affairs, *Nationalism,* London, 1939, p. 9; A. P. Usher, *Economic History of England,* Boston, 1920, pp. 20-21.

7. For a discussion of the chances of linguistic disintegration following upon the dissolution of a universal empire, see Ramón Menéndez Pidal, *Castilla, la tradición, el idioma,* Buenos Aires, 1945, pp. 191-94.

8. For the Graeco-Roman and medieval civilizations, this point has been stressed by Gordon Childe, *What Happened in History,* Harmondsworth, Eng., Penguin Books, 1950, pp. 279-82.

9. Toynbee, *op. cit.,* V, p. 79, and *passim.*

10. "By the end of the [eighteenth] century many village notables (*knez*) began to come into contact as hog exporters with foreign lands, especially with the supply services of the Austrian armies. Among this class the leaders of the Serbian uprising of 1804 were found . . . [who] started the movement for Serbian independence and beyond that for Southern Slav unification . . ." (Hans Kohn, *The Idea of Nationalism,* New York, 1944, p. 549). Cf. also S. Mladenov, *Die Geschichte der bulgarischen Sprache,* Berlin, 1929; Alfred Fischel, *Der Panslawismus bis zum Weltkrieg,* Stuttgart, 1919; etc. For some general social and political aspects of the shift to an exchange economy, see Karl Polanyi, *The Great Transformation,* New York, 1944.

11. For core areas and population clusters, see D. Whittlesey, *The Earth and the State,* New York, 1939, pp. 11-12, 142-52; and Preston James, *Latin America,* New York, 1942, pp. 4-8. For the nodal location of London, see Sir Halford Mackinder, *Britain and the British Seas,* New York, 1902.

12. D. Whittlesey, *The Earth and the State, op. cit.,* pp. 138-39, 151. Cf. W. von Wartburg, *Evolution et structure de la langue française,* Leipzig, 1934, and *Les origines des peuples romans,* Paris, 1941.

13. Cf., on China, G. B. Cressey, *The Geographic Foundations of China,* New York, 1934; Percy M. Roxby, "China as an Entity: The Comparison with Europe," *Geography,* XIX, No. 1 (1934), pp. 1-20; John de Francis, *Nationalism and Language in China,* Princeton, N.J., 1950; etc. On Russia, see Robert Kerner, *The Urge to the Sea: The Role of Rivers, Portages, Ostrogs, Monasteries and Furs,* Berkeley, Calif., 1942; V. O. Kluchevskii, *A History of Russia,* Vol. 1, New York, 1911; J. W. Thompson, *Economic and Social History of the Middle Ages, A.D. 300-1300,* New York, 1931; etc. On Switzerland, see Aloys Schulte, *Geschichte des mittelalterlichen Handels und Verkehrs zwischen Westdeutschland und Italien,* Vol. 1, Leipzig, 1900; Lüdtke und Mackensen, *op. cit.;* Hans Nabholz, *Geschichte der Schweiz,* Vol. I, Zurich, 1932; C. Englert-Faye, *Vom Mythus zur Idee der Schweiz,* Zurich, 1940; Richard Weiss, *Volkskunde der Schweiz,* Zurich, 1946; etc.

14. Cf. Charles A. Beard, *The Idea of the National Interest,* New York, 1934, pp. 22-25. I am indebted to Professor Hans Kohn for valuable suggestions on this point.

15. ". . . our citizens should . . . deal with foreigners as Greeks now deal with one another" (Plato, *Republic,* v, 469-70, Cornford trans., New York, 1945, p. 174). Cf. also Glenn R. Morrow, *Plato's Law of Slavery in Its Relation to Greek Law,* Urbana, Ill., 1935.

16. Hans Kohn, *The Idea of Nationalism, op. cit.,* pp. 98, 601 (Petrarch); p. 127 (Machiavelli); pp. 239, 659 (Rousseau); p. 294 (Jefferson). On the problem of individual self-awareness and identification with groups, cf. also Chr. Bay, I. Gullavg, H. Ofstad, and H. Toenessen, *Nationalism: A Study of Identification with People and Power, I. Problems and Theoretical Framework,* Oslo, Institute of Social Research, 1950, mimeographed.

17. Detailed documentation here would be unnecessary. On the Swiss symbols, see Englert-Faye, *op. cit.* For a novelist's description of the singing of the Negro anthem in South Africa, cf. Alan Paton, *Cry the Beloved Country: A Story of Comfort in Desolation,* New York, 1948.
18. Cf. Carlton H. Hayes, *Essays on Nationalism,* New York, 1926, and *The Historical Evolution of Modern Nationalism,* New York, 1931; F. L. Schuman, *International Politics,* 3d ed., New York, 1941, pp. 300-365; etc.
19. For some problems of conservative aristocratic leadership in undeveloped nations, cf., for the Arabs, the writings of H. A. R. Gibb; for an example from Tibet, Nicholas Mansergh, "The Asian Conference, 1947," in *The Commonwealth and the Nations,* London, 1948, pp. 115-16; and for Southeast Asia, Cora Du Bois, *Social Forces in Southeast Asia,* Minneapolis, Minn., 1949, pp. 33-36, 59. On the contrast, e.g., between French and American business investment policies, cf. David S. Landes, "French Entrepreneurship and Industrial Growth in the Nineteenth Century," *Journal of Economic History,* IX (May 1949), pp. 45-61.
20. Cf. Toynbee, *op. cit., passim;* Kohn, *op. cit., passim;* Carlton H. Hayes, "Nationalism," *Encyclopedia of the Social Sciences;* etc.

The central question to which the above study is addressed is "What are the preconditions for political integration and what are the factors affecting it?" Couched in these terms, the analysis Deutsch provides is necessarily explanatory in emphasis. Whenever we postulate general laws stipulating the causes of the phenomena we are exploring, we devise nomological explanations. Thus, Deutsch's identification of the sources of integration—political and social—serves as explanations of it because it tells us what factors promote it.

Deutsch's study presented here is essentially exploratory. While most of his other research on integration between and among nations has been empirical and rigorous, the treatment at hand is based on the author's reading of history and impressionistic generalizations about presumed historical regularities in the process by which formerly independent units become united into a single unit. The observational base has been confined largely to Western Europe and the North Atlantic region, on the assumption that the process of integration is a general rather than regionally specific one; thus, the insights and lessons that are derived about the process of building nations and empires at the international level are assumed to be representative of the process that is likely to occur everywhere. It should be noted, however, that Deutsch has subsequently revised many of his views about integration to take account of new developments and the research findings of others on the problem. For instance, he gathered data on transactions among societies—trade, mail flows, travel, and student exchanges—and collected public-opinion data, and his analysis of this empirical evidence enabled him to revise some of his conclusions and refine others. Some of this reconceptualization has led Deutsch to attach greater stress to the impact made on the integration potential of interacting communities by compatibility of central values, a perceived distinctive way of life, a multiplicity of ranges of communication and transaction, and the mobility of persons from the politically relevant strata. Thus, his continuing research into the problem of creating conditions of peace through political integration serves as an example of how new data exert pressure for the refinement of theory, as well as how theoretical explanations of the sort provided in this selection exert pressure for new data. It is through the juxtaposition of theory with data that we are able to improve our ability to explain phenomena.

Our next selection focuses on yet another substantive issue related to the maintenance of the international system: the problem of the relationship between the structure of alliance systems in the international environment and international stability. Here the empirical question is what type of alliance, or coalition, configuration is most conducive to the maintenance of international equilibrium and peace. By implication, much of the inquiry on this problem has been phrased in terms of the kinds of alignment networks that best enhance the prospects for a viable balance-of-power system. Essentially, the question tends to be posed in terms of the polarity of the international system's structure—that is, in terms of the number of poles, or interstate blocs, in the system. In the selection that follows, Karl Deutsch and J. David Singer combine their creative research talents to investigate the relationship between the polarity of the system and the consequent likelihood of international stability.

MULTIPOLAR POWER SYSTEMS AND INTERNATIONAL STABILITY

Karl W. Deutsch and J. David Singer

In the classical literature of diplomatic history, the balance-of-power concept occupies a central position. Regardless of one's interpretation of the term or one's preference for or antipathy to it, the international relations scholar cannot escape dealing with it. The model is, of course, a multifaceted one, and it produces a fascinating array of corollaries; among these, the relationship between the number of actors and the stability of the system is one of the most widely accepted and persuasive. That is, as

---

Karl W. Deutsch and J. David Singer, "Multipolar Power Systems and International Stability," *World Politics* 16, 3 (April 1964): 390-406. Copyright, 1964, by Princeton University Press. Reprinted by permission of the authors and publisher.

Research used in this article has been supported in part by the Carnegie Corporation.

the system moves away from bipolarity toward multipolarity, the frequency and intensity of war should be expected to diminish.

To date, however, that direct correlation has not been subjected to rigorous scrutiny by either abstract or empirical test. For the most part, it has seemed so intuitively reasonable that a few historical illustrations have been accepted as sufficient. This is, on balance, not enough to support a lawful generalization; it must eventually be put to the historical test. This will be done eventually,[1] but in the interim this hypothesis should at least be examined on formal, abstract grounds. The purpose of this article, therefore, is to present two distinct—but related—lines of formal, semi-quantitative, argument as to why the diffusion-stability relationship should turn out as the theoretician has generally assumed and as the historian has often found to be the case.

I. A PROBABILISTIC CONCEPT OF INTERNATIONAL POLITICAL STABILITY

Stability may, of course, be considered from the vantage point of both the total system and the individual states comprising it. From the broader, or systemic, point of view, we shall define stability as the probability that the system retains all of its essential characteristics; that no single nation becomes dominant; that most of its members continue to survive; and the large-scale war does not occur. And from the more limited perspective of the individual nations, stability would refer to the probability of their continued political independence and territorial integrity without any significant probability of becoming engaged in a "war for survival." The acceptable level of this probability—such as 90, or 95, or 99 per cent—seems to be intuitively felt by political decision-makers, without necessarily being made explicit, but it could be inferred by investigators in the analysis of particular cases. A more stringent definition of stability would require also a low probability of the actors' becoming engaged even in limited wars.

This probabilistic concept of political stability differs from the stability concept used by L. F. Richardson, which was that of classical mechanics. Richardson's stability referred simply to any set of conditions under which the system would return to its equilibrium state; instability meant to him any state of affairs that would not so return, but rather would continue to change until reaching some limit or breakdown point of the system. A low rate of exponential growth of arms expenditures, of two competing powers—say, of 2 to 4 per cent a year—would be "unstable" in Richardson's terms, but might be compatible with a political stability for the indefinite future, as long as national per capita income or other indicators of the system's absorption capacity grew at least at the same rate. In that case, of course, the per cent for defense taken from the average per capita income would remain unchanging or might decline, with no untoward effects upon the internal financial or political stability of the states concerned—or upon the stability of the relation between them, as long as both continued to grow at similar rates.[2]

Richardson's essentially non-political stability concept and the political and probabilistic concept proposed here will lead to more closely similar results, however, if we reformulate Richardson's increments of arms expenditure of two rival states not in terms of dollars but in terms of per cent of national income. An arms race proper would then be defined as one in which the rival states stimulate one another to divert *increasing proportions of their national income* to military preparations—a practice with obvious political and economic limits, well before the entire 100 per cent of national income is consumed by military spending. The chief practical case investigated by Richardson, the arms race preceding World War I, was in fact of this nature, since the growth rate of the aggregate arms budgets of the two main coalitions was of the order of 15 per cent per year, in contrast to income growth rates of the order of only 5 per cent in the principal countries.

The political definition of equilibrium that we have just proposed is quite compatible with the language used by Morton Kaplan.[3] In Kaplan's formulation, equilibrium and stability can be defined only in terms of particular variables, which must be chosen in advance. Thus, if we focus our attention upon the absolute level of armaments—say, in terms of a constant dollar expenditure at constant prices—the system would be stable, and a system in which the rival powers allocated constant proportions of their gross national products to armaments would appear to be unstable in these terms. If, however, these percentages of GNP themselves were chosen as the critical variables, the system would once again appear as stable.

The rest of this article will be presented in four sections. In the first, we link up the independent variable (number of independent actors) with the dependent one (stability of the system) by means of an emphasis on "interaction opportunity"—our intervening variable. In the second section, the interaction opportunity concept is extended to the point where it impinges on the degree of attention that any nation in the system may allocate to all of the other nations or to possible coalitions of nations. In the third, the multipolar and bipolar models are connected with Richardson's model of arms races and similar kinds of escalating conflicts. In the final section, these arguments are subjected to a new scrutiny, with the time scale introduced as a limiting factor.

II. THE ACCELERATED RISE OF INTERACTION OPPORTUNITIES

The most obvious effect of an increase in the number of independent actors is an increase in the number of possible pairs or dyads in the total system. This assumes, of course, that the number of independent actors is responsive to the general impact of coalition membership, and that as a nation enters into the standard coalition it is much less of a free agent than it was while non-aligned. That is, its alliance partners now exercise an inhibiting effect—or perhaps even a veto—upon its freedom to interact with non-alliance nations.

This reduction in the number of possible dyadic relations produces, both for any individual nation and for the totality of those in the system, a corresponding diminution in the number of opportunities for interaction with other actors. Although it must be recognized at the outset, that, in the international system of the nineteenth and twentieth centuries, such opportunities are as likely to be competitive as they are to be cooperative, the overall effect is nevertheless destabilizing. The argument is nothing more than a special case of the widely employed pluralism model.

In that model, our focus is on the degree to which the system exhibits negative feedback as well as cross-pressuring. By negative—as distinguished from positive or amplifying—feedback, we refer to the phenomenon of self-correction: as stimuli in one particular direction increase, the system exhibits a decreasing response to those stimuli, and increasingly exhibits tendencies that counteract them. This is the self-restraining system, manifested in the automatic pilot, the steam-engine governor, and most integrated social systems, and it stands in contrast to the self-aggravating system as seen in forest fires, compound interest, nuclear fission, runaway inflation or deflation, and drug addiction.[4]

The pluralistic model asserts that the amplifying feedback tendency is strengthened, and the negative feedback tendency is weakened, to the extent that conflict positions are superimposed or reinforcing. Thus, if all clashes and incompatibilities in the system produce the same divisions and coalitions—if all members in class Blue line up *with* one another and *against* all or most of those in class Red—the line of cleavage will be wide and deep, with positive feedback operating both within and between the two classes or clusters. But if some members of class Blue have some incompatible interests with others in their class, and an overlap of interests with some of those in Red, there will be some degree of negative or self-correcting feedback both within and between the two classes.

This notion is analogous to that of cross-cutting pressure familiar to the student of politics. Here we observe that every individual plays a fairly large number of politically relevant roles and that most of these pull him in somewhat different attitudinal, behavioral, and organizational directions. For example, if an individual is (1) a loving parent, (2) a member of a militant veterans' organization, (3) owner of a factory, and (4) a Catholic, the first and third factors will tend to deflect him toward a "coexistence" foreign policy, the second will pull him toward a "holy war" orientation, and his religious affiliation will probably (in the 1960's) produce a deep ambivalence. Likewise, following Ralf Dahrendorf's formulation, if status difference is a major determinant of conflict exacerbation, and an individual is head of a family, a bank teller, and president of the lodge, he will coalesce with and against different people on different issues.[5] In each of these cases, his relatively large number of interaction opportunities produces a set of cross-pressures such as largely to inhibit any superimposition or reinforcement. The consequence would seem to favor social stability and to inhibit social cleavage; increasing differentiation and role specialization in industrial society has, in a sense, counteracted the Marxian expectation of class warfare.

Thus, in any given bilateral relationship, a rather limited range of possible interactions obtains, even if the relationship is highly symbiotic. But as additional actors are brought into the system, the range of possible interactions open to each—and hence to the total system—increases. In economics, this accretion produces the transformation from barter to market, and in any social setting it produces a comparable increase in the range and flexibility of possible interactions. Traditionally, social scientists have believed—and observed—that as the number of possible exchanges increases, so does the probability that the "invisible hand" of pluralistic interests will be effective. One might say that one of the greatest threats to the stability of any impersonal social system is the shortage of alternative partners.

If we assume, then, that any increase in the number of independent actors *is* conducive to stability, the question remains as to the quantitative nature of this correlation. Is there any particular level at which the system cannot be made more stable by the addition of new actors, or less stable by the loss of existing actors? Is there, furthermore, some critical level at which small changes become crucial? Our response must be based, of course, on the degree to which each single increment or decrement affects the number of possible dyads, or bilateral interaction opportunities, in the system. That effect is found by applying the standard formula for possible pairs: $\frac{N(N-1)}{2}$; thus, in a purely bipolar system, only one dyad or pair is possible, while a tripolar situation produces three pairs, four actors produce six pairs, five produce ten possible pairings, and so on, as shown in Figure 1.

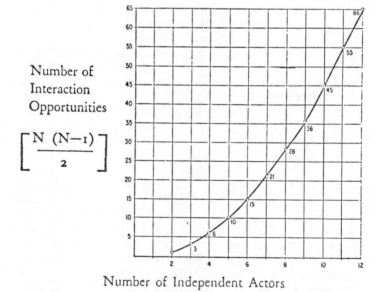

Number of
Interaction
Opportunities

$$\left[\frac{N\,(N-1)}{2}\right]$$

Number of Independent Actors

FIGURE 1
Interaction Opportunity

This figure indicates rather dramatically the degree to which the number of independent actors affects the possible number of dyads, and thus interaction opportunities. Even as we move from bipolarity to a tripolar system, the interaction opportunities within the system triple, and when another single actor is added the possible dyadic relations increase by three, and so on, with each addition in the actor column producing an increment of $N-1$ in the interaction opportunity column. Intuitively, the student of international politics would note that until N reaches five, there is an insufficient number of possible dyads, and that beyond that level the stability-enchancing increment begins to grow very sharply.

So far, we have operated from the conservative assumption that all nations have identical interests, concerns, and goals, and though we would not want to exaggerate in the opposite direction, one cannot overlook the diversity that does exist. A landlocked nation can hardly offer fishing rights in its coastal waters, an agricultural surplus nation will seldom purchase those same foodstuffs, two underdeveloped nations are most unlikely to exchange machine tools, and a permanent member of the Security Council cannot be expected to give much for assurance of a seat in that organ. Every nation's needs and supplies differ, and the more nations there are, the greater will be the number and diversity of trade-offs available to the total system. As possible trade-offs increase, the greater the possibility for compensatory and stabilizing interactions to occur. That is, in a system characterized by conflict-generating scarcities, each and every increase in opportunities for cooperation (i.e., to engage in a mutually advantageous trade-off) will diminish the tendency to pursue a conflict up to, and over, the threshold of war.

Finally, membership in an alliance not only exercises a negative quantitative impact on a nation's interaction opportunities, but affects the quality of those that do continue to exist. On the one hand, the pattern-maintenance needs of the alliance will be such as to *minimize* (a) the range of issues over which it will conflict with an alliance partner, and (b) the intensity of such intra-alliance conflicts as are permitted. On the other hand, the establishment of such a clear-cut in-group-outgroup division can only lead to an *increase* in the range and intensity of any conflcts with non-alliance actors.

To summarize, one logical explanation for the correlation between number of independent actors and the probability of armed conflict lies in the realm of enhanced interaction opportunities, observed in terms of their quantity, diversity, and qualities.

III. THE ACCELERATED DIMINUTION IN THE ALLOCATION OF ATTENTION

A second line of argument that should also support the hypothesized correlation between multipolarity and stability revolves around the notion of attention available for conflict. Here we assume that, as the number of independent actors in the system increases, the share of its attention that any nation can devote to any other must of necessity diminish. The argument need not, of course, postulate that each additional actor will attract an equal share of the attention of each of the other actors, or necessarily attract the same share as those already in the system. That share will be a function of many considerations and may vary rather widely. Let us assume, then, that any nation's total external attention—that is, its information-processing and resource-allocating capabilities—will be distributed among all others in the system according to a normal distribution, as illustrated in Figure 2.

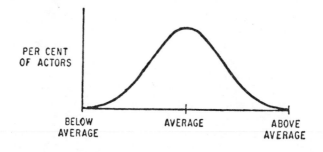

FIGURE 2
Share of Attention

In this figure, we suggest that a very few of the total number of actors in the system receive very little of A's attention, that most of them receive a moderate share of that attention, and that a very few receive an impressively heavy share of it. But regardless of the shape of this attention distribution curve, the fact is that every actor claims *some*.

If those receiving a minimal share of A's attention were to disappear into a coalition, this would have only a minor impact on the amount of attention now left over for A to redistribute among the remaining independent actors. But if coalition were to occur among some of those receiving a greater share of that original attention, A would then be able to deal with the members of that coalition with fewer demands on its information-processing and energy-allocating capabilities; as a consequence, that remaining for allocation to the other actors in the system would be appreciably increased.

Now the limited attention capability of each nation in the system must be allocated between two different sets of relationships. First priority will tend to go to all of those dyadic relationships in which it is a partner, while the dyads of which it is not a member will receive a lesser, but not insignificant, degree of attention. Some recent illustrations of this latter demand might be found in the attention which the United States has expended on the Soviet-Yugoslavian, British-Egyptian, or Indian-Pakistan dyads, or which the USSR devoted to the Arab-Israeli, Cuban-American, or Franco-Algerian pairings. Regardless of membership or non-membership, each nation must spread its attention among most of the dyads in the system.

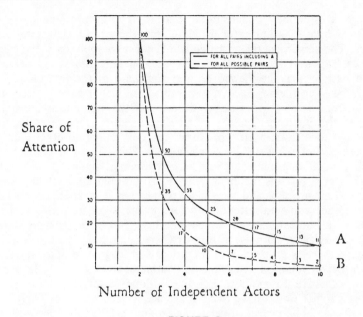

Share of
Attention

Number of Independent Actors

FIGURE 3
Allocation of Attention

What, then, is the effect of any trend toward or away from bipolarity upon that distribution of attention? In Figure 3, we plot that distribution according to the assumption that, with each single addition to the number of independent actors, the total number of dyads in which Nation A is a member will also increase by one, following the formula $N-1$. With each increment in the number of dyads of which A may be a member, the amount of attention available for any one such pairing will drop, as shown in the upper (solid line) curve. Thus three actors produce two possible dyads that include A, with an average of 50 per cent of A's attention available for each; four actors produce three such pairs and 33 percent of A's attention for each; and five actors produce four A-inclusive dyads, with only 25 per cent of his attention available to each.

When we drop the condition that only those dyads of which A (any actor) is a member can constitute a drain on A's attention, and assume that *every* possible dyad will make some such demand, the attention curve responds even more rapidly to an increase in the number of independent actors. As the lower (dotted line) curve indicates, each new actor increases the total number of dyads by the $\frac{N(N-1)}{2}$ formula, as already used earlier

in Figure 1, with the percentage of share of attention available to each dyad dropping even more sharply.

Why should these rapid decreases in percentage of available attention exercise any effect upon the stability of the system? In communication theory, it is generally recognized that below a certain signal-to-noise ratio, the signal is essentially undetectable; that is, it loses prominence as its strength vis-à-vis the noise (or random disturbance) in the system diminishes. The same general principle would seem to apply to social interaction; as Rapoport and Schelling have pointed out, interaction between any two nations may be viewed as a special case of the interchange of messages between them.[6] Each state in this case would have to treat the messages from its most prominent adversary of the moment as the signal relevant to this incipient conflict in or before its early stage of escalation; and it would tend to treat all other messages, concerning all other pairs of states, as noise of relatively little relevance to this particular conflict.[7]

The general requirement of at least a minimal signal-to-noise ratio would then hold for this incipient conflict, as it would hold for any other communication process; and we shall assume that it is approximated by the ratio of governmental attention to foreign messages from this particular rival, to all other messages concerning other states or pairs of states. Just what this signal-to-noise ratio—or, here, minimal attention ratio—would have to be is a question of empirical fact. Signal-to-noise ratios of 100:1 are not uncommon in electronic communication systems. It is perhaps not excessive to assume that the minimal attention ratio for an escalating conflict would have to be 1:9, since it does not seem likely that any country could be provoked very far into an escalating conflict with less than 10 per cent of the foreign policy attention of its government devoted to the matter.[8]

If we require a minimal attention of 10 per cent for an escalating conflict, the likelihood of such conflicts thus will decline sharply with the decline of the average attention that any one government has available for any one of the remaining actors in the international system.

The decline of this average available attention with an increasing number of actors in the system has been graphed in curves A and B in Figure 3, as discussed earlier. We can now show on the same graph the lines of minimal attention ratios required to permit average probabilities of, say, 20, 10, or 5 per cent for an escalating conflict between any two actors in the system. Several such lines, at the 10, 20, 30 . . . per cent levels of an assumed minimum attention ratio, have been drawn in Figure 3. Their intersections with curves A and B show how quickly the increase of the number of actors will remove an international system from the danger zone, or how fast a diminution in the number of actors will increase the average risk of escalating conflict among the remainder.

As far as it goes, this graphic representation confirms the greater stability of multipolar systems, and it suggests some quantitative findings. It shows that the average share of available attention for any one conflict drops sharply as soon as there are more than three power centers in the system, and more gently after there are more than five such centers; and it further suggests that the stability of the system may depend critically on the *critical attention ratio*—that is, on the proneness of countries to enter into escalating conflicts even if only a small part of their government's attention is engaged in this particular quarrel.

Thus, if some minimum percentage of a nation's external attention is required for that nation to engage in behavior tending toward armed conflict, and the increase in number of independent actors diminishes the share that any nation can allocate to any other single actor, such an increase is likely to have a stabilizing effect upon the system.

IV. SOME IMPLICATIONS FOR RICHARDSON'S MODEL OF ESCALATING CONFLICT

The task of this section will be to correlate the propositions concerning the greater stability of multipolar systems in international politics, especially as recently formalized by Morton Kaplan, with the Richardson model of conflict;[9] and to show that the former proposition can be treated as a special case of the general Richardson model.

In the Richardson model of the arms race, or of similar competitive relations, conflict behavior of each of two parties is seen as growing at an exponential rate, similar to the growth of compound interest or to the progress of an explosion. The rate of this growth is described by a pair of differential equations in which one party's increase in armaments—or of other competitive behavior—is perceived as a threat and becomes the motivating input for the corresponding reciprocal or retaliatory response of the other. Thus, if country A had spent in the previous year $90 million on armaments, while its rival B had spent $100, and if A now tries to equal B and increases its armaments budgets from $90 million to $100, and if country B, which previously had spent $100 million, tries to maintain the previous ratio of arms budgets, then B must now spend $11 million in the following year; whereupon A, if its rulers still aim at parity with B, will now increase its budget accordingly to $111 million, forcing B to defend its old proportionate lead by raising its arms budget by $12.3 million to $123.3 million, so that not only the absolute amounts but also the *increases* in arms spending on both sides are growing in every round, and the arms race will accelerate in ever-growing steps until some limit or breakdown is attained.

The simple model would hold equally for bipolar and multipolar systems. In the latter systems, one might imagine that it could apply to every possible pair of nations in rivalry, and thus to 10 pairs in a five-power system, to 15 pairs in a six-power world, and generally to $N(N-1)/2$ powers in a N-power system. If country A wanted at least to keep its proportionate lead against *each* of its rivals, it would have to maintain its level in an exponentially growing arms race with the most quickly growing of these rivals, because this would automatically increase its lead over all the rest. If all powers followed this type of policy, the total pace of arms competition for all countries would be set by the fastest growing competitor.

This model, however, seems too simple. It may be more reasonable to assume that a country is most likely to respond to an increase in the arms expenditure of a rival only in regard to that part which appears likely to be deployed or directed against itself.

In the case of a bipolar world, this consideration would make very little difference. The strongest country, A, would have to fear almost the full amount of the increment in the strength of the next strongest power, B, since in this bipolar world the third and fourth ranking powers, C and D, and all the lesser powers down to N, are almost negligible in their strength in comparison to A and B. These negligible lesser powers would thus not require any significant allocation of B's resources to ensure against the risk of having to fight them, and practically all of B's strength would remain available for use against A, forcing A in turn to increase its own efforts to the full extent required to maintain its own margin of strength in relation to B's growth.

Matters are quite different, however, in a multipolar world. In a four-power system, C and D, the third and fourth ranking nations, are already nearly as strong as A and B, the top and second-rank powers. Accordingly, B may have to allocate more than one-half of its resources—and of its increment in these—to the possibility of having to fight C or D, and thus B may have left less than one-half of its increment for a credible increase in its threat against A. The effect on A's behavior, according to the Richardson model, would be correspondingly less, since A would have to raise its arms budget only to the extent needed to hold its proportionate lead in regard to one-half or less of B's increment in arms expenditure. The arms race in a completely rational world would thus tend to be slower under multipolar conditions than under bipolar ones.

A different line of reasoning suggests the same result. Richardson's original model assumed that the motivation for a state to try to maintain its proportionate lead over the arms level of another was autonomously generated within the state itself. Once the national subsystems of the international political system had this motivation, in Richardson's model, then the consequences of an escalating arms race followed under the conditions that he specified. It was the competitive motivations of the national states, in Richardson's thought, that produced the competitive character of the international system. Many writers on international politics, from Machiavelli onward, have taken the opposite view. The larger system, they have maintained, is itself competitive to start with, in that it rewards appropriate competitive behavior and penalizes the failure to compete by the pitiless elimination of the laggards and the weak. Machiavelli's princes, Adam Smith's businessmen, and Charles Darwin's animal all must compete for survival in their respective systems, on pain of being wiped out otherwise, regardless of their subjective motivation. In time, each of these systems is expected to select for survival primarily those subsystems that have responded most adequately to its competitive pressure. Which rival subsystem happened to exercise this competitive pressure at the moment is secondary in each of these theories. If this particular rival had been absent, another would have taken his place and served the same function of offering a compelling challenge to competitive behavior.

This type of thinking has remained familiar in the popular rhetoric of arms competition. The world is such, the argument used to run—or the adversary is such, it has run more recently—that "there is no choice" but arms competition or national doom through surrender or defeat. Regardless of the motivations of its own people, its own political system, and its own decision-makers, any state in such a situation must respond to the challenge of an arms race or else perish.

How strong is this externally derived pressure upon a state to increase its own armaments for the sake of survival, regardless of any other values or motivations produced by its domestic political system? Clearly, it is proportional only to that part of the increment in a rival's armament that is not likely to be balanced by a shift in alliances under a balance-of-power policy. In a bipolar world, a 10 per cent increase in the arms spending of power A must be answered by an equal increment in the arms of B, and the escalation process may then proceed at 10 per cent increments for each cycle. In a world of four approximately equal powers, a rise in the arms level of power A from 100 to 110 would give A's coalition, I—consisting, say, of A plus C—only a strength of 210 against the rival coalition II, consisting of B and D, with a strength of 200. The superiority of coalition I over coalition II would thus be not 10 but 5 per cent; the offsetting armaments needed by coalition II would only have to be of 5 per cent; the subsequent increments of the escalation would likewise be of this lesser order of magnitude; and escalation would proceed more slowly.

In a similar six-power world, a 10 per cent increase in the armament of one power would compel an increment of only about 3 per cent in the arms spending of the three members of the rival coalition. A ten-power world in the same situation would only be forced to a 2 per cent arms rise for each of five powers. Generally, every increase in the number of powers would slow down the speed of Richardsonian escalation.

If we drop the assumption of approximately equal powers in a multipolar world, the same general result follows. So long as most powers are free to move laterally from one coalition or alignment to another, their self-interest will favor such balance-of-power policies as to produce very nearly evenly matched coalitions, each of them composed quite possibly of members of unequal power. In such a mobile multipolar world, no government needs to fear a moderate decline in national power as potentially disastrous. It can survive as a second-class power as safely or precariously as it did as a first-class one, provided only that it joins in time the appropriate new alliance or alignment. Arms increases by a rival power, which in a bipolar world might pose a fatal threat, might call in a multipolar world for little more than a quick adjustment of alliances.

V. SOME IMPLICATIONS FOR THE DIFFUSION OF NUCLEAR WEAPONS

If an increase in the number and diplomatic mobility of actors may slow down the process of arms escalation, it would by the same reasoning also slow down any process of de-escalation. Here, too, a one-sided arms reduction in a two-power world may elicit an equal response by the other power, while in a multipolar world the effect of any such unilateral initiative would be much weaker.

If we are chiefly interested in rapid de-escalation—that is, in partial or complete disarmament—a multipolar world may prove more intractable than a bipolar one; and we may view the emergence of French, German, Japanese, or Communist Chinese national power with justified alarm. If we are mainly concerned, on the contrary, with preventing any rapid escalation of the two-power arms competition between the United States and the Soviet Union, a shift toward a multipolar world may appear preferable.

At this point, of course, the bare and abstract arguments pursued thus far become quite insufficient. In our analysis of alternative international power systems we have abstracted from all other qualities of the states, governments, and national political systems within them. At the point of policy choice, however, these hitherto neglected aspects may be the decisive ones. A bipolar system in which each of the two rival powers is likely to be moderate and cautious in its policy initiatives and responses might be a great deal safer than a multipolar world containing one or several well-armed powers whose governments or politically relevant strata were inclined to incompetence or recklessness. As elsewhere, so also in international politics a stable general system could be wrecked by the introduction of unstable components.

At the present time, the importance of this latter point may well be decisive. Each of the present major nuclear powers—the United States, Britain, and the Soviet Union—has been politically stable, in the sense that each has retained its particular type of government for over forty years. None of these three countries has been notable for initiating large and reckless military enterprises. Among the middle-level and smaller powers most likely to press for nuclear weapons during the next decade—which include France, Germany, Japan, Mainland China, Nationalist China, and perhaps Egypt and others—there are several whose recent history lacks any comparable evidence of stability in domestic institutions and caution in international affairs. If this stage should be followed by the dissemination of nuclear weapons among a still larger number of countries, including inevitably at least some with still less stable domestic regimes and less cautious military policies, the instability of the international system would be still more dangerous. For these reasons, any successful efforts by the United States and other powers to slow down the dissemination of nuclear weapons would tend to increase the stability of the entire international system. In the present article, devoted to an abstract argument, these matters can only be indicated, but they must not be forgotten.

One other problem, however, should be discussed here: the time horizon under which the stability of international systems is evaluated. A multipolar world, though often more stable in the short run than a bipolar one, has its own problem of long-run political stability, and it is to this that we must now turn our attention.

VI. THE LONG-RUN INSTABILITY OF MULTIPOLAR SYSTEMS

On the basis of these considerations, it might seem that a multipolar system could last forever, or for a very long time, by always opposing the ambitions of its currently top-ranking member; and this is indeed what some writers have claimed as a virtue of the balance-of-power system. In each of the sections above, however, we have dealt with considerations of an essentially short or middle-run nature, with a rather incomplete view as the natural consequence.

There are at least two analytic reasons why this relatively benign long-run outcome cannot be expected. For one thing, if we accept the usual zero-sum assumption of Machiavelli and the classic theory of games—according to which any gain by one contender can occur only through an equal loss by one or more of his rivals—then we must assume that each contending power ordinarily will try to acquire all the territory and population it can at the expense of its rivals, and that it will do nothing to create new rivals for itself. The model thus provides for the possibility of the destruction of states whose rulers misjudged the precise balance of strength at the moment, or whose economies and populations no longer yielded the increasing increments in arms spending and military effort required by the competition, but this model does not provide for the creation of new states. If the probability of states' perishing is small, but larger than zero, and the probability of substantial new powers' arising is zero in terms of this model, then the model will predict a diminishing number of effective contenders, leading eventually to a two-power world or to the survival of a single power, as in the case of the reduction of the many governments of classic antiquity to the two-power clash of Rome and Carthage, and of Rome's final long monopoly of power in the Mediterranean world until new forces entered from outside the region.

The second line of reasoning is based on considerations of statistics. Thus far we have taken probabilities only in terms of their central tendencies, rather than in terms of the variance of possible outcomes and their distribution. If we assume these outcomes to be normally distributed around some mean, then the usual outcome of an increment in threat by power A against power B in a multipolar system will consist in both A's and B's finding enough allies, respectively, to match the power of their respective coalitions and to produce the relatively moderate outcomes predicted by the classic balance-of-power model. In rare cases, however, corresponding to one tail of the distribution, state A will find a great preponderance of allies and become able to destroy its current enemy, B, completely; and in other rare cases—corresponding to the other tail of the distribution—A must expect to find itself facing an overwhelming coalition of adversaries that will destroy it. In the short run, only the moderate central tendencies of the distribution of outcomes of the coalition-forming process will be frequent enough to be taken into account, but in the long run the balance-of-power world must be expected to produce eventually dramatic and catastrophic changes, both locally and at last at the system level. The number of years after which long-run rather than short-run phenomena are likely to prevail will depend on the frequency of international crises, and on the shape of the distribution of balanced and unbalanced coalitions, respectively, as outcomes of the coalition-forming process.

This expectation seems in good agreement with the historical data. No balance-of-power system has lasted longer than a few centuries, and most of the original powers contending in such systems have survived as independent powers only for much shorter periods.[10]

The classic descriptive and analytical views of two-power confrontations and of the balance of power among several contenders have been formalized by several writers. The most prominent models, of the tight bipolar and multipolar world, respectively, can be interpreted in terms of the dynamic model of conflict by Lewis F. Richardson. The results suggest that the Richardson model, with very simple assumptions, can be made to include the bipolar and multipolar models as special cases. This combined model then suggests some general inferences in predictions about trends that appear to accord well with historical data. In the long run, according to this model, even multipolar systems operating under the rules of balance-of-power policies are shown to be self-destroying, but both in the short and the long run the instability of tight bipolar systems appears to be substantially greater. It seems plausible that, *if the spread of nuclear weapons could be slowed down or controlled,* a transition from the bipolar international system of the early 1950's to an increasingly multipolar system in the 1960's might buy mankind some valuable time to seek some more dependable bases for world order.

NOTES

[1] Data-gathering on this topic is currently being carried on by David Singer.

[2] This argument does not take into account, of course, the effects of any radical changes in the quantity or effectiveness of weapons, or of the quantitative increase of currently available weapons of mass destruction to very high levels.

[3] Morton A. Kaplan, *System and Process in International Relations* (New York 1957), 6-8. Kaplan has formalized many classic formulations of balance-of-power theory. For outstanding examples of these, see Hans Morgenthau, *Politics Among Nations* (3rd edn., New York 1960), 167-226; Inis Claude, *Power and International Relations* (New York 1962), 11-93; Frederick L. Schuman, *International Politics* (6th edn., New York 1958), 70-72, 275-78, 577-79, 591-92; Arnold Wolfers, *Discord and Collaboration* (Baltimore 1962), 117-32; and Quincy Wright, *A Study of War* (Chicago 1942), II, 743-46. For other attempts at formalization, see George Liska, *International Equilibrium* (Cambridge, Mass., 1957), 23-56, 187-202; Edward V. Gulick, *Europe's Classical Balance of Power* (Ithaca 1955); and, for significant recent contributions, see Anatol Rapoport, *Fights, Games and Debates* (Ann Arbor 1960), and Richard Rosecrance, *Action and Reaction in World Politics* (Boston 1963).

[4] For an application of these and related concepts to a range of political questions, see Karl W. Deutsch, *The Nerves of Government* (New York 1963).

[5] Ralf Dahrendorf, "Toward a Theory of Social Conflict," *Journal of Conflict Resolution,* II (June 1958), 176-77.

[6] Rapoport, 213-22; Thomas C. Schelling, *The Strategy of Conflict* (Cambridge, Mass., 1960), 83-118.

[7]Cf. Colin Cherry, *On Human Communication: A Review, a Survey, and a Criticism* (Cambridge-New York 1957), 42 and *passim*.

[8]For an earlier version of a related argument about mass attitudes to quarrels with a foreign country, see Karl W. Deutsch, "Mass Communication and the Loss of Freedom in National Decision-Making," *Journal of Conflict Resolution,* I (July 1957), 200-11.

[9]Kaplan, 21-53; Rapoport, 15-47; and the same author's essay, "L. F. Richardson's Mathematical Theory of War," *Journal of Conflict Resolution,* I (September 1957), 249-99. See also L. F. Richardson, *Arms and Insecurity* (Chicago 1960).

[10]For some historical data, see the discussion of the reduction of Italian city states during the years 1300-1527 from 70 or 80 to 10, in A. J. Toynbee, *A Study of History* (London-New York 1945), III, 355-56; cf. also 301-4, 345-48. In addition, see Wright, II, 762-63 ("The Disappearance of Small States").

The preceding article by Deutsch and Singer attempts to assess the consequences of multipolarity and bipolarity for the incidence and magnitude of war. The explanatory conclusion reached is that, "as the system moves away from bipolarity toward multipolarity, the frequency of war should be expected to diminish." This conclusion stems from a number of theoretical premises the authors make, which they state in mathematical form in order to derive the deduction that, at least in the short run, a multipolar system is likely to be more stable, with a declining level in the frequency and intensity of war.

Note how the explanations the authors provide are contingent upon the premises they take as axiomatic givens. The argument assumes that alliances, or blocs of states, diminish the freedom of coalition members to interact with outside countries; moreover, the assumption is made that the more nations remain "unentangled" in alliances, the greater will be the number of potential interaction opportunities in the international system. It follows from this logic that conflict within and among the membership of the coalition will decline, while there will be a concomitant increase in the number of conflicts with states outside the coalition.

As intuitively appealing and convincing as this reasoning is, it is important to note that competing theoretical explanations of the question exist. For instance, Kenneth Waltz has written a widely known article entitled "The Stability of a Bipolar World," which contends that the bipolar structure is not as unstable as some assume, because it encourages states to use caution and assume greater responsibility for their actions in foreign affairs. Employing rather unsystematic observation and descriptive procedures, Waltz points out that, as ironic as it may seem, the Cold War period was marked by relatively little actual violence between states, despite the tension that marked the period. He deduced that the perpetual competition between the superpowers and their overwhelming power made for relative stability in the midst of potential chaos and mass destruction:

Empires dissolved, and numerous new states appeared in the world. Strategic nuclear weapons came into the possession of four separate countries. Tactical nuclear weapons were developed and to some extent dispersed. The manned bomber gave way to the missile. Vulnerable missiles were hardened, made mobile and hidden. A revolution in military technology occurred on an average of once every five years and at an accelerating pace. Two "losses" of China, each a qualified loss but both traumatic, were accommodated without seriously distorting—or even greatly affecting—the balance between America and Russia.

Nevertheless, despite this potential for destruction and mutual hostility, Waltz found stability to result from these conditions. Part of this was due, he argued, to the fact that the superpower stalemate and mutual antagonism gave less developed nations more room for maneuver and thereby made for more over-all flexibility in the system. Thus, Waltz felt that peace and stability are most effectively produced when conditions reach the brink of war.

Attention is drawn to Waltz's study because its conclusion is diametrically opposed to that reached by Deutsch and Singer. The results of the two studies contradict each other. This raises the question of their validity: Which of them is more meaningful? In assessing the articles' validity, the approaches of the authors become crucial. Waltz's position is based on a large number of assumptions that are not systematically tested in the article, and that are implicitly related to each other. To determine the validity of Waltz's explanation, then, one would be confronted with the enormous task of investigating each assumption about the world and evaluating the relationship posited among the various assumptions. In contrast, the Deutsch-Singer approach is based on a small number of premises, the two most important of which are that multipolarity would lead to a substantial rise in interaction opportunity, and that this, in turn, would lead, in the short run, to less severe international conflict. In evaluating a presentation such as the Deutsch-Singer article, one need only to evaluate premises and logical deductions made by the authors extending the premises. Consequently, the Deutsch-Singer argument is much less difficult to assess than the Waltz approach.

Yet, to say that a highly deductive approach focused on a small number of premises is less difficult to assess than an approach that depends on a large number of interrelated theoretical concepts says nothing about the correctness of the explanation. The deductive approach is easier to disprove than the more complex approach because one need only to discredit the few explicitly stated assumptions. But because the Deutsch-Singer approach is so much more succinct, we might expect that it is less qualified and more abstract than the Waltz argument. In this case, those using the deductive approach are trading off theoretical richness and complexity for parsimony and the chance to have the argument systematically evaluated. Conversely, approaches such as that represented in the Waltz article, since they employ neither systematic observation nor a precise focus on crucial assumptions, trade off parsimony and verifiability for theoretical complexity.

A final point comparing the Waltz with the Deutsch-Singer article has to do with prescription. Both articles imply policy prescriptions, with Waltz advocating a continuation of the bipolar structure of international politics and Deutsch-Singer implying that a multipolar structure would be more stable. In both cases, the authors are employing the same criteria of international stability in evaluating the different types of international patterns—that is, the absence of widespread and highly destructive conflict. This agreement on goals, or criteria of success, makes the contrast between the two articles all the more striking, since, in spite of the agreement, the prescriptive implications are clearly different.

What the foregoing comments and contrasts suggest is that our knowledge claims and explanations of reality are inevitably dependent on the research methodologies that produced them. Different investigative techniques are frequently able to produce different and often contradictory conclusions. This suggests that no single study should ever be considered authoritative or definitive, and that the ultimate test of the veracity of any explanation is whether it holds up across many studies using different techniques and different sets of data.

The last three selections in this chapter are all exemplary of scholarly efforts to explain the conditions promoting the maintenance of the international system. They range from the conceptual discussion of Deutsch on political and social integration to theoretical explanations and predictions by Singer-Wallace and Deutsch-Singer. The important point is that there is a place for each of these types of analysis in the study of the international system. Moreover, there is need for discussions of concepts to be related to theoretical explanations, whether they be of the deductive variety or the more traditional theoretical exposition. In addition, systematic descriptions need to be used in evaluating theoretical explanations. Without tying conceptual and theoretical discussions to empirical reality, we cannot develop extensive explanatory knowledge of the international system.

In the remaining portions of the chapter, we will turn to studies that are primarily prescriptive in emphasis. Like the preceding ones, the following articles deal with the international system as a whole. What distinguishes them from the former, however, is that they address themselves to the way the global environment might and should be changed. They thus are typical of "advocacy" pieces in the literature that attempt to persuade the reader that certain values should be maximized and suggest the means by which those value preferences might be realized.

The first prescriptive reading is by a man who certainly requires no introduction—Henry Kissinger. While he was a professor of international relations at Harvard, Kissinger wrote extensively on strategic policy and bureaucratic sources of foreign policy. Since 1968, he has been a policy-maker, first as Assistant to the President and then as Secretary of State. His success in the world of practical politics suggests that not all "academics find difficulties with solutions, but solutions for difficulties." In the following piece, Kissinger seeks to offer policy prescriptions for the United States that would enable it to achieve creation of a world conducive to American interests.

THE WORLD AS IT IS
AND THE WORLD WE SEEK

Henry A. Kissinger

Dramatic changes in recent years have transformed America's position and role in the world:

• For most of the postwar period, America enjoyed predominance in physical resources and political power. Now, like most other nations in history, we find that our most difficult task is how to apply limited means to the accomplishment of carefully defined ends. We can no longer overwhelm our problems; we must master them with imagination, understanding, and patience.

• For a generation our preoccupation was to prevent the Cold War from degenerating into a hot war. Today, when the danger of global conflict has diminished, we face the more profound problem of defining what we mean by peace and determining the ultimate purpose of improved international relations.

• For two decades the solidarity of our alliances seemed as constant as the threats to our security. Now our allies have regained strength and self-confidence, and relations with adversaries have improved. All this has given rise to uncertainties over the sharing of burdens with friends and the impact of reduced tensions on the cohesion of alliances.

• Thus even as we have mastered the art of continuing crises, our concern with the nature of a more permanent international order has grown. Questions once obscured by more insistent needs now demand our attention: What is true national interest? To what end stability? What is the relationship of peace to justice?

It is characteristic of periods of upheaval that to those who live through them they appear as a series of haphazard events. Symptoms obscure basic issues and historical trends. The urgent tends to dominate the important. Too often goals are presented as abstract utopias, safe havens from pressing events.

But a debate to be fruitful must define what can reasonably be asked of foreign policy and at what pace progress can be achieved. Otherwise it turns into competing catalogues of the desirable rather than informed comparisons of the possible. Dialogue degenerates into tactical skirmishing.

Henry A. Kissinger, "The Nature of the National Dialogue," address delivered to the Pacem in Terris III Conference, Washington, D.C., October 8, 1973. Copyright 1973, Henry A. Kissinger. Reprinted by permission of the author.
Kissinger is currently U. S. Secretary of State.

The current public discussion reflects some interesting and significant shifts in perspective:

• A foreign policy once considered excessively moralistic is now looked upon by some as excessively pragmatic.
• The government was criticized in 1969 for holding back East-West trade with certain countries until there was progress in their foreign policies. Now we are criticized for not holding back East-West trade until there are changes in those same countries' domestic policies.
• The administration's foreign policy, once decried as too Cold War–oriented, is now attacked as too insensitive to the profound moral antagonism between Communism and freedom. One consequence of this intellectual shift is a gap between conception and performance on some major issues of policy.
• The desirability of peace and détente is affirmed, but both the inducements to progress and the penalties to confrontation are restricted by legislation.
• Expressions of concern for human values in other countries are coupled with failure to support the very programs designed to help developing areas improve their economic and social conditions.
• The declared objective of maintaining a responsible American international role clashes with nationalistic pressures in trade and monetary negotiations and with calls for unilateral withdrawal from alliance obligations.

It is clear that we face genuine moral dilemmas and important policy choices. But it is also clear that we need to define the framework of our dialogue more perceptively and understandingly.

I

Foreign policy must begin with the understanding that it involves relationships between sovereign countries. Sovereignty has been defined as a will uncontrolled by others; that is what gives foreign policy its contingent and ever incomplete character. For disagreements among sovereign states can be settled only by negotiation or by power, by compromise or by imposition. Which of these methods prevails depends on the values, the strengths, and the domestic systems of the countries involved. A nation's values define what is just; its strength determines what is possible; its domestic structure decides what policies can in fact be implemented and sustained.

Thus foreign policy involves two partially conflicting endeavors: defining the interests, purposes, and values of a society and relating them to the interests, purposes, and values of others.

The policy-maker, therefore, must strike a balance between what is desirable and what is possible. Progress will always be measured in partial steps and in the relative satisfaction of alternative goals. Tension is unavoidable between values, which are invariably cast in maximum terms, and efforts to promote them, which of necessity involve compromise. Foreign policy is explained domestically in terms of justice. But what is defined as justice at home becomes the subject of negotiation abroad. It is thus no accident that many nations, including our own, view the international arena as a forum in which virtue is thwarted by the clever practice of foreigners.

In a community of sovereign states, the quest for peace involves a paradox: The attempt to impose absolute justice by one side will be seen as absolute injustice by all others; the quest for total security for some turns into total insecurity for the remainder. Stability depends on the relative satisfaction and therefore also the relative dissatisfaction of the various states. The pursuit of peace must therefore begin with a pragmatic concept of coexistence—especially in a period of ideological conflict.

We must, of course, avoid becoming obsessed with stability. An excessively pragmatic policy will be empty of vision and humanity. It will lack not only direction, but also roots and heart. General de Gaulle wrote in his memoirs that "France cannot be France without greatness." By the same token, America cannot be true to itself without moral purpose. This country has always had a sense of mission. Americans have always held the view that America stood for something above and beyond its material achievements. A purely pragmatic policy provides no criteria for other nations to assess our performance and no standards to which the American people can rally.

But when policy becomes excessively moralistic, it may turn quixotic or dangerous. A presumed monopoly on truth obstructs negotiation and accommodation. Good results may be given up in the quest for ever-elusive ideal solutions. Policy may fall prey to ineffectual posturing or adventuristic crusades.

The prerequisite for a fruitful national debate is that the policy-makers and critics appreciate each other's perspectives and respect each other's purposes. The policy-maker must understand that the critic is obliged to stress imperfections in order to challenge assumptions and to goad actions. But equally the critic should acknowledge the complexity and inherent ambiguity of the policy-maker's choices. The policy-maker must be concerned with the best that can be achieved, not just the best that can be imagined. He has to act in a fog of incomplete knowledge without the information that will be available later to the analyst. He knows—or should know—that he is responsible for the consequences of disaster as well as for the benefits of success. He may have to qualify some goals not because they would be undesirable if reached, but because the risks of failure outweigh potential gains. He must often settle for the gradual, much as he might prefer the immediate. He must compromise with others, and this means to some extent compromising with himself.

The outsider demonstrates his morality by the precision of his perceptions and the loftiness of his ideals. The policy-maker expresses his morality by implementing a sequence of imperfections and partial solutions in pursuit of *his* ideals.

There must be understanding, as well, of the crucial importance of timing. Opportunities cannot be hoarded; once past, they are usually irretrievable. New relationships in a fluid transitional period—such as today—are delicate and vulnerable; they must be nurtured if they are to thrive. We cannot pull up young shoots periodically to see whether the roots are still there or whether there is some marginally better location for them.

We are now at such a time of tenuous beginnings. Western Europe and Japan have joined us in an effort to reinvigorate our relationships. The Soviet Union has begun to practice foreign policy—at least partially—as a relationship between states rather than as international civil war. The People's Republic of China has emerged from two decades of isolation. The developing countries are impatient for economic and social change. A new dimension of unprecedented challenges—in food, oceans, energy, environment—demands global cooperation.

We are at one of those rare moments where through a combination of fortuitous circumstances and design man seems in a position to shape his future. What we need is the confidence to discuss issues without bitter strife, the wisdom to define together the nature of our world, as well as the vision to chart together a more just future.

II

Nothing demonstrates this need more urgently than our relationship with the Soviet Union.

This administration has never had any illusions about the Soviet system. We have always insisted that progress in technical fields, such as trade, had to follow—and reflect—progress toward more stable international relations. We have maintained a strong military balance and a flexible defense posture as a buttress to stability. We have insisted that disarmament had to be mutual. We have judged movement in our relations with the Soviet Union, not by atmospherics, but by how well concrete problems are resolved and by whether there is responsible international conduct.

Coexistence to us continues to have a very precise meaning:

• We will oppose the attempt by any country to achieve a position of predominance either globally or regionally.

• We will resist any attempt to exploit a policy of détente to weaken our alliances.

• We will react if relaxation of tensions is used as a cover to exacerbate conflicts in international trouble spots.

The Soviet Union cannot disregard these principles in any area of the world without imperiling its entire relationship with the United States.

On this basis we have succeeded in transforming U.S.-Soviet relations in many important ways. Our two countries have concluded an historic accord to limit strategic arms. We have substantially reduced the risk of direct U.S.-Soviet confrontation in crisis areas. The problem of Berlin has been resolved by negotiation. We and our allies have engaged the Soviet Union in negotiations on major issues of European security, including a reduction of military forces in Central Europe. We have reached a series of bilateral agreements on cooperation—health, environment, space, science and technology, as well as trade. These accords are designed to create a vested interest in cooperation and restraint.

Until recently the goals of détente were not an issue. The necessity of shifting from confrontation toward negotiation seemed so overwhelming that goals beyond the settlement of international disputes were never raised. But now progress has been made—and already taken for granted. We are engaged in an intense debate on whether we should make changes in Soviet society a precondition for further progress—or indeed for following through on commitments already made. The cutting edge of this problem is the congressional effort to condition most-favored-nation trade status for other countries on changes in their domestic systems.

This is a genuine moral dilemma. There are genuine moral concerns —on both sides of the argument. So let us not address this as a debate between those who are morally sensitive and those who are not, between those who care for justice and those who are oblivious to humane values. The attitude of the American people and government has been made emphatically clear on countless occasions, in ways that have produced effective results. The exit tax on emigration is not being collected and we have received assurances that it will not be reapplied; hardship cases submitted to the Soviet government are being given specific attention; the rate of Jewish emigration has been in the terms of thousands where it was once a trickle. We will continue our vigorous efforts on these matters.

But the real debate goes far beyond this: Should we now tie demands which were never raised during negotiations to agreements that have already been concluded? Should we require as a formal condition internal changes that we heretofore sought to foster in an evolutionary manner?

Let us remember what the MFN question specifically involves. The very term "most favored nation" is misleading in its implication of preferential treatment. What we are talking about is whether to allow *normal* economic relations to develop—of the kind we now have with over one hundred other countries and which the Soviet Union enjoyed until 1951. The issue is whether to abolish discriminatory trade restrictions that were imposed at the height of the Cold War. Indeed, at that time the Soviet government discouraged commerce because it feared the domestic impact of normal trading relations with the West on its society.

The demand that Moscow modify its domestic policy as a precondition for MFN or détente was never made while we were negotiating; now it is inserted after both sides have carefully shaped an overall mosaic. Thus it raises questions about our entire bilateral relationship.

Finally the issue affects not only our relationship with the Soviet Union, but also with many other countries whose internal structures we find incompatible with our own. Conditions imposed on one country could inhibit expanding relations with others, such as the People's Republic of China.

We shall never condone the suppression of fundamental liberties. We shall urge humane principles and use our influence to promote justice. But the issue comes down to the limits of such efforts. How hard can we press without provoking the Soviet leadership into returning to practices in its foreign policy that increase international tensions? Are we ready to face the crises and increased defense budgets that a return to Cold War conditions would spawn? And will this encourage full emigration or enhance the well-being or nourish the hope for liberty of the peoples of Eastern Europe and the Soviet Union? Is it détente that has prompted repression—or is it détente that has generated the ferment and the demand for openness which we are now witnessing?

For half a century we have objected to Communist efforts to alter the domestic structures of other countries. For a generation of Cold War we sought to ease the risks produced by competing ideologies. Are we now to come full circle and *insist* on domestic compatibility as a condition of progress?

These questions have no easy answers. The government may underestimate the margin of concessions available to us. But a fair debate must admit that they *are* genuine questions, the answers to which could affect the fate of all of us.

Our policy with respect to détente is clear: We shall resist aggressive foreign policies. Détente cannot survive irresponsibility in any area, including the Middle East. As for the internal policies of closed systems, the United States will never forget that the antagonism between freedom and its enemies is part of the reality of the modern age. We are not neutral in that struggle. As long as we remain powerful we will use our influence to promote freedom, as we always have. But in the nuclear age we are obliged to recognize that the issue of war and peace also involves human lives and that the attainment of peace is a profound moral concern.

III

Addressing the United Nations General Assembly two weeks ago, I described our goal as a world where power blocs and balances are no longer relevant; where justice, not stability, can be our overriding preoccupation; where countries consider cooperation in the world interest to be in their national interest.

But we cannot move toward the world of the future without first maintaining peace in the world as it is. These very days we are vividly reminded that this requires vigilance and a continuing commitment.

So our journey must start from where we are now. This is a time of lessened tension, of greater equilibrium, of diffused power. But if the world is better than our earlier fears, it still falls far short of our hopes. To deal with the present does not mean that we are content with it.

The most striking feature of the contemporary period—the feature that gives complexity as well as hope—is the radical transformation in the nature of power. Throughout history power has generally been homogeneous. Military, economic, and political potential were closely related. To be powerful a nation had to be strong in all categories. Today the vocabulary of strength is more complex. Military muscle does not guarantee political influence. Economic giants can be militarily weak, and military strength may not be able to obscure economic weakness. Countries can exert political influence even when they have neither military nor economic strength.

It is wrong to speak of only one balance of power, for there are several which have to be related to each other. In the military sphere, there are two superpowers. In economic terms, there are at least five major groupings. Politically, many more centers of influence have emerged; some eighty new nations have come into being since the end of World War II and regional groups are assuming ever increasing importance.

Above all, whatever the measure of power, its political utility has changed. Throughout history increases in military power—however slight—could be turned into specific political advantage. With the overwhelming arsenals of the nuclear age, however, the pursuit of marginal advantage is both pointless and potentially suicidal. Once sufficiency is reached, additional increments of power do not translate into usable political strength; and attempts to achieve tactical gains can lead to cataclysm.

This environment both puts a premium on stability and makes it difficult to maintain. Today's striving for equilibrium should not be compared to the balance of power of previous periods. The very notion of "operating" a classical balance of power disintegrates when the change required to upset the balance is so large that it cannot be achieved by limited means.

More specifically, there is no parallel with the nineteenth century. Then, the principal countries shared essentially similar concepts of legitimacy and accepted the basic structure of the existing international order. Small adjustments in strength were significant. The "balance" operated in a relatively confined geographic area. None of these factors obtain today.

Nor when we talk of equilibrium do we mean a simplistic mechanical model devoid of purpose. The constantly shifting alliances that maintained equilibrium in previous centuries are neither appropriate nor possible in our time. In an age of ideological schism the distinction between friends and adversaries is an objective reality. We share ideals as well as interests with our friends, and we know that the strength of our friendship is crucial to the lowering of tensions with our opponents.

When we refer to five or six or seven major centers of power, the point being made is not that others are excluded but that a few short years ago everyone agreed that there were only two. The diminishing tensions and the emergence of new centers of power has meant greater freedom of action and greater importance for all other nations. In this setting, our immediate aim has been to build a stable network of relationships that offers hope of sparing mankind the scourges of war. An interdependent world community cannot tolerate either big power confrontations or recurrent regional crises.

But peace must be more than the absence of conflict. We perceive stability as the bridge to the realization of human aspirations, not an end in itself. We have learned much about containing crises, but we have not removed their roots. We have begun to accommodate our differences, but we have not affirmed our commonality. We may have improved the mastery of equilibrium, but we have not yet attained justice.

In the encyclical *Pacem in Terris,* Pope John sketched a greater vision. He foresaw "that no political community is able to pursue its own interests and develop itself in isolation," for "there is a growing awareness of all human beings that they are members of a world community."

The opportunities of mankind now transcend nationalism, and can only be dealt with by nations acting in concert:

. For the first time in generations mankind is in a position to shape a new and peaceful international order. But do we have the imagination and determination to carry forward this still fragile task of creation?
. For the first time in history we may have the technical knowledge to satisfy man's basic needs. The imperatives of the modern world respect no national borders and must inevitably open all societies to the world around them. But do we have the political will to join together to accomplish this great end?

If this vision is to be realized, America's active involvement is inescapable. History will judge us by our deeds, not by our good intentions.

But it cannot be the work of any one country. And it cannot be the undertaking of any one administration or one branch of government or one party. To build truly is to chart a course that will be carried on by future leaders because it has the enduring support of the American people.

So let us search for a fresh consensus. Let us restore a spirit of understanding between the legislative and the executive, between the government and the press, between the people and their public servants. Let us learn once again to debate our methods and not our motives, to focus on our destiny and not on our divisions. Let us all contribute our different views and perspectives but let us, once again, see ourselves as engaged in a common enterprise. If we are to shape a world community we must first restore community at home.

With Americans working together, America can work with others toward man's eternal goal of *pacem in terris*—peace abroad, peace at home, and peace within ourselves.

Kissinger's speech was delivered while he occupied the role of policy-maker. Consequently, he was necessarily motivated to couch his arguments in prescriptive terms, contending that particular policy options are desirable for the United States. While we must take cognizance of the fact that such an address by a policy spokesman often tends to be delivered for public consumption, we must also note that the cogency of any advocacy argument is amenable to evaluation by clear criteria. Several points about his statements deserve comment.

First, it is apparent that many of his prescriptions regarding the appropriate course of action for the United States are derived from often implicit assumptions. For instance, the contention that policy "must strike a balance between what is desirable and what is possible" stems from the conviction that it is unrealistic for foreign-policy behavior to be value-maximizing, in the sense of searching for the full realization of ideal goals. Kissinger's image of foreign policy conforms to the notion that policy decisions must be the product of adjustments among conflicting interests and therefore tend to be compromises. To search for the achievement of one goal necessarily precludes or diminishes the opportunity to achieve others. Thus, the conclusion that foreign policy should not be guided by the search for ideal solutions stems from the assumption that policy, of necessity, must be a compromise among alternative goals.

Second, the policies advocated in this piece all stem from Kissinger's assessment of the world as it currently is. Notice that the address begins with a description of the world. How one defines empirical reality goes far in determining how one proposes to deal with it and perhaps change it. The point illustrated by this arrangement is that descriptions tend to precede prescriptions.

Third, we note that the descriptions offered are based on the author's personal impressions of today's international system. The accuracy of those descriptions is crucial to the reasonableness of the policy advice that follows; for, if his assessment of the current international milieu is erroneous, then his recommendations for behavior with respect to it become dubious. For instance, the descriptive assumption that "the danger of global conflict has diminished" has serious implications for the subsequent analysis.

Fourth, it is worth noting that the policy recommendations are couched in explicitly normative terms. For example, when Kissinger attacks moralistic policy as dangerous, he does so by reference to value judgments.

And finally, but certainly not exhaustively, we should take cognizance of the fact that intrinsic to Kissinger's presentation is a mental model, or pretheory, of international relations that stresses certain features as important and regards others as relatively insignificant. He introduces many variables in his interpretation of the world environment, such as the presence and behavior of other superpowers, timing, and domestic constraints; but he dismisses others, such as international legal norms and intergovernmental organizational actors, as of secondary concern and relevance. Thus, in stipulating what is central to the international system and what is relatively insignificant, he bases his argument on a set of assumptions about the underlying characteristics of the global community and the factors that serve to modify its structure. These assumptions constitute a theoretical posture toward the world. Kissinger's theory of the foundations of international relations thereby influences his preferences for the kind of world the United States should seek to create. This suggests that prescriptions about the kinds of behavior that are most appropriate, such as détente with the Soviet Union and the fragmentation of power blocs, are ultimately tied to the theoretical framework and conceptual lens one employs to interpret the world.

With these epistemological points about prescriptive analysis in mind, let us turn to a final example of prescriptive inquiry at the level of the international system. The preceding article by Kissinger dealt with the international system in terms of the kind of international environment one national actor, the United States, should seek to create. The following article approaches the same problem but from a more theoretical and general perspective. Instead of examining how a particular actor might constructively and realistically deal with the international milieu, the final selection considers sets of national images, or attitudes, to be a crucial determinant of the evolving structure of the international system and explores how the perceptions people in general hold about reality are related to the behavior of states in the system. This emphasis serves as a takeoff point, or framework, for analyzing the international system as a set of interacting images. Its author, Kenneth E. Boulding, is one of the leading students of international phenomena and has contributed much to that subject through his interdisciplinary approach.

NATIONAL IMAGES AND INTERNATIONAL SYSTEMS

Kenneth E. Boulding

An international system consists of a group of interacting behavior units called "nations" or "countries," to which may sometimes be added certain supra-national organizations, such as the United Nations.

Each of the behavior units in the system can be described in terms of a set of "relevant variables." Just what is relevant and what is not is a matter of judgment of the system-builder, but we think of such things as states of war or peace, degrees of hostility or friendliness, alliance or enmity, arms budgets, geographic extent, friendly or hostile communications, and so on. Having defined our variables, we can then proceed to

Kenneth E. Boulding, "National Images and International Systems," *Journal of Conflict Resolution* 3, 2 (June, 1959): 120-131. Copyright, 1959, by the University of Michigan. Reprinted by permission of the author and publisher.

This paper was presented to a meeting of the American Psychological Association in Washington, D.C., on August 30, 1958.

Boulding is currently director of the Institute of Behavioral Science at the University of Colorado and has served as president of the American Economic Association and the International Studies Association.

postulate certain relationships between them, sufficient to define a path for all the variables through time. Thus we might suppose, with Lewis Richardson,[1] that the rate of change of hostility of one nation toward a second depends on the level of hostility in the second and that the rate of change of hostility of the second toward the first depends on the level of hostility of the first. Then, if we start from given levels of hostility in each nation, these equations are sufficient to spell out what happens to these levels in succeeding time periods. A system of this kind may (or may not) have an *equilibrium* position at which the variables of one period produce an identical set in the next period, and the system exhibits no change through time.

Mechanical systems of this kind, though they are frequently illuminating, can be regarded only as very rough first approximations to the immensely complex truth. At the next level of approximation we must recognize that the people whose decisions determine the policies and actions of nations do not respond to the "objective" facts of the situation, whatever that may mean, but to their "image" of the situation. It is what we think the world is like, not what it is really like, that determines our behavior. If our image of the world is in some sense "wrong," of course, we may be disappointed in our expectations, and we may therefore revise our image; if this revision is in the direction of the "truth" there is presumably a long-run tendency for the "image" and the "truth" to coincide. Whether this is so or not, it is always the image, not the truth, that immediately determines behavior. We act according to the way the world appears to us, not necessarily according to the way it "is." Thus in Richardson's models it is one nation's image of the hostility of another, not the "real" hostility, which determines its reaction. The "image," then, must be thought of as the total cognitive, affective, and evaluative structure of the behavior unit, or its internal view of itself and its universe.[2]

Generally speaking, the behavior of complex organizations can be regarded as determined by *decisions,* and a decision involves the selection of the most preferred position in a contemplated field of choice. Both the field of choice and the ordering of this field by which the preferred position is identified lie in the image of the decision-maker. Therefore, in a system in which decision-makers are an essential element, the study of the ways in which the image grows and changes, both of the field of choice and of the valuational ordering of this field, is of prime importance. The image is always in some sense a product of messages received in the past. It is not, however, a simple inventory or "pile" of such messages but a highly structured piece of information-capital, developed partly by its inputs and outputs of information and partly by internal messages and its own laws of growth and stability.

The images which are important in international systems are those which a nation has of itself and of those other bodies in the system which constitute its international environment. At once a major complication suggests itself. A nation is some complex of the images of the persons who contemplate it, and as there are many different persons, so there are many different images. The complexity is increased by the necessity for inclusion in the image of each person, or at least of many persons, his image of the image of others. This complexity, however, is a property of the real world, not to be evaded or glossed over. It can be reduced to simpler terms if we distinguish between two types of persons in a nation— the powerful, on the one hand, and the ordinary, on the other. This is not, of course, a sharp distinction. The power of a decision-maker may be measured roughly by the number of people which his decisions potentially affect, weighted by some measure of the effect itself. Thus the head of a state is powerful, meaning that his decisions affect the lives of millions of people; the ordinary person is not powerful, for his decisions affect only himself and the lives of a few people around him. There is usually a continuum of power among the persons of a society: thus in international relations there are usually a few very powerful individuals in a state—the chief executive, the prime minister, the secretary of state or minister of foreign affairs, the chiefs of staff of the armed forces. There will be some who are less powerful but still influential—members of the legislature, of the civil service, even journalists, newspaper owners, prominent businessmen, grading by imperceptible degrees down to the common soldier, who has no power of decision even over his own life. For purposes of the model, however, let us compress this continuum into two boxes, labeled the "powerful" and the "ordinary," and leave the refinements of power and influence for later studies.

We deal, therefore, with two representative images, (1) the image of the small group of powerful people who make the actual decisions which lead to war or peace, the making or breaking of treaties, the invasions or withdrawals, alliances, and enmities which make up the major events of international relations, and (2) the image of the mass of ordinary people who are deeply affected by these decisions but who take little or no direct part in making them. The tacit support of the mass, however, is of vital importance to the powerful. The powerful are always under some obligation to represent the mass, even under dictatorial regimes. In democratic societies the aggregate influence of the images of ordinary people is very great; the image of the powerful cannot diverge too greatly from the image of the mass without the powerful losing power. On the other hand, the powerful also have some ability to manipulate the images of the mass toward those of the powerful. This is an important object of instruments as diverse as the public education system, the public relations departments of the armed services, the Russian "agitprop," and the Nazi propaganda ministry.

In the formation of the national images, however, it must be emphasized that impressions of nationality are formed mostly in childhood and usually in the family group. It would be quite fallacious to think of the images as being cleverly imposed on the mass by the powerful. If anything, the reverse is the case: the image is essentially a mass image, or what might be called a "folk image," transmitted through the family and the intimate face-to-face group, both in the case of the powerful and in the case of ordinary persons. Especially in the case of the old, long-established nations, the powerful share the mass image rather than impose it; it is passed on from the value systems of the parents to those of the children, and agencies of public instruction and propaganda merely reinforce the images which derived essentially from the family culture. This is much less true in new nations which are striving to achieve nationality, where the family culture frequently does not include strong elements of national allegiance but rather stresses allegiance to religious ideals or to the family as such. Here the powerful are frequently inspired by a national image derived not from family tradition but from a desire to imitate other nations, and here they frequently try to impose their images on the mass of people. Imposed images, however, are fragile by comparison with those which are deeply internalized and transmitted through family and other intimate sources.

Whether transmitted orally and informally through the family or more formally through schooling and the written word, the national image is essentially a *historical* image—that is, an image which extends through time, backward into a supposedly recorded or perhaps mythological past and forward into an imagined future. The more conscious a people is of its history, the stronger the national image is likely to be. To be an Englishman is to be conscious of "1066 and All That" rather than of "Constantine and All That," or "1776 and All That." A nation is the creation of its historians, formal and informal. The written word and public education contribute enormously to the stability and persistence of the national images. The Jews, for instance, are a creation of the Bible and the Talmud, but every nation has its bible, whether formed into a canon or not—noble words like the Declaration of Independence and the Gettysburg Address—which crystallize the national image in a form that can be transmitted almost unchanged from generation to generation. It is no exaggeration to say that the function of the historian is to pervert the truth in directions favorable to the images of his readers or hearers. Both history and geography as taught in national schools are devised to give "perspective" rather than truth: that is to say, they present the world as seen from the vantage point of the nation. The national geography is learned in great detail, and the rest of the world is in fuzzy outline; the national history is emphasized and exalted; the history of the rest of the world is neglected or even falsified to the glory of the national image.

It is this fact that the national image is basically a lie, or at least a perspective distortion of the truth, which perhaps accounts for the ease with which it can be perverted to justify monstrous cruelties and wickednesses. There is much that is noble in the national image. It has lifted man out of the narrow cage of self-centeredness, or even family-centeredness, and has forced him to accept responsibility, in some sense, for people and events far beyond his face-to-face cognizance and immediate experience. It is a window of some sort on both space and time and extends a man's concern far beyond his own little lifetime and petty interests. Nevertheless, it achieves these virtues usually only at the cost of untruth, and this fatal flaw constantly betrays it. Love of country is perverted into hatred of the foreigner, and peace, order, and justice at home are paid for by war, cruelty, and injustice abroad.

In the formation of the national image the consciousness of great *shared* events and experiences is of the utmost importance. A nation is a body of people who are conscious of having "gone through something" together. Without the shared experience, the national image itself would not be shared, and it is of vital importance that the national image be highly similar. The sharing may be quite vicarious; it may be an experience shared long ago but constantly renewed by the ritual observances and historical memory of the people, like the Passover and the Captivity in the case of the Jews. Without the sharing, however, there is no nation. It is for this reason that war has been such a tragically important element in the creation and sustenance of the national image. There is hardly a nation that has not been cradled in violence and nourished by further violence. This is not, I think, a necessary property of war itself. It is rather that, especially in more primitive societies, war is the one experience which is dramatic, obviously important, and shared by everybody. We are now witnessing the almost unique phenomenon of a number of new nations arising without war in circumstances which are extremely rare in history, for example, India, Ghana, and the new West Indian Federation, though even here there are instances of severe violence, such as the disturbances which accompanied partition in India. It will be interesting to see the effect, if any, on their national images.

We now come to the central problem of this paper, which is that of the impact of national images on the relations among states, that is, on the course of events in international relations. The relations among states can be described in terms of a number of different dimensions. There is, first of all, the dimension of simple geographical space. It is perhaps the most striking single characteristic of the national state as an organization, by contrast with organizations such as firms or churches, that it thinks of itself as occupying, in a "dense" and exclusive fashion, a certain area of the globe. The schoolroom maps which divide the world into colored shapes which are identified as nations have a profound effect on the national image. Apart from the very occasional condominium, it is impossible for a given plot of land on the globe to be associated with two nations at the same time. The territories of nations are divided sharply by frontiers carefully surveyed and frequently delineated by a chain of customs houses, immigration stations, and military installations. We are so accustomed to this arrangement that we think of it as "natural" and take it completely for granted. It is by no means the only conceivable arrangement, however. In primitive societies the geographical image is not sharp enough to define clear frontiers; there may be a notion of the rough territory of a tribe, but, especially among nomadic peoples, there is no clear concept of a frontier and no notion of a nation as something that has a shape on a map. In our own society the shape on the map that symbolizes the nation is constantly drilled into the minds of both young and old, both through formal teaching in schools and through constant repetition in newspapers, advertisements, cartoons, and so on. A society is not inconceivable, however, and might even be desirable, in which nations governed people but not territories and claimed jurisdiction over a defined set of citizens, no matter where on the earth's surface they happened to live.

The territorial aspect of the national state is important in the dynamics of international relations because of the *exclusiveness* of territorial occupation. This means that one nation can generally expand only at the expense of another; an increase in the territory of one is achieved only at the expense of a decrease in the territory of another. This makes for a potential conflict situation. This characteristic of the nation does not make conflict inevitable, but it does make it likely and is at least one of the reasons why the history of international relations is a history of perpetual conflict.

The territorial aspect of international relations is complicated by the fact that in many cases the territories of nations are not homogeneous but are composed of "empires," in which the populations do not identify themselves with the national image of the dominant group. Thus when one nation conquers another and absorbs the conquered territory into an empire, it does not thereby automatically change the culture and allegiances of the conquered nation. The Poles remained Polish for a hundred and twenty-five years of partition between Germany, Austria, and Russia. The Finns retained their nationality through eight hundred years of foreign rule and the Jews, through nearly two thousand years of dispersion. If a nation loses territory occupied by disaffected people, this is much less damaging than the loss of territory inhabited by a well-disposed and loyal population. Thus Turkey, which was the "sick man of Europe" as long as it retained its heterogeneous empire, enjoyed a substantial renewal of national health when stripped of its empire and pushed back to the relatively homogeneous heartland of Anatolia. In this case the loss of a disaffected empire actually strengthened the national unit.

The image of the map-shape of the nations may be an important factor affecting the general frame of mind of the nation. There is a tendency for nations to be uneasy with strong irregularities, enclaves, detached portions, and protuberances or hollows. The ideal shape is at least a convex set, and there is some tendency for nations to be more satisfied if they have regularly round or rectangular outlines. Thus the detachment of East Prussia from the body of Germany by the Treaty of Versailles was an important factor in creating the fanatical discontent of the Nazis.

A second important dimension of the national image is that of hostility or friendliness. At any one time a particular national image includes a rough scale of the friendliness or hostility of, or toward, other nations. The relationship is not necessarily either consistent or reciprocal—in nation A the prevailing image may be that B is friendly, whereas in nation B itself the prevailing image may be one of hostility toward A; or again in both nations there may be an image of friendliness of A toward B but of hostility of B toward A. On the whole, however, there is a tendency toward both consistency and reciprocation—if a nation A pictures itself as hostile toward B, it usually also pictures B as hostile toward it, and the image is likely to be repeated in B. One exception to this rule seems to be observable: most nations seem to feel that their enemies are more hostile toward them than they are toward their enemies. This is a typical paranoid reaction; the nation visualizes itself as surrounded by hostile nations toward which it has only the nicest and friendliest of intentions.

An important subdimension of the hostility-friendliness image is that of the stability or security of the relationship. A friendly relationship is frequently formalized as an alliance. Alliances, however, are shifting; some friendly relations are fairly permanent, others change as the world kaleidoscope changes, as new enemies arise, or as governments change. Thus a bare fifteen or twenty years ago most people in the United States visualized Germany and Japan, even before the outbreak of the war, as enemies, and after Hitler's invasion of Russia, Russia was for a while regarded as a valuable friend and ally. Today the picture is quite changed: Germany and Japan are valuable friends and allies; Russia is the great enemy. We can roughly classify the reciprocal relations of nations along some scale of friendliness-hostility. At one extreme we have stable friendliness, such as between Britain and Portugal or between Britain and the Commonwealth countries. At the other extreme we have stable hostility— the "traditional enemies" such as France and Germany. Between these extremes we have a great many pairs characterized by shifting alliances. On the whole, stable friendly relations seem to exist mainly between strong nations and weaker nations which they have an interest in preserving and stable hostile relations between adjacent nations each of which has played a large part in the formation of the other.

Another important dimension both of the image and of the "reality" of the nation-state is its strength or weakness. This is, in turn, a structure made up of many elements—economic resources and productivity, political organization and tradition, willingness to incur sacrifice and inflict cruelties, and so on. It still makes some kind of sense to assess nations on a strength-weakness scale at any one time. Strength is frequently thought of in military terms as the ability to hurt an opponent or to prevent one's self from being hurt by him. There are also more subtle elements in terms of symbolic loyalties and affections which are hard to assess but which must be included in any complete picture. Many arrays of bristling armaments have been brought low by the sheer inability of their wielders to attract any lasting respect or affection. No social organization can survive indefinitely unless it can command the support of its members, and a continuing sense of the significance of the organization or group as such is much more durable a source of support than is the fleeting booty of war or monopoly. The Jews have outlasted an impressive succession of conquerors. These questions regarding the ultimate sources of continuing strength or weakness are difficult, and we shall neglect them in this paper.

In order to bring together the variables associated with each nation or pair of nations into an international system, we must resort to the device of a matrix, as in Figure 1. Here the hostility-friendliness variable is used as an example. Each cell, a_{ij}, indicates the degree of hostility or friendliness of nation I (of the row) toward nation J (of the column). For purposes of illustration, arbitrary figures have been inserted on a scale from 5 to -5, -5 meaning very hostile, 5 very friendly, and 0 neutral.[3] A matrix

	A	B	C	D	E	Totals
A		−5	+3	0	+2	0
B	−3		−2	−1	−2	−8
C	+2	−4		0	+1	−1
D	−1	−1	0		0	−2
E	+4	−3	+2	0		+3
Totals	+2	−13	+3	−1	+1	−8
X	2	−5	4	+1	−2	0
Y	1	−10½	1	−1½	2	−8

FIGURE 1

of this kind has many interesting properties, not all of which can be worked out here but which depend on the kind of restraints that we impose on it. If we suppose, for instance, that the relations of nations are reciprocal, so that I's attitude toward J is the same as J's toward I, the matrix becomes symmetrical about its major diagonal—that is, the lower left-hand triangle is a mirror image of the upper right-hand triangle. This is a very severe restriction and is certainly violated in fact: there are unrequited loves and hates among the nations as there are among individuals. We can recognize a *tendency*, however, for the matrix to become symmetrical. There is a certain instability about an unrequited feeling. If I loves J and J hates I, then either J's constant rebuff of I's affections will turn I's love to hate, or I's persistent wooing will break down J's distaste and transform it into affection. Unfortunately for the history of human relations, the former seems to be the more frequent pattern, but the latter is by no means unknown.[4]

The sum totals of the rows represent the overall friendliness or hostility of the nation at the head of the row; the sum totals of the columns represent the degree of hostility or friendliness *toward* the nation at the head of the column. The sum of either of these sums (which must be equal, as each represents a way of adding up all the figures of the matrix) is a measure of the overall friendliness or hostility of the system. In the example of Figure 1, B is evidently a "paranoid" nation, feeling hostile toward everyone and receiving hostility in return; D is a "neutral" nation, with low values for either hostility or friendliness; E is a "friendly" nation, reciprocating B's general hostility but otherwise having positive relations with everyone. In this figure it is evident that A, C, and E are likely to be allied against B, and D is likely to be uncommitted.

In the matrix of Figure 1 no account is taken of the relative size or power of the different nations. This dimension of the system can easily be accommodated, however. All that is necessary is to take the power of the smallest nation as a convenient unit and express the power of the others in multiples of this unit. Then in the matrix we simply give each nation a number of places along the axes equal to the measure of its power. Thus in Figure 2 we suppose a system of three nations, where B is twice as powerful as C and A is three times as powerful as $C;$ A is then allotted three spaces along the axes, B two, and C one. The analysis of the matrix proceeds as before, with the additional constraint that all the figures in the larger boxes bounded by the lines which divide the nations should be the same, as in the figure.

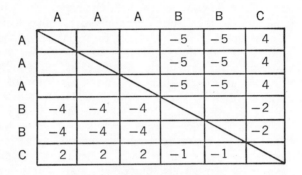

	A	A	A	B	B	C
A				−5	−5	4
A				−5	−5	4
A				−5	−5	4
B	−4	−4	−4			−2
B	−4	−4	−4			−2
C	2	2	2	−1	−1	

FIGURE 2

The difference between the sum of a nation's column, representing the general degree of support or affection it *receives,* and the sum of a nation's row, representing the sum of support or affection it *gives,* might be called its *affectional balance.* This is shown in the row X in Figure 1. It is a necessary property of a matrix of this kind that the sum of all these balances shall be zero. They measure the relative position of each nation in regard to the degree of support it can expect from the international system as a whole. Thus in Figure 1 it is clear that B is in the worst position, and C in the best position, vis-à-vis the system as a whole. Another figure of some interest might be called the *affectional contribution,* shown in the line Y. This is the mean of the column and row totals for each nation. The total affectional contribution is equal to the total of all the figures of the matrix, which measures the general hostility or friendliness of the whole system. The affectional contribution is then a rough measure of how much each nation contributes to the general level of hostility of the whole system. Thus in the example of Figure 1 we see that nation B (the paranoid) actually contributes more than 100 per cent to the total hostility of the system, its extreme hostility being offset to some extent by other nations' friendliness.

One critical problem of an international system, then, is that of the *dynamics* of the hostility matrix. We can conceive of a succession of such matrices at successive points of time. If there is a system with a "solution," we should be able to predict the matrix at t_1 from the knowledge we have of the matrix at t_0 or at various earlier times. The matrix itself will not, in general, carry enough information to make such predictions possible, even though it is easy to specify theoretical models in which a determinate dynamic system can be derived from the information in the matrix alone.[5]

The difficulty with "simple" systems of this nature is that they are very much more simple than the reality which they symbolize. This is because, in reality, the variables of the system consist of the innumerable dimensions of the images of large numbers of people, and the dynamics of the image are much more complex than the dynamics of mechanical systems. This is because of the structural nature of the image; it cannot be represented simply by a set of quantities or variables. Because of this structural nature, it is capable occasionally of very dramatic changes as a message hits some vital part of the structure and the whole image reorganizes itself. Certain events—like the German invasion of Belgium in 1914, the Japanese attack on Pearl Harbor in 1941, the American use of the atom bomb at Hiroshima and Nagasaki, the merciless destruction of Dresden, and the Russian success with Sputnik I—have profound effects and possibly long-run effects on reorganizing the various national images. The "reorganizing" events are hard both to specify and to predict; they introduce, however, a marked element of uncertainty into any dynamic international system which does not exist, for instance, in the solar system!

In spite of this difficulty, which, oddly enough, is particularly acute in short-term prediction, one gets the impression from the observation of history that we are in the presence of a true system with a real dynamic of its own. We do observe, for instance, cumulative processes of hostility. If we had some measures of the hostility matrix, however crude, it would be possible to identify these processes in more detail, especially the "turning points." There is an analogy here with the business cycle, which also represents a system of cumulative stochastic processes subject to occasional "reorganizations" of its basic equations. Just as we can trace cumulative upward and downward movements in national income, the downward movements often (though not always) culminating in financial crisis and the upward movements often leading to inflation and a subsequent downturn, so we can trace cumulative movements in the hostility matrix. We have "prewar" periods corresponding to downswings, in which things go from bad to worse and hostility constantly increases. The total of all the hostility figures (e.g., -8 on Fig. 1) is a striking analogue of the national-income concept. It might be called the "international temperature." Just as there is a certain critical point in a deflation at which a financial crisis is likely to ensue because of the growing insolvency of heavily indebted businesses, so there is a critical point in the rise of hostility at which war breaks out. This critical point itself depends on a number of different factors and may not be constant. Some nations may be more tolerant of hostility than others; as the cost of war increases, the tolerance of hostility also increases, as we see today in the remarkable persistence of the "cold war." A deflation or downturn, however, *may* reverse itself without a crisis, and a "prewar" period may turn into a "postwar" period without a war. Indeed, in the period since 1945 we might identify almost as many small international cycles as there have been business cycles! The "upturn" may be a result of a change of government, the death of certain prominent individuals, or even a change of heart (or image!) on the part of existing rulers. The catharsis of a war usually produces the typical "postwar" period following, though this is often tragically short, as it was after the end of World War II, when a "downturn" began after the revolution in Czechoslovakia. The downturn is often the result of the reassertion of a persistent, long-run character of the system after a brief interlude of increasing friendliness. There seems to be a certain long-run tendency of an international system toward hostility, perhaps because of certain inescapable flaws in the very concept of a national image, just as there also seems to be a long-run tendency of an unregulated and undisturbed market economy toward deflation.

In considering the dynamics of an international system, the essential properties of the image matrix might be summed up in a broad concept of "compatibility." If the change in the system makes for greater compatibility the system may move to an equilibrium. The "balance-of-power" theory postulates the existence of an equilibrium of this nature. The record of history, however, suggests that, in the past at least, international systems have usually been unstable. The incompatibility of various national images has led to changes in the system which have created still greater incompatibility, and the system has moved to less and less stable situations until some crisis, such as war, is reached, which represents a discontinuity in the system. After a war the system is reorganized; some national units may disappear, others change their character, and the system starts off again. The incompatibility may be of many kinds, and it is a virtue of this kind of rather loose model that the historian can fill in the endlessly various details in the special situations which he studies. The model is a mere dress form on which the historian swathes the infinite variations of fashion and fact.

In the model we can distinguish two very different kinds of incompatibility of images. The first might be called "real" incompatibility, where we have two images of the future in which realization of one would prevent the realization of the other. Thus two nations may both claim a certain piece of territory, and each may feel dissatisfied unless the territory is incorporated into it. (One thinks of the innumerable irredenta which have stained the pages of history with so much blood!) Or two nations may both wish to feel stronger than, or superior to, each other. It is possible for two nations to be in a position where each is stronger than the other *at home,* provided that they are far enough apart and that the "loss of .power gradient" (which measures the loss of power of each as we remove the point of application farther and farther from the home base) is large enough. It is rarely possible, however, for two nations each to dominate the other, except in the happy situation where each suffers from delusions of grandeur.

The other form of incompatibility might be called "illusory" incompatibility, in which there exists a condition of compatibility which would satisfy the "real" interests of the two parties but in which the dynamics of the situation or the illusions of the parties create a situation of perverse dynamics and misunderstandings, with increasing hostility simply as a result of the reactions of the parties to each other, not as a result of any basic differences of interest. We must be careful about this distinction: even "real" incompatibilities are functions of the national images rather than of physical fact and are therefore subject to change and control. It is hard for an ardent patriot to realize that his country is a mental, rather than a physical, phenomenon, but such indeed is the truth! It is not unreasonable to suppose, however, that "real" incompatibilities are more intractable and less subject to "therapy" than illusory ones.

One final point of interest concerns what might be called the impact of "sophistication" or "self-consciousness" on national images and the international system. The process of sophistication in the image is a very general one, and we cannot follow all its ramifications here. It occurs in every person in greater or less degree as he grows into adult awareness of himself as part of a larger system. It is akin almost to a Copernican revolution: the unsophisticated image sees the world only from the viewpoint of the viewer; the sophisticated image sees the world from many imagined viewpoints, as a system in which the viewer is only a part. The child sees everything through his own eyes and refers everything to his own immediate comfort. The adult learns to see the world through the eyes of others; his horizon extends to other times, places, and cultures than his own; he learns to distinguish between those elements in his experience which are universal and those which are particular. Many grown people, of course, never become adults in this sense, and it is these who fill our mental hospitals with themselves and their children.

The scientific subculture is an important agency in the sophistication of images. In the physical world we no longer attribute physical phenomena to spirits analogous to our own. In the social sciences we have an agency whereby men reach self-consciousness about their own cultures and institutions and therefore no longer regard these as simply given to them by "nature." In economics, for instance, we have learned to see the system as a whole, to realize that many things which are true of individual behavior are not true of the system and that the system itself is not incapable of a modicum of control. We no longer, for instance, regard depressions as "acts of God" but as system-made phenomena capable of control through relatively minor system change.

The national image, however, is the last great stronghold of unsophistication. Not even the professional international relations experts have come very far toward seeing the system as a whole, and the ordinary citizen and the powerful statesman alike have naïve, self-centered, and unsophisticated images of the world in which their nation moves. Nations are divided into "good" and "bad"—the enemy is all bad, one's own nation is of spotless virtue. Wars are either acts of God or acts of the other nations, which always catch us completely by surprise. To a student of international systems the national image even of respectable, intellectual, and powerful people seems naïve and untrue. The patriotism of the sophisticated cannot be a simple faith. There is, however, in the course of human history a powerful and probably irreversible movement toward sophistication. We can wise up, but we cannot wise down except at enormous cost in the breakdown of civilizations, and not even a major breakdown results in much loss of knowledge. This movement must be taken into account in predicting the future of the international system. The present system as we have known it for the past hundreds or even thousands of years is based on the widespread acceptance of unsophisticated images, such as, for instance, that a nation can be made more secure *merely* by increasing its armaments. The growth of a systems-attitude toward international relations will have profound consequences for the dynamics of the system itself, just as the growth of a systems-attitude in economics has profound consequences for the dynamics of the economic system.

If, as I myself believe, we live in an international system so unstable that it threatens the very existence of life on earth, our main hope for change may lie in the rapid growth of sophistication, especially at the level of the images of the powerful. Sophistication, of course, has its dangers also. It is usually but a hair's-breadth removed from sophistry, and a false sophistication (of which Marxism in some respects is a good example) can be even more destructive to the stability of a system than a naïve image. Whichever way we move, however, there is danger. We have no secure place to stand where we are, and we live in a time when intellectual investment in developing more adequate international images and theories of international systems may bear an enormous rate of return in human welfare.

NOTES

[1]See Anatol Rapoport, "Lewis F. Richardson's Mathematical Theory of War," *Journal of Conflict Resolution*, I (September, 1957), 249, for an excellent exposition.

[2]See K. E. Boulding, *The Image* (Ann Arbor: University of Michigan Press, 1956), for an exposition of the theory on which this paper is based.

[3]The problem of the measurement of hostility (or friendliness) is a very interesting one which we cannot go into extensively here but which is not so hopeless of solution as might at first sight appear. Possible avenues are as follows: (1) A historical approach. Over a period of years two nations have been at war, threatening war, allied, bound by treaty, and so on. Each relation would be given an arbitrary number, and each year assigned a number accordingly: the average of the years' numbers would be the index. This would always yield a symmetrical matrix—that is, the measure of I's relation to J would be the same as J's relation to I, or $a_{if} = a_{ji}$. (2) An approach by means of content analysis of public communications (official messages, newspaper editorials, public speeches, cartoons, etc.). This seems likely to be most immediately useful and fruitful, as it would give current information and would also yield very valuable dynamic information about the *changes* in the matrix, which may be much more important than the absolute figures. The fact that any measure of this kind is highly arbitrary is no argument against it, provided that it is qualitatively reliable— that is, moves generally in the same direction as the variable which it purports to measure— and provided also that the limitations of the measure are clearly understood. It would probably be advisable to check the second type of measure against the more objective measures derived from the first method. The difficulty of the first method, however, is the extreme instability of the matrix. The affections of nations are ephemeral!

[4]George F. Kennan once said: "It is an undeniable privilege of every man to prove himself in the right in the thesis that the world is his enemy; for if he reiterates it frequently enough and makes it the background of his conduct, he is bound eventually to be right" ("The Roots of Soviet Conduct," *Foreign Affairs,* July, 1947). If for "enemy" we read "friend" in this statement, the proposition seems to be equally true but much less believed.

[5]As a very simple example of such a system, let $(a_{ij})t$ be a cell of the matrix at time t and $(a_{ij})t + 1$ be the corresponding value at time $t + 1$. Then if for each cell we can postulate a function $(a_{ij})t+1 = F(a_{ij})_t$ we can derive the whole $t + 1$ matrix from the t matrix. This is essentially the dynamic method of Lewis F. Richardson, and in fairly simple cases it provides an interesting way of formulating certain aspects of the system, especially its tendency toward *cumulative* movements of hostility (arms races) or occasionally of friendliness.

As one begins reading this selection, he might get the idea that the author is attempting to develop an explanation for the instability and hostility that appear to have been characteristic of the international political system in the contemporary world. The author argues that, since people's attitudes and perceptions are what determines their behavior, the present nature of the international political system is a consequence of their images. In talking about the future, Boulding concludes that there may be a trend away from the dangerous national images that have caused so much hostility and instability to a "systems-attitude" that may result in a change in the basic nature of the international political system.

A careful reading of the selection, however, might lead one to conclude that the author's purpose is not to build a systematic explanation upon which to project the evolution of the international political system but to argue for replacing national images with system-oriented images. In addition to ignoring systematic observation as a method of testing his basic explanatory propositions, Boulding's attempt to trace the basic features of the international system to one general cause, the images of people, shows a greater concern for convincing the reader with a self-contained and relatively simple argument than providing a scholarly set of explanations and predictions. No matter how appealing we find Boulding's explanation, we would not be unjustified in concluding that his choice of images as the key to change is as much a result of his desire to change people's images as it is of his belief that images can be used to explain and project trends in the international political system.

At issue here is the question of how much reliance can be placed on a single concept in discussing general features of the international political system. Given the difficulty one might have in identifying changing images, as well as the problem that Boulding almost totally ignores, namely, whose images are changing or need to be changed, it seems unreasonable to invest such a large amount of explanation in an important but highly inarticulated concept. If one argues that Boulding was attempting to provide a discussion of the evolving international political system, criticism of his reliance on a single concept would be justified.

If, however, one viewed the selection as a sermon to mankind that there is a need for men to become more sophisticated in viewing the world around them, then the article may be viewed as prescription. Clearly, Boulding has illustrated the consequences of national images even though he has not systematically tested their role in the contemporary world. Similarly, he has shown the possible effect of more system-oriented images, although he has not provided any evidence that such images are on the increase. Nevertheless, the selection may be viewed as the contribution of a brilliant mind attempting to deal with what he perceives to be mankind's central problem—the peaceful management of international affairs. Thus, like Kissinger, Boulding is concerned with international conflict, with its effect on the international system and its cure. While both authors seem to agree that the actions and beliefs of actors with respect to the world community can make an impact on the type of system that exists, they differ somewhat on the kinds of behavior and attitudes that are most conducive to the creation of a peaceful world environment. Neither is content with the system as it exists, and both believe that a nationalistic orientation is detrimental to the construction of a more peaceful world, although there are subtle and major differences in the options each proposes for bringing about that world. Nevertheless, the style of argumentation is very similar; both present their prescriptive evaluations in terms of logical critiques and appeals to a sense of justice. Such a style is typical of prescriptive analysis found in the literature, although other modes of prescriptive inquiry exist, as the Harkavy reading in Chapter 2 illustrates.

5

Description, Explanation, and Prescription in Perspective

In addition to providing an overview for the entire book, this discussion of the readings in Chapters 2 through 4 is designed to help you weigh the strengths and weaknesses of various approaches employed in the study for contemporary international politics. In the table below, the readings

TABLE 3
Classification of Readings by Task and Level Analysis

	Description	Explanation	Prescription
ACTORS	Holsti Rosenau	Allison Wittkopf Wilkenfeld	Morgenthau Harkavy
INTER- ACTIONS	Angell Bronfen- brenner	Azar Russett	Kelman Singer- Small
SYSTEM	Kaplan Coplin	Singer- Wallace Deutsch- Singer Deutsch	Boulding Kissinger

are classified for review. The columns identify, somewhat arbitrarily, the readings that focus primarily on observation, explanation, and prescription. The rows divide the readings into the three levels of analysis by which the book is organized: actors, interactions, and system. The levels of analysis are not very distinct but are useful in delineating the major units of analysis employed in international relations research.

DESCRIPTION

In the introductory chapter, we pointed out that the student of international politics is far removed from direct observation of events comprised by the field. The readings clearly illustrate how various authors have dealt with the fact that they are relatively isolated from the phenomena. For purposes of discussion, we might identify three approaches to description in the study of international politics.

First, some scholars do not attempt to provide systematic descriptions because they are more concerned with some other type of analysis, usually prescription. For example, although Morgenthau has a definite view of modern international politics, he does not spend much time on demonstrating that his image corresponds to reality. He cites some isolated events to support his descriptive assumptions, but he does not seriously consider the possibility that his view of international politics is reliable or accurate. Many scholars have pursued such a course in describing international politics. In addition to using isolated events to support their view, they sometimes cite other scholars. But, for the most part, they do little to demonstrate the adequateness of their descriptions.

Another approach to description is to concentrate primarily on the development of concepts. Illustrating this pattern are selections by Rosenau and Kaplan, who identify classes or categories that can be used in describing specific aspects of international politics. For example, Rosenau suggest ways of classifying the factors that might contribute to foreign-policy decisions, while Kaplan postulates six types of systems, four of which might correspond to past and present international systems. In providing a conceptual map that serves as a guide to the objects of observation, these authors hope to be able to develop categories and distinctions that will lead to more systematic observation and more valid explanations. Although concepts developed by authors cannot be evaluated until they are employed in research, this concept-development approach is a prerequisite to the third approach, systematic observation.

Using this third approach to observation are writers such as Holsti, Angell, Wittkopf, and Azar. They are concerned not only with developing concepts but also with collecting data according to specific rules that relate the concepts to empirical reality. Their data sources and their procedures are greatly varied—from Wittkopf and Wilkenfeld's uses of aggregate data from sources such as the *United Nations Statistical Yearbook,* to Holsti's content analysis of the speeches of John Foster Dulles, to Angell's study of the flow of transactions among states, to, finally, Russett's and Azar's coding of historical events. Some are willing to be satisfied with identifying patterns through observation (for example, Angell), while others seek to relate two or more sets of systematic observations to each other (as in Wittkopf, Russett, and Azar). Regardless of the ends to which they are directed, these procedures for systematic observation greatly enhance the accuracy and precision of observations and thereby increase our confidence in them.

Before one concludes too quickly that systematic observation is preferable to the other two patterns of observation, two factors ought to be considered. First, if the scholar's purpose is to explain or prescribe, he may have neither the resources (such as time, money, or methodoligical tools) nor the inclination to perform systematic observations. In this case, the author is trading off his obligation to be as open as possible to reality with his desire to provide explanation or to "set the world straight." All too often in the past, scholars have been too willing to make that trade, and the study of international politics has suffered. Nevertheless, the tension between explanation and prescription, on the one hand, and systematic observation, on the other, clearly exists. It ought to be recognized as endemic in most international relations research, given the limitation on resources that plague all scholars.

The second factor to consider when judging scholars' description procedures in international politics is the progress of the discipline and the availability of data. For example, when Rosenau wrote the article excerpted in this book, scholarly activity was not sufficiently advanced to warrant the systematic collecting of data. In fact, the primary consequence of Rosenau's work during the 1960's was to stimulate scholars to develop methods for systematic data collection on the foreign-policy behavior of states.

Moreover, some international political concepts may never be suceptible to systematic observation techniques, because the phenomena are so remote from the scholar. Conditions such as the mental state of the individual who is making foreign-policy decisions or the political bargaining within specific international conferences that takes place behind closed doors may only be observed through unsystematic methods such as anecdotes in memoirs or hearsay information. Recognizing this fact, however, does not mean that one should ignore the problems of observation, or that he should study only what he can observe systematically. Rather, he should make clear to the reader and himself the basis for, and the tentative nature of, his observations.

EXPLANATION

In the first chapter, we noted the variety of ways in which explanation has been conceived. There is little agreement on what kind of explanation is sufficient. Most scholars would agree that explanation is the process of attaching cause to effect. But the selections throughout the book are testimony to the diversity of approaches scholars have employed to explain different aspects of international politics. This section will discuss four dimensions that appear to affect how scholars approach explanation in international relations research.

The first dimension concerns the sample of phenomena about which the scholar attempts to generalize. The sample size can range from only one case to the entire universe of relevant cases. For example, Allison's discussion of the Cuban Missile Crisis or Azar's discussion of the Suez crisis, in contrast to Wilkenfeld's analysis of seventy-four nations and Singer and Wallace's examination of thirty historical periods between 1816 and 1964. Somewhere in the middle are studies of ten to twenty cases by Russett.

The size of the sample greatly affects the nature of the resulting explanations. Other things being equal, with fewer cases the complexity of the explanation will be greater; that is, with a larger number of variables and a greater complexity of relationships among them, the detail and sufficiency of explanation for those cases will be greater. The Allison selection involved a large number of variables, such as the nature of the problem, information processes, bureaucratic structure, and the like. It related each to the other in numerous ways. In contrast, the Wilkenfeld study employed only four variables and searched for relatively simple relationships among them that held cross-nationally for many cases. The Russett study contains fewer and more simply related variables than Allison's study but substantially more complexity than Wilkenfeld's. By focusing on one or a few cases, a scholar is better able to explain them in depth and discover their unique features.

One should not conclude, however, that single-case studies are somehow superior to studies employing many cases. The latter are preferable if one is willing to sacrifice highly complex and relatively complete explanations. This is because, with more cases, one can have more confidence that explanations are generalizable to, and valid for, similar phenomena. For the higher level of generality rises, the greater becomes our ability to find widely applicable generalizations about cause and effect that are necessary to develop abstract theory. Thus, because Russett attempted to generalize about the factors related to deterrence from a number of cases, we have more confidence in his findings than we would have had if he had done a single-case study. Although we can never be sure that a generalization will hold for every case, our confidence is increased if these theoretical explanations are tested in a large number of cases.

There appears to be a clear trade-off of this confidence between single-case studies and those involving a large number of cases. The figure below represents this trade-off in terms of a conflict between the desire for complete and complex explanations, on the one hand, and the desire for highly generalizable and testable explanations, on the other. There are costs and benefits to the choice that the international relations scholar makes, and these should be borne in mind when considering how a subject should be investigated.

A second dimension apparent in scholars' explanations is the mixture of deductive and inductive logic. At one extreme are the Deutsch-Singer and Kaplan studies that posit a few premises to suggest future patterns of international activity. A shade less deductive is the Allison article, which attempts to apply three complex models of foreign-policy behavior to the same set of data. At the other extreme are the Wilkenfeld and Deutsch selections, which examine empirical reality to suggest and to test specific theoretical propositions. The Russett selection represents

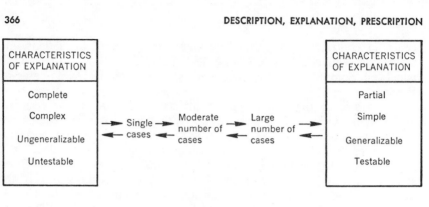

FIGURE 1
Trade-Offs in Number of Cases Selected for Study

almost an equal balance between deductive and inductive procedures because it applies specific theoretical ideas to a moderately large sample.

One of the long-standing debates among scholars in all the social sciences is the proper balance between theory and data. Although few scholars would advocate that either is acceptable without reference to the other, debate continues over how much theory and how much data are appropriate. Since the answer depends in part on the nature of the research question, no universal guideline can be presented. The most that can be said is that scholars should strive to give their theoretical explanations empirical content and should undertake inductive observation of reality with the aim of generating and testing theoretical explanations.

A third dimension of scholarly approaches to explanation is the kinds of general theoretical frameworks, or, more specifically, explanatory procedures, that are employed. In general, scholars have approached explanation through the following seven frameworks.

Some authors say they are merely inductively *searching for patterns,* but implicit in their search is the hope that the patterns will suggest explanatory relationships. Hence, Angell's attempt to identify the growth of transnational participation is structured by his underlying assumption that this particular pattern will affect the behavior of states and the future of the international political system.

Others concentrate on *correlation analysis of variables.* While correlation certainly does not denote causation, it helps investigations see the relationship of factors that may be causally linked and thus aids explanation. Wittkopf, for example, uses correlation analysis to investigate relationships between the characteristics of aid recipients and the pattern of aid-giving by the United States, on the assumption that these characteristics may help to explain why the United States gives foreign aid. Wilkenfeld uses correlation to identify relationships between internal characteristics of states and their foreign-policy behaviors. Singer and Wallace attempt to see whether growth of intergovernmental organizations is correlated with the outbreak of war.

Some explanations are set in terms of *cause and effect*. That is, scholars search for antecedent conditions that are necessary and sufficient for the resultant condition. Two examples are Bronfenbrenner's attempt to attribute hostility between the United States and the Soviet Union to the so-called mirror-image effect and Harkavy's attempt to demonstrate that economic development is related to reduced population growth rates.

Other scholars seek *functional explanations:* They frame their explanations in terms of functions by relating the structure and behavior of certain entities to the performance of particular functions or tasks. We explain something by noting its purpose and the role it performs, including the consequences of those functions for the larger structure in which it is imbedded. For example, Coplin describes international law in terms of its function of communicating the shared assumptions about the international system held by national leaders.

Explanations may be cast in a *predictive* framework, although some explanations may in no way be predictive and statistical prediction is possible without an answer to the question why. Explanatory prediction is provided when prediction involves identifying the antecedent variables, or determinants, that predict or cause consequent conditions. Deutsch and Singer make projections based on certain assumptions about the influence of specific factors on future conditions. These projections are based on theoretical explanations that may or may not be valid.

Some writers seek theoretical explanations in *phenomena analogous to international politics*. For example, Kelman uses a number of works by psychologists on the attitudes of individuals toward a variety of subjects like race relations and American television to generalize about the role of international interchanges on beliefs about other nations. Or, to take another example, Kaplan employs concepts from cybernetics —the study of man and machines—to characterize patterns of international relations. Although the ultimate question is how similar these phenomena are to international politics, it is often useful to search for theoretical explanations in other fields in order to suggest propositions that may be tested in international politics.

Finally, some scholars employ a *systems framework* to generate explanations. Systems analysis enjoys a variety of versions and applications, but its basic idea is to design a simplified model of a complex entity that may then be defined by its systematic characteristics. A system consists of a set of interrelated and interdependent variables and actors, and a description of their interaction provides an explanation of the system's behavior. For instance, Kaplan attempts to identify actors and rules of behavior for different kinds of international systems, focusing on patterns of authority and interactions. His aim is to provide an explanation of the behavior of states by demonstrating that such behavior is attributable to regularities in international patterns of behavior.

These seven approaches to explanation are not mutually exclusive or exhaustive. Scholars often begin in one mode and switch to another. Moreover, it is difficult to say whether one approach is any better than another. Two modes that should be avoided in a study of two simple variables are functional and system description, because their use creates excess jargon. In more complex cases, however, it is not always advisable to reject one mode entirely at the expense of the other. Each mode has its assets and liabilities. The important thing to keep in mind is that each framework, or explanatory procedure, carries certain implicit assumptions that should be continuously watched if one is going to avoid being led unwittingly to the wrong conclusion.

A final dimension characterizing scholarly explanations is the level of analysis at which the study is focused. The threefold classification of actors, interaction, and system is particularly useful in this respect, because it distinguishes three major focal points in the study of international politics.

Although a particular study may focus on the actor level, it must also be concerned with the other two levels. Most studies that focus on one level make certain assumptions about other levels. For example, the Boulding selection attempts to relate explicitly the actor level to the system level by arguing that images held by people affect the way things happen in the international political system. Boulding can be faulted for failing to be clear about what actors he is talking about (i.e., mass or elites), but he is clear in his attempt to relate the levels.

Frequently, scholars fail to be clear about the relationship among the three levels. For example, Bronfenbrenner cites his personal experience while a visitor to the Soviet Union as evidence of the mirror-image effect in governmental perceptions. He also implies that perceptions of governmental officials may affect the interaction patterns among states and even the general level of tension in the international system.

To deal with the impact of various levels on the particular level with which they are most concerned, some writers hold the other levels constant. For example, the Deutsch-Singer essay treats all actors as if they were the same and builds its projections and explanations on assumptions about the way states interact and the implications of that interaction for the international political system. Their attempt to hold the actor level constant does not mean that they assume that level to be irrelevant or unrelated to the phenomena they are attempting to understand. Rather, it shows their care in explicitly defining the level of analysis from which they are working.

Thus, the choice of level of analysis involves a choice in the focus of one's study, not a theoretical assumption that other levels are irrelevant. Those interested in the behavior of actors would make a grave mistake if they did not consider the impact of interactions among states and the general conditions in the international political system as determinants of that actor's behavior. Those interested in interactions must be concerned with the nature of the system and the impact of events within specific societies. Finally, those concerned with the international political system cannot ignore the fact that the system is the product, over a long period of time, of the behavior of states and the interactions between them.

These four dimensions help us to understand how scholars develop explanations about international politics. Knowing the author's reason for choosing a particular sample size, the role of deductive and inductive analysis, the type of language and general theoretical framework employed, and the level of analysis and its relation to other levels is critical for understanding the author's research. We have tried to show that in each dimension there are no single correct choices. The scholar's purposes and style ought to determine, for example, whether he uses few or many cases, or whether he employs correlational techniques or systems terminology. The important thing for you as a reader of the scholarly works of others is to determine where the author stands on each of these dimensions. Even more important, when you undertake research in the area of international politics, it is imperative that you be as clear about these factors as possible.

PRESCRIPTION

In the first chapter, we noted that an inevitable aspect of our study is concern for the consequences of international politics in terms of the values of the human beings who will be affected by those consequences. The prescriptive analyses provided in these readings indicate that the purpose and style of prescription vary substantially from scholar to scholar. We will discuss four aspects of the variation.

The first has to do with the purposes of the scholar and can be discussed most fruitfully by asking at whom the prescription is directed. In order to answer this question, one must distinguish methodological prescription from substantive prescription. The former is directed at other scholars; for example, Rosenau's suggestions on how to approach the study of foreign policy comparatively. The latter is directed at some actor in the political arena; for example, Morgenthau's attack on American foreign policy in Vietnam and Kissinger's speech on the evolving international system.

Although one might assume that it is impossible to confuse prescriptions to scholars about methods or concepts with prescriptions to actors about foreign policy, the confusion appears frequently in the international politics literature. The Boulding article, for example, might be viewed as a discussion of the proper approach to the study of international politics, but it may be viewed with as much or more justification as an attack on the nationalistic xenophobia that Boulding assumes to be part of the conditions leading to instability in international politics. In fact, scholars frequently confuse discussions of the usefulness of concepts with discussions of the substance of foreign policy. This confusion is difficult to avoid in a field that borrows many of its concepts from the usage of practitioners.

Assuming the scholar is trying to prescribe conditions in international politics (as opposed to prescribing how to study international politics), some variation in prescriptive analysis also exists, primarily in terms of the level-of-analysis distinction discussed earlier. Morgenthau makes suggestions about the policy of a state (the United States) in a particular area of the world (Vietnam), while Kelman calls for an alteration in the way states interact, and Kissinger calls for specific changes at the international system level. Boulding operates at even broader level when he calls for a change in the basic attitudes of all people, especially those most influential in the making of foreign policy.

A second aspect of prescription in our field has to do with the degree to which the values underlying the prescription are made explicit. Singer and Small call for the need to be explicit about criteria employed to evaluate international relations and demonstrate how such indicators might be developed with respect to the value predisposition against warfare. In contrast, Morgenthau, with his implicit emphasis on particular values, represents the type of prescription frequently found in the international politics literature.

The identification of value orientations ought to be made clearly in any attempt at prescriptive analysis. Without such clear identification, one cannot determine the author's position. In the Morgenthau essay, for example, what underlying values does the author hold? We might assume that he abhors war, but we know from his other writings that Morgenthau considers war to be an appropriate foreign-policy tool under certain circumstances. Similarly, a reading of Kissinger's selection reveals a number of explicitly stated values like peace and human justice, but it also demonstrates a very strong, hidden commitment to the maintenance of a major American presence in many areas of the world. While Kissinger might be excused for failing to make this prescription clear because he wrote the selection as part of an address by the Secretary of State, scholars who are writing for nonofficial purposes cannot be excused. Without clearly specifying goals, prescription provides little by which to judge the author's argument.

A third aspect of prescription concerns the amount of effort put into description and explanation. Many articles throughout the book contain prescriptive sections, not for a major purpose but to extend implications of the study. Holsti, for example, developed some prescriptive implications from his systematic observations of Dulles's foreign-policy statements. Similarly, Singer and Small demonstrate how systematic research can be used to evaluate conditions resulting from the interactions of states. These two studies contrast sharply with the lack of systematic description underlying the prescriptions rendered by Morgenthau on U.S. policy in Vietnam and Bronfenbrenner's personal observations that led him to criticize the mirror image he saw operating in Soviet-American relations.

Policy prescription should be based on prior scholarly attempts at systematic description and explanation. The polemicist is short on facts and long on rhetoric. The scholar must learn, instead, to recognize the possible consequences and policy implications of his research. This suggestion applies clearly to scholars concerned with prescription but less so to those concerned with the day-to-day operation of foreign policy. The latter may not have the time to make the systematic description and evaluate the scholarly explanations. Therefore, it is even more important for scholars to take the time and share their part of the burden of designing foreign policy.

The above discussion is based on an implicit value that again should be made clear. We place a high value on tentativeness as a prescriptive style, and, with limitations, it is very much in order. Like the medieval alchemist who attempted to provide medical advice with little data and poor explanatory theory, scholars have the right and obligation to provide policy advice, but uncertainty and defensiveness should not be cloaked in dogmatism. If our goal is to create a better world, we must first be prepared to look and understand before we leap. Our prescriptive judgments should be recognized as opinions that are not subject to proof or disconfirmation, and it is pretentious to present them as more conclusive, valid, or worthy than any other evaluation.

Selected Bibliography

1. Alger, Chadwick F. "Intergovernmental Relations in Organizations and Their Significance for International Conflict." In *The Nature of Human Conflict,* ed., Elton M. McNeil. Englewood Cliffs, N.J.: Prentice-Hall, 1965.
2. Alger, Chadwick F.; and Brams, Steven J. "Patterns of Representation in National Capitals and Intergovernmental Organizations." *World Politics* 19 (July 1967): 646-63.
3. Alker, Hayward R., Jr.; and Puchala, Donald. "Trends in Economic Partnership: The North Atlantic Area, 1928-1963." In *Quantitative International Politics: Insights and Evidence,* ed., J. David Singer. New York: Free Press, 1968, 287-316.
4. Alker, Hayward R., Jr.; and Russett, Bruce M. *World Politics in the General Assembly.* New Haven, Conn.: Yale University Press, 1965.
5. Almond, Gabriel A. *The American People and Foreign Policy.* New York: Harcourt, Brace and World, 1950.
6. Aron, Raymond. *The Century of Total War.* Garden City, N.Y.: Doubleday, 1954.
7. ———. *Peace and War: A Theory of International Relations,* trans. Richard Howard and Annette Baker Fox. Garden City, N.Y.: Doubleday, 1966.
8. Azar, Edward. "Analysis of International Events." *Peace Research Reviews* 4 (November 1970).
9. Baldwin, William L. *The Structure of the Defense Market, 1955-1964.* Durham, N.C.: Duke University Press, 1967.
10. Ball, George W. *The Discipline of Power: Essentials of a Modern World Structure.* Boston: Little, Brown, 1968.
11. Banfield, Edward C. "The Decision-Making Scheme." *Public Administration Review* PS-11 (1957): 278-85.
12. Banks, A. S.; and Textor, R. B., eds. *A Cross-Polity Survey.* 2d ed. Cambridge, Mass.: MIT Press, 1963.
13. Barkun, Michael. "Conflict Resolution Through Implicit Mediation." *Journal of Conflict Resolution* 8 (1964): 121-30.
14. Becker, Howard S. "Notes on the Concept of Commitment." *American Journal of Sociology* 66 (1960): 32-40.
15. Black, Joseph E.; and Thompson, Kenneth W., eds. *Foreign Policies in a World of Change.* New York: Harper & Row, 1963.

16. Bloomfield, Lincoln F., ed. *International Military Forces*. Boston: Little, Brown, 1964.
17. Boulding, Kenneth E. *Conflict and Defense: A General Theory*. New York: Harper & Row, 1962.
18. Bozeman, Adda B. *The Future of Law in a Multicultural World*. Princeton, N.J.: Princeton University Press, 1971.
19. Brams, Steven J. "Transaction Flows in the International System." *American Political Science Review* 60 (December 1966): 880-98.
20. Braybrooke, David; and Lindblom, Charles E. *A Strategy for Decision: Policy Evaluation as a Social Process*. New York: Free Press, 1963.
21. Brecher, Michael; Steinberg, Blema; and Stein, Janice. "A Framework for Research on Foreign Policy Behavior." *Journal of Conflict Resolution* 13 (1969): 75-101.
22. Brody, Richard A. "Some Systemic Effects of the Spread of Nuclear Weapons Technology: A Study Through Simulation of a Multi-Nuclear Future." *Journal of Conflict Resolution* 7 (December 1963): 663-753.
23. Burgess, Philip M.; and Lawton, R. W. "Indicators of International Behavior: An Assessment of Events Data Research," *Sage Professional Papers in International Studies*, Vol. 1. Beverly Hills: Sage Publications, 1972.
24. Burton, John Wear. *Peace Theory*. New York: Knopf, 1963.
25. Carr, Edward H. *The Twenty Years' Crisis, 1919-1939*. London: Macmillan, 1946.
26. Cherry, Colin. *World Communication: Threat or Promise? A Socio-Technical Approach*. New York: Wiley, 1971.
27. Chittick, William O. *State Department, Press and Pressure Groups: A Role Analysis*. New York: Wiley-Interscience, 1970.
28. Clark, Greenville; and Sohn, Louis B. *World Peace Through World Law*. Cambridge, Mass.: Harvard University Press, 1960.
29. Claude, Inis L., Jr. *Swords into Plowshares: The Problems and Prospects of International Organization*. 3d ed. New York: Random House, 1964.
30. ————. *Power and International Relations*. New York: Random House, 1962.
31. Cohen, Bernard C. *The Press and Foreign Policy*. Princeton, N.J.: Princeton University Press, 1963.
32. Coplin, William D. *The Functions of International Law*. Chicago: Rand McNally, 1966.
33. ————. "The World Court and the International Bargaining Process." In *The United Nations System and Its Functions*, ed., Michael A. Barkun and Robert W. Gregg. Princeton, N.J.: Van Nostrand, 1968, 317-33.
34. ————. "Current Studies of the Functions of International Law." In *Political Science Annual II*, ed., James A. Robinson. Indianapolis: Bobbs Merrill, 1969, 149-207.
35. Coplin, William D.; and Rochester, J. Martin. "The Permanent Court of Justice, the League of Nations, and the United Nations: A Comparative Empirical Survey." *American Political Science Review* (June 1972): 529-50.
36. Cyert, Richard M.; and March, James G. *A Behavioral Theory of the Firm*. Englewood Cliffs, N.J.: Prentice-Hall, 1963.

37. deRivera, Joseph H. *The Psychological Dimension of Foreign Policy.* Columbus, Ohio: Merrill, 1968.

38. Deutsch, Karl W.; Burrell, Sidney A.; Kann, Robert A.; Lee, Maurice, Jr.; Lichtermann, Martin; Lindgren, Raymond E.; Loewenhein, Francis L.; and Van Wagenen, Richard W. "Political Community and the North Atlantic Area." In *International Political Communities: An Anthology.* Garden City, N.Y.: Doubleday, 1966.

39. ————. *Nationalism and Social Communication.* 2d ed. Cambridge, Mass.: MIT Press, 1966.

40. Earle, Edward Mead, ed. *Makers of Modern Strategy.* Princeton, N.J.: Princeton University Press, 1948.

41. East, Maurice A. "Size and Foreign Policy Behavior: A Test of Two Models." *World Politics* 25 (July 1973): 556-77.

42. East, Maurice A.; and Gregg, Philip M. "Factors Influencing Cooperation and Conflict in the International System." *International Studies Quarterly* 3 (September 1967): 244-69.

43. Edwards, David. *Arms Control in International Relations.* New York: Holt, Rinehart & Winston, 1968.

44. Falk, Richard A.; and Barnet, Richard J., eds. *Security in Disarmament.* Princeton, N.J.: Princeton University Press, 1965.

45. Farrell, R. Barry, ed. *Approaches to Comparative and International Politics.* Evanston, Ill.: Northwestern University Press, 1966.

46. Fink, Clinton F. "More Calculations About Deterrence," *Journal of Conflict Resolution* 9 (March 1965): 54-66.

47. Fisher, Roger. *International Conflict for Beginners.* New York: Harper & Row, 1970.

48. Fox, William T. R. "Atomic Energy and International Relations." In *Technology and International Relations,* ed., William F. Ogburn. Chicago: University of Chicago Press, 1949.

49. Galbraith, John Kenneth. *The New Industrial State.* Boston: Houghton Mifflin, 1967.

50. Galtung, Johan. "On the Effects of International Economic Sanctions, with Examples from the Case of Rhodesia." *World Politics* 3 (April 1967): 378-416.

51. Gareau, Frederick H. *The Balance of Power and Nuclear Deterrence.* Boston: Houghton Mifflin, 1962.

52. Gladstone, Arthur. "The Conception of the Enemy." *Journal of Conflict Resolution* 3 (June 1959): 132-37.

53. Goldwin, Robert A., ed. *Why Foreign Aid?* Chicago: Rand McNally, 1963.

54. Gregg, Robert W.; and Kegley, Charles, Jr., eds. *After Vietnam: The Future of American Foreign Policy.* Garden City, N.Y.: Doubleday, Anchor, 1971.

55. Gulick, Edward Vose. *Europe's Classical Balance of Power.* Ithaca, N.Y.: Cornell University Press, 1955.

56. Haas, Ernst B. "The Balance of Power as a Guide to Policy-Making." *Journal of Politics* 15 (1953): 370-98.

57. ————. "The Balance of Power: Prescription, Concept, or Propaganda?" *World Politics* 5 (1953): 442-77.

58. ————. *Beyond the Nation-State: Functionalism and International Organization.* Stanford, Calif.: Stanford University Press, 1964.

59. ———. *The Uniting of Europe: Political, Social and Economic Forces, 1950-1957*. Stanford, Calif.: Stanford University Press, 1968.

60. Halperin, Morton. "The Limiting Process in the Korean War." *Political Science Quarterly* 78 (1965): 13-39.

61. Hanrieder, Wolfram F. *Comparative Foreign Policy: Theoretical Essays*. New York: McKay, 1971.

62. Harmon, Robert B. *The Art and Practice of Diplomacy: A Selected and Annotated Guide*. Metuchen, N.J.: Scarecrow, 1971.

63. Heilbroner, Robert L. *The Making of Economic Society*. Englewood Cliffs, N.J.: Prentice-Hall, 1962.

64. Herrmann, Charles F. *International Crisis: Insights from Behavioral Research*. New York: Free Press, 1972.

65. ———. "Policy Classification: A Key to the Comparative Study of Foreign Policy." In *The Analysis of International Politics*, eds., James N. Rosenau, Vincent Davis, and Maurice A. East. New York: Free Press, 1972, 58-79.

66. Herz, John H. *International Politics in the Atomic Age*. New York: Columbia University Press, 1959.

67. Hirschman, Albert O. *National Power and the Structure of Foreign Trade*. Berkeley, Calif.: University of California Press, 1945.

68. Holsti, Ole R.; and North, Robert C. "Comparative Data from Content Analysis: Perceptions of Hostility and Economic Variables in the 1914 Crisis." In *Comparing Nations: The Uses of Quantitative Data in Cross-National Research*, ed., Richard L. Merritt and Stein Rokkan. New Haven, Conn.: Yale University Press, 1966, 169-99.

69. Horowitz, Irving Louis. *Three Worlds of Development: The Theory and Practice of International Stratification*. New York: Oxford University Press, 1966.

70. Ikle, Fred C. *How Nations Negotiate*. New York: Harper & Row, 1964.

71. Jacob, Philip E.; and Atherton, A. L. *The Dynamics of International Organization*. Homewood, Ill.: Dorsey, 1965.

72. Jacob, Philip E.; and Toscano, James V., eds. *The Integration of Political Communities*. Philadelphia: Lippincott, 1964.

73. Jensen, Lloyd. "Soviet-American Bargaining Behavior in the Postwar Disarmament Negotiations." *Journal of Conflict Resolution* 7 (September 1963): 522-41.

74. ———. "Military Capabilities and Bargaining Behavior." *Journal of Conflict Resolution* 9 (June 1965): 155-63.

75. Kahn, Herman. *On Thermonuclear War*. Princeton, N.J.: Princeton University Press, 1960.

76. Kahn, Herman; and Wiener, Anthony J. *The Year 2000*. New York: Macmillan, 1967.

77. Kaplan, Morton A. *System and Process in International Politics*. New York: Wiley, 1957.

78. Kaufmann, W. W. *The McNamara Strategy*. New York: Harper & Row, 1964.

79. Kegley, Charles W. "A General Typology of Foreign Policy Behavior," *Sage Professional Papers in International Studies*, Vol. 1. Beverly Hills: Sage Publications, 1972.

80. Kegley, Charles W.; et al., eds. *International Events and the Comparative Analysis of Foreign Policy*. Columbia: University of South Carolina Press, 1975.

81. Kegley, Charles W.; Salmore, Stephen A.; and Rosen, David. "Convergences in the Measurement of Interstate Behavior." In *The Sage International Yearbook of Foreign Policy Studies*, Vol. 2. Beverly Hills: Sage Publications, 1974: 309-39.

82. Kelman, Herbert C., ed. *International Behavior: A Social-Psychological Analysis*. New York: Holt, Rinehart & Winston, 1965.

83. Kennan, George F. *Realities of American Foreign Policy*. Princeton, N.J.: Princeton University Press, 1954.

84. Kindleberger, Charles P. *Power and Money: The Economics of International Politics and the Politics of International Economics*. New York: Basic Books, 1970.

85. Kissinger, Henry A. *Nuclear Weapons and Foreign Policy*. New York: Harper & Brothers, 1957.

86. ———. "Domestic Structure and Foreign Policy," *Daedalus* 95 (Spring 1966): 503-29.

87. Klineberg, Frank L. "Studies in Measurement of the Relations Among Sovereign States." *Psychometrika* 6 (1941): 335-52.

88. Knorr, Klaus. *The War Potential of Nations*. Princeton, N.J.: Princeton University Press, 1956.

89. Lall, Armand S. *Modern International Negotiations*. New York: Columbia University Press, 1966.

90. Lerche, Charles O., Jr. "Contrasting Strategic Styles in the Cold War." *U.S. Naval Institute Proceedings* 88 (May 1962): 23-34.

91. Lindblom, Charles E. "The Science of Muddling Through." *Public Administration Review* 19 (Spring 1959): 79-88.

92. Liska, George. *International Equilibrium: A Theoretical Essay on the Politics and Organization of Security*. Cambridge, Mass.: Harvard University Press, 1957.

93. ———. *Nations in Alliance: The Limits of Interdependence*. Baltimore: Johns Hopkins University Press, 1962.

94. Macridis, Roy C., ed. *Foreign Policy in World Politics*. Englewood Cliffs, N.J.: Prentice-Hall, 1967.

95. Mattingly, Garrett. *Renaissance Diplomacy*. London: Jonathan Cape, 1955.

96. McClelland, Charles A. "Access to Berlin: The Quantity and Variety of Events, 1948-1963." In *Quantitative International Politics: Insights and Evidence*, ed., J. David Singer. New York: Free Press, 1968, 159-87.

97. McClelland, Charles A.; and Hoggard, Gary D. "Conflict Patterns in the Interactions Among Nations." In *International Politics and Foreign Policy*, ed., James N. Rosenau. Rev. ed. New York: Free Press, 1969, 711-24.

98. McGowan, Patrick J., ed. *The Sage International Yearbook of Foreign Policy Studies*. Beverly Hills: Sage Publications, 1973.

99. McGowan, Patrick J.; and Shapiro, Howard B. *The Comparative Study of Foreign Policy: A Survey of Scientific Findings*. Beverly Hills: Sage Publications, 1974.

100. McKenna, Joseph C. *Diplomatic Protest in Foreign Policy*. Chicago: Loyola University Press, 1962.

101. Merritt, Richard L. *The Growth of the American Community*. New Haven, Conn.: Yale University Press, 1966.

102. Milbrath, Lester W. "Interest Groups and Foreign Policy." In *Domestic*

Sources of Foreign Policy, ed., James N. Rosenau. New York: Free Press, 1967, 231-51.

103. Millikan, Max F.; and Blackmer, Donald L., eds. *The Emerging Nations: Their Growth and United States Policy.* Boston: Little, Brown, 1961.

104. Mitrany, David. *A Working Peace System: An Argument for the Functional Development of International Organization.* London: Royal Institute of International Affairs, 1943.

105. Modeleski, George, "Agraria and Industria: Two Models of the International System." *World Politics* 14 (1961): 118-43.

106. Morgenthau, Hans J. *In Defense of the National Interest.* New York: Knopf, 1951.

107. Mueller, John E., *Approaches to Measurement in International Relations: A Non-Evangelical Survey.* New York: Appleton-Century-Crofts, 1969.

108. North, Robert C.; Holsti, Ole R.; Zaninovich, M. George; and Zinnes, Dina A. *Content Analysis: A Handbook with Application for the Study of International Crisis.* Evanston, Ill.: Northwestern University Press, 1963.

109. Organski, A. F. K. *World Politics.* 2d ed. New York: Knopf, 1968.

110. Orwell, George. *1984.* New York: Harcourt, Brace, 1949.

111. Osgood, Robert E. *Ideals and Self-Interest in American Foreign Relations.* Chicago: Chicago University Press, 1953.

112. Osgood, Robert E.; and Tucker, Robert. *Force, Order, and Justice.* Baltimore: Johns Hopkins University Press, 1967.

113. Paige, Glenn D. *The Korean Decision: June 24-30, 1950.* New York: Free Press, 1968.

114. Petrie, Sir Charles, *Diplomatic History, 1713-1933.* London: Hollis & Carter, 1946.

115. Plano, Jack C.; and Riggs, Robert E. *Forging World Order: The Politics of International Organization.* New York: Macmillan, 1967.

116. Pruitt, Dean G. "An Analysis of Responsiveness Between Nations." *Journal of Conflict Resolution* 6 (1962): 5-18.

117. Quester, George. "The Bargaining and Bombing During World War II in Europe." *World Politics* 15 (1963): 417-39.

118. Rapoport, Anatol. *Fights, Games and Debates.* Ann Arbor: University of Michigan Press, 1960.

119. ———. *Two-Person Game Theory: The Essential Ideals.* Ann Arbor: University of Michigan Press, 1966.

120. Rapoport, Anatol; and Guyer, Melvin. "A Taxonomy of 2X2 Games." *Peace Research Society Papers (International)* 6 (1966): 11-26.

121. Richardson, Lewis F. "Generalized Foreign Politics." *British Journal of Psychology.* Monograph 23 (1939).

122. ———. *Arms and Insecurity.* Chicago: Quadrangle Books, 1960.

123. ———. *Statistics of Deadly Quarrels.* Chicago: Quadrangle Books, 1960.

124. Ridgeway, James. *The Last Play: The Struggle to Monopolize the World's Energy Resources.* New York: E. P. Dutton, 1973.

125. Riker, William H. *The Theory of Political Coalitions.* New Haven, Conn.: Yale University Press, 1962.

126. Robinson, James A.; and Snyder, Richard C. "Decision-Making in International Politics." In *International Behavior: A Social-Psychologi-*

cal Analysis, ed., Herbert C. Kelman. New York: Holt, Rinehart & Winston, 1965, 435-63.

127. Rohn, Peter H. "Institutionalism in the Law of Treaties: A Case of Combining Teaching and Research." *Proceedings of the American Society of International Law* (1965): 93-98.

128. Rosecrance, Richard N. *Action and Reaction in World Politics.* Boston: Little, Brown, 1963.

129. ————. *The Dispersion of Nuclear Weapons.* New York: Columbia University Press, 1964.

130. ————, ed. *Domestic Sources of Foreign Policy.* New York: Free Press, 1967.

131. ————, ed. *Linkage Politics.* New York: Free Press, 1969.

132. ————. *The Scientific Study of Foreign Policy.* New York: Free Press, 1972.

133. Rostow, W. W. *The Stages of Economic Growth.* New York: Cambridge University Press, 1960.

134. Rummel, Rudolph J. "Dimensions of Conflict Behavior Within and Between Nations." *Yearbook of the Society for General Systems Research* 8 (1962): 1-50.

135. ————. "A Foreign Conflict Code Sheet." *World Politics* 18 (1966): 283-97.

136. Russett, Bruce M. "The Calculus of Deterrence." *Journal of Conflict Resolution* 7 (June 1963): 97-109.

137. ————. *Trends in World Politics.* New York: Macmillan, 1965.

138. ————, ed. *Economic Theories of International Politics.* Chicago: Markham, 1968.

139. Russett, Bruce M.; Alker, Hayward, Jr.; Deutsch, Karl W.; and Lasswell, Harold D. *World Handbook of Political and Social Indicators.* 2d ed. New Haven, Conn.: Yale University Press, 1965.

140. Sawyer, Jack. "Dimensions of Nations: Size, Wealth, and Politics." *American Journal of Sociology* 73 (1967): 145-72.

141. Sawyer, Jack; and Guetzkow, Harold. "Bargaining and Negotiation in International Relations." In *International Behavior: A Social-Psychological Analysis,* ed., Herbert C. Kelman. New York: Holt, Rinehart & Winston, 1965, 466-52.

142. Schelling, Thomas C. *The Strategy of Conflict.* New York: Oxford University Press, 1960.

143. ————. *Arms and Influence.* New Haven, Conn.: Yale University Press, 1966.

144. Seabury, Paul, ed. *Balance of Power.* San Francisco: Chandler, 1965.

145. Sewell, James P. *Functionalism and World Politics: A Study Based on United Nations Programs Financing Economic Development.* Princeton, N.J.: Princeton University Press, 1966.

146. Shubik, Martin, ed. *Game Theory and Related Approaches to Social Behavior.* New York: Wiley, 1964.

147. Simon, Herbert A. *Administrative Behavior.* 2d ed. New York: Free Press, 1957.

148. ————. "The Decision-Making Schema: A Reply." *Public Administration Review* 18 (Winter 1958): 60-63.

149. Singer, J. David. *Deterrence, Arms Control and Disarmament.* Columbus: Ohio State University Press, 1962.

150. Singer, J. David; and Small, Melvin. "The Composition and Status

Ordering of the International System, 1815-1940." *World Politics* 18 (1966): 236-83.

151. ———. "Formal Alliances, 1815-1939: A Quantitative Description." *Journal of Peace Research* 3 (1966): 1-32.

152. ———. *The Wages of War.* New York: Wiley, 1972.

153. Smoker, Paul. "Nation-State Escalation and International Integration." *Journal of Peace Research* 4 (1967): 61-75.

154. ———. "Sino-Indian Relations: A Study of Trade, Communication and Defense." *Journal of Peace Research* 2 (1965): 65-76.

155. Snyder, Richard C. "Game Theory and the Analysis of Political Behavior." In *Research Frontiers in Politics and Government,* ed., Stephan K. Bailey et al. Washington: Brookings Institution, 1955, 70-103.

156. Snyder, Richard C.; Bruck, H. W.; and Sapin, Burton, eds. "Decision-Making as an Approach to the Study of International Politics." In *Foreign Policy Decision-Making,* eds. Richard C. Snyder, H. W. Bruck, and Burton Sapin. New York: Free Press, 1962, 14-186.

157. Snyder, Glenn H. *Stockpiling Strategic Materials: Politics and National Defense.* San Francisco: Chandler, 1966.

158. Sprout, Harold; and Sprout, Margaret. *Toward a Politics of the Planet Earth.* New York: Van Nostrand Reinhold, 1971.

159. Stagner, Ross. *Dimensions of Human Conflict.* Detroit: Wayne State University Press, 1967.

160. Taylor, A. J. P. *The Struggle for Mastery in Europe.* Oxford, England: Clarendon Press, 1954.

161. ———. *The Origins of the Second World War.* Rev. ed. New York: Fawcett World, 1968.

162. *Toward the Year Two Thousand Eighteen.* New York: Cowles, 1968.

163. Triska, Jan F.; and Finley, David D. *Soviet Foreign Policy.* New York: Macmillan, 1968.

164. Verba, Sidney. "Assumptions of Rationality and Non-Rationality in Models of the International System." In *The International System: Theoretical Essays,* ed., Klaus Knorr and Sidney Verba. Princeton, N.J.: Princeton University Press, 1967, 93-117.

165. Wainhouse, David W.; et al. *International Peace Observation.* Baltimore: Johns Hopkins University Press, 1966.

166. Wallensteen, Peter. "Characteristics of Economic Sanctions." *Journal of Peace Research* 3 (1966): 248-67.

167. Waltz, Kenneth. *Man, the State, and War.* New York: Columbia University Press, 1959.

168. ———. "Electoral Punishment and Foreign Policy Crises." In *Domestic Sources of Foreign Policy,* ed., James N. Rosenau. New York: Free Press, 1967, 263-93.

169. Whiting, Allen S. *China Crosses the Yalu: The Decision to Enter the Korean War.* New York: Macmillan, 1960.

170. Wight, Martin. *Power Politics.* London: Royal Institute of International Affairs, 1946.

171. Wilkenfeld, Jonathan, ed. *Conflict Behavior and Linkage Politics.* New York: McKay, 1973.

172. Wilkinson, David O. *Comparative Foreign Relations: Framework and Methods.* Belmont, Calif.: Dickenson, 1969.

173. Wohlstetter, Albert; and Wohlstetter, Roberta. "Controlling the Risks in Cuba." *Adelphi Papers* 17. London: Institute for Strategic Studies, 1965.
174. Wolf, Charles, Jr. *United States Policy and the Third World: Problems and Analysis.* Boston: Little, Brown, 1967.
175. Wolfers, Arnold, ed. *Alliance Policy and the Cold War.* Baltimore: Johns Hopkins University Press, 1959.
176. Wright, Quincy. *A Study of War.* 2d ed. Chicago: University of Chicago Press, 1965.
177. Wright, Quincy; Evans, William M.; and Deutsch, Morton, eds. *Preventing World War III.* New York: Simon & Schuster, 1962.
178. Yalem, Ronald J. "The Study of International Organization, 1920-1965: A Survey of the Literature." *Background* 10 (May 1966): 1-56.

THE EDITORS

William D. Coplin is Professor of International Relations and Director of the International Relations Program at Syracuse University. He is the author of numerous articles and books on international relations, including *Introduction to International Politics,* and is a co-author of many simulations for American-government and international-politics courses.

Charles W. Kegley, Jr., is Associate Professor of International Relations and Chairman of the International Studies Program at the University of South Carolina. Author of *International Events and the Comparative Analysis of Foreign Policy* and co-editor of *After Vietnam: The Future of American Foreign Policy,* he has also contributed to numerous journals.